EXECUTIVE OFFICE OF THE PRESIDENT
OFFICE OF MANAGEMENT AND BUDGET

STANDARD
OCCUPATIONAL
CLASSIFICATION
MANUAL

2010

Standard Occupational Classification Manual

This Publication was prepared by the Executive Office of the President, Office of Management and Budget and is distributed by the:

National Technical Information Service
U.S. Department of Commerce
5301 Shawnee Rd.
Alexandria, VA 22312

ISBN-978-1-935239-04-8

To order a copy:

www.ntis.gov
orders@ntis.gov
Tel. 1-800-553-6847, 703-605-6000
Fax. 703-605-6900

For sale by the Superintendent of Documents, U.S. Government Printing Office
Internet: bookstore.gpo.gov   Phone: toll free (866) 512-1800;   DC area (202) 512-1800
Fax: (202) 512-2104 Mail: Stop IDCC, Washington, DC 20402-0001

ISBN 978-1-935239-04-8

Contents

11-0000   Management Occupations
    11-1000   Top Executives
    11-2000   Advertising, Marketing, Promotions, Public Relations, and Sales Managers
    11-3000   Operations Specialties Managers
    11-9000   Other Management Occupations

13-0000   Business and Financial Operations Occupations
    13-1000   Business Operations Specialists
    13-2000   Financial Specialists

15-0000   Computer and Mathematical Occupations
    15-1100   Computer Occupations
    15-2000   Mathematical Science Occupations

17-0000   Architecture and Engineering Occupations
    17-1000   Architects, Surveyors, and Cartographers
    17-2000   Engineers
    17-3000   Drafters, Engineering Technicians, and Mapping Technicians

19-0000   Life, Physical, and Social Science Occupations
    19-1000   Life Scientists
    19-2000   Physical Scientists
    19-3000   Social Scientists and Related Workers
    19-4000   Life, Physical, and Social Science Technicians

21-0000   Community and Social Service Occupations

55-0000   Military Specific Occupations
     55-1000 Military Officer Special and Tactical Operations Leaders
     55-2000 First-Line Enlisted Military Supervisors
     55-3000 Military Enlisted Tactical Operations and Air/Weapons Specialists and Crew Members

Introduction

Purpose of the Standard Occupational Classification

The 2010 Standard Occupational Classification (SOC) system is used by Federal statistical agencies to classify workers and jobs into occupational categories for the purpose of collecting, calculating, analyzing, or disseminating data.

Users of occupational data include government program managers, industrial and labor relations practitioners, students considering career training, job seekers, career and employment counselors, educational institutions, and employers wishing to set salary scales or to locate to a new facility. Federal agencies use the SOC system to collect occupational data. The implementation of the 2000 SOC meant that for the first time, all major occupational data sources produced by the Federal statistical system provided data that are comparable, greatly improving the usefulness of the data. The 2010 SOC continues to serve this purpose and has been revised to improve data collection and maintain currency.

The SOC is designed to reflect the current occupational structure of the United States; it classifies all occupations in which work is performed for pay or profit. The SOC covers all jobs in the national economy, including occupations in the public, private, and military sectors. All Federal agencies that publish occupational data for statistical purposes are required to use the SOC to increase data comparability across Federal programs. State and local government agencies are strongly encouraged to use this national system to promote a common language for categorizing and analyzing occupations.

To facilitate classification and presentation of data, the SOC is organized in a tiered system with four levels, ranging from major groups to detailed occupations. There are 23 major groups, broken into 97 minor groups. Each minor group is broken into broad groups, of which there are 461. There are, at the most specified level, 840 detailed occupations. Detailed occupations in the SOC with similar job duties, and in some cases skills, education, and/or training, are grouped together. Each worker is classified into only one of the 840 detailed occupations based on the tasks he or she performs.

Overview of SOC Manual 2010

This manual describes the occupational structure showing the different levels of aggregation, as well as the occupation titles and definitions. Illustrative examples of job titles used in an occupation are listed. The *SOC Manual 2010* also discusses the principles of classification, guidelines for coding jobs to the classification, and answers to Frequently Asked Questions. Detailed occupation descriptions begin on page 1.

Information in this manual also can be found on the SOC homepage at http://www.bls.gov/soc. To obtain a CD-ROM version or additional print copies, contact:

US Department of Commerce
National Technical Information Service
5301 Shawnee Road
Alexandria, VA 22312
(703) 605-6000 or 1-800-553-NTIS (6847)
Order Number: PB2010-105544 (paper)
Order Number: PB2010-500061 (CD-ROM)

Historical background

The Standard Occupational Classification (SOC) was first published in 1980, but was rarely used. The Office of Management and Budget (OMB) created the SOC Revision Policy Committee (SOCRPC) to revise the SOC for 2000 with the purpose of creating a system of classification that would allow all government agencies and private industry to produce comparable data.

Completed in 1998, the 2000 SOC resulted from 4 years of research by the SOCRPC and workgroups composed of members of more than 15 government agencies. The SOCRPC used the Bureau of Labor Statistics' (BLS) Occupational Employment Statistics (OES) occupational classification system as the starting point for the new SOC framework.

The *SOC Manual 2010* replaces the 2000 edition, and will be adopted by all Federal agencies that use the *SOC Manual 2000*.

Revision process for the 2010 edition

In 2005, the Office of Management and Budget first met with the Standard Occupational Classification Policy Committee (SOCPC) which includes representatives from the following agencies:

- o Department of Labor, Bureau of Labor Statistics and Employment and Training Administration
- o Department of Commerce, Census Bureau
- o Department of Defense, Defense Manpower Data Center
- o Department of Education, National Center for Education Statistics
- o Equal Employment Opportunity Commission
- o Department of Health and Human Services, Health Resources and Services Administration
- o National Science Foundation, Division of Science Resources Statistics
- o Office of Personnel Management
- o Office of Management and Budget, Office of Information and Regulatory Affairs

To initiate the formal 2010 SOC revision process, OMB and the SOCPC requested public comment in a May 16, 2006, *Federal Register* notice (71 FR 28536) on: (1) the Standard Occupational Classification Principles, (2) corrections to the *Standard Occupational Classification Manual 2000*, (3) the intention to retain the current SOC major group structure, (4) changes to the existing detailed occupations, and (5) new detailed occupations to be added to the revised 2010 SOC.

To carry out the bulk of the revision effort, the SOCPC created six workgroups comprised of agency staff to examine occupations in the following major groups:

- o Management, Professional, and Related Occupations (major groups 11-29)
- o Service Occupations (major groups 31-39)
- o Sales and Office Occupations (major groups 41-43)
- o Natural Resources, Construction, and Maintenance Occupations (major groups 45-49)
- o Production, Transportation, and Material Moving Occupations (major groups 51-53) and
- o Military Specific Occupations (major group 55).

The workgroups were charged with reviewing comments received in response to the May 16, 2006, *Federal Register* notice (71 FR 28536) and providing recommendations to the SOCPC. Guided by the Classification Principles, the SOCPC reviewed the recommendations from the workgroups and reached decisions by consensus.

OMB announced the proposed new structure in a *Federal Register* notice on May 22, 2008 (73 FR 29930). OMB, in conjunction with the SOCPC, reviewed and carefully considered the comments received in response to these notices in the process of making its final decisions. The final 2010 occupation changes were announced in a *Federal Register* notice on January 21, 2009 (74 FR 3920).

Future of the SOC

The SOC Policy Committee will continue to serve as a standing committee after publication of the *SOC Manual 2010*, to perform maintenance functions such as recommending clarifications of SOC definitions, placement of new occupations within the existing structure, and updates to title files, including the newly-created Direct Match Title File.

The Direct Match Title File lists associated job titles for many detailed SOC occupations. Each of these titles is a direct match to a single SOC occupation. All workers with a job title listed in the Direct Match Title File are classified in only one detailed SOC occupation code. All Federal agencies that use the SOC will adopt the Direct Match Title File, although some may maintain separate program-specific title files. The Direct Match Title File, available on the SOC Web site at http://www.bls.gov/soc, allows data users to compare occupational information for these titles across Federal statistical agencies.

The SOCPC will continue to update the Direct Match Title File on a regular basis. Interested parties may suggest additional job titles to the SOCPC by e-mailing SOC@bls.gov.

The SOCPC has proposed that the next revision of the SOC will result in a 2018 edition, with the next major review and revision of the SOC expected to begin in 2013. The intent of this revision schedule is to minimize disruption to data providers, producers, and users by promoting simultaneous adoption of revised occupational and industry classification systems for those data series that use both. Given the multiple interdependent programs that rely on the SOC, this is best accomplished by timing revisions of the SOC for the years following North American Industry Classification System (NAICS) revisions, which occur for years ending in 2 and 7. The next such year is 2018, which has the additional benefit of coinciding with the beginning year of the American Community Survey 5-year set of surveys that bracket the 2020 Decennial Census. Thus, OMB intends to consider revisions of the SOC for 2018 and every 10 years thereafter.

What's New in the 2010 Edition

The 2010 SOC system contains 840 detailed occupations, aggregated into 461 broad occupations. In turn, the SOC combines these 461 broad occupations into 97 minor groups and 23 major groups. Of the 840 detailed occupations in the 2010 SOC, 359 remained exactly the same as in 2000, 452 had definition changes, 21 had a title change only, and 9 had a code change without a change in definition. Most of the definition changes (392) were editorial revisions that did not change occupational content. Therefore, no substantive changes occurred in occupational coverage for about 90 percent of the detailed occupations in the 2010 SOC.

Occupational areas with significant revisions and additions included

- Information technology (minor group 15-1100 Computer Occupations)
- Healthcare (major groups 29-0000 Healthcare Practitioners and Technical Occupations and 31-0000 Healthcare Support Occupations)
- Printing (minor group 51-5100 Printing Workers) and
- Human resources (minor group 13-1000 Business Operations Specialists)

In comparison to the 2000 SOC, the 2010 SOC realized a net gain of 19 detailed occupations, 12 broad occupations, and 1 minor group. The nature of the changes in detailed occupations is indicated in table 1 and in the table in appendix C of this manual.

Table 1: Distribution of detailed 2010 occupations, by type of change, 2000-2010

Type of change			2010 SOC detailed occupations	
Code changed?	Title revised?	Definition revised?	Number	Percent[1]
No	No	No	359	42.7
No	No	Yes[2]	356	42.4
No	Yes	Yes[2]	44	5.2
Yes	Yes	Yes[2]	41	4.9
No	Yes	No	21	2.5
Yes	No	Yes[2]	11	1.3
Yes	No	No	7	0.8
Yes	Yes	No	1	0.1
All occupations			840	100.0

[1] May not add to total due to rounding
[2] Of the 452 definition changes, 392 were editorial or to account for changes in technology. The remaining 60 occupations with revisions to definitions affected occupational coverage and are embedded in these rows. See page xiii, Revised Occupational Definitions.

New occupations

The 2010 SOC contains 24 new occupations and codes that were broken out of the 2000 SOC occupations. These occupations are as follows:

The number of detailed occupations (821) in the 2000 SOC increased to 845 with the addition of these 24 new occupations. The final count of 2010 SOC occupations (840) was due to a number of other changes.

- o The 2010 detailed occupation 51-9151 Photographic Process Workers and Processing Machine Operators resulted from combining two detailed 2000 occupations into one.
- o The 2010 detailed occupation 11-9013 Farmers, Ranchers, and Other Agricultural Managers resulted from combining two detailed 2000 occupations into one.
- o The 2010 detailed occupations in minor group 51-5110 Printing Workers, 51-5111 Prepress Technicians and Workers, 51-5112 Printing Press Operators, and 51-5113 Print Binding and Finishing Workers, resulted from combining five detailed 2000 occupations into three.
- o Three 2000 SOC computer occupations were revised to six detailed occupations in the 2010 SOC, four of which are included in the list of new occupations above.

For more information on the relationships between detailed occupations in the 2000 and 2010 SOC, see the table in appendix C or the crosswalks in appendices A and B. These tables are also available in electronic format at http://www.bls.gov/soc.

Occupations that moved within the SOC structure

As another indicator of the scope of changes, the nine detailed occupations listed below moved from one major group in the 2000 SOC to another in the 2010 SOC.

o Emergency Management Directors (11-9161) moved into major group 11-0000 Management Occupations from major group 13-0000 Business and Financial Operations Occupations, where it was previously Emergency Management Specialists (13-1061)

o Farm Labor Contractors (13-1074) moved into major group 13-0000 Business and Financial Operations Occupations from major group 45-0000 Farming, Fishing, and Forestry Occupations

o Fundraisers (13-1131) moved into major group 13-0000 Business and Financial Operations Occupations from Sales and Related Workers, All Other (41-9099) in major group 41-0000 Sales and Related Occupations

o Market Research Analysts and Marketing Specialists (13-1161) moved into major group 13-0000 Business and Financial Operations Occupations from multiple SOC occupations including Market Research Analysts in major group 19-0000 Life, Physical, and Social Science Occupations and Public Relations Specialists in major group 27-0000 Arts, Design, Entertainment, Sports, and Media Occupations

o Workers in the newly-created Transportation Security Screeners (33-9093) were previously classified in multiple SOC occupations including Compliance Officers, Except Agriculture, Construction, Health and Safety, and Transportation in major group 13-0000 Business and Financial Operations

o Workers in the newly-created Morticians, Undertakers, and Funeral Directors (39-4031) were previously classified with Funeral Directors (11-9061) in major group 11-0000 Management Occupations

o Workers in the newly-created Solar Photovoltaic Installers (47-2231) were previously classified in multiple SOC occupations including two in major group 49-0000 Installation, Maintenance, and Repair Occupations—Heating, Air Conditioning, and Refrigeration Mechanics and Installers (49-9021) and Installation, Maintenance, and Repair Workers, All Other (49-9099)

o Flight Attendants (53-2031) moved into major group 53-0000 Transportation and Material Moving Occupations from major group 39-0000 Personal Care and Service Occupations

o Transportation Attendants, Except Flight Attendants (53-6061) moved into major group 53-0000 Transportation and Material Moving Occupations from major group 39-0000 Personal Care and Service Occupations

Revised occupational definitions

There were 60 instances of revisions to definitions that affected occupational coverage. These 60 detailed occupations are listed below and include the 24 new occupations denoted by an asterisk (*). This list encompasses collapsed occupations, as well as 2010 occupations that resulted from a split. Other occupations had editorial changes or modifications to account for changes in technology. A table describing the nature of the changes, by detailed occupation, is available in appendix C or at http://www.bls.gov/soc.

2010 SOC
Code   *2010 SOC Title*

11-9013	Farmers, Ranchers, and Other Agricultural Managers
11-9061	Funeral Service Managers
13-1041	Compliance Officers
13-1071	Human Resources Specialists
13-1075	Labor Relations Specialists
13-1121	Meeting, Convention, and Event Planners
13-1131	Fundraisers *
13-1161	Market Research Analysts and Marketing Specialists
13-1199	Business Operations Specialists, All Other
15-1121	Computer Systems Analysts
15-1122	Information Security Analysts *
15-1134	Web Developers*
15-1142	Network and Computer Systems Administrators
15-1143	Computer Network Architects *
15-1152	Computer Network Support Specialists *
21-1091	Health Educators
21-1094	Community Health Workers *
21-1099	Community and Social Service Specialists, All Other
23-1012	Judicial Law Clerks
23-2011	Paralegals and Legal Assistants
25-2051	Special Education Teachers, Preschool *
25-2052	Special Education Teachers, Kindergarten and Elementary School
25-2059	Special Education Teachers, All Other *
25-3099	Teachers and Instructors, All Other
29-1128	Exercise Physiologists *
29-1129	Therapists, All Other
29-1141	Registered Nurses
29-1151	Nurse Anesthetists*
29-1161	Nurse Midwives *
29-1171	Nurse Practitioners *
29-2034	Radiologic Technologists
29-2035	Magnetic Resonance Imaging Technologists *
29-2057	Ophthalmic Medical Technicians *
29-2092	Hearing Aid Specialists *
29-2099	Health Technologists and Technicians, All Other
29-9092	Genetic Counselors *
29-9099	Healthcare Practitioners and Technical Workers, All Other
31-1014	Nursing Assistants
31-1015	Orderlies *
31-9097	Phlebotomists *

31-9099	Healthcare Support Workers, All Other
33-9032	Security Guards
33-9093	Transportation Security Screeners *
33-9099	Protective Service Workers, All Other
39-4031	Morticians, Undertakers, and Funeral Directors*
41-9099	Sales and Related Workers, All Other
43-3099	Financial Clerks, All Other *
43-9199	Office and Administrative Support Workers, All Other
47-2111	Electricians
47-2181	Roofers
47-2231	Solar Photovoltaic Installers*
47-4099	Construction and Related Workers, All Other
49-9021	Heating, Air Conditioning, and Refrigeration Mechanics and Installers
49-9081	Wind Turbine Service Technicians*
49-9099	Installation, Maintenance, and Repair Workers, All Other
51-3099	Food Processing Workers, All Other *
51-5112	Printing Press Operators
51-5113	Print Binding and Finishing Workers
51-9151	Photographic Process Workers and Processing Machine Operators
51-9199	Production Workers, All Other

SOC codes no longer in use

Of the 821 detailed SOC codes in the 2000 SOC, the 40 listed in table 2 are not used in the 2010 SOC. For each detailed 2000 SOC occupation, the corresponding 2010 codes and titles are also shown.

Table 2: 2000 SOC codes no longer in use and their 2010 replacements

2000 SOC code	2000 SOC title	2010 SOC code	2010 SOC title
11-3041	Compensation and Benefits Managers	11-3111	Compensation and Benefits Managers
11-3042	Training and Development Managers	11-3131	Training and Development Managers
11-3049	Human Resources Managers, All Other	11-3121	Human Resources Managers
11-9011	Farm, Ranch, and Other Agricultural Managers	11-9013	Farmers, Ranchers, and Other Agricultural Managers
11-9012	Farmers and Ranchers	11-9013	Farmers, Ranchers, and Other Agricultural Managers
13-1061	Emergency Management Specialists	11-9161	Emergency Management Directors
13-1072	Compensation, Benefits, and Job Analysis Specialists	13-1141	Compensation, Benefits, and Job Analysis Specialists
13-1073	Training and Development Specialists	13-1151	Training and Development Specialists
13-1079	Human Resources, Training, and Labor Relations Specialists, All Other	13-1075	Labor Relations Specialists
15-1011	Computer and Information Scientists, Research	15-1111	Computer and Information Research Scientists
15-1021	Computer Programmers	15-1131	Computer Programmers
15-1031	Computer Software Engineers, Applications	15-1132	Software Developers, Applications

Table 2 (con't): 2000 SOC codes no longer in use and their 2010 replacements

15-1032	Computer Software Engineers, Systems Software	15-1133	Software Developers, Systems Software
15-1041	Computer Support Specialists	15-1151	Computer User Support Specialists
15-1051	Computer Systems Analysts	15-1143	Computer Network Architects (part)
		15-1121	Computer Systems Analysts
15-1061	Database Administrators	15-1141	Database Administrators
15-1071	Network and Computer Systems Administrators	15-1142	Network and Computer Systems Administrators (part)
15-1081	Network Systems and Data Communications Analysts	15-1122	Information Security Analysts
		15-1134	Web Developers
		15-1142	Network and Computer Systems Administrators (part)
		15-1143	Computer Network Architects (part)
		15-1152	Computer Network Support Specialists
15-1099	Computer Specialists, All Other	15-1199	Computer Occupations, All Other
19-3021	Market Research Analysts	13-1161	Market Research Analysts and Marketing Specialists
23-2092	Law Clerks	23-1012	Judicial Law Clerks
		23-2011	Paralegals and Legal Assistants (part)
25-2041	Special Education Teachers, Preschool, Kindergarten, and Elementary School	25-2051	Special Education Teachers, Preschool
		25-2052	Special Education Teachers, Kindergarten and Elementary School
25-2042	Special Education Teachers, Middle School	25-2053	Special Education Teachers, Middle School
25-2043	Special Education Teachers, Secondary School	25-2054	Special Education Teachers, Secondary School
29-1111	Registered Nurses	29-1141	Registered Nurses
29-1121	Audiologists	29-1181	Audiologists
31-1012	Nursing Aides, Orderlies, and Attendants	31-1014	Nursing Assistants
		31-1015	Orderlies
39-6021	Tour Guides and Escorts	39-7011	Tour Guides and Escorts
39-6022	Travel Guides	39-7012	Travel Guides
39-6031	Flight Attendants	53-2031	Flight Attendants
39-6032	Transportation Attendants, Except Flight Attendants and Baggage Porters	53-6061	Transportation Attendants, Except Flight Attendants
45-1012	Farm Labor Contractors	13-1074	Farm Labor Contractors
49-9042	Maintenance and Repair Workers, General	49-9071	Maintenance and Repair Workers, General
51-5011	Bindery Workers	51-5113	Print Binding and Finishing Workers (part)
51-5012	Bookbinders	51-5113	Print Binding and Finishing Workers (part)
51-5021	Job Printers	51-5112	Printing Press Operators (part)
		51-5113	Print Binding and Finishing Workers (part)
51-5022	Prepress Technicians and Workers	51-1111	Prepress Technicians and Workers
51-5023	Printing Machine Operators	51-5112	Printing Press Operators (part)
51-9131	Photographic Process Workers	51-9151	Photographic Process Workers and Processing Machine Operators
51-9132	Photographic Processing Machine Operators	51-9151	Photographic Process Workers and Processing Machine Operators

Classification Principles

The SOC Classification Principles form the basis on which the SOC system is structured.

1. The SOC covers all occupations in which work is performed for pay or profit, including work performed in family-operated enterprises by family members who are not directly compensated. It excludes occupations unique to volunteers. Each occupation is assigned to only one occupational category at the lowest level of the classification.

2. Occupations are classified based on work performed and, in some cases, on the skills, education, and/or training needed to perform the work at a competent level.

3. Workers primarily engaged in planning and directing are classified in management occupations in Major Group 11-0000. Duties of these workers may include supervision.

4. Supervisors of workers in Major Groups 13-0000 through 29-0000 usually have work experience and perform activities similar to those of the workers they supervise, and therefore are classified with the workers they supervise.

5. Workers in Major Group 31-0000 Healthcare Support Occupations assist and are usually supervised by workers in Major Group 29-0000 Healthcare Practitioners and Technical Occupations. Therefore, there are no first-line supervisor occupations in Major Group 31-0000.

6. Workers in Major Groups 33-0000 through 53-0000 whose primary duty is supervising are classified in the appropriate first-line supervisor category because their work activities are distinct from those of the workers they supervise.

7. Apprentices and trainees are classified with the occupations for which they are being trained, while helpers and aides are classified separately because they are not in training for the occupation they are helping.

8. If an occupation is not included as a distinct detailed occupation in the structure, it is classified in an appropriate "All Other," or residual, occupation. "All Other" occupations are placed in the structure when it is determined that the detailed occupations comprising a broad occupation group do not account for all of the workers in the group. These occupations appear as the last occupation in the group with a code ending in "9" and are identified in their title by having "All Other" appear at the end.

9. The U.S. Bureau of Labor Statistics and the U.S. Census Bureau are charged with collecting and reporting data on total U.S. employment across the full spectrum of SOC major groups. Thus, for a detailed occupation to be included in the SOC, either the Bureau of Labor Statistics or the Census Bureau must be able to collect and report data on that occupation.

Coding Guidelines

The SOC Coding Guidelines are intended to assist users in consistently assigning SOC codes and titles to survey responses and in other coding activities.

1. A worker should be assigned to an SOC occupation code based on work performed.

2. When workers in a single job could be coded in more than one occupation, they should be coded in the occupation that requires the highest level of skill. If there is no measurable difference in skill requirements, workers should be coded in the occupation in which they spend the most time. Workers whose job is to teach at different levels (e.g., elementary, middle, or secondary) should be coded in the occupation corresponding to the highest educational level they teach.

3. Data collection and reporting agencies should assign workers to the most detailed occupation possible. Different agencies may use different levels of aggregation, depending on their ability to collect data. For more information on data produced using the SOC, see the Frequently Asked Questions (FAQs) section.

4. Workers who perform activities not described in any distinct detailed occupation in the SOC structure should be coded in an appropriate "All Other" or residual occupation. These residual occupational categories appear as the last occupation in a group with a code ending in "9" and are identified by having the words "All Other" appear at the end of the title.

5. Workers in Major Groups 33-0000 through 53-0000 who spend 80 percent or more of their time performing supervisory activities are coded in the appropriate first-line supervisor category in the SOC. In these same Major Groups (33-0000 through 53-0000), persons with supervisory duties who spend less than 80 percent of their time supervising are coded with the workers they supervise.

6. Licensed and non-licensed workers performing the same work should be coded together in the same detailed occupation, except where specified otherwise in the SOC definition.

Standard Occupational Classification and Coding Structure

The occupations in the SOC are classified at four levels of aggregation to suit the needs of various data users: major group, minor group, broad occupation, and detailed occupation. Each lower level of detail identifies a more specific group of occupations. The 23 major groups, listed below, are divided into 97 minor groups, 461 broad occupations, and 840 detailed occupations.

2010 SOC Major Groups

Code	Title
11-0000	Management Occupations
13-0000	Business and Financial Operations Occupations
15-0000	Computer and Mathematical Occupations
17-0000	Architecture and Engineering Occupations
19-0000	Life, Physical, and Social Science Occupations
21-0000	Community and Social Service Occupations
23-0000	Legal Occupations
25-0000	Education, Training, and Library Occupations
27-0000	Arts, Design, Entertainment, Sports, and Media Occupations
29-0000	Healthcare Practitioners and Technical Occupations
31-0000	Healthcare Support Occupations
33-0000	Protective Service Occupations
35-0000	Food Preparation and Serving Related Occupations
37-0000	Building and Grounds Cleaning and Maintenance Occupations
39-0000	Personal Care and Service Occupations
41-0000	Sales and Related Occupations
43-0000	Office and Administrative Support Occupations
45-0000	Farming, Fishing, and Forestry Occupations
47-0000	Construction and Extraction Occupations
49-0000	Installation, Maintenance, and Repair Occupations
51-0000	Production Occupations
53-0000	Transportation and Material Moving Occupations
55-0000	Military Specific Occupations

Some users may require aggregations other than the SOC system built on these major groups. Further details on alternate occupational aggregations and approved modifications to the SOC structure are provided in the following section beginning on page xxi.

Major groups are broken into minor groups, which, in turn, are divided into broad occupations. Broad occupations are then divided into one or more detailed occupations.

> 29-0000 Healthcare Practitioners and Technical Occupations
> 29-1000 Health Diagnosing and Treating Practitioners
> 29-1060 Physicians and Surgeons
> 29-1062 Family and General Practitioners

- o Major group codes end with 0000 (e.g., 29-0000 Healthcare Practitioners and Technical Occupations).

- Minor groups generally end with 000 (e.g., 29-1000 Health Diagnosing and Treating Practitioners)—the exceptions are minor groups 15-1100 Computer Occupations and 51-5100 Printing Workers, which end with 00.
- Broad occupations end with 0 (e.g., 29-1060 Physicians and Surgeons).
- Detailed occupations end with a number other than 0 (e.g., 29-1062 Family and General Practitioners).

Each item in the SOC is designated by a six-digit code. The hyphen between the second and third digit is used only for clarity (see figure 1).

Figure 1.

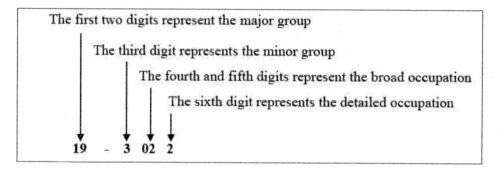

As shown in figure 2, all residuals ("Other," "Miscellaneous," or "All Other" occupations), whether at the detailed or broad occupation or minor group level, contain a "9" at the level of the residual. Minor groups that are major group residuals end in 9000 (e.g., 33-9000, Other Protective Service Workers). Broad occupations that are minor group residuals end in 90 (e.g., 33-9090, Miscellaneous Protective Service Workers). Detailed residual occupations end in 9 (e.g., 33-9099, Protective Service Workers, All Other).

Figure 2.

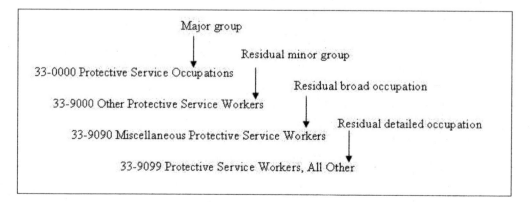

If there are more than nine broad occupations in a minor group (e.g., 51-9000 Other Production Occupations); or more than eight, if there is no residual (e.g., 47-2000 Construction Trades Workers), then the code xx-x090 is skipped (reserved for residuals), the code xx-x000 is skipped (reserved for minor groups), and the numbering system will continue with code xx-x110. The residual broad occupation is then code xx-x190 or xx-x290 (e.g., 51-9190, Miscellaneous Production Workers).

The structure is comprehensive, and encompasses all occupations in the U.S. economy. If a specific occupation is not listed, it is included in a residual category with similar occupations.

Detailed occupations are identified and defined so that each occupation includes workers who perform similar job tasks as described in Classification Principle 2. Definitions begin with the duties all workers in the occupation perform. Some definitions include a sentence at the end describing tasks workers in an occupation *may*, but do not necessarily *have to* perform, in order to be included in the occupation. Where the definitions include tasks also performed by workers in another occupation, cross-references to that occupation are provided in the definition.

Figure 3 identifies the eight elements that appear in detailed SOC occupations. All six-digit, detailed occupations have a SOC code (1), a title (2), and a definition (3). All workers classified in an occupation are required to perform the duties described in the first sentence of each definition (4). Some definitions also have a "may" statement (5), an "includes" statement (6), and/or an "excludes" statement (7). Many occupations have one or more "illustrative examples" (8), presented in alphabetical order. Illustrative examples are job titles classified in only that occupation, and were selected from the Direct Match Title File described on page vii.

Figure 3.

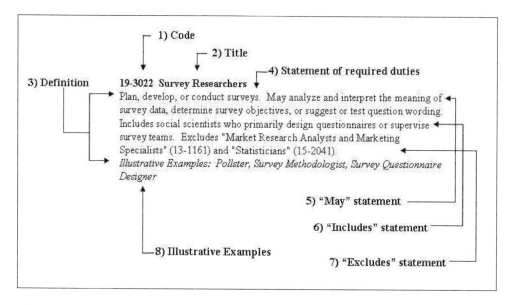

The "may" statement describes tasks that workers in that occupation may – but are not required to – perform in order to be classified with Survey Researchers. The "includes" statement identifies particular workers who should be classified with Survey Researchers. The "excludes" statement indicates other detailed occupations that may be similar to Survey Researchers and clarifies that workers who fall into those occupations should be excluded from Survey Researchers.

Approved Modifications to the Structure

Agencies may use the SOC or parts of the SOC at varying levels of the system. For example, data may be collected at the broad occupation level in some areas and at the detailed level in others.

Occupations below the detailed level

The coding system is designed to allow SOC users desiring a delineation of occupations below the detailed occupation level to use a decimal point and additional digit(s) after the sixth digit. For example, Secondary School Teachers, Except Special and Career/Technical Education (25-2031) is a detailed occupation. Agencies wishing to collect more particular information on teachers by subject matter might use 25-2031.1 for secondary school science teachers or 25-2031.12 for secondary school biology teachers. Additional levels of detail also may be used to distinguish workers who have different training or years of experience.

OMB recommends that those needing extra detail use the structure of the Department of Labor's Employment and Training Administration's Occupational Information Network (O*NET). For more information, see http://online.onetcenter.org.

Higher levels of aggregation

Some users may wish to present occupational data at higher levels of aggregation than the SOC major groups. To meet this need and to maintain consistency and comparability across data sets, either the intermediate or the high-level aggregations presented in tables 3 and 4 should be used for data tabulation purposes.

Table 3. Intermediate aggregation to 13 groups, 2010 SOC

Intermediate aggregation	Major groups included	Intermediate aggregation title
1	11-13	Management, Business, and Financial Occupations
2	15-19	Computer, Engineering, and Science Occupations
3	21-27	Education, Legal, Community Service, Arts, and Media Occupations
4	29	Healthcare Practitioners and Technical Occupations
5	31-39	Service Occupations
6	41	Sales and Related Occupations
7	43	Office and Administrative Support Occupations
8	45	Farming, Fishing, and Forestry Occupations
9	47	Construction and Extraction Occupations
10	49	Installation, Maintenance, and Repair Occupations
11	51	Production Occupations
12	53	Transportation and Material Moving Occupations
13	55	Military Specific Occupations

Table 4. High-level aggregation to 6 groups, 2010 SOC

High-level aggregation	Major groups included	High-level aggregation title
1	11-29	Management, Business, Science, and Arts Occupations
2	31-39	Service Occupations
3	41-43	Sales and Office Occupations
4	45-49	Natural Resources, Construction, and Maintenance Occupations
5	51-53	Production, Transportation, and Material Moving Occupations
6	55	Military Specific Occupations

Alternate aggregations

Data collection issues or confidentiality concerns may prevent agencies from reporting all the detail indicated in the SOC. For example, an agency might report the detail of at least one occupational category at a particular level of the SOC structure but must aggregate the other occupations at that level. In such cases, the agency may adjust the occupational categories so long as these adjustments permit aggregation to the next higher SOC level. In such a situation, agencies must distinguish such groups from the official SOC aggregation. If agencies choose this option they must obtain approval from the Standard Occupational Classification Policy Committee for their proposed aggregation scheme.

Frequently Asked Questions

1. How do the U.S. Bureau of Labor Statistics and the Census Bureau determine if they can collect and report on an occupation? (See Classification Principle 9.)

The Bureau of Labor Statistics (BLS) develops estimates of occupational employment and wages for wage and salary workers in nonfarm establishments in its Occupational Employment Statistics (OES) Survey. This survey collects information from business establishments sampled by industry and geographic area. BLS looks at the definition, and at the size and dispersion of (estimated) employment, in determining whether it can collect and report data on an occupation. For OES survey respondents to report on an occupation, the duties or work performed of the occupation must be uniquely defined, i.e., clearly differentiated from those of any other occupations. If the occupation is widely dispersed across areas and/or industries, employment in an occupation must be sizeable to be reliably measured. If the occupation is highly concentrated in a single industry or area, smaller levels of employment can be reliably measured.

The Census Bureau develops estimates of occupational employment of the population with its household-based Current Population (a joint program with BLS) and American Community Surveys. As with BLS above, the Census Bureau is concerned about the size and dispersion of employment in an occupation in determining if it can collect and report data on that occupation. In addition, the Census Bureau considers whether the respondents to its household surveys, who may provide information for themselves as well as for other household members, are likely to report the job titles and job activities associated with an occupation accurately and completely. Household survey respondents tend to give general or informal, rather than specific or technical, occupational titles. For example, a household survey respondent may report "doctor," rather than "pediatrician." This makes it difficult for the Census Bureau to report on such specialized occupations.

2. What is the difference between an occupation and a job?

An occupation is a category of jobs that are similar with respect to the work performed and the skills possessed by the incumbents. A job is the specific set of tasks performed by an individual worker. "Turnpike toll collector" is an example of a job that corresponds to the occupation 41-2011 Cashiers.

3. Why doesn't every job title have its own code in the SOC?

Occupational classification schemes examine and organize the millions of jobs and tens of thousands of job titles in the economy into occupations based upon their similarities as determined by the scheme's classification principles. The organizing principle of the SOC system is work performed rather than job title so there are many fewer occupation codes in the SOC than there are jobs in the economy.

4. What is the difference between the SOC Classification Principles and the Coding Guidelines?

The SOC Classification Principles form the basis on which the SOC system is structured. The Coding Guidelines are intended to assist SOC users in consistently assigning SOC occupational codes to survey responses.

5. Who uses the SOC?

Government agencies that collect and publish occupational statistical data use the SOC. See FAQ number 6 for more detail. At the Federal level, these agencies and programs include:

> Department of Commerce
>> Census Bureau
>
> Department of Defense
> Department of Education
> Department of Health and Human Services
> Department of Labor
>> Bureau of Labor Statistics
>>> Employment Projections Program
>>> Labor Force Statistics from the Current Population Survey
>>> National Compensation Survey
>>> National Longitudinal Surveys
>>> Occupational Employment Statistics
>>> Occupational Health and Safety Statistics
>>
>> Employment and Training Administration
>> Employment Standards Administration
>
> Department of Transportation
> Department of Veterans Affairs
>> National Center for Veterans Analysis and Statistics
>
> Equal Employment Opportunity Commission
> National Science Foundation
>> Division of Science Resources Statistics
>
> Office of Personnel Management

6. Where can I get information on the occupations in the SOC?

Depending on the type of information you are seeking, you may obtain information from several agencies:

a) The U.S. Census Bureau publishes occupational data annually, collected through the American Community Survey (ACS), for the Nation, all States and the District of Columbia, Puerto Rico, and all counties and places with populations of at least 65,000. The Census Bureau also publishes 3-year ACS data for geographic areas with populations of at least 20,000 and 5-year ACS data for all geographies in the U.S. and Puerto Rico. Census 2010 will collect, classify, and publish occupational data for Guam, American Samoa, the Commonwealth of

Northern Mariana Islands, and the U.S. Virgin Islands. Other household surveys publish occupational data at varying levels of detail and geography. Standard tabulations are available through the American FactFinder via the Internet at http://www.census.gov. Information about occupation coding and written reports on occupational trends can be found at http://www.census.gov/hhes/www/ioindex/ioindex.html. For additional information, contact the Census Bureau's Question and Answer Center at http://ask.census.gov or contact the Call Center at (301) 763-INFO.

b) The Department of Defense publishes data that cross-reference military occupational codes of the Army, Navy, Air Force, Marine Corps, and Coast Guard with civilian equivalent occupations. Additional information on available data products can be obtained on the Internet at http://www.dmdc.osd.mil; or by writing to Director, Defense Manpower Data Center, 1600 Wilson Blvd., Suite 400, Arlington, VA 22209-2593.

c) The National Center for Education Statistics (NCES) publishes data collected through the School and Staffing Survey (SASS) on the employment of elementary and secondary teachers, principals, and other school staff, as well as detailed information on their education, training, and background characteristics. NCES publishes detailed data on postsecondary instructors and professors collected through the Integrated Postsecondary Education Data System (IPEDS). In addition, NCES conducts various longitudinal studies that follow high school and college students into their working years and uses the SOC to classify their occupations. Products based on data from these various surveys and programs are available from the specific surveys and programs, which can be found at http://nces.ed.gov/surveys.

d) Biennially, the Bureau of Labor Statistics' Employment Projections (EP) Program publishes the *Occupational Outlook Handbook* and *Career Guide to Industries*. In addition, EP publishes the *Occupational Outlook Quarterly*. For more information about these publications, visit the EP Web site at http://www.bls.gov/emp or contact the Chief, Division of Occupational Outlook, Bureau of Labor Statistics, 2 Massachusetts Ave. NE., Room 2135, Washington, DC 20212, telephone (202) 691-5700.

e) The Current Population Survey (CPS), a joint program of the Census Bureau and the Bureau of Labor Statistics, uses the 2002 Census occupational classification system, which is derived from the 2000 Standard Occupational Classification. CPS data series are available on this classification beginning with year 2000. The CPS previously used the 1990 Census occupational classification, which was adapted from the 1980 SOC. CPS data series on the earlier classification are available from 1983-2002; these data are not directly comparable with the current series. The Bureau of Labor Statistics publishes national-level estimates of occupational employment, unemployment, and earnings with demographic detail from the CPS. The CPS homepage on the BLS website is at http://www.bls.gov/cps/home.htm; contact information for the BLS CPS program can be found at http://www.bls.gov/cps/contact.htm.

f) The Bureau of Labor Statistics' National Compensation Survey (NCS) program provides comprehensive measures of occupational wages; employment cost trends; and benefit incidence and detailed plan provisions. Detailed occupational earnings are available for selected metropolitan and nonmetropolitan areas, nine Census divisions, and on a National basis. Employment cost trends and information on the incidence and detailed provision of employee benefit plans are published for major occupational groups. For more information, see the NCS Web site at http://www.bls.gov/ncs/home.htm, call (202) 691-6199, or send an e-mail to NCSInfo@bls.gov. Correspondence may be sent to U.S. Bureau of Labor Statistics National Compensation Survey, 2 Massachusetts Ave., NE., Room 4175, Washington, DC 20212-0001.

g) The Bureau of Labor Statistics' Occupational Employment Statistics (OES) program produces cross-industry occupational employment and wage estimates for the Nation, all States, the District of Columbia, Guam, Puerto Rico, the U.S. Virgin Islands, metropolitan areas, metropolitan divisions, and nonmetropolitan areas. OES also publishes national industry-specific occupational employment and wage estimates for sectors and 3-, 4-, and selected 5-digit North American Industry Classification System (NAICS) industries. Data are available from the OES home page at http://www.bls.gov/oes/home.htm. For assistance with these data, contact the OES program at (202) 691-6569 or oesinfo@bls.gov. Industry-specific data for States and metropolitan and nonmetropolitan areas may be available from the State workforce agencies by contacting the individual State or States for which information is needed. Contact information for the State workforce agencies is available at http://www.bls.gov/bls/ofolist.htm.

h) The Employment and Training Administration's (ETA) Occupational Information Network (O*NET) system is a comprehensive database of occupational competency profiles. ETA sponsors the development, updating, and dissemination of O*NET information through a grant with the North Carolina Employment Security Commission. The O*NET system is based on the Standard Occupational Classification (SOC) system and also provides information on additional detailed occupations within a SOC category in selected instances. The O*NET Content Model of occupational descriptors is the foundation for a series of survey questionnaires that go out to incumbent workers in various occupations which form the basis for the O*NET occupational competency profiles. The O*NET system is the successor to the Dictionary of Occupational Titles, which was last published by the Department of Labor in 1991. O*NET information is available via the Internet at http://online.onetcenter.org and also as a downloadable electronic database from the O*NET Resource Center: http://www.onetcenter.org/database.html. For more information, contact O*NET Customer Support at onet@ncmail.net or contact the Department of Labor at o-net@dol.gov . You can also write to the O*NET project director at Office of

Workforce Investment, Employment and Training Administration, U.S. Department of Labor, FPB Room S 4231, 200 Constitution Ave., NW., Washington, DC 20210.

i) The Equal Employment Opportunity Commission (EEOC) uses SOC occupational classifications, and equivalent Census occupational classifications, to create broader categories as part of the Commission's data survey and enforcement programs. Under the survey program, employer workforce information is collected periodically from private-sector firms on the Employer Information Report (EEO-1), and public sector employers on the State and Local Government Report (EEO-4). More information may be obtained from the Commission's Web site at http://www.eeoc.gov.

j) The National Science Foundation (NSF) Division of Science and Resources Statistics (SRS) Web site provides access to the Scientists and Engineers Statistical Data System (SESTAT), a comprehensive and integrated system of information about the employment, educational and demographic characteristics of scientists and engineers in the United States. It is intended for both policy analysis and general research, having features for both the casual and more intensive data user. More information may be obtained from the SESTAT Web site at http://www.nsf.gov/statistics/sestat.

7. Whom should I contact if I have a question about the SOC?

You may call the SOC information line at 202-691-6500, or send an e-mail to SOC@bls.gov.

8. Why are there different levels of detail in the SOC?

The four-tiered levels in the SOC enable users to choose the level or levels of detail corresponding to their interest and ability to collect data on different occupations. Users needing different levels of detail will still be able to compare data at the defined levels. Please see the description of alternative aggregations beginning on page xxi for more information.

9. Why can't I find my job title in the SOC?

This volume lists occupations that may have many different job titles. It does not attempt to provide an exhaustive list of job titles. A list of additional titles called the Direct Match title file is available at http://www.bls.gov/soc. If your title is not listed, you may e-mail SOC@bls.gov to suggest its inclusion.

10. Which occupations in the SOC cover "professionals"?

The 2010 SOC does not classify or identify workers using the term "professional", or other similar terms such as "skilled" or "unskilled." The SOC was created solely for statistical purposes (see FAQ number 13) and the classification structure is not intended to rank or group occupations by education, credentials, earnings, or any other similar user-defined indicator of status. However, government agencies or private users may define and use various terms to suit their own purposes. For example, the Employment and Training Administration's O*NET program classifies occupations into 1 of 5 "job zones," based on data regarding the levels of education, experience, and training needed for work in an occupation, ranging from "little or no" to "extensive" preparation (for more information, see http://online.onetcenter.org/help/online/zones).

11. Why are supervisors of workers in Major Groups 13-0000 through 31-0000 not listed? Where should they be classified?

Supervisors of workers in Major Groups 13-0000 through 29-0000 are classified with the occupations they supervise because they often must have the same type of training, education, and experience as the workers they supervise. Supervisors of workers in Major Group 31-0000 are usually classified in Major Group 29-0000. See Classification Principles 4 and 5 on page xv.

12. When is the next revision of the SOC scheduled?

The next major review and revision of the SOC is expected to begin in 2013 in preparation for the 2018 SOC. The intent of this revision schedule is to minimize disruption to data providers, producers, and users by promoting simultaneous adoption of revised occupational and industry classification systems for those data series that use both. Given the multiple interdependent programs that rely on the SOC, this is best accomplished by timing revisions of the SOC for the years following North American Industry Classification System (NAICS) revisions, which occur for years ending in 2 and 7. The next such year is 2018, which has the additional benefit of coinciding with the beginning year of the American Community Survey 5-year set of surveys that bracket the 2020 Decennial Census. Thus, OMB intends to consider revisions of the SOC for 2018 and every 10 years thereafter.

To ensure that the successful efforts of the SOCPC continue and that the SOC reflects the structure of the changing workforce, the SOCPC will continue its service as a standing committee. The SOCPC will meet periodically to monitor the implementation of the 2010 SOC across Federal agencies. This consultation will include regularly scheduled interagency communication to ensure a smooth transition to the 2010 SOC. The SOCPC will also perform SOC maintenance functions, such as recommending clarifications of the SOC occupational definitions, placement of new occupations within the existing structure, and updating title files.

13. Can the SOC be used for nonstatistical purposes?

The 2010 SOC was designed solely for statistical purposes. Although it is likely that the 2010 SOC also will be used for various nonstatistical purposes (e.g., for administrative, regulatory, or taxation functions), the requirements of government agencies or private users that choose to use the 2010 SOC for nonstatistical purposes have played no role in its development, nor will OMB modify the classification to meet the requirements of any nonstatistical program.

Consequently, the 2010 SOC is not to be used in any administrative, regulatory, or tax program unless the head of the agency administering that program has first determined that the use of such occupational definitions is appropriate to the implementation of the program's objectives.

14. Where can I find how the 2010 SOC relates to the 2000 SOC?

The official crosswalks can be found in appendices A and B and at http://www.bls.gov/soc. Occupations are crosswalked from the 2010 SOC to the 2000 SOC and from the 2000 SOC to the 2010 SOC.

15. Where can I obtain an electronic version or additional printed versions of the SOC?

Information in this manual can be found on the SOC homepage at http://www.bls.gov/soc. To obtain a CD-ROM version or additional print copies, contact

> U.S. Department of Commerce
> National Technical Information Service
> 5301 Shawnee Road
> Alexandria, VA 22312
> (703) 605-6000 or 1-800-553-NTIS (6847)
> Order Number: PB2000-105544 (paper)
> Order Number: PB2000-500061 (CD-ROM)

16. When will Federal statistical agencies begin using the 2010 SOC in survey collection?

Federal statistical agencies will begin using the 2010 SOC for occupational data they publish for reference years beginning on or after January 1, 2010. However, it is important to note that for some programs, full implementation of the 2010 SOC will occur in stages, as sufficient data are needed to produce estimates at the full level of occupational detail. Contact an agency or program directly for specific information on implementation. A schedule of implementation dates for programs within the Bureau of Labor Statistics will be available at http://www.bls.gov/soc.

Acknowledgements

SOCPC Members
John Galvin, Bureau of Labor Statistics, Chair

Andrea Bright, Office of Personnel Management
Paul Bugg, Office of Management and Budget
Jennifer Cheeseman Day, Census Bureau
Joseph Donovan, Equal Employment Opportunity Commission
Barbara Downs, Census Bureau
Phil Doyle, Bureau of Labor Statistics
Pam Frugoli, Employment and Training Administration
Nimmi Kannankutty, National Science Foundation
Mary Kirk, Census Bureau (retired)
Roslyn Korb, National Center for Education Statistics
Mary McCarthy, Bureau of Labor Statistics (retired)
Mike McElroy, Bureau of Labor Statistics (retired)
Stephen Provasnik, National Center for Education Statistics
Sabrina Ratchford, National Center for Education Statistics
Steve Reardon, Defense Manpower Data Center
Tara Ricci, Office of Personnel Management
Sarah Richards, Health Resources and Services Administration
Marc Rosenblum, Equal Employment Opportunity Commission
Dixie Sommers, Bureau of Labor Statistics
George Stamas, Bureau of Labor Statistics

SOC Coordinating Team
Theresa Cosca, Bureau of Labor Statistics
Alissa Emmel, Bureau of Labor Statistics
Anne Louise Marshall, Bureau of Labor Statistics
Wendy Price, Bureau of Labor Statistics, Administrative Support

Workgroup Members

Bureau of Labor Statistics

Shane Stephens	Jim Smith
Richard Yeast	Sam Meyer
John Morton	Mark Doucette
Dee McCarthy	Reid VanNattan
Janice Windau	Laurie Salmon
Audrey Watson	Benjamin Cover
Patrick Kilcoyne	John I. Jones
Zachary Warren	Michael Soloy
Dina Itkin	Jeffrey Holt
Carrie Jones	Amy Bierer
Kinna Brewington	Fatemeh Hajiha
Jeffrey LaPointe	Mark Maggi
Cori Martinelli	Phillip Bastian
Sadie Blanchard	Douglas Braddock
Olivia Crosby	Lauren Csorny

Conley Hall Dillon
Thomas DiVincenzo
Diana Gelhaus
Sam Greenblatt
Elka Torpey
Jonathan Kelinson
T. Alan Lacey
Chester Levine
Kevin McCarron
Gregory Niemesh
Brian Roberts
Jon Sargent
Kristina Bartsch
Patricia Tate
David Terkanian
Michael Wolf
Ian Wyatt

Tamara Dillon
Arlene Dohm
Kathleen Green
Jeffrey Gruenert
Henry Kasper
Jill Lacey
William Lawhorn
C. Brett Lockard
Roger Moncarz
Alice Ramey
Erik Savisaar
Terry Schau
Lynn Shniper
Colleen Teixeira Moffat
Nicholas Terrell
Benjamin Wright

Census Bureau
Marisa Hotchkiss

Defense Manpower Data Center
Dawn De-iongh
Sue Hay

Employment and Training Administration
Tracie Hamilton

Health Resources and Services Administration
Jim Cultice
Annette Debisette
Jerilyn Glass
Anjum Rishi
Young Song

National Center for Education Statistics
Michelle Coon

National Center for O*NET Development
Phil Lewis
David Rivkin
John Nottingham

National Science Foundation
Kelly Kang

Office of Personnel Management
Mark Doboga

11-1000 Top Executives

11-1010 Chief Executives This broad occupation is the same as the detailed occupation: 11-1011 Chief Executives

> **11-1011 Chief Executives**Determine and formulate policies and provide overall direction of companies or private and public sector organizations within guidelines set up by a board of directors or similar governing body. Plan, direct, or coordinate operational activities at the highest level of management with the help of subordinate executives and staff managers.
>
> *Illustrative examples: Governor*

11-1020 General and Operations Managers

This broad occupation is the same as the detailed occupation:
11-1021 General and Operations Managers

> **11-1021 General and Operations Managers**
> Plan, direct, or coordinate the operations of public or private sector organizations. Duties and responsibilities include formulating policies, managing daily operations, and planning the use of materials and human resources, but are too diverse and general in nature to be classified in any one functional area of management or administration, such as personnel, purchasing, or administrative services. Excludes First-Line Supervisors.
>
> *Illustrative examples: General Superintendent, Radio Station Manager, Television Station Manager*

11-1030 Legislators

This broad occupation is the same as the detailed occupation:
11-1031 Legislators

> **11-1031 Legislators**
> Develop, introduce or enact laws and statutes at the local, tribal, State, or Federal level. Includes only workers in elected positions.
>
> *Illustrative examples: City Council Member, Senator, Tribal Council Member*

11-2000 Advertising, Marketing, Promotions, Public Relations, and Sales Managers

11-2010 Advertising and Promotions Managers

This broad occupation is the same as the detailed occupation:
11-2011 Advertising and Promotions Managers

> **11-2011 Advertising and Promotions Managers**
> Plan, direct, or coordinate advertising policies and programs or produce collateral materials, such as posters, contests, coupons, or give-aways, to create extra interest in the purchase of a product or service for a department, an entire organization, or on an account basis.

Illustrative examples: Advertising Director, Advertising Executive, Promotions Director

11-2020 Marketing and Sales Managers
This broad occupation includes the following two detailed occupations:
11-2021 Marketing Managers
11-2022 Sales Managers

11-2021 Marketing Managers
Plan, direct, or coordinate marketing policies and programs, such as determining the demand for products and services offered by a firm and its competitors, and identify potential customers. Develop pricing strategies with the goal of maximizing the firm's profits or share of the market while ensuring the firm's customers are satisfied. Oversee product development or monitor trends that indicate the need for new products and services.

Illustrative examples: Internet Marketing Manager, Marketing Administrator, Marketing Director

11-2022 Sales Managers
Plan, direct, or coordinate the actual distribution or movement of a product or service to the customer. Coordinate sales distribution by establishing sales territories, quotas, and goals and establish training programs for sales representatives. Analyze sales statistics gathered by staff to determine sales potential and inventory requirements and monitor the preferences of customers.

Illustrative examples: District Sales Manager, Export Manager, Regional Sales Manager, Sales Director

11-2030 Public Relations and Fundraising Managers
This broad occupation is the same as the detailed occupation:
11-2031 Public Relations and Fundraising Managers

11-2031 Public Relations and Fundraising Managers
Plan, direct, or coordinate activities designed to create or maintain a favorable public image or raise issue awareness for their organization or client; or if engaged in fundraising, plan, direct, or coordinate activities to solicit and maintain funds for special projects or nonprofit organizations.

Illustrative examples: Fundraising Director, Public Affairs Director, Publicity Director

11-3000 Operations Specialties Managers

11-3010 Administrative Services Managers
This broad occupation is the same as the detailed occupation:

11-3011 Administrative Services Managers

11-3011 Administrative Services Managers
Plan, direct, or coordinate one or more administrative services of an organization, such as records and information management, mail distribution, facilities planning and maintenance, custodial operations, and other office support services. Medical records administrators are included in "Medical and Health Services Managers" (11-9111). Excludes "Purchasing Managers" (11-3061).

Illustrative examples: Facilities Manager, Records and Information Manager, Records Management Director

11-3020 Computer and Information Systems Managers
This broad occupation is the same as the detailed occupation:
11-3021 Computer and Information Systems Managers

11-3021 Computer and Information Systems Managers
Plan, direct, or coordinate activities in such fields as electronic data processing, information systems, systems analysis, and computer programming. Excludes "Computer Occupations" (15-1111 through 15-1199).

Illustrative examples: Chief Technology Officer, Information Technology Systems Director, Management Information Systems Director

11-3030 Financial Managers
This broad occupation is the same as the detailed occupation:
11-3031 Financial Managers

11-3031 Financial Managers
Plan, direct, or coordinate accounting, investing, banking, insurance, securities, and other financial activities of a branch, office, or department of an establishment.

Illustrative examples: Comptroller, Financial Director

11-3050 Industrial Production Managers
This broad occupation is the same as the detailed occupation:
11-3051 Industrial Production Managers

11-3051 Industrial Production Managers
Plan, direct, or coordinate the work activities and resources necessary for manufacturing products in accordance with cost, quality, and quantity specifications.
Illustrative examples: Manufacturing Director, Plant Manager, Production Control Manager

11-3060 Purchasing Managers
This broad occupation is the same as the detailed occupation:

11-3061 Purchasing Managers

11-3061 Purchasing Managers
Plan, direct, or coordinate the activities of buyers, purchasing officers, and related workers involved in purchasing materials, products, and services. Includes wholesale or retail trade merchandising managers and procurement managers.

Illustrative examples: Contracting Manager, Procurement Manager, Purchasing Director

11-3070 Transportation, Storage, and Distribution Managers
This broad occupation is the same as the detailed occupation:
11-3071 Transportation, Storage, and Distribution Managers

11-3071 Transportation, Storage, and Distribution Managers
Plan, direct, or coordinate transportation, storage, or distribution activities in accordance with organizational policies and applicable government laws or regulations. Includes logistics managers.

Illustrative examples: Distribution Center Manager, Traffic Safety Administrator, Warehouse Manager

11-3110 Compensation and Benefits Managers
This broad occupation is the same as the detailed occupation:
11-3111 Compensation and Benefits Managers

11-3111 Compensation and Benefits Managers
Plan, direct, or coordinate compensation and benefits activities of an organization. Job analysis and position description managers are included in "Human Resource Managers" (11-3121).

Illustrative examples: Compensation Director, Employee Benefits Director, Wage and Salary Administrator

11-3120 Human Resources Managers
This broad occupation is the same as the detailed occupation:
11-3121 Human Resources Managers

11-3121 Human Resources Managers
Plan, direct, or coordinate human resources activities and staff of an organization. Excludes managers who primarily focus on compensation and benefits (11-3111) and training and development (11-3131).

Illustrative examples: Job Analysis Manager, Labor Relations Director, Personnel Manager, Position Description Manager

11-3130 Training and Development Managers

This broad occupation is the same as the detailed occupation:
11-3131 Training and Development Managers

11-3131 Training and Development Managers
Plan, direct, or coordinate the training and development activities and staff of an organization.

Illustrative examples: E-Learning Manager, Employee Development Director, Labor Training Manager

11-9000 Other Management Occupations

11-9010 Farmers, Ranchers, and Other Agricultural Managers
This broad occupation is the same as the detailed occupation:
11-9013 Farmers, Ranchers, and Other Agricultural Managers

11-9013 Farmers, Ranchers, and Other Agricultural Managers
Plan, direct, or coordinate the management or operation of farms, ranches, greenhouses, aquacultural operations, nurseries, timber tracts, or other agricultural establishments. May hire, train, and supervise farm workers or contract for services to carry out the day-to-day activities of the managed operation. May engage in or supervise planting, cultivating, harvesting, and financial and marketing activities. Excludes "First-Line Supervisors of Farming, Fishing, and Forestry Workers" (45-1011).

Illustrative examples: Animal Husbandry Manager, Dairy Farm Manager, Fish Hatchery Manager, Orchard Manager

11-9020 Construction Managers
This broad occupation is the same as the detailed occupation:
11-9021 Construction Managers

11-9021 Construction Managers
Plan, direct, or coordinate, usually through subordinate supervisory personnel, activities concerned with the construction and maintenance of structures, facilities, and systems. Participate in the conceptual development of a construction project and oversee its organization, scheduling, budgeting, and implementation. Includes managers in specialized construction fields, such as carpentry or plumbing.

Illustrative examples: Construction Coordinator, Construction Superintendent, General Contractor

11-9030 Education Administrators
This broad occupation includes the following four detailed occupations:
11-9031 Education Administrators, Preschool and Childcare Center/Program
11-9032 Education Administrators, Elementary and Secondary School

11-9033 Education Administrators, Postsecondary
11-9039 Education Administrators, All Other

11-9031 Education Administrators, Preschool and Childcare Center/Program

Plan, direct, or coordinate the academic and nonacademic activities of preschool and childcare centers or programs. Excludes "Preschool Teachers" (25-2011).

Illustrative examples: Childcare Center Administrator, Head Start Director, Preschool Director

11-9032 Education Administrators, Elementary and Secondary School

Plan, direct, or coordinate the academic, administrative, or auxiliary activities of public or private elementary or secondary level schools.

Illustrative examples: Elementary School Principal, High School Principal, Middle School Principal

11-9033 Education Administrators, Postsecondary

Plan, direct, or coordinate research, instructional, student administration and services, and other educational activities at postsecondary institutions, including universities, colleges, and junior and community colleges.

Illustrative examples: Provost, University Administrator

11-9039 Education Administrators, All Other

All education administrators not listed separately.

11-9040 Architectural and Engineering Managers

This broad occupation is the same as the detailed occupation:
11-9041 Architectural and Engineering Managers

11-9041 Architectural and Engineering Managers

Plan, direct, or coordinate activities in such fields as architecture and engineering or research and development in these fields. Excludes "Natural Sciences Managers" (11-9121).

Illustrative examples: Engineering Design Manager, Global Engineering Manager, Mechanical Engineering Director

11-9050 Food Service Managers

This broad occupation is the same as the detailed occupation:
11-9051 Food Service Managers

11-9051 Food Service Managers

Plan, direct, or coordinate activities of an organization or department that serves food and beverages. Excludes "Chefs and Head Cooks" (35-1011).

Illustrative examples: Banquet Director, Food Service Director, Tavern Operator

11-9060 Funeral Service Managers
This broad occupation is the same as the detailed occupation:
11-9061 Funeral Service Managers

11-9061 Funeral Service Managers
Plan, direct, or coordinate the services or resources of funeral homes. Includes activities such as determining prices for services or merchandise and managing the facilities of funeral homes. Excludes "Morticians, Undertakers, and Funeral Directors" (39-4031).

Illustrative examples: Funeral Home Director, Funeral Home Manager

11-9070 Gaming Managers
This broad occupation is the same as the detailed occupation:
11-9071 Gaming Managers

11-9071 Gaming Managers
Plan, direct, or coordinate gaming operations in a casino. May formulate house rules.

Illustrative examples: Casino Manager, Slot Operations Director, Table Games Manager

11-9080 Lodging Managers
This broad occupation is the same as the detailed occupation:
11-9081 Lodging Managers

11-9081 Lodging Managers
Plan, direct, or coordinate activities of an organization or department that provides lodging and other accommodations. Excludes "Food Service Managers" (11-9051) in lodging establishments.

Illustrative examples: Bed and Breakfast Innkeeper, Hotel Manager, Innkeeper

11-9110 Medical and Health Services Managers
This broad occupation is the same as the detailed occupation:
11-9111 Medical and Health Services Managers

11-9111 Medical and Health Services Managers
Plan, direct, or coordinate medical and health services in hospitals, clinics, managed care organizations, public health agencies, or similar organizations.

Illustrative examples: Clinic Director, Hospital Administrator, Medical Records Administrator, Mental Health Program Manager

11-9120 Natural Sciences Managers

This broad occupation is the same as the detailed occupation:
11-9121 Natural Sciences Managers

11-9121 Natural Sciences Managers
Plan, direct, or coordinate activities in such fields as life sciences, physical sciences, mathematics, statistics, and research and development in these fields. Excludes "Architectural and Engineering Managers" (11-9041) and "Computer and Information Systems Managers" (11-3021).

Illustrative examples: Agricultural Research Director, Geophysical Manager, Ocean Program Administrator

11-9130 Postmasters and Mail Superintendents
This broad occupation is the same as the detailed occupation:
11-9131 Postmasters and Mail Superintendents

11-9131 Postmasters and Mail Superintendents
Plan, direct, or coordinate operational, administrative, management, and supportive services of a U.S. post office; or coordinate activities of workers engaged in postal and related work in assigned post office.

Illustrative examples: Postal Supervisor, Postmaster

11-9140 Property, Real Estate, and Community Association Managers
This broad occupation is the same as the detailed occupation:
11-9141 Property, Real Estate, and Community Association Managers

11-9141 Property, Real Estate, and Community Association Managers
Plan, direct, or coordinate the selling, buying, leasing, or governance activities of commercial, industrial, or residential real estate properties. Includes managers of homeowner and condominium associations, rented or leased housing units, buildings, or land (including rights-of-way).

Illustrative examples: Apartment Manager, Building Rental Manager, Leasing Property Manager

11-9150 Social and Community Service Managers
This broad occupation is the same as the detailed occupation:
11-9151 Social and Community Service Managers

11-9151 Social and Community Service Managers
Plan, direct, or coordinate the activities of a social service program or community outreach organization. Oversee the program or organization's budget and policies regarding participant

involvement, program requirements, and benefits. Work may involve directing social workers, counselors, or probation officers.

Illustrative examples: Child Welfare Director, Family Service Center Director, Youth Program Director

11-9160 Emergency Management Directors
This broad occupation is the same as the detailed occupation:
11-9161 Emergency Management Directors

11-9161 Emergency Management Directors
Plan and direct disaster response or crisis management activities, provide disaster preparedness training, and prepare emergency plans and procedures for natural (e.g., hurricanes, floods, earthquakes), wartime, or technological (e.g., nuclear power plant emergencies or hazardous materials spills) disasters or hostage situations.

Illustrative examples: Disaster Response Director, Emergency Preparedness Coordinator, Public Safety Director

11-9190 Miscellaneous Managers
This broad occupation is the same as the detailed occupation:
11-9199 Managers, All Other

11-9199 Managers, All Other
All managers not listed separately.

Illustrative examples: Clerk of Court, Social Science Manager, Utilities Manager

13-1000 Business Operations Specialists

13-1010 Agents and Business Managers of Artists, Performers, and Athletes
This broad occupation is the same as the detailed occupation:
13-1011 Agents and Business Managers of Artists, Performers, and Athletes

13-1011 Agents and Business Managers of Artists, Performers, and Athletes
Represent and promote artists, performers, and athletes in dealings with current or prospective employers. May handle contract negotiation and other business matters for clients.

Illustrative examples: Band Manager, Literary Agent, Theatrical Agent

13-1020 Buyers and Purchasing Agents
This broad occupation includes the following three detailed occupations:
13-1021 Buyers and Purchasing Agents, Farm Products
13-1022 Wholesale and Retail Buyers, Except Farm Products
13-1023 Purchasing Agents, Except Wholesale, Retail, and Farm Products

13-1021 Buyers and Purchasing Agents, Farm Products
Purchase farm products either for further processing or resale. Includes tree farm contractors, grain brokers and market operators, grain buyers, and tobacco buyers.

Illustrative examples: Cotton Broker, Fruit Buyer, Livestock Buyer

13-1022 Wholesale and Retail Buyers, Except Farm Products
Buy merchandise or commodities, other than farm products, for resale to consumers at the wholesale or retail level, including both durable and nondurable goods. Analyze past buying trends, sales records, price, and quality of merchandise to determine value and yield. Select, order, and authorize payment for merchandise according to contractual agreements. May conduct meetings with sales personnel and introduce new products. Includes assistant wholesale and retail buyers of nonfarm products.

Illustrative examples: Gold Buyer, Merchandise Buyer

13-1023 Purchasing Agents, Except Wholesale, Retail, and Farm Products
Purchase machinery, equipment, tools, parts, supplies, or services necessary for the operation of an establishment. Purchase raw or semi-finished materials for manufacturing. Excludes "Buyers and Purchasing Agents, Farm Products" (13-1021) and "Wholesale and Retail Buyers, Except Farm Products" (13-1022).

Illustrative examples: Equipment, Supplies, and Tools Purchasing Agent; Radio Time Buyer

13-1030 Claims Adjusters, Appraisers, Examiners, and Investigators
This broad occupation includes the following two detailed occupations:
13-1031 Claims Adjusters, Examiners, and Investigators

13-1032 Insurance Appraisers, Auto Damage

13-1031 Claims Adjusters, Examiners, and Investigators
Review settled claims to determine that payments and settlements are made in accordance with company practices and procedures. Confer with legal counsel on claims requiring litigation. May also settle insurance claims. Excludes "Fire Inspectors and Investigators" (33-2021).

Illustrative examples: Fire Claims Adjuster, Health Insurance Adjuster, Property and Casualty Insurance Claims Examiner

13-1032 Insurance Appraisers, Auto Damage
Appraise automobile or other vehicle damage to determine repair costs for insurance claim settlement. Prepare insurance forms to indicate repair cost or cost estimates and recommendations. May seek agreement with automotive repair shop on repair costs.

Illustrative examples: Automobile Damage Appraiser, Vehicle Damage Appraiser

13-1040 Compliance Officers
This broad occupation is the same as the detailed occupation:
13-1041 Compliance Officers

13-1041 Compliance Officers
Examine, evaluate, and investigate eligibility for or conformity with laws and regulations governing contract compliance of licenses and permits, and perform other compliance and enforcement inspection and analysis activities not classified elsewhere. Excludes "Financial Examiners" (13-2061), "Tax Examiners and Collectors, and Revenue Agents" (13-2081), "Occupational Health and Safety Specialists" (29-9011), "Occupational Health and Safety Technicians" (29-9012), Transportation Security Screeners (33-9093), "Agricultural Inspectors" (45-2011), "Construction and Building Inspectors" (47-4011), and "Transportation Inspectors" (53-6051).

Illustrative examples: Driver's License Examiner, Environmental Compliance Inspector, Equal Employment Opportunity Officer

13-1050 Cost Estimators
This broad occupation is the same as the detailed occupation:
13-1051 Cost Estimators

13-1051 Cost Estimators
Prepare cost estimates for product manufacturing, construction projects, or services to aid management in bidding on or determining price of product or service. May specialize according to particular service performed or type of product manufactured.

Illustrative examples: Construction Job Cost Estimator, Crating and Moving Estimator, Production Cost Estimator

13-1070 Human Resources Workers
This broad occupation includes the following three detailed occupations:
13-1071 Human Resources Specialists
13-1074 Farm Labor Contractors
13-1075 Labor Relations Specialists

13-1071 Human Resources Specialists
Perform activities in the human resource area. Includes employment specialists who screen, recruit, interview, and place workers. Excludes "Compensation, Benefits, and Job Analysis Specialists" (13-1141) and "Training and Development Specialists" (13-1151).

Illustrative examples: Human Resources Generalist, Personnel Recruiter, Staffing Coordinator

13-1074 Farm Labor Contractors
Recruit and hire seasonal or temporary agricultural laborers. May transport, house, and provide meals for workers.

Illustrative example: Harvesting Contractor

13-1075 Labor Relations Specialists
Resolve disputes between workers and managers, negotiate collective bargaining agreements, or coordinate grievance procedures to handle employee complaints. Excludes equal employment opportunity (EEO) officers who are included in "Compliance Officers" (13-1041).

Illustrative examples: Employee Relations Specialist, Labor Relations Consultant, Union Representative

13-1080 Logisticians
This broad occupation is the same as the detailed occupation:
13-1081 Logisticians

13-1081 Logisticians
Analyze and coordinate the logistical functions of a firm or organization. Responsible for the entire life cycle of a product, including acquisition, distribution, internal allocation, delivery, and final disposal of resources. Excludes "Transportation, Storage, and Distribution Managers" (11-3071).

Illustrative examples: Logistics Analyst, Logistics Planner, Logistics Specialist

13-1110 Management Analysts
This broad occupation is the same as the detailed occupation:
13-1111 Management Analysts

13-1111 Management Analysts
Conduct organizational studies and evaluations, design systems and procedures, conduct work simplification and measurement studies, and prepare operations and procedures manuals to assist management in operating more efficiently and effectively. Includes program analysts and management consultants. Excludes "Computer Systems Analysts" (15-1121) and "Operations Research Analysts" (15-2031).

Illustrative examples: Business Management Analyst, Business Process Consultant, Industrial Analyst

13-1120 Meeting, Convention, and Event Planners
This broad occupation is the same as the detailed occupation:
13-1121 Meeting, Convention, and Event Planners

13-1121 Meeting, Convention, and Event Planners
Coordinate activities of staff, convention personnel, or clients to make arrangements for group meetings, events, or conventions.

Illustrative examples: Conference Planner, Corporate Meeting Planner, Wedding Planner

13-1130 Fundraisers
This broad occupation is the same as the detailed occupation:
13-1131 Fundraisers

13-1131 Fundraisers
Organize activities to raise funds or otherwise solicit and gather monetary donations or other gifts for an organization. May design and produce promotional materials. May also raise awareness of the organization's work, goals, and financial needs.

Illustrative examples: Campaign Fundraiser, Donor Relations Officer, Fundraising Officer

13-1140 Compensation, Benefits, and Job Analysis Specialists
This broad occupation is the same as the detailed occupation:
13-1141 Compensation, Benefits, and Job Analysis Specialists

13-1141 Compensation, Benefits, and Job Analysis Specialists
Conduct programs of compensation and benefits and job analysis for employer. May specialize in specific areas, such as position classification and pension programs.

Illustrative examples: Employee Benefits Specialist, Job Analyst, Retirement Plan Specialist

13-1150 Training and Development Specialists
This broad occupation is the same as the detailed occupation:
13-1151 Training and Development Specialists

13-1151 Training and Development Specialists
Design and conduct training and development programs to improve individual and organizational performance. May analyze training needs.

Illustrative examples: Computer Training Specialist, Corporate Trainer, Workforce Development Specialist

13-1160 Market Research Analysts and Marketing Specialists
This broad occupation is the same as the detailed occupation:
13-1161 Market Research Analysts and Marketing Specialists

13-1161 Market Research Analysts and Marketing Specialists
Research market conditions in local, regional, or national areas, or gather information to determine potential sales of a product or service, or create a marketing campaign. May gather information on competitors, prices, sales, and methods of marketing and distribution.

Illustrative examples: Market Research Specialist, Marketing Consultant, Marketing Forecaster

13-1190 Miscellaneous Business Operations Specialists
This broad occupation is the same as the detailed occupation:
13-1199 Business Operations Specialists, All Other

13-1199 Business Operations Specialists, All Other
All business operations specialists not listed separately.

Illustrative examples: Mystery Shopper, Ship Purser

13-2000 Financial Specialists

13-2010 Accountants and Auditors
This broad occupation is the same as the detailed occupation:
13-2011 Accountants and Auditors

13-2011 Accountants and Auditors
Examine, analyze, and interpret accounting records to prepare financial statements, give advice, or audit and evaluate statements prepared by others. Install or advise on systems of recording costs or other financial and budgetary data. Excludes "Tax Examiners and Collectors, and Revenue Agents" (13-2081).

Illustrative examples: Certified Public Accountant, Field Auditor, Internal Auditor

13-2020 Appraisers and Assessors of Real Estate
This broad occupation is the same as the detailed occupation:
13-2021 Appraisers and Assessors of Real Estate

13-2021 Appraisers and Assessors of Real Estate
Appraise real property and estimate its fair value. May assess taxes in accordance with prescribed schedules.

Illustrative examples: Land Appraiser, Property Appraiser, Tax Assessor

13-2030 Budget Analysts
This broad occupation is the same as the detailed occupation:
13-2031 Budget Analysts

13-2031 Budget Analysts
Examine budget estimates for completeness, accuracy, and conformance with procedures and regulations. Analyze budgeting and accounting reports.

Illustrative examples: Budget Examiner, Budget Officer, Cost Analyst

13-2040 Credit Analysts
This broad occupation is the same as the detailed occupation:
13-2041 Credit Analysts

13-2041 Credit Analysts
Analyze credit data and financial statements of individuals or firms to determine the degree of risk involved in extending credit or lending money. Prepare reports with credit information for use in decision making.

Illustrative examples: Credit Assessment Analyst, Credit Risk Analyst

13-2050 Financial Analysts and Advisors
This broad occupation includes the following three detailed occupations:
13-2051 Financial Analysts
13-2052 Personal Financial Advisors
13-2053 Insurance Underwriters

13-2051 Financial Analysts
Conduct quantitative analyses of information affecting investment programs of public or private institutions.

Illustrative examples: Corporate Financial Analyst, Corporate Securities Research Analyst, Institutional Commodity Analyst

13-2052 Personal Financial Advisors
Advise clients on financial plans using knowledge of tax and investment strategies, securities, insurance, pension plans, and real estate. Duties include assessing clients' assets, liabilities, cash flow, insurance coverage, tax status, and financial objectives.

Illustrative examples: Estate Planner, Individual Pension Advisor, Personal Investment Advisor

13-2053 Insurance Underwriters
Review individual applications for insurance to evaluate degree of risk involved and determine acceptance of applications.

Illustrative examples: Automobile and Property Underwriter, Bond Underwriter, Insurance Analyst

13-2060 Financial Examiners
This broad occupation is the same as the detailed occupation:
13-2061 Financial Examiners

13-2061 Financial Examiners
Enforce or ensure compliance with laws and regulations governing financial and securities institutions and financial and real estate transactions. May examine, verify, or authenticate records.

Illustrative examples: Bank Examiner, Financial Compliance Examiner, Home Mortgage Disclosure Act Specialist

13-2070 Credit Counselors and Loan Officers
This broad occupation includes the following two detailed occupations:
13-2071 Credit Counselors
13-2072 Loan Officers

13-2071 Credit Counselors
Advise and educate individuals or organizations on acquiring and managing debt. May provide guidance in determining the best type of loan and explaining loan requirements or restrictions. May help develop debt management plans, advise on credit issues, or provide budget, mortgage, and bankruptcy counseling.

Illustrative examples: Debt Management Counselor, Financial Assistance Advisor, Loan Counselor

13-2072 Loan Officers
Evaluate, authorize, or recommend approval of commercial, real estate, or credit loans. Advise borrowers on financial status and payment methods. Includes mortgage loan officers and agents, collection analysts, loan servicing officers, and loan underwriters.

Illustrative examples: Commercial Lender, Loan Reviewer, Real Estate Loan Officer

13-2080 Tax Examiners, Collectors and Preparers, and Revenue Agents
This broad occupation includes the following two detailed occupations:
13-2081 Tax Examiners and Collectors, and Revenue Agents

13-2082 Tax Preparers

13-2081 Tax Examiners and Collectors, and Revenue Agents
Determine tax liability or collect taxes from individuals or business firms according to prescribed laws and regulations.

Illustrative examples: Internal Revenue Service Agent, Revenue Collector, Tax Investigator

13-2082 Tax Preparers
Prepare tax returns for individuals or small businesses. Excludes "Accountants and Auditors" (13-2011).

Illustrative examples: Income Tax Advisor, Income Tax Preparer, Licensed Tax Consultant

13-2090 Miscellaneous Financial Specialists
This broad occupation is the same as the detailed occupation:
13-2099 Financial Specialists, All Other

13-2099 Financial Specialists, All Other
All financial specialists not listed separately.

Illustrative examples: Bail Bondsman, Executor of Estate, Foreign Exchange Trader

15-1100 Computer Occupations 15-1110 Computer and Information Research Scientists

This broad occupation is the same as the detailed occupation:

15-1111 Computer and Information Research Scientists

15-1111 Computer and Information Research Scientists

Conduct research into fundamental computer and information science as theorists, designers, or inventors. Develop solutions to problems in the field of computer hardware and software.

Illustrative examples: Control System Computer Scientist, Computational Theory Scientist, Programming Methodology and Languages Researcher

15-1120 Computer and Information Analysts

This broad occupation includes the following two detailed occupations:

15-1121 Computer Systems Analysts
15-1122 Information Security Analysts

15-1121 Computer Systems Analysts

Analyze science, engineering, business, and other data processing problems to implement and improve computer systems. Analyze user requirements, procedures, and problems to automate or improve existing systems and review computer system capabilities, workflow, and scheduling limitations. May analyze or recommend commercially available software.

Illustrative examples: Applications Analyst, Data Processing Systems Analyst, Information Systems Analyst, Systems Architect

15-1122 Information Security Analysts

Plan, implement, upgrade, or monitor security measures for the protection of computer networks and information. May ensure appropriate security controls are in place that will safeguard digital files and vital electronic infrastructure. May respond to computer security breaches and viruses. Excludes "Computer Network Architects" (15-1143).

Illustrative examples: Computer Security Specialist, Internet Security Specialist, Network Security Analyst

15-1130 Software Developers and Programmers

This broad occupation includes the following four detailed occupations:

15-1131 Computer Programmers
15-1132 Software Developers, Applications
15-1133 Software Developers, Systems Software
15-1134 Web Developers

15-1131 Computer Programmers

Create, modify, and test the code, forms, and script that allow computer applications to run. Work from specifications drawn up by software developers or other individuals. May assist software developers by analyzing user needs and designing software solutions. May develop and write computer programs to store, locate, and retrieve specific documents, data, and information.

Illustrative examples: Applications Programmer, Computer Language Coder, Systems Programmer

15-1132 Software Developers, Applications
Develop, create, and modify general computer applications software or specialized utility programs. Analyze user needs and develop software solutions. Design software or customize software for client use with the aim of optimizing operational efficiency. May analyze and design databases within an application area, working individually or coordinating database development as part of a team. May supervise computer programmers.

Illustrative examples: Computer Applications Engineer, Database Developer, Software Applications Architect, Software Applications Engineer

15-1133 Software Developers, Systems Software
Research, design, develop, and test operating systems-level software, compilers, and network distribution software for medical, industrial, military, communications, aerospace, business, scientific, and general computing applications. Set operational specifications and formulate and analyze software requirements. May design embedded systems software. Apply principles and techniques of computer science, engineering, and mathematical analysis.

Illustrative examples: Computer Systems Software Architect, Embedded Systems Software Developer, Software Systems Engineer

15-1134 Web Developers
Design, create, and modify Web sites. Analyze user needs to implement Web site content, graphics, performance, and capacity. May integrate Web sites with other computer applications. May convert written, graphic, audio, and video components to compatible Web formats by using software designed to facilitate the creation of Web and multimedia content. Excludes "Multimedia Artists and Animators" (27-1014).

Illustrative examples: Internet Developer, Intranet Developer, Web Designer

15-1140 Database and Systems Administrators and Network Architects
This broad occupation includes the following three detailed occupations:
15-1141 Database Administrators
15-1142 Network and Computer Systems Administrators
15-1143 Computer Network Architects

15-1141 Database Administrators

Administer, test, and implement computer databases, applying knowledge of database management systems. Coordinate changes to computer databases. May plan, coordinate, and implement security measures to safeguard computer databases. Excludes "Information Security Analysts" (15-1122).

Illustrative examples: Database Management System Specialist, Database Security Administrator

15-1142 Network and Computer Systems Administrators
Install, configure, and support an organization's local area network (LAN), wide area network (WAN), and Internet systems or a segment of a network system. Monitor network to ensure network availability to all system users and may perform necessary maintenance to support network availability. May monitor and test Web site performance to ensure Web sites operate correctly and without interruption. May assist in network modeling, analysis, planning, and coordination between network and data communications hardware and software. May supervise computer user support specialists and computer network support specialists. May administer network security measures. Excludes "Information Security Analysts"(15-1122), "Computer User Support Specialists" (15-1151), and "Computer Network Support Specialists" (15-1152).

Illustrative examples: Network Coordinator, Network Security Administrator, Wide Area Network Administrator

15-1143 Computer Network Architects
Design and implement computer and information networks, such as local area networks (LAN), wide area networks (WAN), intranets, extranets, and other data communications networks. Perform network modeling, analysis, and planning. May also design network and computer security measures. May research and recommend network and data communications hardware and software. Excludes "Information Security Analysts" (15-1122), "Network and Computer Systems Administrators" (15-1142), and "Computer Network Support Specialists" (15-1152).

Illustrative examples: Computer Network Engineer, Network Designer, Network Developer

15-1150 Computer Support Specialists
This broad occupation includes the following two detailed occupations:
15-1151 Computer User Support Specialists
15-1152 Computer and Network Support Specialists

15-1151 Computer User Support Specialists
Provide technical assistance to computer users. Answer questions or resolve computer problems for clients in person, or via telephone or electronically. May provide assistance concerning the use of computer hardware and software, including printing, installation, word processing, electronic mail, and operating systems. Excludes "Network and Computer Systems Administrators" (15-1142).

Illustrative examples: Desktop Support Specialist, End-User Support Specialist, Help Desk Technician

15-1152 Computer Network Support Specialists

Analyze, test, troubleshoot, and evaluate existing network systems, such as local area network (LAN), wide area network (WAN), and Internet systems or a segment of a network system. Perform network maintenance to ensure networks operate correctly with minimal interruption. Excludes "Network and Computer Systems Administrators" (15-1142) and "Computer Network Architects" (15-1143).

Illustrative examples: Network Diagnostic Support Technician, Network Support Technician, Network Technician

15-1190 Miscellaneous Computer Occupations

This broad occupation is the same as the detailed occupation:
15-1199 Computer Occupations, All Other

15-1199 Computer Occupations, All Other

All computer occupations not listed separately. Excludes "Computer and Information Systems Managers" (11-3021), "Computer Hardware Engineers" (17-2061), "Electrical and Electronics Engineers" (17-2070), "Computer Science Teachers, Postsecondary" (25-1021), "Multimedia Artists and Animators" (27-1014), "Graphic Designers" (27-1024), "Computer Operators" (43-9011), and "Computer, Automated Teller, and Office Machine Repairers" (49-2011).

Illustrative example: Computer Laboratory Technician

15-2000 Mathematical Science Occupations

15-2010 Actuaries

This broad occupation is the same as the detailed occupation:
15-2011 Actuaries

15-2011 Actuaries

Analyze statistical data, such as mortality, accident, sickness, disability, and retirement rates and construct probability tables to forecast risk and liability for payment of future benefits. May ascertain insurance rates required and cash reserves necessary to ensure payment of future benefits.

Illustrative examples: Actuarial Mathematician, Health Actuary, Insurance Actuary

15-2020 Mathematicians

This broad occupation is the same as the detailed occupation:
15-2021 Mathematicians

15-2021 Mathematicians
Conduct research in fundamental mathematics or in application of mathematical techniques to science, management, and other fields. Solve problems in various fields using mathematical methods.

Illustrative examples: Algebraist, Cryptographer, Cryptographic Vulnerability Analyst

15-2030 Operations Research Analysts
This broad occupation is the same as the detailed occupation:
15-2031 Operations Research Analysts

15-2031 Operations Research Analysts
Formulate and apply mathematical modeling and other optimizing methods to develop and interpret information that assists management with decision making, policy formulation, or other managerial functions. May collect and analyze data and develop decision support software, service, or products. May develop and supply optimal time, cost, or logistics networks for program evaluation, review, or implementation.

Illustrative examples: Operations Analyst, Procedure Analyst, Process Analyst

15-2040 Statisticians
This broad occupation is the same as the detailed occupation:
15-2041 Statisticians

15-2041 Statisticians
Develop or apply mathematical or statistical theory and methods to collect, organize, interpret, and summarize numerical data to provide usable information. May specialize in fields such as bio-statistics, agricultural statistics, business statistics, or economic statistics. Includes mathematical and survey statisticians. Excludes "Survey Researchers" (19-3022).

Illustrative examples: Biostatistician, Statistical Analyst, Time Study Statistician

15-2090 Miscellaneous Mathematical Science Occupations
This broad occupation includes the following two detailed occupations:
15-2091 Mathematical Technicians
15-2099 Mathematical Scientists, All Other

15-2091 Mathematical Technicians
Apply standardized mathematical formulas, principles, and methodology to technological problems in engineering and physical sciences in relation to specific industrial and research objectives, processes, equipment, and products.

Illustrative example: Mathematical Engineering Technician

15-2099 Mathematical Science Occupations, All Other

All mathematical scientists not listed separately.

Illustrative example: Harmonic Analyst

17-1000 Architects, Surveyors, and Cartographers

17-1010 Architects, Except Naval
This broad occupation includes the following two detailed occupations:
17-1011 Architects, Except Landscape and Naval
17-1012 Landscape Architects

17-1011 Architects, Except Landscape and Naval
Plan and design structures, such as private residences, office buildings, theaters, factories, and other structural property. Excludes "Landscape Architects" (17-1012) and "Marine Engineers and Naval Architects" (17-2121).

Illustrative examples: Building Architect, Building Architectural Designer, Structural Architect

17-1012 Landscape Architects
Plan and design land areas for projects such as parks and other recreational facilities, airports, highways, hospitals, schools, land subdivisions, and commercial, industrial, and residential sites.

Illustrative examples: Golf Course Architect, Golf Course Designer, Landscape Designer

17-1020 Surveyors, Cartographers, and Photogrammetrists
This broad occupation includes the following two detailed occupations:
17-1021 Cartographers and Photogrammetrists
17-1022 Surveyors

17-1021 Cartographers and Photogrammetrists
Collect, analyze, and interpret geographic information provided by geodetic surveys, aerial photographs, and satellite data. Research, study, and prepare maps and other spatial data in digital or graphic form for legal, social, political, educational, and design purposes. May work with Geographic Information Systems (GIS). May design and evaluate algorithms, data structures, and user interfaces for GIS and mapping systems.

Illustrative examples: Digital Cartographer, Mapper, Topographer

17-1022 Surveyors
Make exact measurements and determine property boundaries. Provide data relevant to the shape, contour, gravitation, location, elevation, or dimension of land or land features on or near the earth's surface for engineering, mapmaking, mining, land evaluation, construction, and other purposes.

Illustrative examples: Geodetic Surveyor, Land Surveyor, Mineral Surveyor

17-2000 Engineers

17-2010 Aerospace Engineers
This broad occupation is the same as the detailed occupation:
17-2011 Aerospace Engineers

17-2011 Aerospace Engineers
Perform engineering duties in designing, constructing, and testing aircraft, missiles, and spacecraft. May conduct basic and applied research to evaluate adaptability of materials and equipment to aircraft design and manufacture. May recommend improvements in testing equipment and techniques.

Illustrative examples: Aeronautical Engineer, Aircraft Design Engineer, Flight Test Engineer

17-2020 Agricultural Engineers
This broad occupation is the same as the detailed occupation:
17-2021 Agricultural Engineers

17-2021 Agricultural Engineers
Apply knowledge of engineering technology and biological science to agricultural problems concerned with power and machinery, electrification, structures, soil and water conservation, and processing of agricultural products.

Illustrative examples: Agricultural Production Engineer, Agricultural Research Engineer, Farm Equipment Engineer

17-2030 Biomedical Engineers
This broad occupation is the same as the detailed occupation:
17-2031 Biomedical Engineers

17-2031 Biomedical Engineers
Apply knowledge of engineering, biology, and biomechanical principles to the design, development, and evaluation of biological and health systems and products, such as artificial organs, prostheses, instrumentation, medical information systems, and heath management and care delivery systems.

Illustrative examples: Biomaterials Engineer, Bio-Mechanical Engineer, Dialysis Engineer

17-2040 Chemical Engineers
This broad occupation is the same as the detailed occupation:
17-2041 Chemical Engineers

17-2041 Chemical Engineers

Design chemical plant equipment and devise processes for manufacturing chemicals and products, such as gasoline, synthetic rubber, plastics, detergents, cement, paper, and pulp, by applying principles and technology of chemistry, physics, and engineering.

Illustrative examples: Fuels Engineer, Plastics Engineer, Polymerization Engineer

17-2050 Civil Engineers

This broad occupation is the same as the detailed occupation:
17-2051 Civil Engineers

17-2051 Civil Engineers

Perform engineering duties in planning, designing, and overseeing construction and maintenance of building structures, and facilities, such as roads, railroads, airports, bridges, harbors, channels, dams, irrigation projects, pipelines, power plants, and water and sewage systems. Includes architectural, structural, traffic, ocean, and geo-technical engineers. Excludes "Hydrologists" (19-2043).

Illustrative examples: Bridge Engineer, Construction Engineer, Highway Engineer

17-2060 Computer Hardware Engineers

This broad occupation is the same as the detailed occupation:
17-2061 Computer Hardware Engineers

17-2061 Computer Hardware Engineers

Research, design, develop, or test computer or computer-related equipment for commercial, industrial, military, or scientific use. May supervise the manufacturing and installation of computer or computer-related equipment and components. Excludes "Software Developers, Applications" (15-1132) and "Software Developers, Systems Software" (15-1133).

Illustrative examples: Computer Hardware Designer, Computer Hardware Developer

17-2070 Electrical and Electronics Engineers

This broad occupation includes the following two detailed occupations:
17-2071 Electrical Engineers
17-2072 Electronics Engineers, Except Computer

17-2071 Electrical Engineers

Research, design, develop, test, or supervise the manufacturing and installation of electrical equipment, components, or systems for commercial, industrial, military, or scientific use. Excludes "Computer Hardware Engineers" (17-2061).

Illustrative examples: Electrical Systems Engineer, Illuminating Engineer, Power Distribution Engineer

17-2072 Electronics Engineers, Except Computer

Research, design, develop, or test electronic components and systems for commercial, industrial, military, or scientific use employing knowledge of electronic theory and materials properties. Design electronic circuits and components for use in fields such as telecommunications, aerospace guidance and propulsion control, acoustics, or instruments and controls. Excludes "Computer Hardware Engineers" (17-2061).

Illustrative examples: Circuit Design Engineer, Electronic Design Automation Engineer, Telecommunication Engineer

17-2080 Environmental Engineers

This broad occupation is the same as the detailed occupation:
17-2081 Environmental Engineers

17-2081 Environmental Engineers

Research, design, plan, or perform engineering duties in the prevention, control, and remediation of environmental hazards using various engineering disciplines. Work may include waste treatment, site remediation, or pollution control technology.

Illustrative examples: Environmental Remediation Engineer, Pollution Control Engineer, Soil Engineer, Water Treatment Plant Engineer

17-2110 Industrial Engineers, Including Health and Safety

This broad occupation includes the following two detailed occupations:
17-2111 Health and Safety Engineers, Except Mining Safety Engineers and Inspectors
17-2112 Industrial Engineers

17-2111 Health and Safety Engineers, Except Mining Safety Engineers and Inspectors

Promote worksite or product safety by applying knowledge of industrial processes, mechanics, chemistry, psychology, and industrial health and safety laws. Includes industrial product safety engineers.

Illustrative examples: Fire Protection Engineer, Industrial Safety Engineer, Product Safety Engineer

17-2112 Industrial Engineers

Design, develop, test, and evaluate integrated systems for managing industrial production processes, including human work factors, quality control, inventory control, logistics and material flow, cost analysis, and production coordination. Excludes "Health and Safety Engineers, Except Mining Safety Engineers and Inspectors" (17-2111).

Illustrative examples: Efficiency Engineer, Manufacturing Engineer, Packaging Engineer, Production Engineer

17-2120 Marine Engineers and Naval Architects
This broad occupation is the same as the detailed occupation:
17-2121 Marine Engineers and Naval Architects

17-2121 Marine Engineers and Naval Architects
Design, develop, and evaluate the operation of marine vessels, ship machinery, and related equipment, such as power supply and propulsion systems.

Illustrative examples: Marine Architect, Marine Structural Designer, Naval Engineer

17-2130 Materials Engineers
This broad occupation is the same as the detailed occupation:
17-2131 Materials Engineers

17-2131 Materials Engineers
Evaluate materials and develop machinery and processes to manufacture materials for use in products that must meet specialized design and performance specifications. Develop new uses for known materials. Includes those engineers working with composite materials or specializing in one type of material, such as graphite, metal and metal alloys, ceramics and glass, plastics and polymers, and naturally occurring materials. Includes metallurgists and metallurgical engineers, ceramic engineers, and welding engineers.

Illustrative examples: Automotive Sheet Metal Engineer, Forensic Materials Engineer, Metallographer

17-2140 Mechanical Engineers
This broad occupation is the same as the detailed occupation:
17-2141 Mechanical Engineers

17-2141 Mechanical Engineers
Perform engineering duties in planning and designing tools, engines, machines, and other mechanically functioning equipment. Oversee installation, operation, maintenance, and repair of equipment such as centralized heat, gas, water, and steam systems.

Illustrative examples: Combustion Engineer, Engine Designer, Heating and Cooling Systems Engineer, Tool and Die Engineer

17-2150 Mining and Geological Engineers, Including Mining Safety Engineers
This broad occupation is the same as the detailed occupation:
17-2151 Mining and Geological Engineers, Including Mining Safety Engineers

17-2151 Mining and Geological Engineers, Including Mining Safety Engineers
Conduct sub-surface surveys to identify the characteristics of potential land or mining development sites. May specify the ground support systems, processes and equipment for safe, economical, and environmentally sound extraction or underground construction activities. May

inspect areas for unsafe geological conditions, equipment, and working conditions. May design, implement, and coordinate mine safety programs. Excludes "Petroleum Engineers" (17-2171).

Illustrative examples: Geophysical Engineer, Mineral Engineer, Seismic Engineer

17-2160 Nuclear Engineers
This broad occupation is the same as the detailed occupation:
17-2161 Nuclear Engineers

17-2161 Nuclear Engineers
Conduct research on nuclear engineering projects or apply principles and theory of nuclear science to problems concerned with release, control, and use of nuclear energy and nuclear waste disposal.

Illustrative examples: Atomic Process Engineer, Nuclear Radiation Engineer, Radiation Engineer, Reactor Engineer

17-2170 Petroleum Engineers
This broad occupation is the same as the detailed occupation:
17-2171 Petroleum Engineers

17-2171 Petroleum Engineers
Devise methods to improve oil and gas extraction and production and determine the need for new or modified tool designs. Oversee drilling and offer technical advice.

Illustrative examples: Natural Gas Engineer, Oil Drilling Engineer, Oil Exploration Engineer

17-2190 Miscellaneous Engineers
This broad occupation is the same as the detailed occupation:
17-2199 Engineers, All Other

17-2199 Engineers, All Other
All engineers not listed separately.

Illustrative examples: Optical Engineer, Ordnance Engineer, Photonics Engineer, Salvage Engineer

17-3000 Drafters, Engineering Technicians, and Mapping Technicians

17-3010 Drafters
This broad occupation includes the following four detailed occupations:
17-3011 Architectural and Civil Drafters
17-3012 Electrical and Electronics Drafters
17-3013 Mechanical Drafters
17-3019 Drafters, All Other

17-3011 Architectural and Civil Drafters

Prepare detailed drawings of architectural and structural features of buildings or drawings and topographical relief maps used in civil engineering projects, such as highways, bridges, and public works. Use knowledge of building materials, engineering practices, and mathematics to complete drawings.

Illustrative examples: Building Drafter, Civil Computer-Aided Design and Drafting Technician, Structural Drafter

17-3012 Electrical and Electronics Drafters

Prepare wiring diagrams, circuit board assembly diagrams, and layout drawings used for the manufacture, installation, or repair of electrical equipment.

Illustrative examples: Electrical Computer Aided Design and Drafting Technician, Electrical Systems Drafter, Printed Circuit Board Drafter

17-3013 Mechanical Drafters

Prepare detailed working diagrams of machinery and mechanical devices, including dimensions, fastening methods, and other engineering information.

Illustrative examples: Aeronautical Drafter, Automotive Design Drafter, Tool and Die Designer

17-3019 Drafters, All Other

All drafters not listed separately.

Illustrative examples: Blueprint Tracer, Geological Drafter, Marine Drafter

17-3020 Engineering Technicians, Except Drafters

This broad occupation includes the following eight detailed occupations:
17-3021 Aerospace Engineering and Operations Technicians
17-3022 Civil Engineering Technicians
17-3023 Electrical and Electronic Engineering Technicians
17-3024 Electro-Mechanical Technicians
17-3025 Environmental Engineering Technicians
17-3026 Industrial Engineering Technicians
17-3027 Mechanical Engineering Technicians
17-3029 Engineering Technicians, Except Drafters, All Other

17-3021 Aerospace Engineering and Operations Technicians

Operate, install, calibrate, and maintain integrated computer/communications systems, consoles, simulators, and other data acquisition, test, and measurement instruments and equipment, which are used to launch, track, position, and evaluate air and space vehicles. May record and interpret test data.

Illustrative examples: Altitude Chamber Technician, Flight Data Technician, Wind Tunnel Technician

17-3022 Civil Engineering Technicians

Apply theory and principles of civil engineering in planning, designing, and overseeing construction and maintenance of structures and facilities under the direction of engineering staff or physical scientists.

Illustrative examples: Geotechnical Engineering Technician, Highway Engineering Technician, Structural Engineering Technician

17-3023 Electrical and Electronic Engineering Technicians

Apply electrical and electronic theory and related knowledge, usually under the direction of engineering staff, to design, build, repair, calibrate, and modify electrical components, circuitry, controls, and machinery for subsequent evaluation and use by engineering staff in making engineering design decisions. Excludes "Broadcast Technicians" (27-4012).

Illustrative examples: Electrical Design Technician, Lighting Engineering Technician, Semiconductor Development Technician

17-3024 Electro-Mechanical Technicians

Operate, test, maintain, or calibrate unmanned, automated, servo-mechanical, or electromechanical equipment. May operate unmanned submarines, aircraft, or other equipment at worksites, such as oil rigs, deep ocean exploration, or hazardous waste removal. May assist engineers in testing and designing robotics equipment.

Illustrative examples: Remotely Piloted Vehicle Engineering Technician, Robotics Testing Technician

17-3025 Environmental Engineering Technicians

Apply theory and principles of environmental engineering to modify, test, and operate equipment and devices used in the prevention, control, and remediation of environmental problems, including waste treatment and site remediation, under the direction of engineering staff or scientist. May assist in the development of environmental remediation devices.

Illustrative examples: Air Analysis Engineering Technician, Environmental Remediation Engineering Technician, Pollution Control Engineering Technician

17-3026 Industrial Engineering Technicians

Apply engineering theory and principles to problems of industrial layout or manufacturing production, usually under the direction of engineering staff. May perform time and motion studies on worker operations in a variety of industries for purposes such as establishing standard production rates or improving efficiency.

Illustrative examples: Motion Study Technician, Production Control Technologist, Time Study Technician

17-3027 Mechanical Engineering Technicians
Apply theory and principles of mechanical engineering to modify, develop, test, or calibrate machinery and equipment under direction of engineering staff or physical scientists.

Illustrative examples: Gyroscope Engineering Technician, Heat Transfer Technician, Optomechanical Technician

17-3029 Engineering Technicians, Except Drafters, All Other
All engineering technicians, except drafters, not listed separately.

Illustrative examples: Agricultural Engineering Technician, Biomedical Engineering Technician, Metallurgical Engineering Technician, Optical Engineering Technician

17-3030 Surveying and Mapping Technicians
This broad occupation is the same as the detailed occupation:
17-3031 Surveying and Mapping Technicians

17-3031 Surveying and Mapping Technicians
Perform surveying and mapping duties, usually under the direction of an engineer, surveyor, cartographer, or photogrammetrist to obtain data used for construction, mapmaking, boundary location, mining, or other purposes. May calculate mapmaking information and create maps from source data, such as surveying notes, aerial photography, satellite data, or other maps to show topographical features, political boundaries, and other features. May verify accuracy and completeness of maps. Excludes "Surveyors" (17-1022), "Cartographers and Photogrammetrists" (17-1021), and "Geoscientists, Except Hydrologists and Geographers" (19-2042).

Illustrative examples: Cartographic Technician, Field Map Technician, GIS Mapping Technician

19-1000 Life Scientists19-1010 Agricultural and Food ScientistsThis broad occupation includes the following three detailed occupations:
19-1011 Animal Scientists
19-1012 Food Scientists and Technologists
19-1013 Soil and Plant Scientists

19-1011 Animal Scientists
Conduct research in the genetics, nutrition, reproduction, growth, and development of domestic farm animals.

Illustrative examples: Animal Nutritionist, Dairy Scientist, Poultry Scientist

19-1012 Food Scientists and Technologists
Use chemistry, microbiology, engineering, and other sciences to study the principles underlying the processing and deterioration of foods; analyze food content to determine levels of vitamins, fat, sugar, and protein; discover new food sources; research ways to make processed foods safe, palatable, and healthful; and apply food science knowledge to determine best ways to process, package, preserve, store, and distribute food.

Illustrative examples: Dairy Bacteriologist, Enologist, Food Safety Scientist

19-1013 Soil and Plant Scientists
Conduct research in breeding, physiology, production, yield, and management of crops and agricultural plants or trees, shrubs, and nursery stock, their growth in soils, and control of pests; or study the chemical, physical, biological, and mineralogical composition of soils as they relate to plant or crop growth. May classify and map soils and investigate effects of alternative practices on soil and crop productivity.

Illustrative examples: Arboreal Scientist, Horticulturist, Plant Physiologist

19-1020 Biological Scientists
This broad occupation includes the following four detailed occupations:
19-1021 Biochemists and Biophysicists
19-1022 Microbiologists
19-1023 Zoologists and Wildlife Biologists
19-1029 Biological Scientists, All Other

19-1021 Biochemists and Biophysicists
Study the chemical composition or physical principles of living cells and organisms, their electrical and mechanical energy, and related phenomena. May conduct research to further understanding of the complex chemical combinations and reactions involved in metabolism, reproduction, growth, and heredity. May determine the effects of foods, drugs, serums, hormones, and other substances on tissues and vital processes of living organisms.
Illustrative examples: Biological Chemist, Clinical Biochemist, Physical Biochemist

19-1022 Microbiologists
Investigate the growth, structure, development, and other characteristics of microscopic organisms, such as bacteria, algae, or fungi. Includes medical microbiologists who study the relationship between organisms and disease or the effects of antibiotics on microorganisms.

Illustrative examples: Bacteriologist, Public Health Microbiologist, Virologist

19-1023 Zoologists and Wildlife Biologists
Study the origins, behavior, diseases, genetics, and life processes of animals and wildlife. May specialize in wildlife research and management. May collect and analyze biological data to determine the environmental effects of present and potential use of land and water habitats.

Illustrative examples: Herpetologist, Ichthyologist, Marine Biologist, Ornithologist

19-1029 Biological Scientists, All Other
All biological scientists not listed separately.

Illustrative examples: Embryologist, Osteologist, Paleobotanist

19-1030 Conservation Scientists and Foresters
This broad occupation includes the following two detailed occupations:
19-1031 Conservation Scientists
19-1032 Foresters

19-1031 Conservation Scientists
Manage, improve, and protect natural resources to maximize their use without damaging the environment. May conduct soil surveys and develop plans to eliminate soil erosion or to protect rangelands. May instruct farmers, agricultural production managers, or ranchers in best ways to use crop rotation, contour plowing, or terracing to conserve soil and water; in the number and kind of livestock and forage plants best suited to particular ranges; and in range and farm improvements, such as fencing and reservoirs for stock watering. Excludes "Zoologists and Wildlife Biologists" (19-1023) and "Foresters" (19-1032).

Illustrative examples: Grassland Conservationist, Range Ecologist, Soil Conservationist

19-1032 Foresters
Manage public and private forested lands for economic, recreational, and conservation purposes. May inventory the type, amount, and location of standing timber, appraise the timber's worth, negotiate the purchase, and draw up contracts for procurement. May determine how to conserve wildlife habitats, creek beds, water quality, and soil stability, and how best to comply with environmental regulations. May devise plans for planting and growing new trees, monitor trees for healthy growth, and determine optimal harvesting schedules.
Illustrative examples: Environmental Protection Forester, Forest Ecologist, Timber Management Specialist

19-1040 Medical Scientists
This broad occupation includes the following two detailed occupations:
19-1041 Epidemiologists
19-1042 Medical Scientists, Except Epidemiologists

19-1041 Epidemiologists
Investigate and describe the determinants and distribution of disease, disability, or health outcomes. May develop the means for prevention and control.

Illustrative examples: Epidemiology Investigator, Malariologist, Pharmacoepidemiologist

19-1042 Medical Scientists, Except Epidemiologists
Conduct research dealing with the understanding of human diseases and the improvement of human health. Engage in clinical investigation, research and development, or other related activities. Includes physicians, dentists, public health specialists, pharmacologists, and medical pathologists who primarily conduct research. Practitioners who primarily provide medical or dental care or dispense drugs are included in "Health Diagnosing and Treating Practitioners" (29-1000).

Illustrative examples: Cancer Researcher, Immunochemist, Toxicologist

19-1090 Miscellaneous Life Scientists
This broad occupation is the same as the detailed occupation:
19-1099 Life Scientists, All Other

19-1099 Life Scientists, All Other
All life scientists not listed separately.

Illustrative example: Life Science Taxonomist

19-2000 Physical Scientists

19-2010 Astronomers and Physicists
This broad occupation includes the following two detailed occupations:
19-2011 Astronomers
19-2012 Physicists

19-2011 Astronomers
Observe, research, and interpret astronomical phenomena to increase basic knowledge or apply such information to practical problems.

Illustrative example: Astrophysicist
19-2012 Physicists

Conduct research into physical phenomena, develop theories on the basis of observation and experiments, and devise methods to apply physical laws and theories. Excludes "Biochemists and Biophysicists" (19-1021).

Illustrative examples: Fluid Dynamicist, Molecular Physicist, Optical Scientist, Rheologist

19-2020 Atmospheric and Space Scientists
This broad occupation is the same as the detailed occupation:
19-2021 Atmospheric and Space Scientists

19-2021 Atmospheric and Space Scientists
Investigate atmospheric phenomena and interpret meteorological data, gathered by surface and air stations, satellites, and radar to prepare reports and forecasts for public and other uses. Includes weather analysts and forecasters whose functions require the detailed knowledge of meteorology.

Illustrative examples: Atmospheric Chemist, Climatologist, Hurricane Tracker, Meteorologist

19-2030 Chemists and Materials Scientists
This broad occupation includes the following two detailed occupations:
19-2031 Chemists
19-2032 Materials Scientists

19-2031 Chemists
Conduct qualitative and quantitative chemical analyses or experiments in laboratories for quality or process control or to develop new products or knowledge. Excludes "Geoscientists, Except Hydrologists and Geographers" (19-2042) and "Biochemists and Biophysicists" (19-1021).

Illustrative examples: Food Chemist, Industrial Chemist, Inorganic Chemist, Research and Development Chemist

19-2032 Materials Scientists
Research and study the structures and chemical properties of various natural and synthetic or composite materials, including metals, alloys, rubber, ceramics, semiconductors, polymers, and glass. Determine ways to strengthen or combine materials or develop new materials with new or specific properties for use in a variety of products and applications. Includes glass scientists, ceramic scientists, metallurgical scientists, and polymer scientists.

Illustrative examples: Metal Alloy Scientist, Plastics Scientist

19-2040 Environmental Scientists and Geoscientists
This broad occupation includes the following three detailed occupations:
19-2041 Environmental Scientists and Specialists, Including Health
19-2042 Geoscientists, Except Hydrologists and Geographers
19-2043 Hydrologists

19-2041 Environmental Scientists and Specialists, Including Health

Conduct research or perform investigation for the purpose of identifying, abating, or eliminating sources of pollutants or hazards that affect either the environment or the health of the population. Using knowledge of various scientific disciplines, may collect, synthesize, study, report, and recommend action based on data derived from measurements or observations of air, food, soil, water, and other sources. Excludes "Zoologists and Wildlife Biologists" (19-1023), "Conservation Scientists" (19-1031), "Forest and Conservation Technicians" (19-4093), "Fish and Game Wardens" (33-3031), and "Forest and Conservation Workers" (45-4011).

Illustrative examples: Hazardous Substances Scientist, Health Environmentalist, Water Pollution Scientist

19-2042 Geoscientists, Except Hydrologists and Geographers

Study the composition, structure, and other physical aspects of the Earth. May use geological, physics, and mathematics knowledge in exploration for oil, gas, minerals, or underground water; or in waste disposal, land reclamation, or other environmental problems. May study the Earth's internal composition, atmospheres, oceans, and its magnetic, electrical, and gravitational forces. Includes mineralogists, crystallographers, paleontologists, stratigraphers, geodesists, and seismologists.

Illustrative examples: Geochemist, Oceanographer, Petrologist, Volcanologist

19-2043 Hydrologists

Research the distribution, circulation, and physical properties of underground and surface waters; and study the form and intensity of precipitation, its rate of infiltration into the soil, movement through the earth, and its return to the ocean and atmosphere.

Illustrative examples: Hydrogeologist, Isotope Hydrologist, Surface Hydrologist

19-2090 Miscellaneous Physical Scientists

This broad occupation is the same as the detailed occupation:
19-2099 Physical Scientists, All Other

19-2099 Physical Scientists, All Other

All physical scientists not listed separately.

19-3000 Social Scientists and Related Workers

19-3010 Economists

This broad occupation is the same as the detailed occupation:
19-3011 Economists

19-3011 Economists

Conduct research, prepare reports, or formulate plans to address economic problems related to the production and distribution of goods and services or monetary and fiscal policy. May collect and process economic and statistical data using sampling techniques and econometric methods. Excludes "Market Research Analysts and Marketing Specialists" (13-1161).

Illustrative examples: Econometrician, Economic Research Analyst, Environmental Economist, Industrial Economist

19-3020 Survey Researchers
This broad occupation is the same as the detailed occupation:
19-3022 Survey Researchers

19-3022 Survey Researchers
Plan, develop, or conduct surveys. May analyze and interpret the meaning of survey data, determine survey objectives, or suggest or test question wording. Includes social scientists who primarily design questionnaires or supervise survey teams. Excludes "Market Research Analysts and Marketing Specialists" (13-1161) and "Statisticians" (15-2041).

Illustrative examples: Pollster, Survey Methodologist, Survey Questionnaire Designer

19-3030 Psychologists
This broad occupation includes the following three detailed occupations:
19-3031 Clinical, Counseling, and School Psychologists
19-3032 Industrial-Organizational Psychologists
19-3039 Psychologists, All Other

19-3031 Clinical, Counseling, and School Psychologists
Diagnose and treat mental disorders; learning disabilities; and cognitive, behavioral, and emotional problems, using individual, child, family, and group therapies. May design and implement behavior modification programs.

Illustrative examples: Child Psychologist, Geropsychologist, School Psychologist, Vocational Psychologist

19-3032 Industrial-Organizational Psychologists
Apply principles of psychology to human resources, administration, management, sales, and marketing problems. Activities may include policy planning; employee testing and selection, training and development; and organizational development and analysis. May work with management to organize the work setting to improve worker productivity.

Illustrative examples: Engineering Psychologist, Human Resources Psychologist, Management Psychologist

19-3039 Psychologists, All Other

All psychologists not listed separately.

Illustrative examples: Forensic Psychologist, Social Psychologist, Sports Psychologist

19-3040 Sociologists
This broad occupation is the same as the detailed occupation:
19-3041 Sociologists

19-3041 Sociologists
Study human society and social behavior by examining the groups and social institutions that people form, as well as various social, religious, political, and business organizations. May study the behavior and interaction of groups, trace their origin and growth, and analyze the influence of group activities on individual members.

Illustrative examples: Criminologist, Family Sociologist, Rural Sociologist

19-3050 Urban and Regional Planners
This broad occupation is the same as the detailed occupation:
19-3051 Urban and Regional Planners

19-3051 Urban and Regional Planners
Develop comprehensive plans and programs for use of land and physical facilities of jurisdictions, such as towns, cities, counties, and metropolitan areas.

Illustrative examples: City Planner, Community Development Planner

19-3090 Miscellaneous Social Scientists and Related Workers
This broad occupation includes the following five detailed occupations:
19-3091 Anthropologists and Archeologists
19-3092 Geographers
19-3093 Historians
19-3094 Political Scientists
19-3099 Social Scientists and Related Workers, All Other

19-3091 Anthropologists and Archeologists
Study the origin, development, and behavior of human beings. May study the way of life, language, or physical characteristics of people in various parts of the world. May engage in systematic recovery and examination of material evidence, such as tools or pottery remaining from past human cultures, in order to determine the history, customs, and living habits of earlier civilizations.

Illustrative examples: Ethonoarcheologist, Political Anthropologist, Research Archeologist

19-3092 Geographers

Study the nature and use of areas of the Earth's surface, relating and interpreting interactions of physical and cultural phenomena. Conduct research on physical aspects of a region, including land forms, climates, soils, plants, and animals, and conduct research on the spatial implications of human activities within a given area, including social characteristics, economic activities, and political organization, as well as researching interdependence between regions at scales ranging from local to global.

Illustrative examples: Economic Geographer, Geomorphologist, GIS Geographer, Political Geographer

19-3093 Historians

Research, analyze, record, and interpret the past as recorded in sources, such as government and institutional records, newspapers and other periodicals, photographs, interviews, films, electronic media, and unpublished manuscripts, such as personal diaries and letters.

Illustrative examples: Genealogist, Historiographer, Protohistorian

19-3094 Political Scientists

Study the origin, development, and operation of political systems. May study topics, such as public opinion, political decision-making, and ideology. May analyze the structure and operation of governments, as well as various political entities. May conduct public opinion surveys, analyze election results, or analyze public documents. Excludes "Survey Researchers" (19-3022).

Illustrative examples: Government Affairs Specialist, Political Consultant, Political Research Scientist

19-3099 Social Scientists and Related Workers, All Other

All social scientists and related workers not listed separately.

Illustrative examples: Demographer, Ethnologist, Linguist

19-4000 Life, Physical, and Social Science Technicians

19-4010 Agricultural and Food Science Technicians

This broad occupation is the same as the detailed occupation:
19-4011 Agricultural and Food Science Technicians

19-4011 Agricultural and Food Science Technicians

Work with agricultural and food scientists in food, fiber, and animal research, production, and processing; and assist with animal breeding and nutrition. Conduct tests and experiments to improve yield and quality of crops or to increase the resistance of plants and animals to disease or insects. Includes technicians who assist food scientists or technologists in the research and development of production technology, quality control, packaging, processing, and use of foods.
Illustrative examples: Dairy Technologist, Feed Research Technician, Seed Analyst

19-4020 Biological Technicians
This broad occupation is the same as the detailed occupation:
19-4021 Biological Technicians

19-4021 Biological Technicians
Assist biological and medical scientists in laboratories. Set up, operate, and maintain laboratory instruments and equipment, monitor experiments, make observations, and calculate and record results. May analyze organic substances, such as blood, food, and drugs.

Illustrative examples: Bacteriology Technician, Marine Fisheries Technician, Wildlife Technician

19-4030 Chemical Technicians
This broad occupation is the same as the detailed occupation:
19-4031 Chemical Technicians

19-4031 Chemical Technicians
Conduct chemical and physical laboratory tests to assist scientists in making qualitative and quantitative analyses of solids, liquids, and gaseous materials for research and development of new products or processes, quality control, maintenance of environmental standards, and other work involving experimental, theoretical, or practical application of chemistry and related sciences.

Illustrative examples: Assayer, Chemical Laboratory Technician, Inorganic Chemical Technician

19-4040 Geological and Petroleum Technicians
This broad occupation is the same as the detailed occupation:
19-4041 Geological and Petroleum Technicians

19-4041 Geological and Petroleum Technicians
Assist scientists or engineers in the use of electronic, sonic, or nuclear measuring instruments in both laboratory and production activities to obtain data indicating potential resources such as metallic ore, minerals, gas, coal, or petroleum. Analyze mud and drill cuttings. Chart pressure, temperature, and other characteristics of wells or bore holes. Investigate and collect information leading to the possible discovery of new metallic ore, minerals, gas, coal, or petroleum deposits.

Illustrative examples: Crude Tester, Geophysical Prospector, Seismic Observer

19-4050 Nuclear Technicians
This broad occupation is the same as the detailed occupation:

19-4051 Nuclear Technicians

Assist nuclear physicists, nuclear engineers, or other scientists in laboratory or production activities. May operate, maintain, or provide quality control for nuclear testing and research equipment. May monitor radiation.

Illustrative examples: Nuclear Monitoring Technician, Radiochemical Technician

19-4060 Social Science Research Assistants
This broad occupation is the same as the detailed occupation:
19-4061 Social Science Research Assistants

19-4061 Social Science Research Assistants
Assist social scientists in laboratory, survey, and other social science research. May help prepare findings for publication and assist in laboratory analysis, quality control, or data management. Excludes "Graduate Teaching Assistants" (25-1191).

Illustrative examples: City Planning Aide, Economic Research Assistant, Historian Research Assistant

19-4090 Miscellaneous Life, Physical, and Social Science Technicians
This broad occupation includes the following four detailed occupations:
19-4091 Environmental Science and Protection Technicians, Including Health
19-4092 Forensic Science Technicians
19-4093 Forest and Conservation Technicians
19-4099 Life, Physical, and Social Science Technicians, All Other

19-4091 Environmental Science and Protection Technicians, Including Health
Perform laboratory and field tests to monitor the environment and investigate sources of pollution, including those that affect health, under the direction of an environmental scientist, engineer, or other specialist. May collect samples of gases, soil, water, and other materials for testing.

Illustrative examples: Groundwater Monitoring Technician, Infectious Waste Technician, Pollution Control Technician, Waste Minimization Technician

19-4092 Forensic Science Technicians
Collect, identify, classify, and analyze physical evidence related to criminal investigations. Perform tests on weapons or substances, such as fiber, hair, and tissue to determine significance to investigation. May testify as expert witnesses on evidence or crime laboratory techniques. May serve as specialists in area of expertise, such as ballistics, fingerprinting, handwriting, or biochemistry.

Illustrative examples: Ballistics Expert, Crime Scene Technician, Trace Evidence Technician

19-4093 Forest and Conservation Technicians

Provide technical assistance regarding the conservation of soil, water, forests, or related natural resources. May compile data pertaining to size, content, condition, and other characteristics of forest tracts, under the direction of foresters; or train and lead forest workers in forest propagation, fire prevention and suppression. May assist conservation scientists in managing, improving, and protecting rangelands and wildlife habitats. Excludes "Conservation Scientists" (19-1031) and "Foresters" (19-1032).

Illustrative examples: Forestry Aide, Soil Conservation Technician, Timber Management Technician

19-4099 Life, Physical, and Social Science Technicians, All Other
All life, physical, and social science technicians not listed separately.

Illustrative examples: Meteorological Aide, Polygraph Examiner

21-1000 Counselors, Social Workers, and Other Community and Social Service Specialists

21-1010 Counselors
This broad occupation includes the following six detailed occupations:
21-1011 Substance Abuse and Behavioral Disorder Counselors
21-1012 Educational, Guidance, School, and Vocational Counselors
21-1013 Marriage and Family Therapists
21-1014 Mental Health Counselors
21-1015 Rehabilitation Counselors
21-1019 Counselors, All Other

21-1011 Substance Abuse and Behavioral Disorder Counselors
Counsel and advise individuals with alcohol, tobacco, drug, or other problems, such as gambling and eating disorders. May counsel individuals, families, or groups or engage in prevention programs. Excludes "Social Workers" (21-1021 through 21-1029), "Psychologists" (19-3031 through 19-3039), and "Mental Health Counselors" (21-1014) providing these services.

Illustrative examples: Addiction Counselor, Alcohol and Drug Counselor, Chemical Dependency Counselor

21-1012 Educational, Guidance, School, and Vocational Counselors
Counsel individuals and provide group educational and vocational guidance services.

Illustrative examples: Career Counselor, Career Technical Counselor, Student Development Advisor

21-1013 Marriage and Family Therapists
Diagnose and treat mental and emotional disorders, whether cognitive, affective, or behavioral, within the context of marriage and family systems. Apply psychotherapeutic and family systems theories and techniques in the delivery of services to individuals, couples, and families for the purpose of treating such diagnosed nervous and mental disorders. Excludes "Social Workers" (21-1021 through 21-1029) and "Psychologists" of all types (19-3031 through 19-3039).

Illustrative examples: Child and Family Counselor, Couples Therapist, Marriage Counselor

21-1014 Mental Health Counselors
Counsel with emphasis on prevention. Work with individuals and groups to promote optimum mental and emotional health. May help individuals deal with issues associated with addictions and substance abuse; family, parenting, and marital problems; stress management; self-esteem; and aging. Excludes "Social Workers" (21-1021 through 21-1029), "Psychiatrists" (29-1066), and "Psychologists" (19-3031 through 19-3039).

Illustrative examples: Licensed Clinical Mental Health Counselor (LCMHC), Licensed Mental Health Counselor (LMHC)

21-1015 Rehabilitation Counselors
Counsel individuals to maximize the independence and employability of persons coping with personal, social, and vocational difficulties that result from birth defects, illness, disease, accidents, or the stress of daily life. Coordinate activities for residents of care and treatment facilities. Assess client needs and design and implement rehabilitation programs that may include personal and vocational counseling, training, and job placement.

Illustrative examples: Psychosocial Rehabilitation Counselor, Veterans Rehabilitation Counselor, Vocational Rehabilitation Counselor

21-1019 Counselors, All Other
All counselors not listed separately.

Illustrative examples: Anger Control Counselor, Grief Counselor, Sexual Assault Counselor

21-1020 Social Workers
This broad occupation includes the following four detailed occupations:
21-1021 Child, Family, and School Social Workers
21-1022 Healthcare Social Workers
21-1023 Mental Health and Substance Abuse Social Workers
21-1029 Social Workers, All Other

21-1021 Child, Family, and School Social Workers
Provide social services and assistance to improve the social and psychological functioning of children and their families and to maximize the family well-being and the academic functioning of children. May assist parents, arrange adoptions, and find foster homes for abandoned or abused children. In schools, they address such problems as teenage pregnancy, misbehavior, and truancy. May also advise teachers.

Illustrative examples: Certified Children, Youth, and Family Social Worker; Child Abuse Worker; Foster Care worker

21-1022 Healthcare Social Workers
Provide individuals, families, and groups with the psychosocial support needed to cope with chronic, acute, or terminal illnesses. Services include advising family care givers, providing patient education and counseling, and making referrals for other services. May also provide care and case management or interventions designed to promote health, prevent disease, and address barriers to access to healthcare.

Illustrative examples: Hospice Social Worker, Oncology Social Worker, Public Health Social Worker

21-1023 Mental Health and Substance Abuse Social Workers

Assess and treat individuals with mental, emotional, or substance abuse problems, including abuse of alcohol, tobacco, and/or other drugs. Activities may include individual and group therapy, crisis intervention, case management, client advocacy, prevention, and education.

Illustrative examples: Community Mental Health Social Worker, Drug Abuse Social Worker, Psychiatric Social Worker

21-1029 Social Workers, All Other

All social workers not listed separately.

Illustrative examples: Criminal Justice Social Worker, Forensic Social Worker, Sexual Assault Social Worker

21-1090 Miscellaneous Community and Social Service Specialists

This broad occupation includes the following five detailed occupations:
21-1091 Health Educators
21-1092 Probation Officers and Correctional Treatment Specialists
21-1093 Social and Human Service Assistants
21-1094 Community Health Workers
21-1099 Community and Social Service Specialists, All Other

21-1091 Health Educators

Provide and manage health education programs that help individuals, families, and their communities maximize and maintain healthy lifestyles. Collect and analyze data to identify community needs prior to planning, implementing, monitoring, and evaluating programs designed to encourage healthy lifestyles, policies, and environments. May serve as a resource to assist individuals, other healthcare workers, or the community, and may administer fiscal resources for health education programs. Excludes "Community Health Workers" (21-1094).

Illustrative examples: Community Health Education Coordinator, Diabetes Educator, Public Health Educator

21-1092 Probation Officers and Correctional Treatment Specialists

Provide social services to assist in rehabilitation of law offenders in custody or on probation or parole. Make recommendations for actions involving formulation of rehabilitation plan and treatment of offender, including conditional release and education and employment stipulations.

Illustrative examples: Juvenile Probation Officer, Parole Agent, Parole Officer

21-1093 Social and Human Service Assistants

Assist in providing client services in a wide variety of fields, such as psychology, rehabilitation, or social work, including support for families. May assist clients in identifying and obtaining available benefits and social and community services. May assist social workers with developing, organizing, and conducting programs to prevent and resolve problems relevant to substance abuse, human relationships, rehabilitation, or dependent care. Excludes "Rehabilitation Counselors" (21-1015), "Psychiatric Technicians" (29-2053), "Personal Care Aides" (39-9021), and "Eligibility Interviewers, Government Programs" (43-4061).

Illustrative examples: Case Work Aide, Family Service Assistant, Human Services Worker

21-1094 Community Health Workers
Assist individuals and communities to adopt healthy behaviors. Conduct outreach for medical personnel or health organizations to implement programs in the community that promote, maintain, and improve individual and community health. May provide information on available resources, provide social support and informal counseling, advocate for individuals and community health needs, and provide services such as first aid and blood pressure screening. May collect data to help identify community health needs. Excludes "Health Educators" (21-1091).

Illustrative examples: Lay Health Advocate, Peer Health Promoter

21-1099 Community and Social Service Specialists, All Other
All community and social service specialists not listed separately.

Illustrative examples: Community Organization Worker, Veterans Service Officer

21-2000 Religious Workers

21-2010 Clergy
This broad occupation is the same as the detailed occupation:
21-2011 Clergy

21-2011 Clergy
Conduct religious worship and perform other spiritual functions associated with beliefs and practices of religious faith or denomination. Provide spiritual and moral guidance and assistance to members.

Illustrative examples: Imam, Priest, Rabbi

21-2020 Directors, Religious Activities and Education
This broad occupation is the same as the detailed occupation:
21-2021 Directors, Religious Activities and Education

21-2021 Directors, Religious Activities and Education
Plan, direct, or coordinate programs designed to promote the religious education or activities of a denominational group. May provide counseling and guidance relative to marital, health, financial, and religious problems.

Illustrative examples: Religious Education Director, Youth Ministry Director

21-2090 Miscellaneous Religious Workers
This broad occupation is the same as the detailed occupation:
21-2099 Religious Workers, All Other

21-2099 Religious Workers, All Other
All religious workers not listed separately.

Illustrative examples: Missionary, Mohel, Verger

23-1000 Lawyers, Judges, and Related Workers 23-1010 Lawyers and Judicial Law Clerks

This broad occupation includes the following two detailed occupations:
23-1011 Lawyers
23-1012 Judicial Law Clerks

23-1011 Lawyers

Represent clients in criminal and civil litigation and other legal proceedings, draw up legal documents, or manage or advise clients on legal transactions. May specialize in a single area or may practice broadly in many areas of law.

Illustrative examples: Attorney, Corporate Counsel, Public Defender

23-1012 Judicial Law Clerks

Assist judges in court or by conducting research or preparing legal documents. Excludes "Lawyers" (23-1011) and "Paralegals and Legal Assistants" (23-2011).

Illustrative example: Judicial Clerk

23-1020 Judges, Magistrates, and Other Judicial Workers

This broad occupation includes the following three detailed occupations:
23-1021 Administrative Law Judges, Adjudicators, and Hearing Officers
23-1022 Arbitrators, Mediators, and Conciliators
23-1023 Judges, Magistrate Judges, and Magistrates

23-1021 Administrative Law Judges, Adjudicators, and Hearing Officers

Conduct hearings to recommend or make decisions on claims concerning government programs or other government-related matters. Determine liability, sanctions, or penalties, or recommend the acceptance or rejection of claims or settlements. Excludes "Arbitrators, Mediators, and Conciliators" (23-1022).

Illustrative example: Appeals Examiner, Justice of the Peace, Traffic Court Referee

23-1022 Arbitrators, Mediators, and Conciliators

Facilitate negotiation and conflict resolution through dialogue. Resolve conflicts outside of the court system by mutual consent of parties involved.

Illustrative examples: Alternative Dispute Resolution Coordinator, Mediation Commissioner, Ombudsman

23-1023 Judges, Magistrate Judges, and Magistrates

Arbitrate, advise, adjudicate, or administer justice in a court of law. May sentence defendant in criminal cases according to government statutes or sentencing guidelines. May determine liability of defendant in civil cases. May perform wedding ceremonies.
Illustrative example: Circuit Court Judge, Justice, Tribal Judge

23-2000 Legal Support Workers

23-2010 Paralegals and Legal Assistants
This broad occupation is the same as the detailed occupation:
23-2011 Paralegals and Legal Assistants

23-2011 Paralegals and Legal Assistants
Assist lawyers by investigating facts, preparing legal documents, or researching legal precedent. Conduct research to support a legal proceeding, to formulate a defense, or to initiate legal action. Excludes "Legal Secretaries" (43-6012).

Illustrative example: Legal Aide

23-2090 Miscellaneous Legal Support Workers
This broad occupation includes the following three detailed occupations:
23-2091 Court Reporters
23-2093 Title Examiners, Abstractors, and Searchers
23-2099 Legal Support Workers, All Other

23-2091 Court Reporters
Use verbatim methods and equipment to capture, store, retrieve, and transcribe pretrial and trial proceedings or other information. Includes stenocaptioners who operate computerized stenographic captioning equipment to provide captions of live or prerecorded broadcasts for hearing-impaired viewers.

Illustrative examples: Court Stenographer, Court Transcriber, Deposition Reporter

23-2093 Title Examiners, Abstractors, and Searchers
Search real estate records, examine titles, or summarize pertinent legal or insurance documents or details for a variety of purposes. May compile lists of mortgages, contracts, and other instruments pertaining to titles by searching public and private records for law firms, real estate agencies, or title insurance companies.

Illustrative example: Escrow Officer, Lien Searcher, Title Officer

23-2099 Legal Support Workers, All Other
All legal support workers not listed separately.

Illustrative example: Legal Technician

25-1000 Postsecondary Teachers 25-1010 Business Teachers, Postsecondary This broad occupation is the same as the detailed occupation: 25-1011 Business Teachers, Postsecondary

25-1011 Business Teachers, Postsecondary
Teach courses in business administration and management, such as accounting, finance, human resources, labor and industrial relations, marketing, and operations research. Includes both teachers primarily engaged in teaching and those who do a combination of teaching and research.

Illustrative examples: Accounting Professor, Finance Professor, Marketing Professor

25-1020 Math and Computer Teachers, Postsecondary
This broad occupation includes the following two detailed occupations:
25-1021 Computer Science Teachers, Postsecondary
25-1022 Mathematical Science Teachers, Postsecondary

25-1021 Computer Science Teachers, Postsecondary
Teach courses in computer science. May specialize in a field of computer science, such as the design and function of computers or operations and research analysis. Includes both teachers primarily engaged in teaching and those who do a combination of teaching and research.

Illustrative example: Computer Information Systems Professor, Information Technology Professor, Java Programming Professor

25-1022 Mathematical Science Teachers, Postsecondary
Teach courses pertaining to mathematical concepts, statistics, and actuarial science and to the application of original and standardized mathematical techniques in solving specific problems and situations. Includes both teachers primarily engaged in teaching and those who do a combination of teaching and research.

Illustrative examples: Actuarial Sciences Professor, Calculus Professor, Statistics Professor

25-1030 Engineering and Architecture Teachers, Postsecondary
This broad occupation includes the following two detailed occupations:
25-1031 Architecture Teachers, Postsecondary
25-1032 Engineering Teachers, Postsecondary

25-1031 Architecture Teachers, Postsecondary
Teach courses in architecture and architectural design, such as architectural environmental design, interior architecture/design, and landscape architecture. Includes both teachers primarily engaged in teaching and those who do a combination of teaching and research.

Illustrative examples: Architectural Design Professor, Landscape Architecture Professor

25-1032 Engineering Teachers, Postsecondary

Teach courses pertaining to the application of physical laws and principles of engineering for the development of machines, materials, instruments, processes, and services. Includes teachers of subjects such as chemical, civil, electrical, industrial, mechanical, mineral, and petroleum engineering. Includes both teachers primarily engaged in teaching and those who do a combination of teaching and research. Excludes "Computer Science Teachers, Postsecondary" (25-1021).

Illustrative examples: Aeronautical Engineering Professor, Civil Engineering Professor, Electrical Engineering Professor, Marine Engineering Professor

25-1040 Life Sciences Teachers, Postsecondary
This broad occupation includes the following three detailed occupations:
25-1041 Agricultural Sciences Teachers, Postsecondary
25-1042 Biological Science Teachers, Postsecondary
25-1043 Forestry and Conservation Science Teachers, Postsecondary

25-1041 Agricultural Sciences Teachers, Postsecondary
Teach courses in the agricultural sciences. Includes teachers of agronomy, dairy sciences, fisheries management, horticultural sciences, poultry sciences, range management, and agricultural soil conservation. Includes both teachers primarily engaged in teaching and those who do a combination of teaching and research. Excludes "Forestry and Conservation Science Teachers, Postsecondary" (25-1043).

Illustrative examples: Agronomy Professor, Aquaculture and Fisheries Professor, Farm Management Professor

25-1042 Biological Science Teachers, Postsecondary
Teach courses in biological sciences. Includes both teachers primarily engaged in teaching and those who do a combination of teaching and research.

Illustrative examples: Bacteriology Professor, Biochemistry Professor, Botany Professor

25-1043 Forestry and Conservation Science Teachers, Postsecondary
Teach courses in forestry and conservation science. Includes both teachers primarily engaged in teaching and those who do a combination of teaching and research. Excludes "Agricultural Science Teachers, Postsecondary" (25-1041) and "Environmental Science Teachers, Postsecondary" (25-1053).

Illustrative examples: Forest Ecology Professor, Timber Management Professor, Wildlife Conservation Professor

25-1050 Physical Sciences Teachers, Postsecondary
This broad occupation includes the following four detailed occupations:
25-1051 Atmospheric, Earth, Marine, and Space Sciences Teachers, Postsecondary

25-1052 Chemistry Teachers, Postsecondary
25-1053 Environmental Science Teachers, Postsecondary
25-1054 Physics Teachers, Postsecondary

25-1051 Atmospheric, Earth, Marine, and Space Sciences Teachers, Postsecondary
Teach courses in the physical sciences, except chemistry and physics. Includes both teachers primarily engaged in teaching, and those who do a combination of teaching and research.

Illustrative examples: Climatology Professor, Geology Professor, Oceanography Professor

25-1052 Chemistry Teachers, Postsecondary
Teach courses pertaining to the chemical and physical properties and compositional changes of substances. Work may include instruction in the methods of qualitative and quantitative chemical analysis. Includes both teachers primarily engaged in teaching, and those who do a combination of teaching and research. Excludes "Biological Science Teachers, Postsecondary" (25-1042) who teach biochemistry.

Illustrative examples: Inorganic Chemistry Professor, Organic Chemistry Professor, Physical Chemistry Professor

25-1053 Environmental Science Teachers, Postsecondary
Teach courses in environmental science. Includes both teachers primarily engaged in teaching and those who do a combination of teaching and research.

Illustrative examples: Environmental Science, Management, and Policy Professor; Environmental Studies Professor

25-1054 Physics Teachers, Postsecondary
Teach courses pertaining to the laws of matter and energy. Includes both teachers primarily engaged in teaching and those who do a combination of teaching and research.

Illustrative examples: Astrophysics Professor, Ballistics Professor, Hydrodynamics Professor, Thermodynamics Professor

25-1060 Social Sciences Teachers, Postsecondary
This broad occupation includes the following eight detailed occupations:
25-1061 Anthropology and Archeology Teachers, Postsecondary
25-1062 Area, Ethnic, and Cultural Studies Teachers, Postsecondary
25-1063 Economics Teachers, Postsecondary
25-1064 Geography Teachers, Postsecondary
25-1065 Political Science Teachers, Postsecondary
25-1066 Psychology Teachers, Postsecondary
25-1067 Sociology Teachers, Postsecondary
25-1069 Social Sciences Teachers, Postsecondary, All Other

25-1061 Anthropology and Archeology Teachers, Postsecondary
Teach courses in anthropology or archeology. Includes both teachers primarily engaged in teaching and those who do a combination of teaching and research.

Illustrative examples: Cultural Anthropology Professor, Ethnoarchaeology Professor, Paleology Professor

25-1062 Area, Ethnic, and Cultural Studies Teachers, Postsecondary
Teach courses pertaining to the culture and development of an area, an ethnic group, or any other group, such as Latin American studies, women's studies, or urban affairs. Includes both teachers primarily engaged in teaching and those who do a combination of teaching and research.

Illustrative examples: Ethnology Professor, Latin American Studies Professor, Women's Studies Professor

25-1063 Economics Teachers, Postsecondary
Teach courses in economics. Includes both teachers primarily engaged in teaching and those who do a combination of teaching and research.

Illustrative examples: Agricultural Economics Professor, Econometrics Professor, Labor Economics Professor

25-1064 Geography Teachers, Postsecondary
Teach courses in geography. Includes both teachers primarily engaged in teaching and those who do a combination of teaching and research.

Illustrative examples: Cartography Professor, Geomatics Professor, GIS Professor

25-1065 Political Science Teachers, Postsecondary
Teach courses in political science, international affairs, and international relations. Includes both teachers primarily engaged in teaching and those who do a combination of teaching and research.

Illustrative examples: Government Professor, International Relations Professor, Public Policy Professor

25-1066 Psychology Teachers, Postsecondary
Teach courses in psychology, such as child, clinical, and developmental psychology, and psychological counseling. Includes both teachers primarily engaged in teaching and those who do a combination of teaching and research.

Illustrative examples: Child Development Professor, Educational Psychology Professor, Industrial/Organizational Psychology Professor

25-1067 Sociology Teachers, Postsecondary

Teach courses in sociology. Includes both teachers primarily engaged in teaching and those who do a combination of teaching and research.

Illustrative example: Comparative Sociology Professor

25-1069 Social Sciences Teachers, Postsecondary, All Other

All postsecondary social sciences teachers not listed separately.

Illustrative examples: Survey Research Professor, Urban Planning Professor

25-1070 Health Teachers, Postsecondary

This broad occupation includes the following two detailed occupations:
25-1071 Health Specialties Teachers, Postsecondary
25-1072 Nursing Instructors and Teachers, Postsecondary

25-1071 Health Specialties Teachers, Postsecondary

Teach courses in health specialties, in fields such as dentistry, laboratory technology, medicine, pharmacy, public health, therapy, and veterinary medicine. Excludes "Nursing Instructors and Teachers, Postsecondary" (25-1072) and "Biological Science Teachers, Postsecondary" (25-1042) who teach medical science.

Illustrative examples: Nutrition Professor, Pharmacology Professor, Public Health Professor

25-1072 Nursing Instructors and Teachers, Postsecondary

Demonstrate and teach patient care in classroom and clinical units to nursing students. Includes both teachers primarily engaged in teaching and those who do a combination of teaching and research.

Illustrative examples: Advanced Nursing Professor, Clinical Nursing Professor, Registered Nursing Professor

25-1080 Education and Library Science Teachers, Postsecondary

This broad occupation includes the following two detailed occupations:
25-1081 Education Teachers, Postsecondary
25-1082 Library Science Teachers, Postsecondary

25-1081 Education Teachers, Postsecondary

Teach courses pertaining to education, such as counseling, curriculum, guidance, instruction, teacher education, and teaching English as a second language. Includes both teachers primarily engaged in teaching and those who do a combination of teaching and research.

Illustrative examples: Primary Education Professor, Special Education Professor

25-1082 Library Science Teachers, Postsecondary

Teach courses in library science. Includes both teachers primarily engaged in teaching and those who do a combination of teaching and research.

Illustrative examples: Library and Information Science Professor, Medical Records Library Professor

25-1110 Law, Criminal Justice, and Social Work Teachers, Postsecondary
This broad occupation includes the following three detailed occupations:
25-1111 Criminal Justice and Law Enforcement Teachers, Postsecondary
25-1112 Law Teachers, Postsecondary
25-1113 Social Work Teachers, Postsecondary

25-1111 Criminal Justice and Law Enforcement Teachers, Postsecondary
Teach courses in criminal justice, corrections, and law enforcement administration. Includes both teachers primarily engaged in teaching and those who do a combination of teaching and research.

Illustrative examples: Criminology Professor, Penology Professor

25-1112 Law Teachers, Postsecondary
Teach courses in law. Includes both teachers primarily engaged in teaching and those who do a combination of teaching and research.

Illustrative examples: Constitutional Law Professor, Environmental Law Professor, Torts Law Professor

25-1113 Social Work Teachers, Postsecondary
Teach courses in social work. Includes both teachers primarily engaged in teaching and those who do a combination of teaching and research.

Illustrative examples: Family Welfare Social Work Professor, Geriatric Social Work Professor, Health Social Work Professor

25-1120 Arts, Communications, and Humanities Teachers, Postsecondary
This broad occupation includes the following six detailed occupations:
25-1121 Art, Drama, and Music Teachers, Postsecondary
25-1122 Communications Teachers, Postsecondary
25-1123 English Language and Literature Teachers, Postsecondary
25-1124 Foreign Language and Literature Teachers, Postsecondary
25-1125 History Teachers, Postsecondary
25-1126 Philosophy and Religion Teachers, Postsecondary

25-1121 Art, Drama, and Music Teachers, Postsecondary

Teach courses in drama, music, and the arts including fine and applied art, such as painting and sculpture, or design and crafts. Includes both teachers primarily engaged in teaching and those who do a combination of teaching and research.

Illustrative examples: Ballet Professor, Photography Professor, Piano Professor

25-1122 Communications Teachers, Postsecondary
Teach courses in communications, such as organizational communications, public relations, radio/television broadcasting, and journalism. Includes both teachers primarily engaged in teaching and those who do a combination of teaching and research.

Illustrative examples: Journalism Professor, Public Speaking Professor

25-1123 English Language and Literature Teachers, Postsecondary
Teach courses in English language and literature, including linguistics and comparative literature. Includes both teachers primarily engaged in teaching and those who do a combination of teaching and research.

Illustrative examples: Contemporary English Literature Professor, Creative Writing English Professor, Etymology Professor

25-1124 Foreign Language and Literature Teachers, Postsecondary
Teach languages and literature courses in languages other than English. Includes teachers of American Sign Language (ASL). Includes both teachers primarily engaged in teaching and those who do a combination of teaching and research.

Illustrative examples: Chinese Language Professor, Russian Language Professor, Spanish Literature Professor

25-1125 History Teachers, Postsecondary
Teach courses in human history and historiography. Includes both teachers primarily engaged in teaching and those who do a combination of teaching and research.

Illustrative examples: African History Professor, American History Professor, Jewish History Professor, Russian History Professor

25-1126 Philosophy and Religion Teachers, Postsecondary
Teach courses in philosophy, religion, and theology. Includes both teachers primarily engaged in teaching and those who do a combination of teaching and research.

Illustrative examples: Divinity Professor, Eastern Philosophy Professor, Theology Professor

25-1190 Miscellaneous Postsecondary Teachers
This broad occupation includes the following five detailed occupations:
25-1191 Graduate Teaching Assistants

25-1192 Home Economics Teachers, Postsecondary
25-1193 Recreation and Fitness Studies Teachers, Postsecondary
25-1194 Vocational Education Teachers, Postsecondary
25-1199 Postsecondary Teachers, All Other

25-1191 Graduate Teaching Assistants

Assist faculty or other instructional staff in postsecondary institutions by performing teaching or teaching-related duties, such as teaching lower level courses, developing teaching materials, preparing and giving examinations, and grading examinations or papers. Graduate teaching assistants must be enrolled in a graduate school program. Graduate assistants who primarily perform non-teaching duties, such as research, should be reported in the occupational category related to the work performed. Excludes "Teacher Assistants" (25-9041).

Illustrative examples: Graduate Student Instructor, Teaching Fellow

25-1192 Home Economics Teachers, Postsecondary

Teach courses in childcare, family relations, finance, nutrition, and related subjects pertaining to home management. Includes both teachers primarily engaged in teaching and those who do a combination of teaching and research.

Illustrative examples: Family and Consumer Sciences Professor, Weaving Professor

25-1193 Recreation and Fitness Studies Teachers, Postsecondary

Teach courses pertaining to recreation, leisure, and fitness studies, including exercise physiology and facilities management. Includes both teachers primarily engaged in teaching and those who do a combination of teaching and research.

Illustrative examples: Kinesiology Professor, Leisure Studies Professor, Physical Education (PE) Professor

25-1194 Vocational Education Teachers, Postsecondary

Teach or instruct vocational or occupational subjects at the postsecondary level (but at less than the baccalaureate) to students who have graduated or left high school. Includes correspondence school, industrial, and commercial instructors; and adult education teachers and instructors who prepare persons to operate industrial machinery and equipment and transportation and communications equipment. Teaching may take place in public or private schools whose primary business is education or in a school associated with an organization whose primary business is other than education.

Illustrative examples: Barbering Instructor, Cosmetology Professor, Mechanical Maintenance Instructor

25-1199 Postsecondary Teachers, All Other

All postsecondary teachers not listed separately.
Illustrative examples: Military Science Teacher, Project Management Professor

25-2000 Preschool, Primary, Secondary, and Special Education School Teachers

25-2010 Preschool and Kindergarten Teachers
This broad occupation includes the following two detailed occupations:
25-2011 Preschool Teachers, Except Special Education
25-2012 Kindergarten Teachers, Except Special Education

25-2011 Preschool Teachers, Except Special Education
Instruct preschool-aged children in activities designed to promote social, physical, and intellectual growth needed for primary school in preschool, day care center, or other child development facility. May be required to hold State certification. Substitute teachers are included in "Teachers and Instructors, All Other" (25-3099). Excludes "Childcare Workers" (39-9011) and "Special Education Teachers" (25-2050).

Illustrative examples: Head Start Teacher, Nursery School Teacher, Pre-Kindergarten Teacher

25-2012 Kindergarten Teachers, Except Special Education
Teach elemental natural and social science, personal hygiene, music, art, and literature to kindergarten students. Promote physical, mental, and social development. May be required to hold State certification. Substitute teachers are included in "Teachers and Instructors, All Other" (25-3099). Excludes "Special Education Teachers" (25-2050).

Illustrative example: Bilingual Kindergarten Teacher

25-2020 Elementary and Middle School Teachers
This broad occupation includes the following three detailed occupations:
25-2021 Elementary School Teachers, Except Special Education
25-2022 Middle School Teachers, Except Special and Career/Technical Education
25-2023 Career/Technical Education Teachers, Middle School

25-2021 Elementary School Teachers, Except Special Education
Teach students basic academic, social, and other formative skills in public or private schools at the elementary level. Substitute teachers are included in "Teachers and Instructors, All Other" (25-3099). Excludes "Special Education Teachers" (25-2050).

Illustrative examples: Elementary School Band Director, 4th Grade Math Teacher

25-2022 Middle School Teachers, Except Special and Career/Technical Education
Teach students in one or more subjects in public or private schools at the middle, intermediate, or junior high level, which falls between elementary and senior high school as defined by applicable laws and regulations. Substitute teachers are included in "Teachers and Instructors, All Other" (25-3099). Excludes "Career/Technical Education Teachers, Middle School" (25-2023) and "Special Education Teachers" (25-2050).

Illustrative examples: Junior High School Teacher, Middle School Science Teacher, 7ᵗʰ Grade Social Studies Teacher

25-2023 Career/Technical Education Teachers, Middle School

Teach occupational, career and technical, or vocational subjects in public or private schools at the middle, intermediate, or junior high level, which falls between elementary and senior high school as defined by applicable laws and regulations. Substitute teachers are included in "Teachers and Instructors, All Other" (25-3099).   Excludes "Special Education Teachers" (25-2050).

Illustrative example: Middle School Vocational Education Teacher

25-2030 Secondary School Teachers

This broad occupation includes the following two detailed occupations:
25-2031 Secondary School Teachers, Except Special and Career/Technical Education
25-2032 Career/Technical Education Teachers, Secondary School

25-2031 Secondary School Teachers, Except Special and Career/Technical Education

Teach students in one or more subjects, such as English, mathematics, or social studies at the secondary level in public or private schools. May be designated according to subject matter specialty. Substitute teachers are included in "Teachers and Instructors, All Other" (25-3099). Excludes "Career/Technical Education Teachers, Secondary School" (25-2032) and "Special Education Teachers" (25-2050).

Illustrative examples: High School English Teacher, High School French Teacher, High School History Teacher

25-2032 Career/Technical Education Teachers, Secondary School

Teach occupational, career and technical, or vocational subjects at the secondary school level in public or private schools. Substitute teachers are included in "Teachers and Instructors, All Other" (25-3099).   Excludes "Special Education Teachers, Secondary School" (25-2054).

Illustrative examples: High School Auto Repair Teacher, High School Vocational Education Teacher

25-2050 Special Education Teachers

This broad occupation includes the following five detailed occupations:
25-2051 Special Education Teachers, Preschool
25-2052 Special Education Teachers, Kindergarten and Elementary School
25-2053 Special Education Teachers, Middle School
25-2054 Special Education Teachers, Secondary School
25-2059 Special Education Teachers, All Other

25-2051 Special Education Teachers, Preschool
Teach preschool school subjects to educationally and physically handicapped students. Includes teachers who specialize and work with audibly and visually handicapped students and those who teach basic academic and life processes skills to the mentally impaired. Substitute teachers are included in "Teachers and Instructors, All Other" (25-3099).

Illustrative examples: Early Childhood Special Education Teacher, Pre-Kindergarten Special Education Teacher

25-2052 Special Education Teachers, Kindergarten and Elementary School
Teach elementary school subjects to educationally and physically handicapped students. Includes teachers who specialize and work with audibly and visually handicapped students and those who teach basic academic and life processes skills to the mentally impaired. Substitute teachers are included in "Teachers and Instructors, All Other" (25-3099).

Illustrative examples: Severe Emotional Disorders Elementary School Teacher, Special Education Kindergarten Teacher

25-2053 Special Education Teachers, Middle School
Teach middle school subjects to educationally and physically handicapped students. Includes teachers who specialize and work with audibly and visually handicapped students and those who teach basic academic and life processes skills to the mentally impaired. Substitute teachers are included in "Teachers and Instructors, All Other" (25-3099).

Illustrative examples: Middle School Special Education Teacher, Middle School Teacher for Students with Moderate Intellectual Disabilities

25-2054 Special Education Teachers, Secondary School
Teach secondary school subjects to educationally and physically handicapped students. Includes teachers who specialize and work with audibly and visually handicapped students and those who teach basic academic and life processes skills to the mentally impaired. Substitute teachers are included in "Teachers and Instructors, All Other" (25-3099).

Illustrative examples: High School Learning Support Teacher, High School Special Education Teacher

25-2059 Special Education Teachers, All Other
All special education teachers not listed separately.

Illustrative examples: Autism Tutor, Special Education Teacher for Adults with Disabilities

25-3000 Other Teachers and Instructors

25-3010 Adult Basic and Secondary Education and Literacy Teachers and Instructors
This broad occupation is the same as the detailed occupation:
25-3011 Adult Basic and Secondary Education and Literacy Teachers and Instructors

25-3011 Adult Basic and Secondary Education and Literacy Teachers and Instructors
Teach or instruct out-of-school youths and adults in remedial education classes, preparatory classes for the General Educational Development test, literacy, or English as a Second Language. Teaching may or may not take place in a traditional educational institution.

Illustrative examples: Adult Education Teacher, Adult Literacy Instructor, General Educational Development (GED) Teacher

25-3020 Self-Enrichment Education Teachers
This broad occupation is the same as the detailed occupation:
25-3021 Self-Enrichment Education Teachers

25-3021 Self-Enrichment Education Teachers
Teach or instruct courses other than those that normally lead to an occupational objective or degree. Courses may include self-improvement, nonvocational, and nonacademic subjects. Teaching may or may not take place in a traditional educational institution. Excludes "Fitness Trainers and Aerobics Instructors" (39-9031). Flight instructors are included with "Aircraft Pilots and Flight Engineers" (53-2010).

Illustrative examples: Citizenship Teacher, Horseback Riding Instructor, Sailing Instructor

25-3090 Miscellaneous Teachers and Instructors
This broad occupation is the same as the detailed occupation:
25-3099 Teachers and Instructors, All Other

25-3099 Teachers and Instructors, All Other
All teachers and instructors not listed separately.

Illustrative example: Tutor, Substitute Teacher

25-4000 Librarians, Curators, and Archivists

25-4010 Archivists, Curators, and Museum Technicians
This broad occupation includes the following three detailed occupations:
25-4011 Archivists
25-4012 Curators
25-4013 Museum Technicians and Conservators

25-4011 Archivists

Appraise, edit, and direct safekeeping of permanent records and historically valuable documents. Participate in research activities based on archival materials.

Illustrative examples: Film Archivist, Historical Records Administrator, Reference Archivist

25-4012 Curators

Administer collections, such as artwork, collectibles, historic items, or scientific specimens of museums or other institutions. May conduct instructional, research, or public service activities of institution.

Illustrative examples: Herbarium Curator, Photography and Prints Curator

25-4013 Museum Technicians and Conservators

Restore, maintain, or prepare objects in museum collections for storage, research, or exhibit. May work with specimens such as fossils, skeletal parts, or botanicals; or artifacts, textiles, or art. May identify and record objects or install and arrange them in exhibits. Includes book or document conservators.

Illustrative examples: Ethnographic Materials Conservator, Museum Exhibit Technician, Textile Conservator

25-4020 Librarians

This broad occupation is the same as the detailed occupation:
25-4021 Librarians

25-4021 Librarians

Administer libraries and perform related library services. Work in a variety of settings, including public libraries, educational institutions, museums, corporations, government agencies, law firms, non-profit organizations, and healthcare providers. Tasks may include selecting, acquiring, cataloguing, classifying, circulating, and maintaining library materials; and furnishing reference, bibliographical, and readers' advisory services. May perform in-depth, strategic research, and synthesize, analyze, edit, and filter information. May set up or work with databases and information systems to catalogue and access information.

Illustrative examples: Law Librarian, Music Librarian, School Librarian

25-4030 Library Technicians

This broad occupation is the same as the detailed occupation:
25-4031 Library Technicians

25-4031 Library Technicians

Assist librarians by helping readers in the use of library catalogs, databases, and indexes to locate books and other materials; and by answering questions that require only brief consultation of standard reference. Compile records; sort and shelve books or other media; remove or repair damaged books or other media; register patrons; and check materials in and out of the circulation process. Replace materials in shelving area (stacks) or files. Includes bookmobile drivers who assist with providing services in mobile libraries.

Illustrative examples: Library Acquisitions Technician, Library Circulation Technician

25-9000 Other Education, Training, and Library Occupations

25-9010 Audio-Visual and Multimedia Collections Specialists
This broad occupation is the same as the detailed occupation:
25-9011 Audio-Visual and Multimedia Collections Specialists

25-9011 Audio-Visual and Multimedia Collections Specialists
Prepare, plan, and operate multimedia teaching aids for use in education. May record, catalogue, and file materials.

Illustrative examples: Audio-Visual Collections Coordinator, Library Media Specialist, Multimedia Services Coordinator

25-9020 Farm and Home Management Advisors
This broad occupation is the same as the detailed occupation:
25-9021 Farm and Home Management Advisors

25-9021 Farm and Home Management Advisors
Advise, instruct, and assist individuals and families engaged in agriculture, agricultural-related processes, or home economics activities. Demonstrate procedures and apply research findings to solve problems; and instruct and train in product development, sales, and the use of machinery and equipment to promote general welfare. Includes county agricultural agents, feed and farm management advisors, home economists, and extension service advisors.

Illustrative examples: Agricultural Extension Educator, Family Resource Management Specialist, Feed Management Advisor

25-9030 Instructional Coordinators
This broad occupation is the same as the detailed occupation:
25-9031 Instructional Coordinators

25-9031 Instructional Coordinators
Develop instructional material, coordinate educational content, and incorporate current technology in specialized fields that provide guidelines to educators and instructors for developing curricula and conducting courses. Includes educational consultants and specialists, and instructional material directors.

Illustrative examples: Curriculum and Assessment Director, Curriculum Specialist, Special Education Curriculum Specialist

25-9040 Teacher Assistants
This broad occupation is the same as the detailed occupation:
25-9041 Teacher Assistants

25-9041 Teacher Assistants
Perform duties that are instructional in nature or deliver direct services to students or parents. Serve in a position for which a teacher has ultimate responsibility for the design and implementation of educational programs and services. Excludes "Graduate Teaching Assistants" (25-1191).

Illustrative examples: Instructional Aide, Special Education Classroom Aide

25-9090 Miscellaneous Education, Training, and Library Workers
This broad occupation is the same as the detailed occupation:
25-9099 Education, Training, and Library Workers, All Other

25-9099 Education, Training, and Library Workers, All Other
All education, training, and library workers not listed separately.

Illustrative examples: General Educational Development (GED) Examiner, Individualized Education Plan (IEP) Aide, Scholastic Aptitude Test (SAT) Grader

27-1000 Art and Design Workers 27-1010 Artists and Related Workers This broad occupation includes the following five detailed occupations: 27-1011 Art Directors
27-1012 Craft Artists
27-1013 Fine Artists, Including Painters, Sculptors, and Illustrators
27-1014 Multimedia Artists and Animators
27-1019 Artists and Related Workers, All Other

27-1011 Art Directors
Formulate design concepts and presentation approaches for visual communications media, such as print, broadcasting, and advertising. Direct workers engaged in art work or layout design.

Illustrative example: Magazine Designer

27-1012 Craft Artists
Create or reproduce hand-made objects for sale and exhibition using a variety of techniques, such as welding, weaving, pottery, and needlecraft.

Illustrative examples: Hand Potter, Metal Arts Production Artist, Quilter

27-1013 Fine Artists, Including Painters, Sculptors, and Illustrators
Create original artwork using any of a wide variety of media and techniques.

Illustrative examples: Ice Sculptor, Political Cartoonist, Scientific Illustrator, Sketch Artist

27-1014 Multimedia Artists and Animators
Create special effects, animation, or other visual images using film, video, computers, or other electronic tools and media for use in products or creations, such as computer games, movies, music videos, and commercials.

Illustrative examples: Special Effects Artist, 3D Animator

27-1019 Artists and Related Workers, All Other
All artists and related workers not listed separately.

Illustrative examples: Calligrapher, Tattoo Artist

27-1020 Designers
This broad occupation includes the following eight detailed occupations:
27-1021 Commercial and Industrial Designers
27-1022 Fashion Designers
27-1023 Floral Designers
27-1024 Graphic Designers
27-1025 Interior Designers
27-1026 Merchandise Displayers and Window Trimmers
27-1027 Set and Exhibit Designers

27-1029 Designers, All Other

27-1021 Commercial and Industrial Designers

Develop and design manufactured products, such as cars, home appliances, and children's toys. Combine artistic talent with research on product use, marketing, and materials to create the most functional and appealing product design.

Illustrative examples: Automobile Designer, Package Designer

27-1022 Fashion Designers

Design clothing and accessories. Create original designs or adapt fashion trends.

Illustrative examples: Costume Designer, Custom Furrier, Dress Designer

27-1023 Floral Designers

Design, cut, and arrange live, dried, or artificial flowers and foliage.

Illustrative examples: Corsage Maker, Florist, Flower Arranger

27-1024 Graphic Designers

Design or create graphics to meet specific commercial or promotional needs, such as packaging, displays, or logos. May use a variety of mediums to achieve artistic or decorative effects.

Illustrative examples: Catalogue Illustrator, Graphic Artist

27-1025 Interior Designers

Plan, design, and furnish interiors of residential, commercial, or industrial buildings. Formulate design which is practical, aesthetic, and conducive to intended purposes, such as raising productivity, selling merchandise, or improving life style. May specialize in a particular field, style, or phase of interior design. Excludes "Merchandise Displayers and Window Trimmers" (27-1026).

Illustrative examples: Home Lighting Advisor, Interior Decorator, Kitchen Designer

27-1026 Merchandise Displayers and Window Trimmers

Plan and erect commercial displays, such as those in windows and interiors of retail stores and at trade exhibitions.

Illustrative examples: Display Artist, Mannequin Decorator, Window Decorator

27-1027 Set and Exhibit Designers

Design special exhibits and movie, television, and theater sets. May study scripts, confer with directors, and conduct research to determine appropriate architectural styles.

Illustrative examples: Set Decorator, Stage Scenery Designer

27-1029 Designers, All Other
All designers not listed separately.

Illustrative example: Memorial Marker Designer

27-2000 Entertainers and Performers, Sports and Related Workers

27-2010 Actors, Producers, and Directors
This broad occupation includes the following two detailed occupations:
27-2011 Actors
27-2012 Producers and Directors

27-2011 Actors
Play parts in stage, television, radio, video, motion picture productions, or other settings for entertainment, information, or instruction. Interpret serious or comic role by speech, gesture, and body movement to entertain or inform audience. May dance and sing.

Illustrative examples: Actress, Dramatic Reader, Voice-Over Artist

27-2012 Producers and Directors
Produce or direct stage, television, radio, video, or motion picture productions for entertainment, information, or instruction. Responsible for creative decisions, such as interpretation of script, choice of actors or guests, set design, sound, special effects, and choreography.

Illustrative examples: Casting Director, Independent Film Maker, Stage Manager

27-2020 Athletes, Coaches, Umpires, and Related Workers
This broad occupation includes the following three detailed occupations:
27-2021 Athletes and Sports Competitors
27-2022 Coaches and Scouts
27-2023 Umpires, Referees, and Other Sports Officials

27-2021 Athletes and Sports Competitors
Compete in athletic events.

Illustrative examples: Football Player, Jockey, Race Car Driver

27-2022 Coaches and Scouts
Instruct or coach groups or individuals in the fundamentals of sports. Demonstrate techniques and methods of participation. May evaluate athletes' strengths and weaknesses as possible

recruits or to improve the athletes' technique to prepare them for competition. Those required to hold teaching degrees should be reported in the appropriate teaching category. Excludes "Athletic Trainers" (29-9091).

Illustrative examples: Baseball Scout, Boxing Trainer, Football Coach

27-2023 Umpires, Referees, and Other Sports Officials
Officiate at competitive athletic or sporting events. Detect infractions of rules and decide penalties according to established regulations. Includes all sporting officials, referees, and competition judges.

Illustrative examples: Athletic Events Scorer, Paddock Judge, Race Starter

27-2030 Dancers and Choreographers
This broad occupation includes the following two detailed occupations:
27-2031 Dancers
27-2032 Choreographers

27-2031 Dancers
Perform dances. May perform on stage, for on-air broadcasting, or for video recording

Illustrative examples: Ballerina, Dance Artist, Tap Dancer

27-2032 Choreographers
Create new dance routines. Rehearse performance of routines. May direct and stage presentations.

Illustrative examples: Dance Director, Dance Master

27-2040 Musicians, Singers, and Related Workers
This broad occupation includes the following two detailed occupations:
27-2041 Music Directors and Composers
27-2042 Musicians and Singers

27-2041 Music Directors and Composers
Conduct, direct, plan, and lead instrumental or vocal performances by musical groups, such as orchestras, bands, choirs, and glee clubs. Includes arrangers, composers, choral directors, and orchestrators.

Illustrative examples: Choirmaster, Jingle Writer, Orchestra Conductor, Songwriter

27-2042 Musicians and Singers
Play one or more musical instruments or sing. May perform on stage, for on-air broadcasting, or for sound or video recording.

Illustrative examples: Instrumentalist, Oboist, Rapper

27-2090 Miscellaneous Entertainers and Performers, Sports and Related Workers
This broad occupation is the same as the detailed occupation:
27-2099 Entertainers and Performers, Sports and Related Workers, All Other

27-2099 Entertainers and Performers, Sports and Related Workers, All Other
All entertainers and performers, sports and related workers not listed separately.

Illustrative examples: Clown, Comedian, Magician

27-3000 Media and Communication Workers

27-3010 Announcers
This broad occupation includes the following two detailed occupations:
27-3011 Radio and Television Announcers
27-3012 Public Address System and Other Announcers

27-3011 Radio and Television Announcers
Speak or read from scripted materials, such as news reports or commercial messages, on radio or television. May announce artist or title of performance, identify station, or interview guests. Excludes "Broadcast News Analysts" (27-3021).

Illustrative examples: Game Show Host, Radio Disk Jockey, Talk Show Host

27-3012 Public Address System and Other Announcers
Make announcements over public address system at sporting or other public events. May act as master of ceremonies or disc jockey at weddings, parties, clubs, or other gathering places.

Illustrative examples: Emcee, Ringmaster, Train Caller

27-3020 News Analysts, Reporters and Correspondents
This broad occupation includes the following two detailed occupations:
27-3021 Broadcast News Analysts
27-3022 Reporters and Correspondents

27-3021 Broadcast News Analysts
Analyze, interpret, and broadcast news received from various sources.

Illustrative examples: News Anchor, Newscaster, News Commentator

27-3022 Reporters and Correspondents

Collect and analyze facts about newsworthy events by interview, investigation, or observation. Report and write stories for newspaper, news magazine, radio, or television. Excludes "Broadcast News Analysts" (27-3021).

Illustrative examples: Columnist, Film Critic, Foreign Correspondent

27-3030 Public Relations Specialists
This broad occupation is the same as the detailed occupation:
27-3031 Public Relations Specialists

27-3031 Public Relations Specialists
Engage in promoting or creating an intended public image for individuals, groups, or organizations. May write or select material for release to various communications media.

Illustrative examples: Lobbyist, Press Secretary, Publicity Writer

27-3040 Writers and Editors
This broad occupation includes the following three detailed occupations:
27-3041 Editors
27-3042 Technical Writers
27-3043 Writers and Authors

27-3041 Editors
Plan, coordinate, or edit content of material for publication. May review proposals and drafts for possible publication. Includes technical editors.

Illustrative examples: Advertising Editor, Copy Editor, Technical Editor

27-3042 Technical Writers
Write technical materials, such as equipment manuals, appendices, or operating and maintenance instructions. May assist in layout work.

Illustrative examples: Documentation Writer, Medical Writer, Specifications Writer

27-3043 Writers and Authors
Originate and prepare written material, such as scripts, stories, advertisements, and other material. Excludes "Public Relations Specialists" (27-3031) and "Technical Writers" (27-3042).

Illustrative examples: Advertising Copy Writer, Playwright, Television Writer

27-3090 Miscellaneous Media and Communication Workers
This broad occupation includes the following two detailed occupations:
27-3091 Interpreters and Translators
27-3099 Media and Communication Workers, All Other
27-3091 Interpreters and Translators

Interpret oral or sign language, or translate written text from one language into another.

Illustrative examples: American Sign Language Interpreter, Court Interpreter, Diplomatic Interpreter

27-3099 Media and Communication Workers, All Other
All media and communication workers not listed separately.

Illustrative example: Stage Technician

27-4000 Media and Communication Equipment Workers

27-4010 Broadcast and Sound Engineering Technicians and Radio Operators
This broad occupation includes the following four detailed occupations:
27-4011 Audio and Video Equipment Technicians
27-4012 Broadcast Technicians
27-4013 Radio Operators
27-4014 Sound Engineering Technicians

27-4011 Audio and Video Equipment Technicians
Set up, or set up and operate audio and video equipment including microphones, sound speakers, video screens, projectors, video monitors, recording equipment, connecting wires and cables, sound and mixing boards, and related electronic equipment for concerts, sports events, meetings and conventions, presentations, and news conferences. May also set up and operate associated spotlights and other custom lighting systems. Excludes "Sound Engineering Technicians" (27-4014).

Illustrative examples: Multimedia Production Assistant, Video Control Operator, Video Production Assistant

27-4012 Broadcast Technicians
Set up, operate, and maintain the electronic equipment used to transmit radio and television programs. Control audio equipment to regulate volume level and quality of sound during radio and television broadcasts. Operate transmitter to broadcast radio or television programs.

Illustrative examples: Audio Engineer, Broadcast Engineer

27-4013 Radio Operators
Receive and transmit communications using radiotelephone equipment in accordance with government regulations. May repair equipment. Excludes "Radio, Cellular, and Tower Equipment Installers and Repairs" (49-2021).

Illustrative examples: Radio Officer, Radiophone Operator

27-4014 Sound Engineering Technicians

Operate machines and equipment to record, synchronize, mix, or reproduce music, voices, or sound effects in sporting arenas, theater productions, recording studios, or movie and video productions.

Illustrative examples: Audio Recording Engineer, Sound Editor, Sound Effects Technician

27-4020 Photographers
This broad occupation is the same as the detailed occupation:
27-4021 Photographers

27-4021 Photographers
Photograph people, landscapes, merchandise, or other subjects, using digital or film cameras and equipment. May develop negatives or use computer software to produce finished images and prints. Includes scientific photographers, aerial photographers, and photojournalists.

Illustrative examples: Marine Photographer, Medical Photographer, Wedding Photographer

27-4030 Television, Video, and Motion Picture Camera Operators and Editors
This broad occupation includes the following two detailed occupations:
27-4031 Camera Operators, Television, Video, and Motion Picture
27-4032 Film and Video Editors

27-4031 Camera Operators, Television, Video, and Motion Picture
Operate television, video, or motion picture camera to record images or scenes for various purposes, such as TV broadcasts, advertising, video production, or motion pictures.

Illustrative examples: Cinematographer, News Videographer

27-4032 Film and Video Editors
Edit moving images on film, video, or other media. May edit or synchronize soundtracks with images. Excludes "Sound Engineering Technicians"(27-4014).

Illustrative examples: Cue Selector, Film Editor, Television News Video Editor

27-4090 Miscellaneous Media and Communication Equipment Workers
This broad occupation is the same as the detailed occupation:
27-4099 Media and Communication Equipment Workers, All Other

27-4099 Media and Communication Equipment Workers, All Other
All media and communication equipment workers not listed separately.

Illustrative examples: Dimmer Board Operator, Satellite Communications Operator, Spotlight Operator

29-1000 Health Diagnosing and Treating Practitioners

29-1010 Chiropractors
This broad occupation is the same as the detailed occupation:
29-1011 Chiropractors

29-1011 Chiropractors
Assess, treat, and care for patients by manipulation of spine and musculoskeletal system. May provide spinal adjustment or address sacral or pelvic misalignment.

Illustrative example: Chiropractic Physician

29-1020 Dentists
This broad occupation includes the following five detailed occupations:
29-1021 Dentists, General
29-1022 Oral and Maxillofacial Surgeons
29-1023 Orthodontists
29-1024 Prosthodontists
29-1029 Dentists, All Other Specialists

29-1021 Dentists, General
Examine, diagnose, and treat diseases, injuries, and malformations of teeth and gums. May treat diseases of nerve, pulp, and other dental tissues affecting oral hygiene and retention of teeth. May fit dental appliances or provide preventive care. Excludes "Prosthodontists" (29-1024), "Orthodontists" (29-1023), "Oral and Maxillofacial Surgeons" (29-1022) and "Dentists, All Other Specialists" (29-1029).

Illustrative example: Family Dentist

29-1022 Oral and Maxillofacial Surgeons
Perform surgery and related procedures on the hard and soft tissues of the oral and maxillofacial regions to treat diseases, injuries, or defects. May diagnose problems of the oral and maxillofacial regions. May perform surgery to improve function or appearance.

Illustrative example: Dental Surgeon

29-1023 Orthodontists
Examine, diagnose, and treat dental malocclusions and oral cavity anomalies. Design and fabricate appliances to realign teeth and jaws to produce and maintain normal function and to improve appearance.

Illustrative example: Dentofacial Orthopedics Dentist, Invisible Braces Orthodontist, Pediatric Orthodontist

29-1024 Prosthodontists

Construct oral prostheses to replace missing teeth and other oral structures to correct natural and acquired deformation of mouth and jaws, to restore and maintain oral function, such as chewing and speaking, and to improve appearance.

Illustrative examples: Maxillofacial Prosthetics Dentist, Reconstructive Dentist

29-1029 Dentists, All Other Specialists

All dentists not listed separately.

Illustrative examples: Endodontist, Oral Pathologist, Periodontist

29-1030 Dietitians and Nutritionists

This broad occupation is the same as the detailed occupation:
29-1031 Dietitians and Nutritionists

29-1031 Dietitians and Nutritionists

Plan and conduct food service or nutritional programs to assist in the promotion of health and control of disease. May supervise activities of a department providing quantity food services, counsel individuals, or conduct nutritional research.

Illustrative examples: Clinical Dietitian, Pediatric Dietitian, Public Health Nutritionist

29-1040 Optometrists

This broad occupation is the same as the detailed occupation:
29-1041 Optometrists

29-1041 Optometrists

Diagnose, manage, and treat conditions and diseases of the human eye and visual system. Examine eyes and visual system, diagnose problems or impairments, prescribe corrective lenses, and provide treatment. May prescribe therapeutic drugs to treat specific eye conditions. Ophthalmologists are included in "Physicians and Surgeons, All Other" (29-1069).

Illustrative example: Doctor of Optometry

29-1050 Pharmacists

This broad occupation is the same as the detailed occupation:
29-1051 Pharmacists

29-1051 Pharmacists

Dispense drugs prescribed by physicians and other health practitioners and provide information to patients about medications and their use. May advise physicians and other health practitioners on the selection, dosage, interactions, and side effects of medications.

Illustrative examples: Apothecary, Hospital Pharmacist

29-1060 Physicians and Surgeons

This broad occupation includes the following eight detailed occupations:

29-1061 Anesthesiologists
29-1062 Family and General Practitioners
29-1063 Internists, General
29-1064 Obstetricians and Gynecologists
29-1065 Pediatricians, General
29-1066 Psychiatrists
29-1067 Surgeons
29-1069 Physicians and Surgeons, All Other

29-1061 Anesthesiologists

Physicians who administer anesthetics prior to, during, or after surgery or other medical procedures.

Illustrative example: Obstetrical Anesthesiologist

29-1062 Family and General Practitioners

Physicians who diagnose, treat, and help prevent diseases and injuries that commonly occur in the general population. May refer patients to specialists when needed for further diagnosis or treatment.

Illustrative example: Family Practice Physician

29-1063 Internists, General

Physicians who diagnose and provide non-surgical treatment of diseases and injuries of internal organ systems. Provide care mainly for adults who have a wide range of problems associated with the internal organs. Subspecialists, such as cardiologists and gastroenterologists, are included in "Physicians and Surgeons, All Other" (29-1069).

Illustrative example: Internal Medicine Physician

29-1064 Obstetricians and Gynecologists

Physicians who provide medical care related to pregnancy or childbirth and those who diagnose, treat, and help prevent diseases of women, particularly those affecting the reproductive system. May also provide general medical care to women.

Illustrative examples: OB/GYN, OB Specialist

29-1065 Pediatricians, General

Physicians who diagnose, treat, and help prevent children's diseases and injuries.

Illustrative examples: Paediatrician, Pediatrist, Primary Care Pediatrician

29-1066 Psychiatrists
Physicians who diagnose, treat, and help prevent disorders of the mind.

Illustrative examples: Addiction Psychiatrist, Geriatric Psychiatrist, Neuropsychiatrist

29-1067 Surgeons
Physicians who treat diseases, injuries, and deformities by invasive, minimally-invasive, or non-invasive surgical methods, such as using instruments, appliances, or by manual manipulation. Excludes "Oral and Maxillofacial Surgeons" (29-1022).

Illustrative examples: Cardiovascular Surgeon, Orthopedic Surgeon, Plastic Surgeon, Thoracic Surgeon

29-1069 Physicians and Surgeons, All Other
All physicians and surgeons not listed separately.

Illustrative examples: Cardiologist, Dermatologist, Gastroenterologist, Ophthalmologist

29-1070 Physician Assistants
This broad occupation is the same as the detailed occupation:
29-1071 Physician Assistants

29-1071 Physician Assistants
Provide healthcare services typically performed by a physician, under the supervision of a physician. Conduct complete physicals, provide treatment, and counsel patients. May, in some cases, prescribe medication. Must graduate from an accredited educational program for physician assistants. Excludes "Emergency Medical Technicians and Paramedics" (29-2041), "Medical Assistants" (31-9092), "Registered Nurses" (29-1141), "Nurse Anesthetists" (29-1151), "Nurse Midwives" (29-1161), and "Nurse Practitioners" (29-1171).

Illustrative examples: Anesthesiologist Assistant, Family Practice Physician Assistant

29-1080 Podiatrists
This broad occupation is the same as the detailed occupation:
29-1081 Podiatrists

29-1081 Podiatrists
Diagnose and treat diseases and deformities of the human foot.

Illustrative examples: Chiropodist, Foot Doctor, Foot Orthopedist

29-1120 Therapists
This broad occupation includes the following eight detailed occupations:
29-1122 Occupational Therapists
29-1123 Physical Therapists

29-1124 Radiation Therapists
29-1125 Recreational Therapists
29-1126 Respiratory Therapists
29-1127 Speech-Language Pathologists
29-1128 Exercise Physiologists
29-1129 Therapists, All Other

29-1122 Occupational Therapists

Assess, plan, organize, and participate in rehabilitative programs that help build or restore vocational, homemaking, and daily living skills, as well as general independence, to persons with disabilities or developmental delays.

Illustrative examples: Registered Occupational Therapist

29-1123 Physical Therapists

Assess, plan, organize, and participate in rehabilitative programs that improve mobility, relieve pain, increase strength, and improve or correct disabling conditions resulting from disease or injury.

Illustrative examples: Geriatric Physical Therapist, Physiotherapist, Pulmonary Physical Therapist

29-1124 Radiation Therapists

Provide radiation therapy to patients as prescribed by a radiologist according to established practices and standards. Duties may include reviewing prescription and diagnosis; acting as liaison with physician and supportive care personnel; preparing equipment, such as immobilization, treatment, and protection devices; and maintaining records, reports, and files. May assist in dosimetry procedures and tumor localization.

Illustrative examples: Dosimetrist, Radiation Therapy Technologist

29-1125 Recreational Therapists

Plan, direct, or coordinate medically-approved recreation programs for patients in hospitals, nursing homes, or other institutions. Activities include sports, trips, dramatics, social activities, and arts and crafts. May assess a patient condition and recommend appropriate recreational activity. Excludes "Recreation Workers" (39-9032).

Illustrative examples: Certified Recreational Therapist, Drama Therapist, Therapeutic Recreation Specialist

29-1126 Respiratory Therapists

Assess, treat, and care for patients with breathing disorders. Assume primary responsibility for all respiratory care modalities, including the supervision of respiratory therapy technicians. Initiate and conduct therapeutic procedures; maintain patient records; and select, assemble, check, and operate equipment.

Illustrative examples: Inhalation Therapist, Oxygen Therapist, Registered Respiratory Therapist

29-1127 Speech-Language Pathologists

Assess and treat persons with speech, language, voice, and fluency disorders. May select alternative communication systems and teach their use. May perform research related to speech and language problems.

Illustrative examples: Public School Speech Therapist, Speech Clinician, Speech Therapist

29-1128 Exercise Physiologists

Assess, plan, or implement fitness programs that include exercise or physical activities such as those designed to improve cardiorespiratory function, body composition, muscular strength, muscular endurance, or flexibility. Excludes "Physical Therapists" (29-1123), "Athletic Trainers" (29-9091), and "Fitness Trainers and Aerobic Instructors" (39-9031).

Illustrative examples: Applied Exercise Physiologist, Clinical Exercise Physiologist, Kinesiotherapist

29-1129 Therapists, All Other

All therapists not listed separately.

Illustrative examples: Hydrotherapist, Music Therapist

29-1130 Veterinarians

This broad occupation is the same as the detailed occupation:
29-1131 Veterinarians

29-1131 Veterinarians

Diagnose, treat, or research diseases and injuries of animals. Includes veterinarians who conduct research and development, inspect livestock, or care for pets and companion animals.

Illustrative examples: Animal Surgeon, Doctor of Veterinary Medicine (DVM), Veterinary Medicine Scientist, Wildlife Veterinarian

29-1140 Registered Nurses

This broad occupation is the same as the detailed occupation:
29-1141 Registered Nurses

29-1141 Registered Nurses

Assess patient health problems and needs, develop and implement nursing care plans, and maintain medical records. Administer nursing care to ill, injured, convalescent, or disabled patients. May advise patients on health maintenance and disease prevention or provide case management. Licensing or registration required. Includes Clinical Nurse Specialists. Excludes "Nurse Anesthetists" (29-1151), "Nurse Midwives" (29-1161), and "Nurse Practitioners" (29-1171).

Illustrative examples: Coronary Care Unit Nurse, Hospice Registered Nurse, Psychiatric Nurse

29-1150 Nurse Anesthetists
This broad occupation is the same as the detailed occupation:
29-1151 Nurse Anesthetists

29-1151 Nurse Anesthetists
Administer anesthesia, monitor patient's vital signs, and oversee patient recovery from anesthesia. May assist anesthesiologists, surgeons, other physicians, or dentists. Must be registered nurses who have specialized graduate education.

Illustrative example: Certified Registered Nurse Anesthetist (CRNA)

29-1160 Nurse Midwives
This broad occupation is the same as the detailed occupation:
29-1161 Nurse Midwives

29-1161 Nurse Midwives
Diagnose and coordinate all aspects of the birthing process, either independently or as part of a healthcare team. May provide well-woman gynecological care. Must have specialized, graduate nursing education.

Illustrative example: Certified Nurse Midwife (CNM)

29-1170 Nurse Practitioners
This broad occupation is the same as the detailed occupation:
29-1171 Nurse Practitioners

29-1171 Nurse Practitioners
Diagnose and treat acute, episodic, or chronic illness, independently or as part of a healthcare team. May focus on health promotion and disease prevention. May order, perform, or interpret diagnostic tests such as lab work and x rays. May prescribe medication. Must be registered nurses who have specialized graduate education.

Illustrative examples: Cardiology Nurse Practitioner, Family Practice Nurse Practitioner, Gerontological Nurse Practitioner

29-1180 Audiologists
This broad occupation is the same as the detailed occupation:
29-1181 Audiologists

29-1181 Audiologists
Assess and treat persons with hearing and related disorders. May fit hearing aids and provide auditory training. May perform research related to hearing problems.

Illustrative examples: Clinical Audiologist, Pediatric Audiologist

29-1190 Miscellaneous Health Diagnosing and Treating Practitioners
This broad occupation is the same as the detailed occupation:
29-1199 Health Diagnosing and Treating Practitioners, All Other

29-1199 Health Diagnosing and Treating Practitioners, All Other
All health diagnosing and treating practitioners not listed separately.

Illustrative examples: Acupuncturist, Hypnotherapist, Naturopathic Physician

29-2000 Health Technologists and Technicians

29-2010 Clinical Laboratory Technologists and Technicians
This broad occupation includes the following two detailed occupations:
29-2011 Medical and Clinical Laboratory Technologists
29-2012 Medical and Clinical Laboratory Technicians

29-2011 Medical and Clinical Laboratory Technologists
Perform complex medical laboratory tests for diagnosis, treatment, and prevention of disease. May train or supervise staff.

Illustrative examples: Blood Bank Laboratory Technologist, Cytogenetic Technologist, Immunohematologist

29-2012 Medical and Clinical Laboratory Technicians
Perform routine medical laboratory tests for the diagnosis, treatment, and prevention of disease. May work under the supervision of a medical technologist.

Illustrative examples: Histology Technician, Pathology Technician, Serology Technician

29-2020 Dental Hygienists
This broad occupation is the same as the detailed occupation:
29-2021 Dental Hygienists

29-2021 Dental Hygienists
Clean teeth and examine oral areas, head, and neck for signs of oral disease. May educate patients on oral hygiene, take and develop x rays, or apply fluoride or sealants.

Illustrative examples: Oral Hygienist, Registered Dental Hygienist

29-2030 Diagnostic Related Technologists and Technicians
This broad occupation includes the following five detailed occupations:
29-2031 Cardiovascular Technologists and Technicians
29-2032 Diagnostic Medical Sonographers

29-2033 Nuclear Medicine Technologists
29-2034 Radiologic Technologists
29-2035 Magnetic Resonance Imaging Technologists

29-2031 Cardiovascular Technologists and Technicians

Conduct tests on pulmonary or cardiovascular systems of patients for diagnostic purposes. May conduct or assist in electrocardiograms, cardiac catheterizations, pulmonary functions, lung capacity, and similar tests. Includes vascular technologists.

Illustrative examples: Cardiac Catheterization Technologist, Echocardiographer, EKG Technician

29-2032 Diagnostic Medical Sonographers

Produce ultrasonic recordings of internal organs for use by physicians.

Illustrative examples: Registered Diagnostic Medical Sonographer, Ultrasound Technologist

29-2033 Nuclear Medicine Technologists

Prepare, administer, and measure radioactive isotopes in therapeutic, diagnostic, and tracer studies using a variety of radioisotope equipment. Prepare stock solutions of radioactive materials and calculate doses to be administered by radiologists. Subject patients to radiation. Execute blood volume, red cell survival, and fat absorption studies following standard laboratory techniques.

Illustrative examples: Certified Nuclear Medicine Technologist, Nuclear Cardiology Technologist, Radioisotope Technologist

29-2034 Radiologic Technologists

Take x rays and CAT scans or administer nonradioactive materials into patient's blood stream for diagnostic purposes. Includes technologists who specialize in other scanning modalities. Excludes "Diagnostic Medical Sonographers"(29-2032) and "Magnetic Resonance Imaging Technologists" (29-2035).

Illustrative examples: Computed Tomography (CT) Scanner Operator, X-Ray Technician

29-2035 Magnetic Resonance Imaging Technologists

Operate Magnetic Resonance Imaging (MRI) scanners. Monitor patient safety and comfort, and view images of area being scanned to ensure quality of pictures. May administer gadolinium contrast dosage intravenously. May interview patient, explain MRI procedures, and position patient on examining table. May enter into the computer data such as patient history, anatomical area to be scanned, orientation specified, and position of entry.
Illustrative examples: Computed Tomography/Magnetic Resonance Imaging Technologist (CT/MRI) Technologist, MRI Technologist

29-2040 Emergency Medical Technicians and Paramedics
This broad occupation is the same as the detailed occupation:
29-2041 Emergency Medical Technicians and Paramedics

29-2041 Emergency Medical Technicians and Paramedics
Assess injuries, administer emergency medical care, and extricate trapped individuals.
Transport injured or sick persons to medical facilities.

Illustrative examples: EMT, Flight Paramedic

29-2050 Health Practitioner Support Technologists and Technicians
This broad occupation includes the following seven detailed occupations:
29-2051 Dietetic Technicians
29-2052 Pharmacy Technicians
29-2053 Psychiatric Technicians
29-2054 Respiratory Therapy Technicians
29-2055 Surgical Technologists
29-2056 Veterinary Technologists and Technicians
29-2057 Ophthalmic Medical Technicians

29-2051 Dietetic Technicians
Assist in the provision of food service and nutritional programs, under the supervision of a
dietitian. May plan and produce meals based on established guidelines, teach principles of food
and nutrition, or counsel individuals.

Illustrative examples: Dietary Technician, Registered Diet Technician

29-2052 Pharmacy Technicians
Prepare medications under the direction of a pharmacist. May measure, mix, count out, label,
and record amounts and dosages of medications according to prescription orders.

Illustrative examples: Certified Pharmacy Technician, Pharmacist Technician

29-2053 Psychiatric Technicians
Care for individuals with mental or emotional conditions or disabilities, following the
instructions of physicians or other health practitioners. Monitor patients' physical and emotional
well-being and report to medical staff. May participate in rehabilitation and treatment
programs, help with personal hygiene, and administer oral or injectable medications.

Illustrative examples: Behavioral Health Technician, Mental Health Technician

29-2054 Respiratory Therapy Technicians
Provide respiratory care under the direction of respiratory therapists and physicians.

Illustrative examples: Certified Respiratory Therapy Technician, Oxygen Therapy Technician

29-2055 Surgical Technologists

Assist in operations, under the supervision of surgeons, registered nurses, or other surgical personnel. May help set up operating room, prepare and transport patients for surgery, adjust lights and equipment, pass instruments and other supplies to surgeons and surgeon's assistants, hold retractors, cut sutures, and help count sponges, needles, supplies, and instruments.

Illustrative examples: Certified Surgical Technologist, Operating Room (OR) Tech, Surgical Scrub Technologist

29-2056 Veterinary Technologists and Technicians

Perform medical tests in a laboratory environment for use in the treatment and diagnosis of diseases in animals. Prepare vaccines and serums for prevention of diseases. Prepare tissue samples, take blood samples, and execute laboratory tests, such as urinalysis and blood counts. Clean and sterilize instruments and materials and maintain equipment and machines. May assist a veterinarian during surgery.

Illustrative examples: Veterinary Laboratory Technician, Veterinary Surgery Technologist, Veterinary X-Ray Operator

29-2057 Ophthalmic Medical Technicians

Assist ophthalmologists by performing ophthalmic clinical functions. May administer eye exams, administer eye medications, and instruct the patient in care and use of corrective lenses.

Illustrative examples: Ocular Care Technologist, Ophthalmic Technologist

29-2060 Licensed Practical and Licensed Vocational Nurses
This broad occupation is the same as the detailed occupation:
29-2061 Licensed Practical and Licensed Vocational Nurses

29-2061 Licensed Practical and Licensed Vocational Nurses

Care for ill, injured, or convalescing patients or persons with disabilities in hospitals, nursing homes, clinics, private homes, group homes, and similar institutions. May work under the supervision of a registered nurse. Licensing required.

Illustrative examples: LVN, LPN, Pediatric Licensed Practical Nurse

29-2070 Medical Records and Health Information Technicians
This broad occupation is the same as the detailed occupation:
29-2071 Medical Records and Health Information Technicians

29-2071 Medical Records and Health Information Technicians

Compile, process, and maintain medical records of hospital and clinic patients in a manner consistent with medical, administrative, ethical, legal, and regulatory requirements of the heath care system. Process, maintain, compile, and report patient information for health requirements and standards in a manner consistent with the healthcare industry's numerical coding system. Excludes "File Clerks" (43-4071).

Illustrative examples: Cancer Registrar, Health Information Coder, Health Information Systems Technician, Medical Records Specialist

29-2080 Opticians, Dispensing
This broad occupation is the same as the detailed occupation:
29-2081 Opticians, Dispensing

29-2081 Opticians, Dispensing
Design, measure, fit, and adapt lenses and frames for client according to written optical prescription or specification. Assist client with inserting, removing, and caring for contact lenses. Assist client with selecting frames. Measure customer for size of eyeglasses and coordinate frames with facial and eye measurements and optical prescription. Prepare work order for optical laboratory containing instructions for grinding and mounting lenses in frames. Verify exactness of finished lens spectacles. Adjust frame and lens position to fit client. May shape or reshape frames. Includes contact lens opticians.

Illustrative examples: Contact Lens Fitter, Eyeglass Fitter

29-2090 Miscellaneous Health Technologists and Technicians
This broad occupation includes the following three detailed occupations:
29-2091 Orthotists and Prosthetists
29-2092 Hearing Aid Specialists
29-2099 Health Technologists and Technicians, All Other

29-2091 Orthotists and Prosthetists
Design, measure, fit, and adapt orthopedic braces, appliances or prostheses, such as limbs or facial parts for patients with disabling conditions.

Illustrative examples: Artificial Limb Fitter, Certified Orthotic Fitter, Pedorthist

29-2092 Hearing Aid Specialists
Select and fit hearing aids for customers. Administer and interpret tests of hearing. Assess hearing instrument efficacy. Take ear impressions and prepare, design, and modify ear molds. Excludes "Audiologists" (29-1181).

Illustrative examples: Hearing Aid Fitter, Hearing Aid Technician, Hearing Instrument Specialist

29-2099 Health Technologists and Technicians, All Other
All health technologists and technicians not listed separately.

Illustrative examples: Dialysis Technician, Electroencephalogram (EEG) Technologist, Electroneurodiagnostic Technologist, Polysomnograph Tech

29-9000 Other Healthcare Practitioners and Technical Occupations

29-9010 Occupational Health and Safety Specialists and Technicians
This broad occupation includes the following two detailed occupations:
29-9011 Occupational Health and Safety Specialists
29-9012 Occupational Health and Safety Technicians

29-9011 Occupational Health and Safety Specialists
Review, evaluate, and analyze work environments and design programs and procedures to control, eliminate, and prevent disease or injury caused by chemical, physical, and biological agents or ergonomic factors. May conduct inspections and enforce adherence to laws and regulations governing the health and safety of individuals. May be employed in the public or private sector. Includes environmental protection officers.

Illustrative examples: Environmental Health Sanitarian, Health and Safety Inspector, Industrial Hygienist

29-9012 Occupational Health and Safety Technicians
Collect data on work environments for analysis by occupational health and safety specialists. Implement and conduct evaluation of programs designed to limit chemical, physical, biological, and ergonomic risks to workers.

Illustrative examples: Construction Health and Safety Technician, Ergonomics Technician, Occupational Health and Safety Technologist (OHST)

29-9090 Miscellaneous Health Practitioners and Technical Workers
This broad occupation includes the following three detailed occupations:
29-9091 Athletic Trainers
29-9092 Genetic Counselors
29-9099 Healthcare Practitioners and Technical Workers, All Other

29-9091 Athletic Trainers
Evaluate and advise individuals to assist recovery from or avoid athletic-related injuries or illnesses, or maintain peak physical fitness. May provide first aid or emergency care.

Illustrative example: Certified Athletic Trainer

29-9092 Genetic Counselors
Assess individual or family risk for a variety of inherited conditions, such as genetic disorders and birth defects. Provide information to other healthcare providers or to individuals and families concerned with the risk of inherited conditions. Advise individuals and families to

support informed decisionmaking and coping methods for those at risk. May help conduct research related to genetic conditions or genetic counseling.

Illustrative examples: Chromosomal Disorders Counselor, Mitochondrial Disorders Counselor, Prenatal Genetic Counselor

29-9099 Healthcare Practitioners and Technical Workers, All Other
All healthcare practitioners and technical workers not listed separately.

Illustrative examples: Podiatric Technician, Traditional Chinese Herbalist

31-1000 Nursing, Psychiatric, and Home Health Aides 31-1010 Nursing, Psychiatric, and Home Health Aides

This broad occupation includes the following four detailed occupations:

31-1011 Home Health Aides
31-1013 Psychiatric Aides
31-1014 Nursing Assistants
31-1015 Orderlies

31-1011 Home Health Aides

Provide routine individualized healthcare such as changing bandages and dressing wounds, and applying topical medications to the elderly, convalescents, or persons with disabilities at the patient's home or in a care facility. Monitor or report changes in health status. May also provide personal care such as bathing, dressing, and grooming of patient.

Illustrative examples: Home Health Attendant, Home Hospice Aide

31-1013 Psychiatric Aides

Assist mentally impaired or emotionally disturbed patients, working under direction of nursing and medical staff. May assist with daily living activities, lead patients in educational and recreational activities, or accompany patients to and from examinations and treatments. May restrain violent patients. Includes psychiatric orderlies.

Illustrative examples: Mental Health Orderly, Psychiatric Nursing Aide, Psychiatric Technician Assistant

31-1014 Nursing Assistants

Provide basic patient care under direction of nursing staff. Perform duties such as feed, bathe, dress, groom, or move patients, or change linens. May transfer or transport patients. Includes nursing care attendants, nursing aides, and nursing attendants. Excludes "Home Health Aides" (31-1011), "Orderlies" (31-1015), "Personal Care Aides" (39-9021), and "Psychiatric Aides" (31-1013).

Illustrative examples: Certified Nurse Aide, Certified Nursing Assistant, Nursing Care Attendant

31-1015 Orderlies

Transport patients to areas such as operating rooms or x-ray rooms using wheelchairs, stretchers, or moveable beds. May maintain stocks of supplies or clean and transport equipment. Psychiatric orderlies are included in "Psychiatric Aides" (31-1013). Excludes "Nursing Assistants" (31-1014).

Illustrative examples: Hospital Orderly, Medical Orderly, Surgical Orderly

31-2000 Occupational Therapy and Physical Therapist Assistants and Aides

31-2010 Occupational Therapy Assistants and Aides
This broad occupation includes the following two detailed occupations:
31-2011 Occupational Therapy Assistants
31-2012 Occupational Therapy Aides

31-2011 Occupational Therapy Assistants
Assist occupational therapists in providing occupational therapy treatments and procedures. May, in accordance with State laws, assist in development of treatment plans, carry out routine functions, direct activity programs, and document the progress of treatments. Generally requires formal training.

Illustrative examples: Certified Occupational Therapy Assistant, Licensed Occupational Therapist Assistant

31-2012 Occupational Therapy Aides
Under close supervision of an occupational therapist or occupational therapy assistant, perform only delegated, selected, or routine tasks in specific situations. These duties include preparing patient and treatment room.

Illustrative examples: Occupational Rehabilitation Aide, Occupational Therapist Aide

31-2020 Physical Therapist Assistants and Aides
This broad occupation includes the following two detailed occupations:
31-2021 Physical Therapist Assistants
31-2022 Physical Therapist Aides

31-2021 Physical Therapist Assistants
Assist physical therapists in providing physical therapy treatments and procedures. May, in accordance with State laws, assist in the development of treatment plans, carry out routine functions, document the progress of treatment, and modify specific treatments in accordance with patient status and within the scope of treatment plans established by a physical therapist. Generally requires formal training.

Illustrative examples: Licensed Physical Therapy Assistant, Physiotherapy Assistant

31-2022 Physical Therapist Aides
Under close supervision of a physical therapist or physical therapy assistant, perform only delegated, selected, or routine tasks in specific situations. These duties include preparing the patient and the treatment area.

Illustrative examples: Clinical Rehabilitation Aide, Physical Therapy Aide

31-9000 Other Healthcare Support Occupations

31-9010 Massage Therapists

This broad occupation is the same as the detailed occupation:

31-9011 Massage Therapists

31-9011 Massage Therapists

Perform therapeutic massages of soft tissues and joints. May assist in the assessment of range of motion and muscle strength, or propose client therapy plans.

Illustrative examples: Deep Tissue Massage Therapist, Licensed Massage Therapist, Swedish Masseuse

31-9090 Miscellaneous Healthcare Support Occupations

This broad occupation includes the following eight detailed occupations:

31-9091 Dental Assistants
31-9092 Medical Assistants
31-9093 Medical Equipment Preparers
31-9094 Medical Transcriptionists
31-9095 Pharmacy Aides
31-9096 Veterinary Assistants and Laboratory Animal Caretakers
31-9097 Phlebotomists
31-9099 Healthcare Support Workers, All Other

31-9091 Dental Assistants

Assist dentist, set up equipment, prepare patient for treatment, and keep records.

Illustrative examples: Certified Dental Assistant, Orthodontic Assistant

31-9092 Medical Assistants

Perform administrative and certain clinical duties under the direction of a physician. Administrative duties may include scheduling appointments, maintaining medical records, billing, and coding information for insurance purposes. Clinical duties may include taking and recording vital signs and medical histories, preparing patients for examination, drawing blood, and administering medications as directed by physician. Excludes "Physician Assistants" (29-1071).

Illustrative examples: Chiropractic Assistant, Morgue Attendant, Orthopedic Cast Specialist

31-9093 Medical Equipment Preparers

Prepare, sterilize, install, or clean laboratory or healthcare equipment. May perform routine laboratory tasks and operate or inspect equipment.

Illustrative examples: Central Sterile Supply Technician, Sterilization Specialist

31-9094 Medical Transcriptionists

Transcribe medical reports recorded by physicians and other healthcare practitioners using various electronic devices, covering office visits, emergency room visits, diagnostic imaging studies, operations, chart reviews, and final summaries. Transcribe dictated reports and translate abbreviations into fully understandable form. Edit as necessary and return reports in either printed or electronic form for review and signature, or correction.

Illustrative examples: Medical Stenographer, Medical Transcriber, Pathology Transcriptionist

31-9095 Pharmacy Aides
Record drugs delivered to the pharmacy, store incoming merchandise, and inform the supervisor of stock needs. May operate cash register and accept prescriptions for filling.

Illustrative examples: Pharmacist Assistant, Pharmacy Clerk, Prescription Clerk

31-9096 Veterinary Assistants and Laboratory Animal Caretakers
Feed, water, and examine pets and other nonfarm animals for signs of illness, disease, or injury in laboratories and animal hospitals and clinics. Clean and disinfect cages and work areas, and sterilize laboratory and surgical equipment. May provide routine post-operative care, administer medication orally or topically, or prepare samples for laboratory examination under the supervision of veterinary or laboratory animal technologists or technicians, veterinarians, or scientists. Excludes "Nonfarm Animal Caretakers" (39-2021).

Illustrative examples: Veterinary Attendant, Veterinarian Helper

31-9097 Phlebotomists
Draw blood for tests, transfusions, donations, or research. May explain the procedure to patients and assist in the recovery of patients with adverse reactions.

Illustrative examples: Phlebotomy Technician, Venipuncturist

31-9099 Healthcare Support Workers, All Other
All healthcare support workers not listed separately.

Illustrative example: Ortho/Prosthetic Aide

33-1000 Supervisors of Protective Service Workers
33-1010 First-Line Supervisors of Law Enforcement Workers
This broad occupation includes the following two detailed occupations:
33-1011 First-Line Supervisors of Correctional Officers
33-1012 First-Line Supervisors of Police and Detectives

33-1011 First-Line Supervisors of Correctional Officers
Directly supervise and coordinate activities of correctional officers and jailers.

Illustrative examples: Corrections Sergeant, Prison Guard Supervisor

33-1012 First-Line Supervisors of Police and Detectives
Directly supervise and coordinate activities of members of police force.

Illustrative examples: Commanding Officer Homicide Squad, Detective Lieutenant, Police Lieutenant, Traffic Sergeant

33-1020 First-Line Supervisors of Fire Fighting and Prevention Workers
This broad occupation is the same as the detailed occupation:
33-1021 First-line Supervisors of Fire Fighting and Prevention Workers

33-1021 First-Line Supervisors of Fire Fighting and Prevention Workers
Directly supervise and coordinate activities of workers engaged in fire fighting and fire prevention and control.

Illustrative examples: Fire Lieutenant, Municipal Fire Fighting and Prevention Supervisor, Supervising Fire Marshal

33-1090 Miscellaneous First-Line Supervisors, Protective Service Workers
This broad occupation is the same as the detailed occupation:
33-1099 First-Line Supervisors of Protective Service Workers, All Other

33-1099 First-Line Supervisors of Protective Service Workers, All Other
All protective service supervisors not listed separately above.

Illustrative examples: Animal Cruelty Investigation Supervisor, Security Guard Supervisor, Transportation Security Administration (TSA) Screener Supervisor

33-2000 Fire Fighting and Prevention Workers

33-2010 Firefighters
This broad occupation is the same as the detailed occupation:
33-2011 Firefighters

33-2011 Firefighters

Control and extinguish fires or respond to emergency situations where life, property, or the environment is at risk. Duties may include fire prevention, emergency medical service, hazardous material response, search and rescue, and disaster assistance.

Illustrative examples: Fire Engine Pump Operator, Forest Firefighter, Marine Firefighter, Smoke Jumper

33-2020 Fire Inspectors
This broad occupation includes the following two detailed occupations:
33-2021 Fire Inspectors and Investigators
33-2022 Forest Fire Inspectors and Prevention Specialists

33-2021 Fire Inspectors and Investigators
Inspect buildings to detect fire hazards and enforce local ordinances and State laws, or investigate and gather facts to determine cause of fires and explosions.

Illustrative examples: Arson Investigator, Certified Vehicle Fire Investigator, Fire Hazard Inspector, Fire Prevention Inspector

33-2022 Forest Fire Inspectors and Prevention Specialists
Enforce fire regulations, inspect forest for fire hazards and recommend forest fire prevention or control measures. May report forest fires and weather conditions.

Illustrative examples: Environmental Protection Fire Control Officer, Forest Fire Control Officer, Wildfire Prevention Specialist

33-3000 Law Enforcement Workers

33-3010 Bailiffs, Correctional Officers, and Jailers
This broad occupation includes the following two detailed occupations:
33-3011 Bailiffs
33-3012 Correctional Officers and Jailers

33-3011 Bailiffs
Maintain order in courts of law.

Illustrative examples: Court Bailiff, Court Security Officer, Deputy Bailiff

33-3012 Correctional Officers and Jailers
Guard inmates in penal or rehabilitative institutions in accordance with established regulations and procedures. May guard prisoners in transit between jail, courtroom, prison, or other point. Includes deputy sheriffs and police who spend the majority of their time guarding prisoners in correctional institutions.

Illustrative examples: Certified Detention Deputy, Juvenile Corrections Officer, Prison Guard

33-3020 Detectives and Criminal Investigators
This broad occupation is the same as the detailed occupation:
33-3021 Detectives and Criminal Investigators

33-3021 Detectives and Criminal Investigators
Conduct investigations related to suspected violations of Federal, State, or local laws to prevent or solve crimes. Excludes "Private Detectives and Investigators" (33-9021).

Illustrative examples: Deputy United States Marshal, Homicide Detective, Narcotics Investigator

33-3030 Fish and Game Wardens
This broad occupation is the same as the detailed occupation:
33-3031 Fish and Game Wardens

33-3031 Fish and Game Wardens
Patrol assigned area to prevent fish and game law violations. Investigate reports of damage to crops or property by wildlife. Compile biological data.

Illustrative examples: Conservation Enforcement Officer, Wildlife and Game Protector, Wildlife Officer

33-3040 Parking Enforcement Workers
This broad occupation is the same as the detailed occupation:
33-3041 Parking Enforcement Workers

33-3041 Parking Enforcement Workers
Patrol assigned area, such as public parking lot or city streets to issue tickets to overtime parking violators and illegally parked vehicles.

Illustrative examples: Meter Maid, Parking Enforcement Officer

33-3050 Police Officers
This broad occupation includes the following two detailed occupations:
33-3051 Police and Sheriff's Patrol Officers
33-3052 Transit and Railroad Police

33-3051 Police and Sheriff's Patrol Officers
Maintain order and protect life and property by enforcing local, tribal, State, or Federal laws and ordinances. Perform a combination of the following duties: patrol a specific area; direct traffic; issue traffic summonses; investigate accidents; apprehend and arrest suspects, or serve legal processes of courts.

Illustrative examples: Border Patrol Officer, Motorcycle Police, Park Police, State Trooper

33-3052 Transit and Railroad Police

Protect and police railroad and transit property, employees, or passengers.

Illustrative examples: Railroad Detective, Track Patrol, Transit Authority Police

33-9000 Other Protective Service Workers

33-9010 Animal Control Workers

This broad occupation is the same as the detailed occupation:
33-9011 Animal Control Workers

33-9011 Animal Control Workers

Handle animals for the purpose of investigations of mistreatment, or control of abandoned, dangerous, or unattended animals.

Illustrative examples: Animal Control Officer, Animal Warden, Dog Catcher, Humane Officer

33-9020 Private Detectives and Investigators

This broad occupation is the same as the detailed occupation:
33-9021 Private Detectives and Investigators

33-9021 Private Detectives and Investigators

Gather, analyze, compile and report information regarding individuals or organizations to clients, or detect occurrences of unlawful acts or infractions of rules in private establishment.

Illustrative examples: Private Eye, Skip Tracer, Store Detective

33-9030 Security Guards and Gaming Surveillance Officers

This broad occupation includes the following two detailed occupations:
33-9031 Gaming Surveillance Officers and Gaming Investigators
33-9032 Security Guards

33-9031 Gaming Surveillance Officers and Gaming Investigators

Act as oversight and security agent for management and customers. Observe casino or casino hotel operation for irregular activities such as cheating or theft by either employees or patrons. May use one-way mirrors above the casino floor, cashier's cage, and from desk. Use of audio/video equipment is also common to observe operation of the business. Usually required to provide verbal and written reports of all violations and suspicious behavior to supervisor.

Illustrative examples: Casino Investigator, Casino Surveillance Officer, Gambling Monitor

33-9032 Security Guards

Guard, patrol, or monitor premises to prevent theft, violence, or infractions of rules. May operate x-ray and metal detector equipment. Excludes "Transportation Security Screeners" (33-9093).

Illustrative examples: Bank Guard, Bodyguard, Bouncer

33-9090 Miscellaneous Protective Service Workers
This broad occupation includes the following four detailed occupations:
33-9091 Crossing Guards
33-9092 Lifeguards, Ski Patrol, and Other Recreational Protective Service Workers
33-9093 Transportation Security Screeners
33-9099 Protective Service Workers, All Other

33-9091 Crossing Guards
Guide or control vehicular or pedestrian traffic at such places as streets, schools, railroad crossings, or construction sites.

Illustrative examples: Construction Site Crossing Guard, School Traffic Guard

33-9092 Lifeguards, Ski Patrol, and Other Recreational Protective Service Workers
Monitor recreational areas, such as pools, beaches, or ski slopes to provide assistance and protection to participants.

Illustrative examples: Beach Lifeguard, Outdoor Emergency Care Technician

33-9093 Transportation Security Screeners
Conduct screening of passengers, baggage, or cargo to ensure compliance with Transportation Security Administration (TSA) regulations. May operate basic security equipment such as x-ray machines and hand wands at screening checkpoints.

Illustrative examples: Airport Baggage Screener, Airport Security Screener, Transportation Security Officer, Transportation Security Administration (TSA) Screener

33-9099 Protective Service Workers, All Other
All protective service workers not listed separately.

Illustrative examples, Playground Monitor, Warrant Server

35-1000 Supervisors of Food Preparation and Serving Workers 35-1010 First-Line Supervisors of Food Preparation and Serving Workers

This broad occupation includes the following two detailed occupations:

35-1011 Chefs and Head Cooks
35-1012 First-Line Supervisors of Food Preparation and Serving Workers

35-1011 Chefs and Head Cooks

Direct and may participate in the preparation, seasoning, and cooking of salads, soups, fish, meats, vegetables, desserts, or other foods. May plan and price menu items, order supplies, and keep records and accounts.

Illustrative examples: Executive Chef, Pastry Chef, Sous Chef

35-1012 First-Line Supervisors of Food Preparation and Serving Workers

Directly supervise and coordinate activities of workers engaged in preparing and serving food.

Illustrative examples: Banquet Supervisor, Bar Manager, Kitchen Supervisor

35-2000 Cooks and Food Preparation Workers

35-2010 Cooks

This broad occupation includes the following six detailed occupations:

35-2011 Cooks, Fast Food
35-2012 Cooks, Institution and Cafeteria
35-2013 Cooks, Private Household
35-2014 Cooks, Restaurant
35-2015 Cooks, Short Order
35-2019 Cooks, All Other

35-2011 Cooks, Fast Food

Prepare and cook food in a fast food restaurant with a limited menu. Duties of these cooks are limited to preparation of a few basic items and normally involve operating large-volume single-purpose cooking equipment.

Illustrative example: Fast Food Fry Cook

35-2012 Cooks, Institution and Cafeteria

Prepare and cook large quantities of food for institutions, such as schools, hospitals, or cafeterias.

Illustrative examples: Camp Cook, Galley Cook, Mess Cook, School Cook

35-2013 Cooks, Private Household

Prepare meals in private homes. Includes personal chefs.
Illustrative examples: Certified Personal Chef, Private Chef

35-2014 Cooks, Restaurant
Prepare, season, and cook dishes such as soups, meats, vegetables, or desserts in restaurants. May order supplies, keep records and accounts, price items on menu, or plan menu.

Illustrative examples: Banquet Cook, Line Cook, Saucier

35-2015 Cooks, Short Order
Prepare and cook to order a variety of foods that require only a short preparation time. May take orders from customers and serve patrons at counters or tables. Excludes "Fast Food Cooks" (35-2011).

Illustrative example: Griddle Cook

35-2019 Cooks, All Other
All cooks not listed separately.

Illustrative examples: Falafal Cart Cook, Fraternity House Cook

35-2020 Food Preparation Workers
This broad occupation is the same as the detailed occupation:
35-2021 Food Preparation Workers

35-2021 Food Preparation Workers
Perform a variety of food preparation duties other than cooking, such as preparing cold foods and shellfish, slicing meat, and brewing coffee or tea.

Illustrative examples: Fruit and Vegetable Parer, Salad Maker, Sandwich Maker

35-3000 Food and Beverage Serving Workers

35-3010 Bartenders
This broad occupation is the same as the detailed occupation:
35-3011 Bartenders

35-3011 Bartenders
Mix and serve drinks to patrons, directly or through waitstaff.

Illustrative examples: Barkeep, Mixologist, Taproom Attendant

35-3020 Fast Food and Counter Workers
This broad occupation includes the following two detailed occupations:

35-3021 Combined Food Preparation and Serving Workers, Including Fast Food

Perform duties which combine preparing and serving food and nonalcoholic beverages.

Illustrative example: Mess Attendant

35-3022 Counter Attendants, Cafeteria, Food Concession, and Coffee Shop
Serve food to diners at counter or from a steam table. Counter attendants who also wait tables are included in "Waiters and Waitresses" (35-3031).

Illustrative examples: Cafeteria Server, Ice Cream Server, Snack Bar Attendant

35-3030 Waiters and Waitresses
This broad occupation is the same as the detailed occupation:
35-3031 Waiters and Waitresses

35-3031 Waiters and Waitresses
Take orders and serve food and beverages to patrons at tables in dining establishment. Excludes "Counter Attendants, Cafeteria, Food Concession, and Coffee Shop" (35-3022).

Illustrative examples: Cocktail Server, Dining Car Server, Wine Steward

35-3040 Food Servers, Nonrestaurant
This broad occupation is the same as the detailed occupation:
35-3041 Food Servers, Nonrestaurant

35-3041 Food Servers, Nonrestaurant
Serve food to individuals outside of a restaurant environment, such as in hotel rooms, hospital rooms, residential care facilities, or cars. Excludes "Door-to-Door Sales Workers, News and Street Vendors, and Related Workers" (41-9091) and "Counter Attendants, Cafeteria, Food Concession, and Coffee Shop" (35-3022).

Illustrative examples: Boat Hop, Hospital Food Service Worker, Room Service Food Server

35-9000 Other Food Preparation and Serving Related Workers

35-9010 Dining Room and Cafeteria Attendants and Bartender Helpers
This broad occupation is the same as the detailed occupation:
35-9011 Dining Room and Cafeteria Attendants and Bartender Helpers

35-9011 Dining Room and Cafeteria Attendants and Bartender Helpers
Facilitate food service. Clean tables, remove dirty dishes, replace soiled table linens; set tables; replenish supply of clean linens, silverware, glassware, and dishes; supply service bar with food; and serve items such as water, condiments, and coffee to patrons.
Illustrative examples: Bar Back, Busser, Lunchroom Attendant

35-9020 Dishwashers

This broad occupation is the same as the detailed occupation:
35-9021 Dishwashers

35-9021 Dishwashers
Clean dishes, kitchen, food preparation equipment, or utensils.

Illustrative examples: Dish Room Worker, Silverware Cleaner

35-9030 Hosts and Hostesses, Restaurant, Lounge, and Coffee Shop
This broad occupation is the same as the detailed occupation:
35-9031 Hosts and Hostesses, Restaurant, Lounge, and Coffee Shop

35-9031 Hosts and Hostesses, Restaurant, Lounge, and Coffee Shop
Welcome patrons, seat them at tables or in lounge, and help ensure quality of facilities and service.

Illustrative examples: Dining Room Host, Maitre D'

35-9090 Miscellaneous Food Preparation and Serving Related Workers
This broad occupation is the same as the detailed occupation:
35-9099 Food Preparation and Serving Related Workers, All Other

35-9099 Food Preparation and Serving Related Workers, All Other
All food preparation and serving related workers not listed separately.

Illustrative example: Kitchen Steward

37-1000 Supervisors of Building and Grounds Cleaning and Maintenance Workers

37-1010 First-Line Supervisors of Building and Grounds Cleaning and Maintenance Workers
This broad occupation includes the following two detailed occupations:
37-1011 First-Line Supervisors of Housekeeping and Janitorial Workers
37-1012 First-Line Supervisors of Landscaping, Lawn Service, and Groundskeeping Workers

37-1011 First-Line Supervisors of Housekeeping and Janitorial Workers
Directly supervise and coordinate work activities of cleaning personnel in hotels, hospitals, offices, and other establishments.

Illustrative examples: Building Cleaning Supervisor, Cleaning Staff Supervisor, Custodial Supervisor

37-1012 First-Line Supervisors of Landscaping, Lawn Service, and Groundskeeping Workers
Directly supervise and coordinate activities of workers engaged in landscaping or groundskeeping activities. Work may involve reviewing contracts to ascertain service, machine, and workforce requirements; answering inquiries from potential customers regarding methods, material, and price ranges; and preparing estimates according to labor, material, and machine costs.

Illustrative examples: Grounds Maintenance Supervisor, Head Greenskeeper, Horticultural Services Supervisor

37-2000 Building Cleaning and Pest Control Workers

37-2010 Building Cleaning Workers
This broad occupation includes the following three detailed occupations:
37-2011 Janitors and Cleaners, Except Maids and Housekeeping Cleaners
37-2012 Maids and Housekeeping Cleaners
37-2019 Building Cleaning Workers, All Other

37-2011 Janitors and Cleaners, Except Maids and Housekeeping Cleaners
Keep buildings in clean and orderly condition. Perform heavy cleaning duties, such as cleaning floors, shampooing rugs, washing walls and glass, and removing rubbish. Duties may include tending furnace and boiler, performing routine maintenance activities, notifying management of need for repairs, and cleaning snow or debris from sidewalk.

Illustrative examples: Industrial Plant Custodian, School Custodian, Window Washer

37-2012 Maids and Housekeeping Cleaners

Perform any combination of light cleaning duties to maintain private households or commercial establishments, such as hotels and hospitals, in a clean and orderly manner. Duties may include making beds, replenishing linens, cleaning rooms and halls, and vacuuming.

Illustrative examples: Chambermaid, House Cleaner, Housekeeping Staff

37-2019 Building Cleaning Workers, All Other

All building cleaning workers not listed separately.

Illustrative examples: Building Pressure Washer, Chimney Sweeper

37-2020 Pest Control Workers

This broad occupation is the same as the detailed occupation:
37-2021 Pest Control Workers

37-2021 Pest Control Workers

Apply or release chemical solutions or toxic gases and set traps to kill or remove pests and vermin that infest buildings and surrounding areas.

Illustrative examples: Exterminator, Fumigator, Rodent Exterminator

37-3000 Grounds Maintenance Workers

37-3010 Grounds Maintenance Workers

This broad occupation includes the following four detailed occupations:
37-3011 Landscaping and Groundskeeping Workers
37-3012 Pesticide Handlers, Sprayers, and Applicators, Vegetation
37-3013 Tree Trimmers and Pruners
37-3019 Grounds Maintenance Workers, All Other

37-3011 Landscaping and Groundskeeping Workers

Landscape or maintain grounds of property using hand or power tools or equipment. Workers typically perform a variety of tasks, which may include any combination of the following: sod laying, mowing, trimming, planting, watering, fertilizing, digging, raking, sprinkler installation, and installation of mortarless segmental concrete masonry wall units. Excludes "Farmworkers and Laborers, Crop, Nursery, and Greenhouse" (45-2092).

Illustrative examples: Greenskeeper, Hedge Trimmer, Lawn Caretaker, Shrub Planter

37-3012 Pesticide Handlers, Sprayers, and Applicators, Vegetation

Mix or apply pesticides, herbicides, fungicides, or insecticides through sprays, dusts, vapors, soil incorporation, or chemical application on trees, shrubs, lawns, or botanical crops. Usually requires specific training and State or Federal certification. Excludes "Commercial Pilots" (53-2012) who dust or spray crops from aircraft.

Illustrative examples: Fruit Sprayer, Weed Sprayer

37-3013 Tree Trimmers and Pruners

Using sophisticated climbing and rigging techniques, cut away dead or excess branches from trees or shrubs to maintain right-of-way for roads, sidewalks, or utilities, or to improve appearance, health, and value of tree. Prune or treat trees or shrubs using handsaws, hand pruners, clippers, and power pruners. Works off the ground in the tree canopy and may use truck-mounted lifts. Excludes workers who primarily perform duties of "Pesticide Handlers, Sprayers, and Applicators, Vegetation" (37-3012) and "Landscaping and Groundskeeping Workers" (37-3011).

Illustrative examples: Tree Specialist, Tree Surgeon

37-3019 Grounds Maintenance Workers, All Other

All grounds maintenance workers not listed separately.

Illustrative example: Trailhead Maintenance Worker, Tree Trimmer Helper

39-1000 Supervisors of Personal Care and Service Workers 39-1010 First-Line Supervisors of Gaming Workers

This broad occupation includes the following two detailed occupations:

39-1011 Gaming Supervisors
39-1012 Slot Supervisors

39-1011 Gaming Supervisors

Supervise and coordinate activities of workers in assigned gaming areas. Circulate among tables and observe operations. Ensure that stations and games are covered for each shift. May explain and interpret operating rules of house to patrons. May plan and organize activities and services for guests in hotels/casinos. May address service complaints. Excludes "Slot Supervisors" (39-1012).

Illustrative examples: Cardroom Supervisor, Pit Boss, Table Games Supervisor

39-1012 Slot Supervisors

Supervise and coordinate activities of slot department workers to provide service to patrons. Handle and settle complaints of players. Verify and pay off jackpots. Reset slot machines after payoffs. Make repairs or adjustments to slot machines or recommend removal of slot machines for repair. Report hazards and enforce safety rules.

Illustrative example: Casino Slot Supervisor, Electronic Gaming Device Supervisor, Slot Key Person

39-1020 First-Line Supervisors of Personal Service Workers

This broad occupation is the same as the detailed occupation:
39-1021 First-Line Supervisors of Personal Service Workers

39-1021 First-Line Supervisors of Personal Service Workers

Directly supervise and coordinate activities of personal service workers, such as flight attendants, hairdressers, or caddies.

Illustrative examples: Animal Trainer Supervisor, Caddy Master, Recreation Attendant Supervisor

39-2000 Animal Care and Service Workers

39-2010 Animal Trainers

This broad occupation is the same as the detailed occupation:
39-2011 Animal Trainers

39-2011 Animal Trainers

Train animals for riding, harness, security, performance, or obedience, or assisting persons with disabilities. Accustom animals to human voice and contact; and condition animals to respond to commands. Train animals according to prescribed standards for show or competition. May train animals to carry pack loads or work as part of pack team.

Illustrative examples: Guide Dog Trainer, Horse Breaker, Marine Mammal Trainer

39-2020 Nonfarm Animal Caretakers
This broad occupation is the same as the detailed occupation:
39-2021 Nonfarm Animal Caretakers

39-2021 Nonfarm Animal Caretakers
Feed, water, groom, bathe, exercise, or otherwise care for pets and other nonfarm animals, such as dogs, cats, ornamental fish or birds, zoo animals, and mice. Work in settings such as kennels, animal shelters, zoos, circuses, and aquariums. May keep records of feedings, treatments, and animals received or discharged. May clean, disinfect, and repair cages, pens, or fish tanks. Excludes "Veterinary Assistants and Laboratory Animal Caretakers" (31-9096).

Illustrative examples: Animal Shelter Worker, Dog Groomer, Kennel Worker, Zookeeper

39-3000 Entertainment Attendants and Related Workers

39-3010 Gaming Services Workers
This broad occupation includes the following three detailed occupations:
39-3011 Gaming Dealers
39-3012 Gaming and Sports Book Writers and Runners
39-3019 Gaming Service Workers, All Other

39-3011 Gaming Dealers
Operate table games. Stand or sit behind table and operate games of chance by dispensing the appropriate number of cards or blocks to players, or operating other gaming equipment. Distribute winnings or collect players' money or chips. May compare the house's hand against players' hands.

Illustrative examples: Blackjack Dealer, Craps Dealer, Poker Dealer, Roulette Dealer

39-3012 Gaming and Sports Book Writers and Runners
Post information enabling patrons to wager on various races and sporting events. Assist in the operation of games such as keno and bingo. May operate random number generating equipment and announce the numbers for patrons. Receive, verify, and record patrons' wagers. Scan and process winning tickets presented by patrons and payout winnings for those wagers.

Illustrative examples: Betting Clerk, Keno Runner, Race Book Writer

39-3019 Gaming Service Workers, All Other
All gaming service workers not listed separately.

Illustrative examples: Pit Clerk, Proposition Player, Shill

39-3020 Motion Picture Projectionists
This broad occupation is the same as the detailed occupation:
39-3021 Motion Picture Projectionists

39-3021 Motion Picture Projectionists
Set up and operate motion picture projection and related sound reproduction equipment.

Illustrative examples: Film Projector Operator, Movie Projectionist

39-3030 Ushers, Lobby Attendants, and Ticket Takers
This broad occupation is the same as the detailed occupation:
39-3031 Ushers, Lobby Attendants, and Ticket Takers

39-3031 Ushers, Lobby Attendants, and Ticket Takers
Assist patrons at entertainment events by performing duties, such as collecting admission tickets and passes from patrons, assisting in finding seats, searching for lost articles, and locating such facilities as rest rooms and telephones.

Illustrative examples: Theater Usher, Ticket Collector

39-3090 Miscellaneous Entertainment Attendants and Related Workers
This broad occupation includes the following four detailed occupations:
39-3091 Amusement and Recreation Attendants
39-3092 Costume Attendants
39-3093 Locker Room, Coatroom, and Dressing Room Attendants
39-3099 Entertainment Attendants and Related Workers, All Other

39-3091 Amusement and Recreation Attendants
Perform variety of attending duties at amusement or recreation facility. May schedule use of recreation facilities, maintain and provide equipment to participants of sporting events or recreational pursuits, or operate amusement concessions and rides.

Illustrative examples: Arcade Attendant, Golf Caddy, Ski Lift Operator

39-3092 Costume Attendants
Select, fit, and take care of costumes for cast members, and aid entertainers. May assist with multiple costume changes during performances.

Illustrative examples: Theatrical Wardrobe Dresser, Wardrobe Attendant

39-3093 Locker Room, Coatroom, and Dressing Room Attendants
Provide personal items to patrons or customers in locker rooms, dressing rooms, or coatrooms.

Illustrative examples: Bathhouse Attendant, Coat Checker, Washroom Attendant

39-3099 Entertainment Attendants and Related Workers, All Other
All entertainment attendants and related workers not listed separately.

39-4000 Funeral Service Workers

39-4010 Embalmers
This broad occupation is the same as the detailed occupation:
39-4011 Embalmers

39-4011 Embalmers
Prepare bodies for interment in conformity with legal requirements.

Illustrative examples: Licensed Embalmer, Restorative Art Embalmer

39-4020 Funeral Attendants
This broad occupation is the same as the detailed occupation:
39-4021 Funeral Attendants

39-4021 Funeral Attendants
Perform variety of tasks during funeral, such as placing casket in parlor or chapel prior to service; arranging floral offerings or lights around casket; directing or escorting mourners; closing casket; and issuing and storing funeral equipment.

Illustrative examples: Funeral Home Assistant, Mortician Helper, Pallbearer

39-4030 Morticians, Undertakers, and Funeral Directors
This broad occupation is the same as the detailed occupation:
39-4031 Morticians, Undertakers, and Funeral Directors

39-4031 Morticians, Undertakers, and Funeral Directors
Perform various tasks to arrange and direct funeral services, such as coordinating transportation of body to mortuary, interviewing family or other authorized person to arrange details, selecting pallbearers, aiding with the selection of officials for religious rites, and providing transportation for mourners. Excludes "Funeral Service Managers" (11-9061).

Illustrative examples: Certified Mortician, Funeral Arranger

39-5000 Personal Appearance Workers

39-5010 Barbers, Hairdressers, Hairstylists and Cosmetologists
This broad occupation includes the following two detailed occupations:
39-5011 Barbers
39-5012 Hairdressers, Hairstylists, and Cosmetologists

39-5011 Barbers

Provide barbering services, such as cutting, trimming, shampooing, and styling hair, trimming beards, or giving shaves.

Illustrative examples: Barber Apprentice, Master Barber

39-5012 Hairdressers, Hairstylists, and Cosmetologists

Provide beauty services, such as shampooing, cutting, coloring, and styling hair, and massaging and treating scalp. May apply makeup, dress wigs, perform hair removal, and provide nail and skin care services. Excludes "Makeup Artists, Theatrical and Performance" (39-5091), "Manicurists and Pedicurists" (39-5092), and "Skincare Specialists" (39-5094).

Illustrative examples: Beautician, Wig Stylist

39-5090 Miscellaneous Personal Appearance Workers

This broad occupation includes the following four detailed occupations:
39-5091 Makeup Artists, Theatrical and Performance
39-5092 Manicurists and Pedicurists
39-5093 Shampooers
39-5094 Skincare Specialists

39-5091 Makeup Artists, Theatrical and Performance

Apply makeup to performers to reflect period, setting, and situation of their role.

Illustrative example: Special Effects Makeup Artist

39-5092 Manicurists and Pedicurists

Clean and shape customers' fingernails and toenails. May polish or decorate nails.

Illustrative examples: Fingernail Sculptor, Nail Technician

39-5093 Shampooers

Shampoo and rinse customers' hair.

Illustrative examples: Scalp Treatment Specialist, Shampoo Assistant

39-5094 Skincare Specialists

Provide skincare treatments to face and body to enhance an individual's appearance. Includes electrologists and laser hair removal specialists.

Illustrative examples: Facialist, Medical Esthetician

39-6000 Baggage Porters, Bellhops, and Concierges

39-6010 Baggage Porters, Bellhops, and Concierges
This broad occupation includes the following two detailed occupations:
39-6011 Baggage Porters and Bellhops
39-6012 Concierges

39-6011 Baggage Porters and Bellhops
Handle baggage for travelers at transportation terminals or for guests at hotels or similar establishments.

Illustrative examples: Bellstaff, Hotel Baggage Handler, Skycap

39-6012 Concierges
Assist patrons at hotel, apartment, or office building with personal services. May take messages, arrange or give advice on transportation, business services or entertainment, or monitor guest requests for housekeeping and maintenance.

Illustrative examples: Activities Concierge, Hotel Concierge, Hotel Guest Service Agent

39-7000 Tour and Travel Guides

39-7010 Tour and Travel Guides
This broad occupation includes the following two detailed occupations:
39-7011 Tour Guides and Escorts
39-7012 Travel Guides

39-7011 Tour Guides and Escorts
Escort individuals or groups on sightseeing tours or through places of interest, such as industrial establishments, public buildings, and art galleries.

Illustrative examples: Historical Site Guide, Museum Guide, Sightseeing Guide

39-7012 Travel Guides
Plan, organize, and conduct long distance travel, tours, and expeditions for individuals and groups.

Illustrative examples: Cruise Director, River Expedition Guide

39-9000 Other Personal Care and Service Workers

39-9010 Childcare Workers
This broad occupation is the same as the detailed occupation:
39-9011 Childcare Workers

39-9011 Childcare Workers
Attend to children at schools, businesses, private households, and childcare institutions. Perform a variety of tasks, such as dressing, feeding, bathing, and overseeing play. Excludes "Preschool Teachers, Except Special Education" (25-2011) and "Teacher Assistants" (25-9041).

Illustrative examples: Au Pair, Daycare Provider, Nanny

39-9020 Personal Care Aides
This broad occupation is the same as the detailed occupation:
39-9021 Personal Care Aides

39-9021 Personal Care Aides
Assist the elderly, convalescents, or persons with disabilities with daily living activities at the person's home or in a care facility. Duties performed at a place of residence may include keeping house (making beds, doing laundry, washing dishes) and preparing meals. May provide assistance at non-residential care facilities. May advise families, the elderly, convalescents, and persons with disabilities regarding such things as nutrition, cleanliness, and household activities.

Illustrative examples: Blind Escort, Elderly Companion, Geriatric Personal Care Aide

39-9030 Recreation and Fitness Workers
This broad occupation includes the following two detailed occupations:
39-9031 Fitness Trainers and Aerobics Instructors
39-9032 Recreation Workers

39-9031 Fitness Trainers and Aerobics Instructors
Instruct or coach groups or individuals in exercise activities. Demonstrate techniques and form, observe participants, and explain to them corrective measures necessary to improve their skills. Excludes teachers classified in 25-0000 Education, Training, and Library Occupations. Excludes "Coaches and Scouts" (27-2022) and "Athletic Trainers" (29-9091).

Illustrative examples: Personal Trainer, Yoga Instructor

39-9032 Recreation Workers
Conduct recreation activities with groups in public, private, or volunteer agencies or recreation facilities. Organize and promote activities, such as arts and crafts, sports, games, music, dramatics, social recreation, camping, and hobbies, taking into account the needs and interests of individual members.

Illustrative examples: Activities Aide, Camp Counselor, Playground Worker

39-9040 Residential Advisors
This broad occupation is the same as the detailed occupation:
39-9041 Residential Advisors

39-9041 Residential Advisors

Coordinate activities in residential facilities in secondary and college dormitories, group homes, or similar establishments. Order supplies and determine need for maintenance, repairs, and furnishings. May maintain household records and assign rooms. May assist residents with problem solving or refer them to counseling resources.

Illustrative examples: Dormitory Counselor, House Parent, Residence Life Coordinator

39-9090 Miscellaneous Personal Care and Service Workers

This broad occupation is the same as the detailed occupation:
39-9099 Personal Care and Service Workers, All Other

39-9099 Personal Care and Service Workers, All Other

All personal care and service workers not listed separately.

Illustrative examples: Butler, House Sitter, Shoe Shiner, Valet

41-1000 Supervisors of Sales Workers

41-1010 First-Line Supervisors of Sales Workers
This broad occupation includes the following two detailed occupations:
41-1011 First-Line Supervisors of Retail Sales Workers
41-1012 First-Line Supervisors of Non-Retail Sales Workers

41-1011 First-Line Supervisors of Retail Sales Workers
Directly supervise and coordinate activities of retail sales workers in an establishment or department. Duties may include management functions, such as purchasing, budgeting, accounting, and personnel work, in addition to supervisory duties.

Illustrative examples: Cashier Supervisor, Delicatessen Department Manager

41-1012 First-Line Supervisors of Non-Retail Sales Workers
Directly supervise and coordinate activities of sales workers other than retail sales workers. May perform duties such as budgeting, accounting, and personnel work, in addition to supervisory duties.

Illustrative examples: Insurance Sales Supervisor, Real Estate Sales Supervisor, Telemarketer Supervisor

41-2000 Retail Sales Workers

41-2010 Cashiers
This broad occupation includes the following two detailed occupations:
41-2011 Cashiers
41-2012 Gaming Change Persons and Booth Cashiers

41-2011 Cashiers
Receive and disburse money in establishments other than financial institutions. May use electronic scanners, cash registers, or related equipment. May process credit or debit card transactions and validate checks. Excludes "Gaming Cage Persons and Booth Cashiers" (41-2012).

Illustrative examples: Cash Register Operator, Grocery Checker, Toll Collector

41-2012 Gaming Change Persons and Booth Cashiers
Exchange coins, tokens, and chips for patrons' money. May issue payoffs and obtain customer's signature on receipt. May operate a booth in the slot machine area and furnish change persons with money bank at the start of the shift, or count and audit money in drawers. Excludes "Cashiers" (41-2011).

Illustrative example: Mutuel Teller, Slot Attendant

41-2020 Counter and Rental Clerks and Parts Salespersons
This broad occupation includes the following two detailed occupations:
41-2021 Counter and Rental Clerks
41-2022 Parts Salespersons

41-2021 Counter and Rental Clerks
Receive orders, generally in person, for repairs, rentals, and services. May describe available options, compute costs, and accept payment. Excludes "Counter Attendants, Cafeteria, Food Concession, and Coffee Shop" (35-3022), "Hotel, Motel, and Resort Desk Clerks" (43-4081), "Order Clerks" (43-4151), and "Reservation and Transportation Ticket Agents and Travel Clerks" (43-4181).

Illustrative examples: Car Rental Agent, Dry Cleaning Counter Clerk

41-2022 Parts Salespersons
Sell spare and replacement parts and equipment in repair shop or parts store.

Illustrative examples: Auto Parts Salesperson, Electronic Parts Salesperson

41-2030 Retail Salespersons
This broad occupation is the same as the detailed occupation:
41-2031 Retail Salespersons

41-2031 Retail Salespersons
Sell merchandise, such as furniture, motor vehicles, appliances, or apparel to consumers. Excludes "Cashiers" (41-2011).

Illustrative examples: Used Car Salesperson, Women's Apparel Salesperson

41-3000 Sales Representatives, Services

41-3010 Advertising Sales Agents
This broad occupation is the same as the detailed occupation:
41-3011 Advertising Sales Agents

41-3011 Advertising Sales Agents
Sell or solicit advertising space, time, or media in publications, signage, TV, radio, or the Internet. Includes individuals who obtain leases for outdoor advertising sites or persuade retailers to use sales promotion display items.

Illustrative examples: Advertising Account Executive, Display Advertising Sales Representative, Yellow Pages Space Salesperson

41-3020 Insurance Sales Agents
This broad occupation is the same as the detailed occupation:

41-3021 Insurance Sales Agents

41-3021 Insurance Sales Agents
Sell life, property, casualty, health, automotive, or other types of insurance. May refer clients to independent brokers, work as an independent broker, or be employed by an insurance company.

Illustrative examples: Life Insurance Salesperson, Pension Agent

41-3030 Securities, Commodities, and Financial Services Sales Agents
This broad occupation is the same as the detailed occupation:
41-3031 Securities, Commodities, and Financial Services Sales Agents

41-3031 Securities, Commodities, and Financial Services Sales Agents
Buy and sell securities or commodities in investment and trading firms, or provide financial services to businesses and individuals. May advise customers about stocks, bonds, mutual funds, commodities, and market conditions.

Illustrative examples: Investment Banker, Securities Trader, Stock Broker

41-3040 Travel Agents
This broad occupation is the same as the detailed occupation:
41-3041 Travel Agents

41-3041 Travel Agents
Plan and sell transportation and accommodations for travel agency customers. Determine destination, modes of transportation, travel dates, costs, and accommodations required. May also describe, plan, and arrange itineraries and sell tour packages. May assist in resolving clients' travel problems.

Illustrative examples: Corporate Travel Expert, Travel Service Consultant

41-3090 Miscellaneous Sales Representatives, Services
This broad occupation is the same as the detailed occupation:
41-3099 Sales Representatives, Services, All Other

41-3099 Sales Representatives, Services, All Other
All services sales representatives not listed separately.

Illustrative examples: Business Services Sales Representative, Membership Solicitor, Pest Control Service Sales Agent

41-4000 Sales Representatives, Wholesale and Manufacturing

41-4010 Sales Representatives, Wholesale and Manufacturing
This broad occupation includes the following two detailed occupations:

41-4011 Sales Representatives, Wholesale and Manufacturing, Technical and Scientific Products
41-4012 Sales Representatives, Wholesale and Manufacturing, Except Technical and Scientific Products

41-4011 Sales Representatives, Wholesale and Manufacturing, Technical and Scientific Products

Sell goods for wholesalers or manufacturers where technical or scientific knowledge is required in such areas as biology, engineering, chemistry, and electronics, normally obtained from at least 2 years of post-secondary education. Excludes "Sales Engineers" (41-9031).

Illustrative examples: Pharmaceutical Sales Representative, Surgical Instruments Sales Representative, Wholesale Ultrasonic Equipment Salesperson

41-4012 Sales Representatives, Wholesale and Manufacturing, Except Technical and Scientific Products

Sell goods for wholesalers or manufacturers to businesses or groups of individuals. Work requires substantial knowledge of items sold.

Illustrative examples: Hotel Supplies Salesperson, Pulpwood Dealer, Wholesale Diamond Broker

41-9000 Other Sales and Related Workers

41-9010 Models, Demonstrators, and Product Promoters
This broad occupation includes the following two detailed occupations:
41-9011 Demonstrators and Product Promoters
41-9012 Models

41-9011 Demonstrators and Product Promoters
Demonstrate merchandise and answer questions for the purpose of creating public interest in buying the product. May sell demonstrated merchandise.

Illustrative examples: Home Demonstrator, In-Store Demonstrator

41-9012 Models
Model garments or other apparel and accessories for prospective buyers at fashion shows, private showings, or retail establishments. May pose for photos to be used in magazines or advertisements. May pose as subject for paintings, sculptures, and other types of artistic expression.

Illustrative examples: Fashion Model, Hand Model, Photographer's Model

41-9020 Real Estate Brokers and Sales Agents
This broad occupation includes the following two detailed occupations:
41-9021 Real Estate Brokers

41-9022 Real Estate Sales Agents

41-9021 Real Estate Brokers
Operate real estate office, or work for commercial real estate firm, overseeing real estate transactions. Other duties usually include selling real estate or renting properties and arranging loans.

Illustrative example: Licensed Real Estate Broker

41-9022 Real Estate Sales Agents
Rent, buy, or sell property for clients. Perform duties, such as study property listings, interview prospective clients, accompany clients to property site, discuss conditions of sale, and draw up real estate contracts. Includes agents who represent buyer.

Illustrative examples: Apartment Rental Agent, Right of Way Agent

41-9030 Sales Engineers
This broad occupation is the same as the detailed occupation:
41-9031 Sales Engineers

41-9031 Sales Engineers
Sell business goods or services, the selling of which requires a technical background equivalent to a baccalaureate degree in engineering. Excludes "Engineers" (17-2011 through 17-2199) whose primary function is not marketing or sales.

Illustrative examples: Aerospace Products Sales Engineer, Missile Navigation Systems Sales Engineer, Nuclear Equipment Sales Engineer

41-9040 Telemarketers
This broad occupation is the same as the detailed occupation:
41-9041 Telemarketers

41-9041 Telemarketers
Solicit donations or orders for goods or services over the telephone.

Illustrative examples: Telemarketing Sales Representative, Telephone Solicitor

41-9090 Miscellaneous Sales and Related Workers
This broad occupation includes the following two detailed occupations:
41-9091 Door-to-Door Sales Workers, News and Street Vendors, and Related Workers
41-9099 Sales and Related Workers, All Other

41-9091 Door-to-Door Sales Workers, News and Street Vendors, and Related Workers
Sell goods or services door-to-door or on the street.

Illustrative examples: Newspaper Carrier, Peddler, Souvenir Street Vendor

41-9099 Sales and Related Workers, All Other
All sales and related workers not listed separately.

Illustrative examples: Auctioneer, Blood Donor Recruiter, Personal Shopper, Store Gift Wrap Associate

43-1000 Supervisors of Office and Administrative Support Workers

43-1010 First-Line Supervisors of Office and Administrative Support Workers
This broad occupation is the same as the detailed occupation:
43-1011 First-Line Supervisors of Office and Administrative Support Workers

43-1011 First-Line Supervisors of Office and Administrative Support Workers
Directly supervise and coordinate the activities of clerical and administrative support workers.

Illustrative examples: Clerical Supervisor, Payroll Supervisor, Teller Supervisor

43-2000 Communications Equipment Operators

43-2010 Switchboard Operators, Including Answering Service
This broad occupation is the same as the detailed occupation:
43-2011 Switchboard Operators, Including Answering Service

43-2011 Switchboard Operators, Including Answering Service
Operate telephone business systems equipment or switchboards to relay incoming, outgoing, and interoffice calls. May supply information to callers and record messages.

Illustrative examples: Private Branch Exchange Operator, Telephone Answering Service Operator, Telephone Switchboard Operator

43-2020 Telephone Operators
This broad occupation is the same as the detailed occupation:
43-2021 Telephone Operators

43-2021 Telephone Operators
Provide information by accessing alphabetical, geographical, or other directories. Assist customers with special billing requests, such as charges to a third party and credits or refunds for incorrectly dialed numbers or bad connections. May handle emergency calls and assist children or people with physical disabilities to make telephone calls.

Illustrative examples: Directory Assistance Operator, Long Distance Operator, Information Operator

43-2090 Miscellaneous Communications Equipment Operators
This broad occupation is the same as the detailed occupation:
43-2099 Communications Equipment Operators, All Other

43-2099 Communications Equipment Operators, All Other
All communications equipment operators not listed separately.

Illustrative example: Fax Machine Operator

43-3000 Financial Clerks

43-3010 Bill and Account Collectors
This broad occupation is the same as the detailed occupation:
43-3011 Bill and Account Collectors

43-3011 Bill and Account Collectors
Locate and notify customers of delinquent accounts by mail, telephone, or personal visit to solicit payment. Duties include receiving payment and posting amount to customer's account; preparing statements to credit department if customer fails to respond; initiating repossession proceedings or service disconnection; and keeping records of collection and status of accounts.

Illustrative examples: Collection Agent, Debt Collector, Repossessor

43-3020 Billing and Posting Clerks
This broad occupation is the same as the detailed occupation:
43-3021 Billing and Posting Clerks

43-3021 Billing and Posting Clerks
Compile, compute, and record billing, accounting, statistical, and other numerical data for billing purposes. Prepare billing invoices for services rendered or for delivery or shipment of goods.

Illustrative examples: Invoice Control Clerk, Patient Account Representative, Statement Processor

43-3030 Bookkeeping, Accounting, and Auditing Clerks
This broad occupation is the same as the detailed occupation:
43-3031 Bookkeeping, Accounting, and Auditing Clerks

43-3031 Bookkeeping, Accounting, and Auditing Clerks
Compute, classify, and record numerical data to keep financial records complete. Perform any combination of routine calculating, posting, and verifying duties to obtain primary financial data for use in maintaining accounting records. May also check the accuracy of figures, calculations, and postings pertaining to business transactions recorded by other workers. Excludes "Payroll and Timekeeping Clerks" (43-3051).

Illustrative examples: Accounts Receivable Clerk, Bookkeeper, Mortgage Accounting Clerk

43-3040 Gaming Cage Workers
This broad occupation is the same as the detailed occupation:
43-3041 Gaming Cage Workers

43-3041 Gaming Cage Workers

In a gaming establishment, conduct financial transactions for patrons. May reconcile daily summaries of transactions to balance books. May accept patron's credit application and verify credit references to provide check-cashing authorization or to establish house credit accounts. May sell gambling chips, tokens, or tickets to patrons, or to other workers for resale to patrons. May convert gaming chips, tokens, or tickets to currency upon patron's request. May use a cash register or computer to record transaction.

Illustrative examples: Cage Cashier, Casino Cashier

43-3050 Payroll and Timekeeping Clerks

This broad occupation is the same as the detailed occupation:
43-3051 Payroll and Timekeeping Clerks

43-3051 Payroll and Timekeeping Clerks

Compile and record employee time and payroll data. May compute employees' time worked, production, and commission. May compute and post wages and deductions, or prepare paychecks. Excludes "Bookkeeping, Accounting, and Auditing Clerks" (43-3031).

Illustrative example: Time and Attendance Clerk, Timekeeper

43-3060 Procurement Clerks

This broad occupation is the same as the detailed occupation:
43-3061 Procurement Clerks

43-3061 Procurement Clerks

Compile information and records to draw up purchase orders for procurement of materials and services.

Illustrative examples: Procurement Assistant, Purchasing Clerk

43-3070 Tellers

This broad occupation is the same as the detailed occupation:
43-3071 Tellers

43-3071 Tellers

Receive and pay out money. Keep records of money and negotiable instruments involved in a financial institution's various transactions.

Illustrative examples: Foreign Exchange Clerk, Money Order Clerk, Securities Teller

43-3090 Miscellaneous Financial Clerks

This broad occupation is the same as the detailed occupation:
43-3099 Financial Clerks, All Other

43-3099 Financial Clerks, All Other
All financial clerks not listed separately.

Illustrative examples: Bank Vault Attendant, Financial Reserve Clerk, Safety Deposit Clerk

43-4000 Information and Record Clerks

43-4010 Brokerage Clerks
This broad occupation is the same as the detailed occupation:
43-4011 Brokerage Clerks

43-4011 Brokerage Clerks
Perform duties related to the purchase, sale or holding of securities. Duties include writing orders for stock purchases or sales, computing transfer taxes, verifying stock transactions, accepting and delivering securities, tracking stock price fluctuations, computing equity, distributing dividends, and keeping records of daily transactions and holdings.

Illustrative examples: Commodities Clerk, Dividend Clerk

43-4020 Correspondence Clerks
This broad occupation is the same as the detailed occupation:
43-4021 Correspondence Clerks

43-4021 Correspondence Clerks
Compose letters or electronic correspondence in reply to requests for merchandise, damage claims, credit and other information, delinquent accounts, incorrect billings, or unsatisfactory services. Duties may include gathering data to formulate reply and preparing correspondence.

Illustrative examples: Fan Mail Editor, Medicare Correspondence Representative

43-4030 Court, Municipal, and License Clerks
This broad occupation is the same as the detailed occupation:
43-4031 Court, Municipal, and License Clerks

43-4031 Court, Municipal, and License Clerks
Perform clerical duties for courts of law, municipalities, or governmental licensing agencies and bureaus. May prepare docket of cases to be called; secure information for judges and court; prepare draft agendas or bylaws for town or city council; answer official correspondence; keep fiscal records and accounts; issue licenses or permits; and record data, administer tests, or collect fees. Clerks of Court are classified in "Managers, All Other" (11-9199).

Illustrative examples: Circuit Court Clerk, Motor Vehicle License Clerk, Warrant Clerk

43-4040 Credit Authorizers, Checkers, and Clerks
This broad occupation is the same as the detailed occupation:

43-4041 Credit Authorizers, Checkers, and Clerks

43-4041 Credit Authorizers, Checkers, and Clerks

Authorize credit charges against customers' accounts. Investigate history and credit standing of individuals or business establishments applying for credit. May interview applicants to obtain personal and financial data; determine credit worthiness; process applications; and notify customers of acceptance or rejection of credit.

Illustrative examples: Charge Authorizer, Commercial Credit Reviewer, Credit Rating Checker

43-4050 Customer Service Representatives

This broad occupation is the same as the detailed occupation:
43-4051 Customer Service Representatives

43-4051 Customer Service Representatives

Interact with customers to provide information in response to inquiries about products and services and to handle and resolve complaints. Excludes individuals whose duties are primarily installation, sales, or repair.

Illustrative examples: Customer Complaint Clerk, Passenger Relations Representative, Warranty Clerk

43-4060 Eligibility Interviewers, Government Programs

This broad occupation is the same as the detailed occupation:
43-4061 Eligibility Interviewers, Government Programs

43-4061 Eligibility Interviewers, Government Programs

Determine eligibility of persons applying to receive assistance from government programs and agency resources, such as welfare, unemployment benefits, social security, and public housing.

Illustrative examples: Medical Interviewer, Public Housing Interviewer, Unemployment Benefits Claims Taker

43-4070 File Clerks

This broad occupation is the same as the detailed occupation:
43-4071 File Clerks

43-4071 File Clerks

File correspondence, cards, invoices, receipts, and other records in alphabetical or numerical order or according to the filing system used. Locate and remove material from file when requested.

Illustrative examples: Document Clerk, Records Clerk

43-4080 Hotel, Motel, and Resort Desk Clerks
This broad occupation is the same as the detailed occupation:
43-4081 Hotel, Motel, and Resort Desk Clerks

43-4081 Hotel, Motel, and Resort Desk Clerks
Accommodate hotel, motel, and resort patrons by registering and assigning rooms to guests, issuing room keys or cards, transmitting and receiving messages, keeping records of occupied rooms and guests' accounts, making and confirming reservations, and presenting statements to and collecting payments from departing guests.

Illustrative examples: Hotel Front Desk Clerk, Hotel Registration Clerk

43-4110 Interviewers, Except Eligibility and Loan
This broad occupation is the same as the detailed occupation:
43-4111 Interviewers, Except Eligibility and Loan

43-4111 Interviewers, Except Eligibility and Loan
Interview persons by telephone, mail, in person, or by other means for the purpose of completing forms, applications, or questionnaires. Ask specific questions, record answers, and assist persons with completing form. May sort, classify, and file forms.

Illustrative examples: Census Taker, Market Research Interviewer, Outpatient Interviewing Clerk

43-4120 Library Assistants, Clerical
This broad occupation is the same as the detailed occupation:
43-4121 Library Assistants, Clerical

43-4121 Library Assistants, Clerical
Compile records, sort, shelve, issue, and receive library materials such as books, electronic media, pictures, cards, slides and microfilm. Locate library materials for loan and replace material in shelving area, stacks, or files according to identification number and title. Register patrons to permit them to borrow books, periodicals, and other library materials. Excludes "Library Technicians" (25-4031).

Illustrative examples: Braille and Talking Books Clerk, Circulation Clerk, Microfilm Clerk

43-4130 Loan Interviewers and Clerks
This broad occupation is the same as the detailed occupation:
43-4131 Loan Interviewers and Clerks

43-4131 Loan Interviewers and Clerks
Interview loan applicants to elicit information; investigate applicants' backgrounds and verify references; prepare loan request papers; and forward findings, reports, and documents to

appraisal department. Review loan papers to ensure completeness, and complete transactions between loan establishment, borrowers, and sellers upon approval of loan.

Illustrative examples: Loan Processor, Mortgage Loan Closer

43-4140 New Accounts Clerks
This broad occupation is the same as the detailed occupation:
43-4141 New Accounts Clerks

43-4141 New Accounts Clerks
Interview persons desiring to open accounts in financial institutions. Explain account services available to prospective customers and assist them in preparing applications.

Illustrative examples: Banking Services Clerk, New Accounts Banking Representative

43-4150 Order Clerks
This broad occupation is the same as the detailed occupation:
43-4151 Order Clerks

43-4151 Order Clerks
Receive and process incoming orders for materials, merchandise, classified ads, or services such as repairs, installations, or rental of facilities. Generally receives orders via mail, phone, fax, or other electronic means. Duties include informing customers of receipt, prices, shipping dates, and delays; preparing contracts; and handling complaints. Excludes "Dispatchers, Except Police, Fire, and Ambulance" (43-5032) who both dispatch and take orders for services.

Illustrative examples: Catalogue Clerk, Classified Ad Clerk, Subscription Clerk

43-4160 Human Resources Assistants, Except Payroll and Timekeeping
This broad occupation is the same as the detailed occupation:
43-4161 Human Resources Assistants, Except Payroll and Timekeeping

43-4161 Human Resources Assistants, Except Payroll and Timekeeping
Compile and keep personnel records. Record data for each employee, such as address, weekly earnings, absences, amount of sales or production, supervisory reports, and date of and reason for termination. May prepare reports for employment records, file employment records, or search employee files and furnish information to authorized persons.

Illustrative examples: HR Clerk, Personnel Clerk

43-4170 Receptionists and Information Clerks
This broad occupation is the same as the detailed occupation:
43-4171 Receptionists and Information Clerks

43-4171 Receptionists and Information Clerks
Answer inquiries and provide information to the general public, customers, visitors, and other interested parties regarding activities conducted at establishment and location of departments, offices, and employees within the organization. Excludes "Switchboard Operators, Including Answering Service" (43-2011).

Illustrative examples: Appointment Clerk, Front Desk Receptionist, Land Leasing Information Clerk

43-4180 Reservation and Transportation Ticket Agents and Travel Clerks
This broad occupation is the same as the detailed occupation:
43-4181 Reservation and Transportation Ticket Agents and Travel Clerks

43-4181 Reservation and Transportation Ticket Agents and Travel Clerks
Make and confirm reservations for transportation or lodging, or sell transportation tickets. May check baggage and direct passengers to designated concourse, pier, or track; deliver tickets, contact individuals and groups to inform them of package tours; or provide tourists with travel or transportation information. Excludes "Travel Agents" (41-3041), "Hotel, Motel, and Resort Desk Clerks" (43-4081), and "Cashiers" (41-2011) who sell tickets for local transportation.

Illustrative examples: Airline Ticket Agent, Gate Agent, Hotel Reservationist, Train Reservation Clerk

43-4190 Miscellaneous Information and Record Clerks
This broad occupation is the same as the detailed occupation:
43-4199 Information and Record Clerks, All Other

43-4199 Information and Record Clerks, All Other
All information and record clerks not listed separately.

Illustrative examples: Election Clerk, Probate Clerk, Student Admissions Clerk

43-5000 Material Recording, Scheduling, Dispatching, and Distributing Workers

43-5010 Cargo and Freight Agents
This broad occupation is the same as the detailed occupation:
43-5011 Cargo and Freight Agents

43-5011 Cargo and Freight Agents
Expedite and route movement of incoming and outgoing cargo and freight shipments in airline, train, and trucking terminals, and shipping docks. Take orders from customers and arrange pickup of freight and cargo for delivery to loading platform. Prepare and examine bills of lading to determine shipping charges and tariffs.

Illustrative examples: Cargo Router, Freight Shipping Agent, Ramp Service Agent

43-5020 Couriers and Messengers
This broad occupation is the same as the detailed occupation:
43-5021 Couriers and Messengers

43-5021 Couriers and Messengers
Pick up and deliver messages, documents, packages, and other items between offices or departments within an establishment or directly to other business concerns, traveling by foot, bicycle, motorcycle, automobile, or public conveyance. Excludes "Light Truck or Delivery Services Drivers" (53-3033).

Illustrative examples: Bicycle Messenger, Laboratory Courier, Office Runner

43-5030 Dispatchers
This broad occupation includes the following two detailed occupations:
43-5031 Police, Fire, and Ambulance Dispatchers
43-5032 Dispatchers, Except Police, Fire, and Ambulance

43-5031 Police, Fire, and Ambulance Dispatchers
Operate radio, telephone, or computer equipment at emergency response centers. Receive reports from the public of crimes, disturbances, fires, and medical or police emergencies. Relay information to law enforcement and emergency response personnel. May maintain contact with caller until responders arrive.

Illustrative examples: Emergency Operator, 911 Operator, Police Radio Dispatcher

43-5032 Dispatchers, Except Police, Fire, and Ambulance
Schedule and dispatch workers, work crews, equipment, or service vehicles for conveyance of materials, freight, or passengers, or for normal installation, service, or emergency repairs rendered outside the place of business. Duties may include using radio, telephone, or computer to transmit assignments and compiling statistics and reports on work progress.

Illustrative examples: Taxicab Dispatcher, Tow Truck Dispatcher, Train Dispatcher

43-5040 Meter Readers, Utilities
This broad occupation is the same as the detailed occupation:
43-5041 Meter Readers, Utilities

43-5041 Meter Readers, Utilities
Read meter and record consumption of electricity, gas, water, or steam.

Illustrative examples: Electric Meter Reader, Gas Meter Reader, Water Meter Reader

43-5050 Postal Service Workers
This broad occupation includes the following three detailed occupations:
43-5051 Postal Service Clerks

43-5052 Postal Service Mail Carriers
43-5053 Postal Service Mail Sorters, Processors, and Processing Machine Operators

43-5051 Postal Service Clerks
Perform any combination of tasks in a post office, such as receive letters and parcels; sell postage and revenue stamps, postal cards, and stamped envelopes; fill out and sell money orders; place mail in pigeon holes of mail rack or in bags; and examine mail for correct postage.

Illustrative examples: Bulk Mail Carrier, Parcel Post Clerk, Postal Service Window Clerk

43-5052 Postal Service Mail Carriers
Sort mail for delivery. Deliver mail on established route by vehicle or on foot.

Illustrative examples: Letter Carrier, Mail Deliverer, Rural Route Carrier

43-5053 Postal Service Mail Sorters, Processors, and Processing Machine Operators
Prepare incoming and outgoing mail for distribution. Examine, sort, and route mail. Load, operate, and occasionally adjust and repair mail processing, sorting, and canceling machinery. Keep records of shipments, pouches, and sacks; and other duties related to mail handling within the postal service. Excludes "Postal Service Clerks" (43-5051) and "Postal Service Mail Carriers" (43-5052).

Illustrative examples: Flat Sorting Machine Clerk, Mail Forwarding System Markup Clerk

43-5060 Production, Planning, and Expediting Clerks
This broad occupation is the same as the detailed occupation:
43-5061 Production, Planning, and Expediting Clerks

43-5061 Production, Planning, and Expediting Clerks
Coordinate and expedite the flow of work and materials within or between departments of an establishment according to production schedule. Duties include reviewing and distributing production, work, and shipment schedules; conferring with department supervisors to determine progress of work and completion dates; and compiling reports on progress of work, inventory levels, costs, and production problems. Excludes "Weighers, Measurers, Checkers, and Samplers, Recordkeeping" (43-5111).

Illustrative examples: Expeditor, Material Control Clerk, Production Scheduler

43-5070 Shipping, Receiving, and Traffic Clerks
This broad occupation is the same as the detailed occupation:
43-5071 Shipping, Receiving, and Traffic Clerks

43-5071 Shipping, Receiving, and Traffic Clerks

Verify and maintain records on incoming and outgoing shipments. Prepare items for shipment. Duties include assembling, addressing, stamping, and shipping merchandise or material; receiving, unpacking, verifying and recording incoming merchandise or material; and arranging for the transportation of products. Excludes "Stock Clerks and Order Fillers" (43-5081) and "Weighers, Measurers, Checkers, and Samplers, Recordkeeping" (43-5111).

Illustrative examples: Incoming Freight Clerk, Route Delivery Clerk, Store Receiving Clerk

43-5080 Stock Clerks and Order Fillers

This broad occupation is the same as the detailed occupation:
43-5081 Stock Clerks and Order Fillers

43-5081 Stock Clerks and Order Fillers

Receive, store, and issue sales floor merchandise, materials, equipment, and other items from stockroom, warehouse, or storage yard to fill shelves, racks, tables, or customers' orders. May mark prices on merchandise and set up sales displays. Excludes "Laborers and Freight, Stock, and Material Movers, Hand" (53-7062), and "Shipping, Receiving, and Traffic Clerks" (43-5071).

Illustrative examples: Inventory Control Clerk, Tool Crib Attendant, Warehouse Clerk

43-5110 Weighers, Measurers, Checkers, and Samplers, Recordkeeping

This broad occupation is the same as the detailed occupation:
43-5111 Weighers, Measurers, Checkers, and Samplers, Recordkeeping

43-5111 Weighers, Measurers, Checkers, and Samplers, Recordkeeping

Weigh, measure, and check materials, supplies, and equipment for the purpose of keeping relevant records. Duties are primarily clerical by nature. Includes workers who collect and keep record of samples of products or materials. Excludes "Inspectors, Testers, Sorters, Samplers, and Weighers" (51-9061).

Illustrative examples: Cheese Weigher, Scale Attendant, Weighing Station Operator

43-6000 Secretaries and Administrative Assistants

43-6010 Secretaries and Administrative Assistants

This broad occupation includes the following four detailed occupations:
43-6011 Executive Secretaries and Executive Administrative Assistants
43-6012 Legal Secretaries
43-6013 Medical Secretaries
43-6014 Secretaries and Administrative Assistants, Except Legal, Medical, and Executive

43-6011 Executive Secretaries and Executive Administrative Assistants
Provide high-level administrative support by conducting research, preparing statistical reports, handling information requests, and performing clerical functions such as preparing correspondence, receiving visitors, arranging conference calls, and scheduling meetings. May also train and supervise lower-level clerical staff. Excludes "Secretaries" (43-6012 through 43-6014).

Illustrative example: Executive Assistant

43-6012 Legal Secretaries
Perform secretarial duties using legal terminology, procedures, and documents. Prepare legal papers and correspondence, such as summonses, complaints, motions, and subpoenas. May also assist with legal research.

Illustrative examples: Law Secretary, Legal Administrative Assistant

43-6013 Medical Secretaries
Perform secretarial duties using specific knowledge of medical terminology and hospital, clinic, or laboratory procedures. Duties may include scheduling appointments, billing patients, and compiling and recording medical charts, reports, and correspondence.

Illustrative examples: Dental Secretary, Psychiatric Secretary

43-6014 Secretaries and Administrative Assistants, Except Legal, Medical, and Executive
Perform routine clerical and administrative functions such as drafting correspondence, scheduling appointments, organizing and maintaining paper and electronic files, or providing information to callers. Excludes legal, medical, and executive secretaries (43-6011 through 43-6013).

Illustrative examples: Office Secretary, Personal Secretary, School Secretary

43-9000 Other Office and Administrative Support Workers

43-9010 Computer Operators
This broad occupation is the same as the detailed occupation:
43-9011 Computer Operators

43-9011 Computer Operators
Monitor and control electronic computer and peripheral electronic data processing equipment to process business, scientific, engineering, and other data according to operating instructions. Monitor and respond to operating and error messages. May enter commands at a computer terminal and set controls on computer and peripheral devices. Excludes "Computer Occupations" (15-1100) and "Data Entry Keyers" (43-9021).

Illustrative examples: Computer Peripheral Equipment Operator, Console Operator

43-9020 Data Entry and Information Processing Workers
This broad occupation includes the following two detailed occupations:
43-9021 Data Entry Keyers
43-9022 Word Processors and Typists

43-9021 Data Entry Keyers
Operate data entry device, such as keyboard or photo composing perforator. Duties may include verifying data and preparing materials for printing. Excludes "Word Processors and Typists" (43-9022).

Illustrative examples: Data Input Clerk, Data Typist

43-9022 Word Processors and Typists
Use word processor, computer or typewriter to type letters, reports, forms, or other material from rough draft, corrected copy, or voice recording. May perform other clerical duties as assigned. Excludes "Data Entry Keyers" (43-9021), "Secretaries and Administrative Assistants" (43-6011 through 43-6014), "Court Reporters" (23-2091), and "Medical Transcriptionists" (31-9094).

Illustrative examples: Clerk Typist, Transcription Typist

43-9030 Desktop Publishers
This broad occupation is the same as the detailed occupation:
43-9031 Desktop Publishers

43-9031 Desktop Publishers
Format typescript and graphic elements using computer software to produce publication-ready material.

Illustrative examples: Desktop Publishing Specialist, Electronic Publisher

43-9040 Insurance Claims and Policy Processing Clerks
This broad occupation is the same as the detailed occupation:
43-9041 Insurance Claims and Policy Processing Clerks

43-9041 Insurance Claims and Policy Processing Clerks
Process new insurance policies, modifications to existing policies, and claims forms. Obtain information from policyholders to verify the accuracy and completeness of information on claims forms, applications and related documents, and company records. Update existing policies and company records to reflect changes requested by policyholders and insurance company representatives. Excludes "Claims Adjusters, Examiners, and Investigators" (13-1031).

Illustrative examples: Insurance Policy Issue Clerk, Underwriting Clerk

43-9050 Mail Clerks and Mail Machine Operators, Except Postal Service
This broad occupation is the same as the detailed occupation:
43-9051 Mail Clerks and Mail Machine Operators, Except Postal Service

43-9051 Mail Clerks and Mail Machine Operators, Except Postal Service
Prepare incoming and outgoing mail for distribution. Use hand or mail handling machines to time stamp, open, read, sort, and route incoming mail; and address, seal, stamp, fold, stuff, and affix postage to outgoing mail or packages. Duties may also include keeping necessary records and completed forms.

Illustrative examples: Direct Mail Clerk, Mailroom Clerk, Packaging Clerk

43-9060 Office Clerks, General
This broad occupation is the same as the detailed occupation:
43-9061 Office Clerks, General

43-9061 Office Clerks, General
Perform duties too varied and diverse to be classified in any specific office clerical occupation, requiring knowledge of office systems and procedures. Clerical duties may be assigned in accordance with the office procedures of individual establishments and may include a combination of answering telephones, bookkeeping, typing or word processing, stenography, office machine operation, and filing.

Illustrative examples: Administrative Clerk, Office Assistant, Real Estate Clerk

43-9070 Office Machine Operators, Except Computer
This broad occupation is the same as the detailed occupation:
43-9071 Office Machine Operators, Except Computer

43-9071 Office Machine Operators, Except Computer
Operate one or more of a variety of office machines, such as photocopying, photographic, and duplicating machines, or other office machines. Excludes "Computer Operators" (43-9011), "Mail Clerks and Mail Machine Operators, Except Postal Service" (43-9051) and "Billing and Posting Clerks" (43-3021).

Illustrative examples: Coin Wrapping Machine Operator, Copy Machine Operator

43-9080 Proofreaders and Copy Markers
This broad occupation is the same as the detailed occupation:
43-9081 Proofreaders and Copy Markers

43-9081 Proofreaders and Copy Markers
Read transcript or proof type setup to detect and mark for correction any grammatical, typographical, or compositional errors. Excludes workers whose primary duty is editing copy. Includes proofreaders of Braille.

Illustrative examples: Braille Proofreader, Copy Reader, Editorial Assistant

43-9110 Statistical Assistants
This broad occupation is the same as the detailed occupation:
43-9111 Statistical Assistants

43-9111 Statistical Assistants
Compile and compute data according to statistical formulas for use in statistical studies. May perform actuarial computations and compile charts and graphs for use by actuaries. Includes actuarial clerks.

Illustrative examples: Actuarial Assistant, Statistical Clerk

43-9190 Miscellaneous Office and Administrative Support Workers
This broad occupation is the same as the detailed occupation:
43-9199 Office and Administrative Support Workers, All Other

43-9199 Office and Administrative Support Workers, All Other
All office and administrative support workers not listed separately.

Illustrative examples: Envelope Stuffer, Fingerprint Clerk, Notary Public

45-1000 Supervisors of Farming, Fishing, and Forestry Workers 45-1010 First-Line Supervisors of Farming, Fishing, and Forestry Workers

This broad occupation is the same as the detailed occupation:
45-1011 First-Line Supervisors of Farming, Fishing, and Forestry Workers

45-1011 First-Line Supervisors of Farming, Fishing, and Forestry Workers

Directly supervise and coordinate the activities of agricultural, forestry, aquacultural, and related workers. Excludes "First-Line Supervisors of Landscaping, Lawn Service, and Groundskeeping Workers" (37-1012).

Illustrative examples: Corral Boss, Cranberry Bog Supervisor, Fish Hatchery Supervisor

45-2000 Agricultural Workers

45-2010 Agricultural Inspectors

This broad occupation is the same as the detailed occupation:
45-2011 Agricultural Inspectors

45-2011 Agricultural Inspectors

Inspect agricultural commodities, processing equipment, and facilities, and fish and logging operations, to ensure compliance with regulations and laws governing health, quality, and safety.

Illustrative examples: Cattle Examiner, Grain Sampler, Milk Tester

45-2020 Animal Breeders

This broad occupation is the same as the detailed occupation:
45-2021 Animal Breeders

45-2021 Animal Breeders

Select and breed animals according to their genealogy, characteristics, and offspring. May require knowledge of artificial insemination techniques and equipment use. May involve keeping records on heats, birth intervals, or pedigree. Excludes "Nonfarm Animal Caretakers" (39-2021) who may occasionally breed animals as part of their other caretaking duties. Excludes "Animal Scientists" (19-1011) whose primary function is research.

Illustrative examples: Dairy Husbandry Worker, Horse Breeder

45-2040 Graders and Sorters, Agricultural Products

This broad occupation is the same as the detailed occupation:
45-2041 Graders and Sorters, Agricultural Products

45-2041 Graders and Sorters, Agricultural Products

Grade, sort, or classify unprocessed food and other agricultural products by size, weight, color, or condition. Excludes "Agricultural Inspectors" (45-2011).

Illustrative examples: Cotton Grader, Egg Grader, Fruit Sorter, Meat Grader

45-2090 Miscellaneous Agricultural Workers
This broad occupation includes the following four detailed occupations:
45-2091 Agricultural Equipment Operators
45-2092 Farmworkers and Laborers, Crop, Nursery, and Greenhouse
45-2093 Farmworkers, Farm, Ranch, and Aquacultural Animals
45-2099 Agricultural Workers, All Other

45-2091 Agricultural Equipment Operators
Drive and control farm equipment to till soil and to plant, cultivate, and harvest crops. May perform tasks, such as crop baling or hay bucking. May operate stationary equipment to perform post-harvest tasks, such as husking, shelling, threshing, and ginning.

Illustrative examples: Combine Operator, Hay Baler, Tractor Operator

45-2092 Farmworkers and Laborers, Crop, Nursery, and Greenhouse
Manually plant, cultivate, and harvest vegetables, fruits, nuts, horticultural specialties, and field crops. Use hand tools, such as shovels, trowels, hoes, tampers, pruning hooks, shears, and knives. Duties may include tilling soil and applying fertilizers; transplanting, weeding, thinning, or pruning crops; applying pesticides; or cleaning, grading, sorting, packing, and loading harvested products. May construct trellises, repair fences and farm buildings, or participate in irrigation activities. Excludes "Graders and Sorters, Agricultural Products" (45-2041) and "Forest, Conservation, and Logging Workers" (45-4011 through 45-4029).

Illustrative examples: Greenhouse Transplanter, Pecan Gatherer, Pepper Picker

45-2093 Farmworkers, Farm, Ranch, and Aquacultural Animals
Attend to live farm, ranch, or aquacultural animals that may include cattle, sheep, swine, goats, horses and other equines, poultry, finfish, shellfish, and bees. Attend to animals produced for animal products, such as meat, fur, skins, feathers, eggs, milk, and honey. Duties may include feeding, watering, herding, grazing, castrating, branding, de-beaking, weighing, catching, and loading animals. May maintain records on animals; examine animals to detect diseases and injuries; assist in birth deliveries; and administer medications, vaccinations, or insecticides as appropriate. May clean and maintain animal housing areas. Includes workers who shear wool from sheep, and collect eggs in hatcheries.

Illustrative examples: Cattle Brander, Sheep Shearer, Shrimp Pond Laborer

45-2099 Agricultural Workers, All Other
All agricultural workers not listed separately.
Illustrative examples: Crop Scout, Irrigation Worker

45-3000 Fishing and Hunting Workers

45-3010 Fishers and Related Fishing Workers
This broad occupation is the same as the detailed occupation:
45-3011 Fishers and Related Fishing Workers

45-3011 Fishers and Related Fishing Workers
Use nets, fishing rods, traps, or other equipment to catch and gather fish or other aquatic animals from rivers, lakes, or oceans, for human consumption or other uses. May haul game onto ship. Aquacultural laborers who work on fish farms are included in "Farmworkers, Farm, Ranch, and Aquacultural Animals" (45-2093).

Illustrative examples: Seaweed Harvester, Wild Oyster Harvester

45-3020 Hunters and Trappers
This broad occupation is the same as the detailed occupation:
45-3021 Hunters and Trappers

45-3021 Hunters and Trappers
Hunt and trap wild animals for human consumption, fur, feed, bait, or other purposes.

Illustrative examples: Bird Trapper, Deer Hunter, Predatory Animal Trapper

45-4000 Forest, Conservation, and Logging Workers

45-4010 Forest and Conservation Workers
This broad occupation is the same as the detailed occupation:
45-4011 Forest and Conservation Workers

45-4011 Forest and Conservation Workers
Under supervision, perform manual labor necessary to develop, maintain, or protect areas such as forests, forested areas, woodlands, wetlands, and rangelands through such activities as raising and transporting seedlings; combating insects, pests, and diseases harmful to plant life; and building structures to control water, erosion, and leaching of soil. Includes forester aides, seedling pullers, and tree planters.

Illustrative examples: Forestry Laborer, Rangelands Conservation Laborer, Reforestation Worker, Wetlands Conservation Laborer

45-4020 Logging Workers
This broad occupation includes the following four detailed occupations:
45-4021 Fallers
45-4022 Logging Equipment Operators
45-4023 Log Graders and Scalers

45-4029 Logging Workers, All Other

45-4021 Fallers
Use axes or chainsaws to fell trees using knowledge of tree characteristics and cutting techniques to control direction of fall and minimize tree damage.

Illustrative examples: Lumberjack, Pulpwood Cutter, Timber Cutter

45-4022 Logging Equipment Operators
Drive logging tractor or wheeled vehicle equipped with one or more accessories such as bulldozer blade, frontal shear, grapple, logging arch, cable winches, hoisting rack, or crane boom, to fell tree; to skid, load, unload, or stack logs; or to pull stumps or clear brush. Logging truck drivers are included in "Heavy and Tractor-Trailer Truck Drivers" (53-3032).

Illustrative examples: Grapple Skidder Operator, Log Hauler, Logging Tractor Operator, Lumber Stacker Operator

45-4023 Log Graders and Scalers
Grade logs or estimate the marketable content or value of logs or pulpwood in sorting yards, millpond, log deck, or similar locations. Inspect logs for defects or measure logs to determine volume. Excludes "Buyers and Purchasing Agents, Farm Products" (13-1021).

Illustrative examples: Log Check Scaler, Timber Estimator, Veneer Grader

45-4029 Logging Workers, All Other
All logging workers not listed separately.

Illustrative examples: Log Roper, Rigging Slinger, Timber Hand

47-1000 Supervisors of Construction and Extraction Workers 47-1010 First-Line Supervisors of Construction Trades and Extraction Workers This broad occupation is the same as the detailed occupation:
47-1011 First-Line Supervisors of Construction Trades and Extraction Workers

47-1011 First-Line Supervisors of Construction Trades and Extraction Workers
Directly supervise and coordinate activities of construction or extraction workers.

Illustrative examples: Carpenter Supervisor, Quarry Boss, Rig Supervisor, Solar Panel Installation Supervisor

47-2000 Construction Trades Workers

47-2010 Boilermakers
This broad occupation is the same as the detailed occupation:
47-2011 Boilermakers

47-2011 Boilermakers
Construct, assemble, maintain, and repair stationary steam boilers and boiler house auxiliaries. Align structures or plate sections to assemble boiler frame tanks or vats, following blueprints. Work involves use of hand and power tools, plumb bobs, levels, wedges, dogs, or turnbuckles. Assist in testing assembled vessels. Direct cleaning of boilers and boiler furnaces. Inspect and repair boiler fittings, such as safety valves, regulators, automatic-control mechanisms, water columns, and auxiliary machines.

Illustrative examples: Boiler Installer, Boiler Mechanic, Boiler Tester

47-2020 Brickmasons, Blockmasons, and Stonemasons
This broad occupation includes the following two detailed occupations:
47-2021 Brickmasons and Blockmasons
47-2022 Stonemasons

47-2021 Brickmasons and Blockmasons
Lay and bind building materials, such as brick, structural tile, concrete block, cinder block, glass block, and terra-cotta block, with mortar and other substances to construct or repair walls, partitions, arches, sewers, and other structures. Excludes "Stonemasons" (47-2022). Installers of mortarless segmental concrete masonry wall units are classified in "Landscaping and Groundskeeping Workers" (37-3011).

Illustrative examples: Adobe Layer, Brick Chimney Builder, Refractory Bricklayer

47-2022 Stonemasons
Build stone structures, such as piers, walls, and abutments. Lay walks, curbstones, or special types of masonry for vats, tanks, and floors.
Illustrative examples: Curbstone Setter, Granite Setter, Monument Mason

47-2030 Carpenters
This broad occupation is the same as the detailed occupation:
47-2031 Carpenters

47-2031 Carpenters
Construct, erect, install, or repair structures and fixtures made of wood, such as concrete forms; building frameworks, including partitions, joists, studding, and rafters; and wood stairways, window and door frames, and hardwood floors. May also install cabinets, siding, drywall and batt or roll insulation. Includes brattice builders who build doors or brattices (ventilation walls or partitions) in underground passageways.

Illustrative examples: Building Carpenter, Custom Wood Stair Builder, Wood Floor Layer

47-2040 Carpet, Floor, and Tile Installers and Finishers
This broad occupation includes the following four detailed occupations:
47-2041 Carpet Installers
47-2042 Floor Layers, Except Carpet, Wood, and Hard Tiles
47-2043 Floor Sanders and Finishers
47-2044 Tile and Marble Setters

47-2041 Carpet Installers
Lay and install carpet from rolls or blocks on floors. Install padding and trim flooring materials. Excludes "Floor Layers, Except Carpet, Wood, and Hard Tiles" (47-2042).

Illustrative examples: Carpet Layer, Wall-to-Wall Carpet Installer

47-2042 Floor Layers, Except Carpet, Wood, and Hard Tiles
Apply blocks, strips, or sheets of shock-absorbing, sound-deadening, or decorative coverings to floors.

Illustrative examples: Composition Floor Layer, Cork Floor Installer, Linoleum Installer, Shock-Absorption Floor Installer

47-2043 Floor Sanders and Finishers
Scrape and sand wooden floors to smooth surfaces using floor scraper and floor sanding machine, and apply coats of finish.

Illustrative examples: Floor Sanding Machine Operator, Floor Scraper, Hardwood Finisher

47-2044 Tile and Marble Setters
Apply hard tile, marble, and wood tile to walls, floors, ceilings, and roof decks.

Illustrative examples: Ceramic Tile Installer, Hard Tile Setter, Marble Ceiling Installer, Parquet Floor Layer

47-2050 Cement Masons, Concrete Finishers, and Terrazzo Workers
This broad occupation includes the following two detailed occupations:
47-2051 Cement Masons and Concrete Finishers
47-2053 Terrazzo Workers and Finishers

47-2051 Cement Masons and Concrete Finishers
Smooth and finish surfaces of poured concrete, such as floors, walks, sidewalks, roads, or curbs using a variety of hand and power tools. Align forms for sidewalks, curbs, or gutters; patch voids; and use saws to cut expansion joints. Installers of mortarless segmental concrete masonry wall units are classified in "Landscaping and Groundskeeping Workers" (37- 3011).

Illustrative examples: Cement Patcher, Concrete Floor Installer, Concrete Swimming Pool Installer

47-2053 Terrazzo Workers and Finishers
Apply a mixture of cement, sand, pigment, or marble chips to floors, stairways, and cabinet fixtures to fashion durable and decorative surfaces.

Illustrative examples: Onyx-Chip Terrazzo Worker, Terrazzo Grinder, Terrazzo Setter

47-2060 Construction Laborers
This broad occupation is the same as the detailed occupation:
47-2061 Construction Laborers

47-2061 Construction Laborers
Perform tasks involving physical labor at construction sites. May operate hand and power tools of all types: air hammers, earth tampers, cement mixers, small mechanical hoists, surveying and measuring equipment, and a variety of other equipment and instruments. May clean and prepare sites, dig trenches, set braces to support the sides of excavations, erect scaffolding, and clean up rubble, debris and other waste materials. May assist other craft workers. Construction laborers who primarily assist a particular craft worker are classified under "Helpers, Construction Trades" (47-3010). Excludes "Hazardous Materials Removal Workers" (47-4041).

Illustrative examples: Air Hammer Operator, Construction Craft Laborer, Construction Trench Digger

47-2070 Construction Equipment Operators
This broad occupation includes the following three detailed occupations:
47-2071 Paving, Surfacing, and Tamping Equipment Operators
47-2072 Pile-Driver Operators
47-2073 Operating Engineers and Other Construction Equipment Operators

47-2071 Paving, Surfacing, and Tamping Equipment Operators

Operate equipment used for applying concrete, asphalt, or other materials to road beds, parking lots, or airport runways and taxiways, or equipment used for tamping gravel, dirt, or other materials. Includes concrete and asphalt paving machine operators, form tampers, tamping machine operators, and stone spreader operators.

Illustrative examples: Asphalt Roller Operator, Blacktop-Paver Operator, Road Grader

47-2072 Pile-Driver Operators

Operate pile drivers mounted on skids, barges, crawler treads, or locomotive cranes to drive pilings for retaining walls, bulkheads, and foundations of structures, such as buildings, bridges, and piers.

Illustrative examples: Hydraulic Pile Hammer Operator, Vibratory Pile Driver

47-2073 Operating Engineers and Other Construction Equipment Operators

Operate one or several types of power construction equipment, such as motor graders, bulldozers, scrapers, compressors, pumps, derricks, shovels, tractors, or front-end loaders to excavate, move, and grade earth, erect structures, or pour concrete or other hard surface pavement. May repair and maintain equipment in addition to other duties. Excludes "Crane and Tower Operators" (53-7021) and "Extraction Workers" (47-5000).

Illustrative examples: Bulldozer Operator, Steam Shovel Operator

47-2080 Drywall Installers, Ceiling Tile Installers, and Tapers

This broad occupation includes the following two detailed occupations:
47-2081 Drywall and Ceiling Tile Installers
47-2082 Tapers

47-2081 Drywall and Ceiling Tile Installers

Apply plasterboard or other wallboard to ceilings or interior walls of buildings. Apply or mount acoustical tiles or blocks, strips, or sheets of shock-absorbing materials to ceilings and walls of buildings to reduce or reflect sound. Materials may be of decorative quality. Includes lathers who fasten wooden, metal, or rockboard lath to walls, ceilings or partitions of buildings to provide support base for plaster, fire-proofing, or acoustical material. Excludes "Carpet Installers" (47-2041), "Carpenters" (47-2031), and "Tile and Marble Setters" (47-2044).

Illustrative examples: Acoustical Ceiling Installer, Drywall Finisher, Sheet Rock Hanger

47-2082 Tapers

Seal joints between plasterboard or other wallboard to prepare wall surface for painting or papering.

Illustrative examples: Drywall Taper, Sheet Rock Taper, Wall Taper

47-2110 Electricians

This broad occupation is the same as the detailed occupation:
47-2111 Electricians

47-2111 Electricians
Install, maintain, and repair electrical wiring, equipment, and fixtures. Ensure that work is in accordance with relevant codes. May install or service street lights, intercom systems, or electrical control systems. Excludes "Security and Fire Alarm Systems Installers" (49-2098).

Illustrative examples: Electrical Sign Wirer, Master Electrician, Solar Photovoltaic Electrician

47-2120 Glaziers
This broad occupation is the same as the detailed occupation:
47-2121 Glaziers

47-2121 Glaziers
Install glass in windows, skylights, store fronts, and display cases, or on surfaces, such as building fronts, interior walls, ceilings, and tabletops.

Illustrative examples: Plate Glass Installer, Stained Glass Joiner

47-2130 Insulation Workers
This broad occupation includes the following two detailed occupations:
47-2131 Insulation Workers, Floor, Ceiling, and Wall
47-2132 Insulation Workers, Mechanical

47-2131 Insulation Workers, Floor, Ceiling, and Wall
Line and cover structures with insulating materials. May work with batt, roll, or blown insulation materials.

Illustrative examples: Ceiling Insulation Blower, Composition Weatherboard Installer, Interior Surface Insulation Worker

47-2132 Insulation Workers, Mechanical
Apply insulating materials to pipes or ductwork, or other mechanical systems in order to help control and maintain temperature.

Illustrative examples: Boiler Coverer, Pipe Coverer, Pipe Insulator

47-2140 Painters and Paperhangers
This broad occupation includes the following two detailed occupations:
47-2141 Painters, Construction and Maintenance
47-2142 Paperhangers

47-2141 Painters, Construction and Maintenance

141

Paint walls, equipment, buildings, bridges, and other structural surfaces, using brushes, rollers, and spray guns. May remove old paint to prepare surface prior to painting. May mix colors or oils to obtain desired color or consistency. Excludes "Paperhangers" (47-2142).

Illustrative examples: Bridge Painter, House Painter, Traffic Line Painter

47-2142 Paperhangers
Cover interior walls or ceilings of rooms with decorative wallpaper or fabric, or attach advertising posters on surfaces such as walls and billboards. May remove old materials or prepare surfaces to be papered.

Illustrative examples: Billboard Poster, Wall Covering Installer, Wallpaperer

47-2150 Pipelayers, Plumbers, Pipefitters, and Steamfitters
This broad occupation includes the following two detailed occupations:
47-2151 Pipelayers
47-2152 Plumbers, Pipefitters, and Steamfitters

47-2151 Pipelayers
Lay pipe for storm or sanitation sewers, drains, and water mains. Perform any combination of the following tasks: grade trenches or culverts, position pipe, or seal joints. Excludes "Welders, Cutters, Solderers, and Brazers" (51-4121).

Illustrative examples: Cast-Iron Drain Pipe Layer, Trench Pipe Layer, Water Main Pipe Layer

47-2152 Plumbers, Pipefitters, and Steamfitters
Assemble, install, alter, and repair pipelines or pipe systems that carry water, steam, air, or other liquids or gases. May install heating and cooling equipment and mechanical control systems. Includes sprinklerfitters.

Illustrative examples: Fire Sprinkler Installer, Solar Thermal Installer, Sprinkler Fitter

47-2160 Plasterers and Stucco Masons
This broad occupation is the same as the detailed occupation:
47-2161 Plasterers and Stucco Masons

47-2161 Plasterers and Stucco Masons
Apply interior or exterior plaster, cement, stucco, or similar materials. May also set ornamental plaster.

Illustrative examples: Ornamental Plasterer, Stucco Worker, Swimming Pool Plasterer

47-2170 Reinforcing Iron and Rebar Workers
This broad occupation is the same as the detailed occupation:
47-2171 Reinforcing Iron and Rebar Workers

47-2171 Reinforcing Iron and Rebar Workers

Position and secure steel bars or mesh in concrete forms in order to reinforce concrete. Use a variety of fasteners, rod-bending machines, blowtorches, and hand tools. Includes rod busters.

Illustrative examples: Post Tensioning Iron Worker, Steel Rod Buster

47-2180 Roofers

This broad occupation is the same as the detailed occupation:
47-2181 Roofers

47-2181 Roofers

Cover roofs of structures with shingles, slate, asphalt, aluminum, wood, or related materials. May spray roofs, sidings, and walls with material to bind, seal, insulate, or soundproof sections of structures.

Illustrative examples: Hot Tar Roofer, Shingles Roofer, Terra Cotta Roofer

47-2210 Sheet Metal Workers

This broad occupation is the same as the detailed occupation:
47-2211 Sheet Metal Workers

47-2211 Sheet Metal Workers

Fabricate, assemble, install, and repair sheet metal products and equipment, such as ducts, control boxes, drainpipes, and furnace casings. Work may involve any of the following: setting up and operating fabricating machines to cut, bend, and straighten sheet metal; shaping metal over anvils, blocks, or forms using hammer; operating soldering and welding equipment to join sheet metal parts; or inspecting, assembling, and smoothing seams and joints of burred surfaces. Includes sheet metal duct installers who install prefabricated sheet metal ducts used for heating, air conditioning, or other purposes.

Illustrative examples: Heating, Ventilation, and Air Conditioning (HVAC) Sheet Metal Installer; Sheet Metal Former; Tinsmith

47-2220 Structural Iron and Steel Workers

This broad occupation is the same as the detailed occupation:
47-2221 Structural Iron and Steel Workers

47-2221 Structural Iron and Steel Workers

Raise, place, and unite iron or steel girders, columns, and other structural members to form completed structures or structural frameworks. May erect metal storage tanks and assemble prefabricated metal buildings. Excludes "Reinforcing Iron and Rebar Workers" (47-2171).

Illustrative examples: Bridge Ironworker, Precast Concrete Ironworker, Wind Turbine Erector

47-2230 Solar Photovoltaic Installers

This broad occupation is the same as the detailed occupation:
47-2231 Solar Photovoltaic Installers

47-2231 Solar Photovoltaic Installers
Assemble, install, or maintain solar photovoltaic (PV) systems on roofs or other structures in compliance with site assessment and schematics. May include measuring, cutting, assembling, and bolting structural framing and solar modules. May perform minor electrical work such as current checks. Excludes solar thermal installers who are included in "Plumbers, Pipefitters, and Steamfitters" (47-2152). Excludes solar PV electricians who are included in "Electricians" (47-2111).

Illustrative examples: Photovoltaic (PV) Installation Technician, Solar PV Installer

47-3000 Helpers, Construction Trades

47-3010 Helpers, Construction Trades
This broad occupation includes the following seven detailed occupations:
47-3011 Helpers–Brickmasons, Blockmasons, Stonemasons, and Tile and Marble Setters
47-3012 Helpers–Carpenters
47-3013 Helpers–Electricians
47-3014 Helpers–Painters, Paperhangers, Plasterers, and Stucco Masons
47-3015 Helpers–Pipelayers, Plumbers, Pipefitters, and Steamfitters
47-3016 Helpers–Roofers
47-3019 Helpers, Construction Trades, All Other

47-3011 Helpers—Brickmasons, Blockmasons, Stonemasons, and Tile and Marble Setters
Help brickmasons, blockmasons, stonemasons, or tile and marble setters by performing duties requiring less skill. Duties include using, supplying or holding materials or tools, and cleaning work area and equipment. Construction laborers who do not primarily assist brickmasons, blockmasons, and stonemasons or tile and marble setters are classified under "Construction Laborers" (47-2061). Apprentice workers are classified with the appropriate skilled construction trade occupation (47-2011 through 47-2231).

Illustrative examples: Brick Carrier, Brick Washer, Refractory Tile Helper

47-3012 Helpers—Carpenters
Help carpenters by performing duties requiring less skill. Duties include using, supplying or holding materials or tools, and cleaning work area and equipment. Construction laborers who do not primarily assist carpenters are classified under "Construction Laborers" (47-2061). Apprentice workers are classified with the appropriate skilled construction trade occupation (47-2011 through 47-2231).

Illustrative examples: Carpenter Assistant, Hardwood Floor Installation Helper

47-3013 Helpers—Electricians

Help electricians by performing duties requiring less skill. Duties include using, supplying or holding materials or tools, and cleaning work area and equipment. Construction laborers who do not primarily assist electricians are classified under "Construction Laborers" (47-2061). Apprentice workers are classified with the appropriate skilled construction trade occupation (47-2011 through 47-2231).

Illustrative examples: Marine Electrician Helper, Stage Electrician Helper

47-3014 Helpers—Painters, Paperhangers, Plasterers, and Stucco Masons
Help painters, paperhangers, plasterers, or stucco masons by performing duties requiring less skill. Duties include using, supplying or holding materials or tools, and cleaning work area and equipment. Construction laborers who do not primarily assist painters, paperhangers, plasterers, or stucco masons are classified under "Construction Laborers" (47-2061). Apprentice workers are classified with the appropriate skilled construction trade occupation (47-2011 through 47-2231).

Illustrative examples: Bridge Painter Helper, Dry Plasterer Helper, Wallpaperer Helper

47-3015 Helpers—Pipelayers, Plumbers, Pipefitters, and Steamfitters
Help plumbers, pipefitters, steamfitters, or pipelayers by performing duties requiring less skill. Duties include using, supplying or holding materials or tools, and cleaning work area and equipment. Construction laborers who do not primarily assist plumbers, pipefitters, steamfitters, or pipelayers are classified under "Construction Laborers" (47-2061). Apprentice workers are classified with the appropriate skilled construction trade occupation (47-2011 through 47-2231).

Illustrative examples: Industrial Gas Fitter Helper, Marine Pipefitter Helper, Plumber Assistant, Water Main Installer Helper

47-3016 Helpers—Roofers
Help roofers by performing duties requiring less skill. Duties include using, supplying or holding materials or tools, and cleaning work area and equipment. Construction laborers who do not primarily assist roofers are classified under "Construction Laborers" (47-2061). Apprentice workers are classified with the appropriate skilled construction trade occupation (47-2011 through 47-2231).

Illustrative examples: Hot Tar Roofer Helper, Shingles Roofer Helper, Slate Roofer Helper, Terra Cotta Roofer Helper

47-3019 Helpers, Construction Trades, All Other
All construction trades helpers not listed separately.

Illustrative examples: Cellulose Insulation Helper, Drywall Hanger Helper, Rod Buster Helper, Terrazzo Finisher Helper

47-4000 Other Construction and Related Workers

47-4010 Construction and Building Inspectors
This broad occupation is the same as the detailed occupation:
47-4011 Construction and Building Inspectors

47-4011 Construction and Building Inspectors
Inspect structures using engineering skills to determine structural soundness and compliance with specifications, building codes, and other regulations. Inspections may be general in nature or may be limited to a specific area, such as electrical systems or plumbing.

Illustrative examples: Electrical Inspector, Elevator Inspector, Highway Inspector

47-4020 Elevator Installers and Repairers
This broad occupation is the same as the detailed occupation:
47-4021 Elevator Installers and Repairers

47-4021 Elevator Installers and Repairers
Assemble, install, repair, or maintain electric or hydraulic freight or passenger elevators, escalators, or dumbwaiters.

Illustrative examples: Elevator Mechanic, Escalator Installer, Hydraulic Elevator Constructor

47-4030 Fence Erectors
This broad occupation is the same as the detailed occupation:
47-4031 Fence Erectors

47-4031 Fence Erectors
Erect and repair fences and fence gates, using hand and power tools.

Illustrative examples: Wire Fence Builder, Wood Fence Installer

47-4040 Hazardous Materials Removal Workers
This broad occupation is the same as the detailed occupation:
47-4041 Hazardous Materials Removal Workers

47-4041 Hazardous Materials Removal Workers
Identify, remove, pack, transport, or dispose of hazardous materials, including asbestos, lead-based paint, waste oil, fuel, transmission fluid, radioactive materials, or contaminated soil. Specialized training and certification in hazardous materials handling or a confined entry permit are generally required. May operate earth-moving equipment or trucks.

Illustrative examples: Asbestos Abatement Worker, Decontamination Worker, Irradiated Fuel Handler

47-4050 Highway Maintenance Workers

This broad occupation is the same as the detailed occupation:
47-4051 Highway Maintenance Workers

47-4051 Highway Maintenance Workers
Maintain highways, municipal and rural roads, airport runways, and rights-of-way. Duties include patching broken or eroded pavement, repairing guard rails, highway markers, and snow fences. May also mow or clear brush from along road or plow snow from roadway. Excludes "Tree Trimmers and Pruners" (37-3013).

Illustrative examples: Road Patcher, Road Sign Installer

47-4060 Rail-Track Laying and Maintenance Equipment Operators
This broad occupation is the same as the detailed occupation:
47-4061 Rail-Track Laying and Maintenance Equipment Operators

47-4061 Rail-Track Laying and Maintenance Equipment Operators
Lay, repair, and maintain track for standard or narrow-gauge railroad equipment used in regular railroad service or in plant yards, quarries, sand and gravel pits, and mines. Includes ballast cleaning machine operators and railroad bed tamping machine operators.

Illustrative examples: Rail Maintenance Worker, Track Repairer, Track Surfacing Machine Operator

47-4070 Septic Tank Servicers and Sewer Pipe Cleaners
This broad occupation is the same as the detailed occupation:
47-4071 Septic Tank Servicers and Sewer Pipe Cleaners

47-4071 Septic Tank Servicers and Sewer Pipe Cleaners
Clean and repair septic tanks, sewer lines, or drains. May patch walls and partitions of tank, replace damaged drain tile, or repair breaks in underground piping.

Illustrative examples: Electric Sewer Cleaning Machine Operator, Septic Tank Cleaner, Sewage Screen Operator

47-4090 Miscellaneous Construction and Related Workers
This broad occupation includes the following two detailed occupations:
47-4091 Segmental Pavers
47-4099 Construction and Related Workers, All Other

47-4091 Segmental Pavers
Lay out, cut, and place segmental paving units. Includes installers of bedding and restraining materials for the paving units.

Illustrative examples: Concrete Pavement Installer, Paving Stone Installer
47-4099 Construction and Related Workers, All Other

All construction and related workers not listed separately.

Illustrative examples: Aluminum Pool Installer, Waterproofer

47-5000 Extraction Workers

47-5010 Derrick, Rotary Drill, and Service Unit Operators, Oil, Gas, and Mining
This broad occupation includes the following three detailed occupations:
47-5011 Derrick Operators, Oil and Gas
47-5012 Rotary Drill Operators, Oil and Gas
47-5013 Service Unit Operators, Oil, Gas, and Mining

47-5011 Derrick Operators, Oil and Gas
Rig derrick equipment and operate pumps to circulate mud through drill hole.

Illustrative examples: Rotary Derrick Operator, Well Service Derrick Worker

47-5012 Rotary Drill Operators, Oil and Gas
Set up or operate a variety of drills to remove underground oil and gas, or remove core samples for testing during oil and gas exploration. Excludes "Earth Drillers, Except Oil and Gas" (47-5021).

Illustrative examples: Oil Well Cable Tool Operator, Oil Well Driller

47-5013 Service Unit Operators, Oil, Gas, and Mining
Operate equipment to increase oil flow from producing wells or to remove stuck pipe, casing, tools, or other obstructions from drilling wells. May also perform similar services in mining exploration operations. Includes fishing-tool technicians.

Illustrative example: Well Servicing Rig Operator

47-5020 Earth Drillers, Except Oil and Gas
This broad occupation is the same as the detailed occupation:
47-5021 Earth Drillers, Except Oil and Gas

47-5021 Earth Drillers, Except Oil and Gas
Operate a variety of drills such as rotary, churn, and pneumatic to tap sub-surface water and salt deposits, to remove core samples during mineral exploration or soil testing, and to facilitate the use of explosives in mining or construction. May use explosives. Includes horizontal and earth boring machine operators.

Illustrative examples: Blast Hole Driller, Churn Driller, Earth Auger Operator

47-5030 Explosives Workers, Ordnance Handling Experts, and Blasters

This broad occupation is the same as the detailed occupation:
47-5031 Explosives Workers, Ordnance Handling Experts, and Blasters

47-5031 Explosives Workers, Ordnance Handling Experts, and Blasters
Place and detonate explosives to demolish structures or to loosen, remove, or displace earth, rock, or other materials. May perform specialized handling, storage, and accounting procedures. Includes seismograph shooters. Excludes "Earth Drillers, Except Oil and Gas" (47-5021) who may also work with explosives.

Illustrative examples: Blast Setter, Dynamiter, Explosive Technician

47-5040 Mining Machine Operators
This broad occupation includes the following three detailed occupations:
47-5041 Continuous Mining Machine Operators
47-5042 Mine Cutting and Channeling Machine Operators
47-5049 Mining Machine Operators, All Other

47-5041 Continuous Mining Machine Operators
Operate self-propelled mining machines that rip coal, metal and nonmetal ores, rock, stone, or sand from the mine face and load it onto conveyors or into shuttle cars in a continuous operation.

Illustrative examples: Continuous Mining Machine Lode Miner, Self-Propelled Mining Machine Operator

47-5042 Mine Cutting and Channeling Machine Operators
Operate machinery such as longwall shears, plows, and cutting machines to cut or channel along the face or seams of coal mines, stone quarries, or other mining surfaces to facilitate blasting, separating, or removing minerals or materials from mines or from the Earth's surface. Includes shale planers.

Illustrative examples: Bore Miner Operator, Clay Mine Cutting Machine Operator, Long Wall Shear Operator

47-5049 Mining Machine Operators, All Other
All mining machine operators not listed separately.

Illustrative examples: Dry Placer Machine Operator, Rock Dust Sprayer

47-5050 Rock Splitters, Quarry
This broad occupation is the same as the detailed occupation:
47-5051 Rock Splitters, Quarry

47-5051 Rock Splitters, Quarry

Separate blocks of rough dimension stone from quarry mass using jackhammer and wedges.

Illustrative examples: Quarry Plug and Feather Driller, Sandstone Splitter

47-5060 Roof Bolters, Mining
This broad occupation is the same as the detailed occupation:
47-5061 Roof Bolters, Mining

47-5061 Roof Bolters, Mining
Operate machinery to install roof support bolts in underground mine.

Illustrative examples: Roof Bolting Coal Miner, Underground Bolting Machine Operator, Underground Roof Bolter

47-5070 Roustabouts, Oil and Gas
This broad occupation is the same as the detailed occupation:
47-5071 Roustabouts, Oil and Gas

47-5071 Roustabouts, Oil and Gas
Assemble or repair oil field equipment using hand and power tools. Perform other tasks as needed.

Illustrative examples: Oil Field Roustabout, Oil Rig Roughneck

47-5080 Helpers—Extraction Workers
This broad occupation is the same as the detailed occupation:
47-5081 Helpers—Extraction Workers

47-5081 Helpers—Extraction Workers
Help extraction craft workers, such as earth drillers, blasters and explosives workers, derrick operators, and mining machine operators, by performing duties requiring less skill. Duties include supplying equipment or cleaning work area. Apprentice workers are classified with the appropriate skilled construction trade occupation (47-2011 through 47-2231).

Illustrative examples: Blaster Helper, Mining Helper, Roof Bolter Helper

47-5090 Miscellaneous Extraction Workers
This broad occupation is the same as the detailed occupation:
47-5099 Extraction Workers, All Other

47-5099 Extraction Workers, All Other
All extraction workers not listed separately.

Illustrative example: Sandfill Operator

49-1000 Supervisors of Installation, Maintenance, and Repair Workers

49-1010 First-Line Supervisors of Mechanics, Installers, and Repairers
This broad occupation is the same as the detailed occupation:
49-1011 First-Line Supervisors of Mechanics, Installers, and Repairers

49-1011 First-Line Supervisors of Mechanics, Installers, and Repairers
Directly supervise and coordinate the activities of mechanics, installers, and repairers. Excludes team or work leaders.

Illustrative example: Automobile Body Repair Supervisor, Fleet Maintenance Supervisor, Railroad Car Repair Supervisor

49-2000 Electrical and Electronic Equipment Mechanics, Installers, and Repairers

49-2010 Computer, Automated Teller, and Office Machine Repairers
This broad occupation is the same as the detailed occupation:
49-2011 Computer, Automated Teller, and Office Machine Repairers

49-2011 Computer, Automated Teller, and Office Machine Repairers
Repair, maintain, or install computers, word processing systems, automated teller machines, and electronic office machines, such as duplicating and fax machines.

Illustrative examples: ATM Servicer, Cash Register Servicer, Data Processing Equipment Repairer

49-2020 Radio and Telecommunications Equipment Installers and Repairers
This broad occupation includes the following two detailed occupations:
49-2021 Radio, Cellular, and Tower Equipment Installers and Repairers
49-2022 Telecommunications Equipment Installers and Repairers, Except Line Installers

49-2021 Radio, Cellular, and Tower Equipment Installers and Repairers
Repair, install or maintain mobile or stationary radio transmitting, broadcasting, and receiving equipment, and two-way radio communications systems used in cellular telecommunications, mobile broadband, ship-to-shore, aircraft-to-ground communications, and radio equipment in service and emergency vehicles. May test and analyze network coverage.

Illustrative examples: Radio Frequency Technician, Radio Mechanic, Two-Way Radio Technician

49-2022 Telecommunications Equipment Installers and Repairers, Except Line Installers
Install, set-up, rearrange, or remove switching, distribution, routing, and dialing equipment used in central offices or headends. Service or repair telephone, cable television, Internet, and other communications equipment on customers' property. May install communications equipment or

communications wiring in buildings. Excludes "Telecommunications Line Installers and Repairers" (49-9052).

Illustrative examples: Fiber Optic Central Office Installer, Private Branch Exchange (PBX) Installer and Repairer

49-2090 Miscellaneous Electrical and Electronic Equipment Mechanics, Installers, and Repairers
This broad occupation includes the following eight detailed occupations:
49-2091 Avionics Technicians
49-2092 Electric Motor, Power Tool, and Related Repairers
49-2093 Electrical and Electronics Installers and Repairers, Transportation Equipment
49-2094 Electrical and Electronics Repairers, Commercial and Industrial Equipment
49-2095 Electrical and Electronics Repairers, Powerhouse, Substation, and Relay
49-2096 Electronic Equipment Installers and Repairers, Motor Vehicles
49-2097 Electronic Home Entertainment Equipment Installers and Repairers
49-2098 Security and Fire Alarm Systems Installers

49-2091 Avionics Technicians
Install, inspect, test, adjust, or repair avionics equipment, such as radar, radio, navigation, and missile control systems in aircraft or space vehicles.

Illustrative examples: Aircraft Electrician, Aircraft Instrument Mechanic, Automatic Pilot Mechanic

49-2092 Electric Motor, Power Tool, and Related Repairers
Repair, maintain, or install electric motors, wiring, or switches.

Illustrative examples: Armature Rewinder, Electrical Parts Reconditioner

49-2093 Electrical and Electronics Installers and Repairers, Transportation Equipment
Install, adjust, or maintain mobile electronics communication equipment, including sound, sonar, security, navigation, and surveillance systems on trains, watercraft, or other mobile equipment. Excludes "Avionics Technicians" (49-2091) and "Electronic Equipment Installers and Repairers, Motor Vehicles" (49-2096).

Illustrative examples: Locomotive Electrician, Marine Electronics Repairer

49-2094 Electrical and Electronics Repairers, Commercial and Industrial Equipment
Repair, test, adjust, or install electronic equipment, such as industrial controls, transmitters, and antennas. Excludes "Avionics Technicians" (49-2091), "Electronic Equipment Installers and Repairers, Motor Vehicles" (49-2096), and "Electrical and Electronics Installers and Repairers, Transportation Equipment" (49-2093).

Illustrative examples: Industrial Robotics Mechanic, Missile Pad Mechanic, Public Address System Mechanic

49-2095 Electrical and Electronics Repairers, Powerhouse, Substation, and Relay

Inspect, test, repair, or maintain electrical equipment in generating stations, substations, and in-service relays.

Illustrative examples: Power Transformer Repairer, Powerhouse Electrician, Relay Technician

49-2096 Electronic Equipment Installers and Repairers, Motor Vehicles

Install, diagnose, or repair communications, sound, security, or navigation equipment in motor vehicles.

Illustrative examples: Automotive Electrician, Car Alarm Installer, Car Stereo Installer, GPS Car Navigation Installer

49-2097 Electronic Home Entertainment Equipment Installers and Repairers

Repair, adjust, or install audio or television receivers, stereo systems, camcorders, video systems, or other electronic home entertainment equipment.

Illustrative examples: Electronic Musical Instrument Repairer, Home Theater Installer, Satellite Dish Installer, Wireless Internet Installer

49-2098 Security and Fire Alarm Systems Installers

Install, program, maintain, or repair security or fire alarm wiring and equipment. Ensure that work is in accordance with relevant codes. Excludes "Electricians" (47-2111) who do a broad range of electrical wiring.

Illustrative examples: Burglar Alarm Installer, Fire Alarm Installer, Home Security Alarm Installer

49-3000 Vehicle and Mobile Equipment Mechanics, Installers, and Repairers

49-3010 Aircraft Mechanics and Service Technicians

This broad occupation is the same as the detailed occupation:
49-3011 Aircraft Mechanics and Service Technicians

49-3011 Aircraft Mechanics and Service Technicians

Diagnose, adjust, repair, or overhaul aircraft engines and assemblies, such as hydraulic and pneumatic systems. Includes helicopter and aircraft engine specialists. Excludes "Avionics Technician" (49-2091).

Illustrative examples: Aircraft Engine Specialist, Airframe Mechanic, Flight Test Mechanic

49-3020 Automotive Technicians and Repairers
This broad occupation includes the following three detailed occupations:
49-3021 Automotive Body and Related Repairers
49-3022 Automotive Glass Installers and Repairers
49-3023 Automotive Service Technicians and Mechanics

49-3021 Automotive Body and Related Repairers
Repair and refinish automotive vehicle bodies and straighten vehicle frames. Excludes "Painters, Transportation Equipment" (51-9122) and "Automotive Glass Installers and Repairers" (49-3022).

Illustrative examples: Auto Body Customizer, Auto Bumper Straightener, Truck Body Repairer

49-3022 Automotive Glass Installers and Repairers
Replace or repair broken windshields and window glass in motor vehicles.

Illustrative examples: Auto Glass Mechanic, Automotive Glazier, Windshield Installer

49-3023 Automotive Service Technicians and Mechanics
Diagnose, adjust, repair, or overhaul automotive vehicles. Excludes "Automotive Body and Related Repairers" (49-3021), "Bus and Truck Mechanics and Diesel Engine Specialists" (49-3031), and "Electronic Equipment Installers and Repairers, Motor Vehicles" (49-2096).

Illustrative examples: Auto Transmission Specialist, Automotive Brake Technician, Automotive Fuel Injection Servicer, Hybrid Car Mechanic

49-3030 Bus and Truck Mechanics and Diesel Engine Specialists
This broad occupation is the same as the detailed occupation:
49-3031 Bus and Truck Mechanics and Diesel Engine Specialists

49-3031 Bus and Truck Mechanics and Diesel Engine Specialists
Diagnose, adjust, repair, or overhaul buses and trucks, or maintain and repair any type of diesel engines. Includes mechanics working primarily with automobile or marine diesel engines.

Illustrative examples: Biodiesel Engine Specialist, Marine Diesel Technician, School Bus Mechanic, Tractor Trailer Mechanic

49-3040 Heavy Vehicle and Mobile Equipment Service Technicians and Mechanics
This broad occupation includes the following three detailed occupations:
49-3041 Farm Equipment Mechanics and Service Technicians
49-3042 Mobile Heavy Equipment Mechanics, Except Engines
49-3043 Rail Car Repairers

49-3041 Farm Equipment Mechanics and Service Technicians

Diagnose, adjust, repair, or overhaul farm machinery and vehicles, such as tractors, harvesters, dairy equipment, and irrigation systems. Excludes "Bus and Truck Mechanics and Diesel Engine Specialists" (49-3031).

Illustrative examples: Combine Mechanic, Dairy Equipment Repairer, Irrigation Equipment Mechanic

49-3042 Mobile Heavy Equipment Mechanics, Except Engines

Diagnose, adjust, repair, or overhaul mobile mechanical, hydraulic, and pneumatic equipment, such as cranes, bulldozers, graders, and conveyors, used in construction, logging, and surface mining. Excludes "Rail Car Repairers" (49-3043) and "Bus and Truck Mechanics and Diesel Engine Specialists" (49-3031).

Illustrative examples: Bulldozer Mechanic, Construction Equipment Mechanic, Forklift Mechanic

49-3043 Rail Car Repairers

Diagnose, adjust, repair, or overhaul railroad rolling stock, mine cars, or mass transit rail cars. Excludes "Bus and Truck Mechanics and Diesel Engine Specialists" (49-3031).

Illustrative examples: Mine Car Mechanic, Street Car Repairer, Subway Car Repairer, Trolley Car Overhauler

49-3050 Small Engine Mechanics

This broad occupation includes the following three detailed occupations:
49-3051 Motorboat Mechanics and Service Technicians
49-3052 Motorcycle Mechanics
49-3053 Outdoor Power Equipment and Other Small Engine Mechanics

49-3051 Motorboat Mechanics and Service Technicians

Repair and adjust electrical and mechanical equipment of inboard or inboard-outboard boat engines. Excludes "Bus and Truck Mechanics and Diesel Engine Specialists" (49-3031).

Illustrative examples: Certified Marine Mechanic, Outboard Motor Mechanic

49-3052 Motorcycle Mechanics

Diagnose, adjust, repair, or overhaul motorcycles, scooters, mopeds, dirt bikes, or similar motorized vehicles.

Illustrative examples: All Terrain Vehicle Technician, Motorcycle Service Technician, Motor Scooter Mechanic

49-3053 Outdoor Power Equipment and Other Small Engine Mechanics

Diagnose, adjust, repair, or overhaul small engines used to power lawn mowers, chain saws, recreational sporting equipment and related equipment.

Illustrative examples: Golf Cart Mechanic, Lawn Mower Repairer, Mobility Scooter Repairer, Power Saw Mechanic

49-3090 Miscellaneous Vehicle and Mobile Equipment Mechanics, Installers, and Repairers

This broad occupation includes the following three detailed occupations:
49-3091 Bicycle Repairers
49-3092 Recreational Vehicle Service Technicians
49-3093 Tire Repairers and Changers

49-3091 Bicycle Repairers
Repair and service bicycles.

Illustrative examples: Bicycle Mechanic, Bicycle Service Technician

49-3092 Recreational Vehicle Service Technicians
Diagnose, inspect, adjust, repair, or overhaul recreational vehicles including travel trailers. May specialize in maintaining gas, electrical, hydraulic, plumbing, or chassis/towing systems as well as repairing generators, appliances, and interior components. Includes workers who perform customized van conversions. Excludes "Automotive Service Technicians and Mechanics" (49-3023) and "Bus and Truck Mechanics and Diesel Engine Specialists" (49-3031) who also work on recreation vehicles.

Illustrative examples: Recreational Vehicle (RV) Repairer, RV Mechanic

49-3093 Tire Repairers and Changers
Repair and replace tires.

Illustrative examples: Tire Balancer, Tire Fixer

49-9000 Other Installation, Maintenance, and Repair Occupations

49-9010 Control and Valve Installers and Repairers
This broad occupation includes the following two detailed occupations:
49-9011 Mechanical Door Repairers
49-9012 Control and Valve Installers and Repairers, Except Mechanical Door

49-9011 Mechanical Door Repairers
Install, service, or repair automatic door mechanisms and hydraulic doors. Includes garage door mechanics.

Illustrative example: Automatic Door Mechanic

49-9012 Control and Valve Installers and Repairers, Except Mechanical Door

Install, repair, and maintain mechanical regulating and controlling devices, such as electric meters, gas regulators, thermostats, safety and flow valves, and other mechanical governors.

Illustrative examples: Air Valve Mechanic, Gas Meter Installer, Thermostat Repairer

49-9020 Heating, Air Conditioning, and Refrigeration Mechanics and Installers

This broad occupation is the same as the detailed occupation:
49-9021 Heating, Air Conditioning, and Refrigeration Mechanics and Installers

49-9021 Heating, Air Conditioning, and Refrigeration Mechanics and Installers

Install or repair heating, central air conditioning, or refrigeration systems, including oil burners, hot-air furnaces, and heating stoves.

Illustrative examples: Gas Furnace Installer; Heating, Ventilation, and Air Conditioning (HVAC) Mechanic; Oil Burner Repairer

49-9030 Home Appliance Repairers

This broad occupation is the same as the detailed occupation:
49-9031 Home Appliance Repairers

49-9031 Home Appliance Repairers

Repair, adjust, or install all types of electric or gas household appliances, such as refrigerators, washers, dryers, and ovens.

Illustrative examples: Vacuum Cleaner Repairer, Washing Machine Installer, Window Air Conditioner Installer

49-9040 Industrial Machinery Installation, Repair, and Maintenance Workers

This broad occupation includes the following four detailed occupations:
49-9041 Industrial Machinery Mechanics
49-9043 Maintenance Workers, Machinery
49-9044 Millwrights
49-9045 Refractory Materials Repairers, Except Brickmasons

49-9041 Industrial Machinery Mechanics

Repair, install, adjust, or maintain industrial production and processing machinery or refinery and pipeline distribution systems. Excludes "Millwrights" (49-9044), "Mobile Heavy Equipment Mechanics, Except Engines" (49-3042), and "Maintenance Workers, Machinery" (49-9043).

Illustrative examples: Boilerhouse Mechanic, Foundry Equipment Mechanic, Hydroelectric Machinery Mechanic

49-9043 Maintenance Workers, Machinery
Lubricate machinery, change parts, or perform other routine machinery maintenance. Excludes "Maintenance and Repair Workers, General" (49-9071).

Illustrative example: Crane Oiler

49-9044 Millwrights
Install, dismantle, or move machinery and heavy equipment according to layout plans, blueprints, or other drawings.

Illustrative examples: Machine Erector, Machinery Dismantler, Maintenance Millwright

49-9045 Refractory Materials Repairers, Except Brickmasons
Build or repair equipment such as furnaces, kilns, cupolas, boilers, converters, ladles, soaking pits and ovens, using refractory materials.

Illustrative examples: Bondactor Machine Repairer, Cupola Repairer, Kiln Door Builder, Ladle Repairer

49-9050 Line Installers and Repairers
This broad occupation includes the following two detailed occupations:
49-9051 Electrical Power-Line Installers and Repairers
49-9052 Telecommunications Line Installers and Repairers

49-9051 Electrical Power-Line Installers and Repairers
Install or repair cables or wires used in electrical power or distribution systems. May erect poles and light or heavy duty transmission towers. Excludes "Electrical and Electronics Repairers, Powerhouse, Substation, and Relay" (49-2095).

Illustrative examples: Electric Powerline Examiner, Electric Utility Lineworker, Electrical High Tension Tester, Electrical Lineworker

49-9052 Telecommunications Line Installers and Repairers
Install and repair telecommunications cable, including fiber optics.

Illustrative examples: Cable Television Installer, FIOS Line Installer, Telephone Cable Splicer

49-9060 Precision Instrument and Equipment Repairers
This broad occupation includes the following five detailed occupations:
49-9061 Camera and Photographic Equipment Repairers
49-9062 Medical Equipment Repairers
49-9063 Musical Instrument Repairers and Tuners
49-9064 Watch Repairers
49-9069 Precision Instrument and Equipment Repairers, All Other

49-9061 Camera and Photographic Equipment Repairers
Repair and adjust cameras and photographic equipment, including commercial video and motion picture camera equipment.

Illustrative example: Aircraft Photographic Equipment Repairer, Camera Repairer, Photographic Equipment Technician

49-9062 Medical Equipment Repairers
Test, adjust, or repair biomedical or electromedical equipment.

Illustrative examples: Biomedical Equipment Technician, Radiology Equipment Servicer, Surgical Instrument Mechanic

49-9063 Musical Instrument Repairers and Tuners
Repair percussion, stringed, reed, or wind instruments. May specialize in one area, such as piano tuning. Excludes "Electronic Home Entertainment Equipment Installers and Repairers" (49-2097) who repair electrical and electronic musical instruments.

Illustrative examples: Brass and Wind Instrument Repairer, Piano Tuner, Violin Repairer

49-9064 Watch Repairers
Repair, clean, and adjust mechanisms of timing instruments, such as watches and clocks. Includes watchmakers, watch technicians, and mechanical timepiece repairers.

Illustrative examples: Antique Clock Repairer, Clock Repair Technician, Horologist

49-9069 Precision Instrument and Equipment Repairers, All Other
All precision instrument and equipment repairers not listed separately.

Illustrative examples: Gyroscope Repairer, Telescope Repairer

49-9070 Maintenance and Repair Workers, General
This broad occupation is the same as the detailed occupation:
49-9071 Maintenance and Repair Workers, General

49-9071 Maintenance and Repair Workers, General
Perform work involving the skills of two or more maintenance or craft occupations to keep machines, mechanical equipment, or the structure of an establishment in repair. Duties may involve pipe fitting; boiler making; insulating; welding; machining; carpentry; repairing electrical or mechanical equipment; installing, aligning, and balancing new equipment; and repairing buildings, floors, or stairs. Excludes "Maintenance Workers, Machinery" (49-9043).

Illustrative example: Building Maintenance Mechanic

49-9080 Wind Turbine Service Technicians
This broad occupation is the same as the detailed occupation:
49-9081 Wind Turbine Service Technicians

49-9081 Wind Turbine Service Technicians
Inspect, diagnose, adjust, or repair wind turbines. Perform maintenance on wind turbine equipment including resolving electrical, mechanical, and hydraulic malfunctions.

Illustrative examples: Wind Energy Technician, Wind Turbine Mechanic

49-9090 Miscellaneous Installation, Maintenance, and Repair Workers
This broad occupation includes the following nine detailed occupations:
49-9091 Coin, Vending, and Amusement Machine Servicers and Repairers
49-9092 Commercial Divers
49-9093 Fabric Menders, Except Garment
49-9094 Locksmiths and Safe Repairers
49-9095 Manufactured Building and Mobile Home Installers
49-9096 Riggers
49-9097 Signal and Track Switch Repairers
49-9098 Helpers—Installation, Maintenance, and Repair Workers
49-9099 Installation, Maintenance, and Repair Workers, All Other

49-9091 Coin, Vending, and Amusement Machine Servicers and Repairers
Install, service, adjust, or repair coin, vending, or amusement machines including video games, juke boxes, pinball machines, or slot machines.

Illustrative examples: Arcade Games Mechanic, Parking Meter Collector, Slot Machine Mechanic, Vending Machine Filler

49-9092 Commercial Divers
Work below surface of water, using scuba gear to inspect, repair, remove, or install equipment and structures. May use a variety of power and hand tools, such as drills, sledgehammers, torches, and welding equipment. May conduct tests or experiments, rig explosives, or photograph structures or marine life. Excludes "Fishers and Related Fishing Workers" (45-3011), "Athletes and Sports Competitors" (27-2021), and "Police and Sheriff's Patrol Officers" (33-3051).

Illustrative examples: Marine Diver, Salvage Diver, Scuba Diver, Underwater Welder

49-9093 Fabric Menders, Except Garment
Repair tears, holes, and other defects in fabrics, such as draperies, linens, parachutes, and tents.

Illustrative examples: Fabric Awning Repairer, Parachute Repairer, Sail Repairer

49-9094 Locksmiths and Safe Repairers
Repair and open locks; make keys; change locks and safe combinations; and install and repair safes.

Illustrative examples: Key Maker, Safe and Vault Installer, Safe and Vault Mechanic

49-9095 Manufactured Building and Mobile Home Installers
Move or install mobile homes or prefabricated buildings.

Illustrative examples: Housetrailer Servicer, Mobile Home Mechanic, Mobile Home Servicer

49-9096 Riggers
Set up or repair rigging for construction projects, manufacturing plants, logging yards, ships and shipyards, or for the entertainment industry.

Illustrative examples: Acrobatic Rigger, Crane Rigger, Yard Rigger

49-9097 Signal and Track Switch Repairers
Install, inspect, test, maintain, or repair electric gate crossings, signals, signal equipment, track switches, section lines, or intercommunications systems within a railroad system.

Illustrative examples: Light Rail Signal Technician, Rail Signal Mechanic, Third Rail Installer

49-9098 Helpers—Installation, Maintenance, and Repair Workers
Help installation, maintenance, and repair workers in maintenance, parts replacement, and repair of vehicles, industrial machinery, and electrical and electronic equipment. Perform duties such as furnishing tools, materials, and supplies to other workers; cleaning work area, machines, and tools; and holding materials or tools for other workers.

Illustrative examples: Automobile Body Repairer Helper, Locksmith Helper, Motorboat Mechanic Helper

49-9099 Installation, Maintenance, and Repair Workers, All Other
All installation, maintenance, and repair workers not listed separately.

Illustrative examples: Bowling Alley Mechanic, Fire Extinguisher Installer, Gasoline Pump Installer, Gunsmith

51-1000 Supervisors of Production Workers51-1010 First-Line Supervisors of Production and Operating Workers

This broad occupation is the same as the detailed occupation:
51-1011 First-Line Supervisors of Production and Operating Workers

51-1011 First-Line Supervisors of Production and Operating Workers

Directly supervise and coordinate the activities of production and operating workers, such as inspectors, precision workers, machine setters and operators, assemblers, fabricators, and plant and system operators. Excludes team or work leaders.

Illustrative examples: Assembly Line Supervisor, Machinist Supervisor, Printing Worker Supervisor

51-2000 Assemblers and Fabricators

51-2010 Aircraft Structure, Surfaces, Rigging, and Systems Assemblers

This broad occupation is the same as the detailed occupation:
51-2011 Aircraft Structure, Surfaces, Rigging, and Systems Assemblers

51-2011 Aircraft Structure, Surfaces, Rigging, and Systems Assemblers

Assemble, fit, fasten, and install parts of airplanes, space vehicles, or missiles, such as tails, wings, fuselage, bulkheads, stabilizers, landing gear, rigging and control equipment, or heating and ventilating systems.

Illustrative examples: Aircraft De-Icer Installer, Aircraft Fuselage Framer, Aircraft Riveter

51-2020 Electrical, Electronics, and Electromechanical Assemblers

This broad occupation includes the following three detailed occupations:
51-2021 Coil Winders, Tapers, and Finishers
51-2022 Electrical and Electronic Equipment Assemblers
51-2023 Electromechanical Equipment Assemblers

51-2021 Coil Winders, Tapers, and Finishers

Wind wire coils used in electrical components, such as resistors and transformers, and in electrical equipment and instruments, such as field cores, bobbins, armature cores, electrical motors, generators, and control equipment.

Illustrative examples: Coil Builder, Motor Winder, Wire Coiler

51-2022 Electrical and Electronic Equipment Assemblers

Assemble or modify electrical or electronic equipment, such as computers, test equipment telemetering systems, electric motors, and batteries.

Illustrative examples: Anode Builder, Battery Builder, Circuit Board Assembler, Electric Motor Controls Assembler

51-2023 Electromechanical Equipment Assemblers
Assemble or modify electromechanical equipment or devices, such as servomechanisms, gyros, dynamometers, magnetic drums, tape drives, brakes, control linkage, actuators, and appliances.

Illustrative examples: Programmable Logic Controller Assembler, Synchronous Motor Assembler, Vacuum Cleaner Assembler, Vending Machine Assembler

51-2030 Engine and Other Machine Assemblers
This broad occupation is the same as the detailed occupation:
51-2031 Engine and Other Machine Assemblers

51-2031 Engine and Other Machine Assemblers
Construct, assemble, or rebuild machines, such as engines, turbines, and similar equipment used in such industries as construction, extraction, textiles, and paper manufacturing.

Illustrative examples: Gas Turbine Assembler, Machine Builder, Steam Turbine Assembler

51-2040 Structural Metal Fabricators and Fitters
This broad occupation is the same as the detailed occupation:
51-2041 Structural Metal Fabricators and Fitters

51-2041 Structural Metal Fabricators and Fitters
Fabricate, position, align, and fit parts of structural metal products. Shipfitters are included in "Layout Workers, Metal and Plastic" (51-4192).

Illustrative examples: Mill Beam Fitter, Protector Plate Attacher

51-2090 Miscellaneous Assemblers and Fabricators
This broad occupation includes the following four detailed occupations:
51-2091 Fiberglass Laminators and Fabricators
51-2092 Team Assemblers
51-2093 Timing Device Assemblers and Adjusters
51-2099 Assemblers and Fabricators, All Other

51-2091 Fiberglass Laminators and Fabricators
Laminate layers of fiberglass on molds to form boat decks and hulls, bodies for golf carts, automobiles, or other products.

Illustrative examples: Fiberglass Boat Builder, Fiberglass Ski Maker

51-2092 Team Assemblers
Work as part of a team having responsibility for assembling an entire product or component of a product. Team assemblers can perform all tasks conducted by the team in the assembly process

and rotate through all or most of them rather than being assigned to a specific task on a permanent basis. May participate in making management decisions affecting the work. Includes team leaders who work as part of the team. Assemblers who continuously perform the same task are classified elsewhere in 51-2000.

Illustrative examples: Team Assembly Line Machine Operator, Lead Team Assembler, Team Automobile Assembler

51-2093 Timing Device Assemblers and Adjusters
Perform precision assembling, adjusting, or calibrating, within narrow tolerances, of timing devices such as digital clocks or timing devices with electrical or electronic components. Excludes watchmakers, which are included in "Watch Repairers" (49-9064).

Illustrative examples: Digital Watch Assembler, Electrical Timing Device Calibrator, Marine Chronometer Assembler

51-2099 Assemblers and Fabricators, All Other
All assemblers and fabricators not listed separately.

Illustrative examples: Air Bag Builder, Crate Builder, Doll Maker

51-3000 Food Processing Workers

51-3010 Bakers
This broad occupation is the same as the detailed occupation:
51-3011 Bakers

51-3011 Bakers
Mix and bake ingredients to produce breads, rolls, cookies, cakes, pies, pastries, or other baked goods. Pastry chefs in restaurants and hotels are included with "Chefs and Head Cooks" (35-1011).

Illustrative examples: Bagel Maker, Bread Baker, Pastry Finisher

51-3020 Butchers and Other Meat, Poultry, and Fish Processing Workers
This broad occupation includes the following three detailed occupations:
51-3021 Butchers and Meat Cutters
51-3022 Meat, Poultry, and Fish Cutters and Trimmers
51-3023 Slaughterers and Meat Packers

51-3021 Butchers and Meat Cutters
Cut, trim, or prepare consumer-sized portions of meat for use or sale in retail establishments.
Illustrative examples: Butcher Apprentice, Kosher Butcher, Meat Carver, Meat Counter Worker

51-3022 Meat, Poultry, and Fish Cutters and Trimmers

Use hand or hand tools to perform routine cutting and trimming of meat, poultry, and seafood.

Illustrative examples: Fish Filleter, Oyster Shucker, Poultry Eviscerator, Shrimp Picker

51-3023 Slaughterers and Meat Packers

Work in slaughtering, meat packing, or wholesale establishments performing precision functions involving the preparation of meat. Work may include specialized slaughtering tasks, cutting standard or premium cuts of meat for marketing, making sausage, or wrapping meats. Excludes "Meat, Poultry, and Fish Cutters and Trimmers" (51-3022) who perform routine meat cutting.

Illustrative examples: Halal Meat Packer, Poultry Slaughter, Shochet

51-3090 Miscellaneous Food Processing Workers

This broad occupation includes the following four detailed occupations:
51-3091 Food and Tobacco Roasting, Baking, and Drying Machine Operators and Tenders
51-3092 Food Batchmakers
51-3093 Food Cooking Machine Operators and Tenders
51-3099 Food Processing Workers, All Other

51-3091 Food and Tobacco Roasting, Baking, and Drying Machine Operators and Tenders

Operate or tend food or tobacco roasting, baking, or drying equipment, including hearth ovens, kiln driers, roasters, char kilns, and vacuum drying equipment.

Illustrative examples: Coffee Roaster, Fish Smoker, Meat Curer, Smokehouse Worker

51-3092 Food Batchmakers

Set up and operate equipment that mixes or blends ingredients used in the manufacturing of food products. Includes candy makers and cheese makers.

Illustrative examples: Frozen Yogurt Maker, Honey Blender, Peanut Butter Maker

51-3093 Food Cooking Machine Operators and Tenders

Operate or tend cooking equipment, such as steam cooking vats, deep fry cookers, pressure cookers, kettles, and boilers, to prepare food products. Excludes "Food and Tobacco Roasting, Baking, and Drying Machine Operators and Tenders" (51-3091).

Illustrative examples: Doughnut Machine Operator, Dumpling Machine Operator, Potato Chip Frier

51-3099 Food Processing Workers, All Other

All food processing workers not listed separately.

Illustrative examples: Olive Pitter, Poultry Hanger, Yeast Maker

51-4000 Metal Workers and Plastic Workers

51-4010 Computer Control Programmers and Operators
This broad occupation includes the following two detailed occupations:
51-4011 Computer-Controlled Machine Tool Operators, Metal and Plastic
51-4012 Computer Numerically Controlled Machine Tool Programmers, Metal and Plastic

51-4011 Computer-Controlled Machine Tool Operators, Metal and Plastic
Operate computer-controlled machines or robots to perform one or more machine functions on metal or plastic work pieces.

Illustrative examples: Computer Numerically Controlled (CNC) Shot Peening Operator, Jig Boring Machine Operator for Metal, Welding Robot Operator

51-4012 Computer Numerically Controlled Machine Tool Programmers, Metal and Plastic
Develop programs to control machining or processing of metal or plastic parts by automatic machine tools, equipment, or systems.

Illustrative examples: Metal Numerical Control Programmer, Metal Numerical Tool Programmer, Sheet Metal Computer Numerically Controlled (CNC) Programmer

51-4020 Forming Machine Setters, Operators, and Tenders, Metal and Plastic
This broad occupation includes the following three detailed occupations:
51-4021 Extruding and Drawing Machine Setters, Operators, and Tenders, Metal and Plastic
51-4022 Forging Machine Setters, Operators, and Tenders, Metal and Plastic
51-4023 Rolling Machine Setters, Operators, and Tenders, Metal and Plastic

51-4021 Extruding and Drawing Machine Setters, Operators, and Tenders, Metal and Plastic
Set up, operate, or tend machines to extrude or draw thermoplastic or metal materials into tubes, rods, hoses, wire, bars, or structural shapes.

Illustrative example: Wire Drawing Machine Tender

51-4022 Forging Machine Setters, Operators, and Tenders, Metal and Plastic
Set up, operate, or tend forging machines to taper, shape, or form metal or plastic parts.

Illustrative examples: Cold Header Operator, Forging Roll Operator, Spike Machine Operator, Swager Operator

51-4023 Rolling Machine Setters, Operators, and Tenders, Metal and Plastic
Set up, operate, or tend machines to roll steel or plastic forming bends, beads, knurls, rolls, or plate or to flatten, temper, or reduce gauge of material.

Illustrative examples: Brass Roller, Forming Roll Operator, Plastic Straightening Roll Operator, Steel Roller

51-4030 Machine Tool Cutting Setters, Operators, and Tenders, Metal and Plastic

This broad occupation includes the following five detailed occupations:
51-4031 Cutting, Punching, and Press Machine Setters, Operators, and Tenders, Metal and Plastic
51-4032 Drilling and Boring Machine Tool Setters, Operators, and Tenders, Metal and Plastic
51-4033 Grinding, Lapping, Polishing, and Buffing Machine Tool Setters, Operators, and Tenders, Metal and Plastic
51-4034 Lathe and Turning Machine Tool Setters, Operators, and Tenders, Metal and Plastic
51-4035 Milling and Planing Machine Setters, Operators, and Tenders, Metal and Plastic

51-4031 Cutting, Punching, and Press Machine Setters, Operators, and Tenders, Metal and Plastic

Set up, operate, or tend machines to saw, cut, shear, slit, punch, crimp, notch, bend, or straighten metal or plastic material.

Illustrative examples: Crimping Machine Operator for Metal, Metal Punch Press Operator, Metal Slitter

51-4032 Drilling and Boring Machine Tool Setters, Operators, and Tenders, Metal and Plastic

Set up, operate, or tend drilling machines to drill, bore, ream, mill, or countersink metal or plastic work pieces.

Illustrative examples: Boring Mill Operator for Metal, Drill Press Operator for Metal, Radial Drill Press Operator for Plastic

51-4033 Grinding, Lapping, Polishing, and Buffing Machine Tool Setters, Operators, and Tenders, Metal and Plastic

Set up, operate, or tend grinding and related tools that remove excess material or burrs from surfaces, sharpen edges or corners, or buff, hone, or polish metal or plastic work pieces.

Illustrative examples: Aluminum Polisher, Jewel Bearing Facer, Metal Grinder, Tool Polishing Machine Operator

51-4034 Lathe and Turning Machine Tool Setters, Operators, and Tenders, Metal and Plastic

Set up, operate, or tend lathe and turning machines to turn, bore, thread, form, or face metal or plastic materials, such as wire, rod, or bar stock.

Illustrative examples: Engine Lathe Operator, Gear Cutter, Screw Machine Operator

51-4035 Milling and Planing Machine Setters, Operators, and Tenders, Metal and Plastic

Set up, operate, or tend milling or planing machines to mill, plane, shape, groove, or profile metal or plastic work pieces.

Illustrative examples: Metal Milling Machine Operator, Plastic Thread Milling Machine Setup Operator

51-4040 Machinists
This broad occupation is the same as the detailed occupation:
51-4041 Machinists

51-4041 Machinists
Set up and operate a variety of machine tools to produce precision parts and instruments. Includes precision instrument makers who fabricate, modify, or repair mechanical instruments. May also fabricate and modify parts to make or repair machine tools or maintain industrial machines, applying knowledge of mechanics, mathematics, metal properties, layout, and machining procedures.

Illustrative examples: Automotive Machinist, Gear Machinist, Production Machinist

51-4050 Metal Furnace Operators, Tenders, Pourers, and Casters
This broad occupation includes the following two detailed occupations:
51-4051 Metal-Refining Furnace Operators and Tenders
51-4052 Pourers and Casters, Metal

51-4051 Metal-Refining Furnace Operators and Tenders
Operate or tend furnaces, such as gas, oil, coal, electric-arc or electric induction, open-hearth, or oxygen furnaces, to melt and refine metal before casting or to produce specified types of steel. Excludes "Heat Treating Equipment Setters, Operators, and Tenders, Metal and Plastic" (51-4191).

Illustrative examples: Electric Arc Furnace Operator, Smelter Operator

51-4052 Pourers and Casters, Metal
Operate hand-controlled mechanisms to pour and regulate the flow of molten metal into molds to produce castings or ingots.

Illustrative examples: Ingot Caster, Molten Iron Pourer, Steel Pourer

51-4060 Model Makers and Patternmakers, Metal and Plastic
This broad occupation includes the following two detailed occupations:
51-4061 Model Makers, Metal and Plastic
51-4062 Patternmakers, Metal and Plastic
51-4061 Model Makers, Metal and Plastic
Set up and operate machines, such as lathes, milling and engraving machines, and jig borers to make working models of metal or plastic objects. Includes template makers.

Illustrative examples: Metal Mockup Maker, Plastic Jig and Fixture Builder

51-4062 Patternmakers, Metal and Plastic
Lay out, machine, fit, and assemble castings and parts to metal or plastic foundry patterns, core boxes, or match plates.

51-4070 Molders and Molding Machine Setters, Operators, and Tenders, Metal and Plastic
This broad occupation includes the following two detailed occupations:
51-4071 Foundry Mold and Coremakers
51-4072 Molding, Coremaking, and Casting Machine Setters, Operators, and Tenders, Metal and Plastic

51-4071 Foundry Mold and Coremakers
Make or form wax or sand cores or molds used in the production of metal castings in foundries.

Illustrative examples: Airset Caster, Green Sand Molder, Wax Pattern Coater

51-4072 Molding, Coremaking, and Casting Machine Setters, Operators, and Tenders, Metal and Plastic
Set up, operate, or tend metal or plastic molding, casting, or coremaking machines to mold or cast metal or thermoplastic parts or products.

Illustrative examples: Aluminum Molding Machine Operator, Blow Mold Operator, Plastic Cup Fabricating Machine Operator

51-4080 Multiple Machine Tool Setters, Operators, and Tenders, Metal and Plastic
This broad occupation is the same as the detailed occupation:
51-4081 Multiple Machine Tool Setters, Operators, and Tenders, Metal and Plastic

51-4081 Multiple Machine Tool Setters, Operators, and Tenders, Metal and Plastic
Set up, operate, or tend more than one type of cutting or forming machine tool or robot.

Illustrative examples: Combination Machine Tool Operator, Multi-operation Forming Machine Setter

51-4110 Tool and Die Makers
This broad occupation is the same as the detailed occupation:
51-4111 Tool and Die Makers

51-4111 Tool and Die Makers

Analyze specifications, lay out metal stock, set up and operate machine tools, and fit and assemble parts to make and repair dies, cutting tools, jigs, fixtures, gauges, and machinists' hand tools.

Illustrative examples: Jig Bore Tool Maker, Metal Die Finisher, Metal Gauge Maker

51-4120 Welding, Soldering, and Brazing Workers
This broad occupation includes the following two detailed occupations:
51-4121 Welders, Cutters, Solderers, and Brazers
51-4122 Welding, Soldering, and Brazing Machine Setters, Operators, and Tenders

51-4121 Welders, Cutters, Solderers, and Brazers
Use hand-welding, flame-cutting, hand soldering, or brazing equipment to weld or join metal components or to fill holes, indentations, or seams of fabricated metal products.

Illustrative examples: Arc Welder, Cutting Torch Operator, Pipe Welder, Silver Solderer

51-4122 Welding, Soldering, and Brazing Machine Setters, Operators, and Tenders
Set up, operate, or tend welding, soldering, or brazing machines or robots that weld, braze, solder, or heat treat metal products, components, or assemblies. Includes workers who operate laser cutters or laser-beam machines.

Illustrative examples: Electric Beam Welder Setter, Ultrasonic Welding Machine Operator

51-4190 Miscellaneous Metal Workers and Plastic Workers
This broad occupation includes the following five detailed occupations:
51-4191 Heat Treating Equipment Setters, Operators, and Tenders, Metal and Plastic
51-4192 Layout Workers, Metal and Plastic
51-4193 Plating and Coating Machine Setters, Operators, and Tenders, Metal and Plastic
51-4194 Tool Grinders, Filers, and Sharpeners
51-4199 Metal Workers and Plastic Workers, All Other

51-4191 Heat Treating Equipment Setters, Operators, and Tenders, Metal and Plastic
Set up, operate, or tend heating equipment, such as heat-treating furnaces, flame-hardening machines, induction machines, soaking pits, or vacuum equipment to temper, harden, anneal, or heat-treat metal or plastic objects.

Illustrative examples: Annealing Furnace Operator, Induction Machine Setter, Wire Temperer

51-4192 Layout Workers, Metal and Plastic
Lay out reference points and dimensions on metal or plastic stock or workpieces, such as sheets, plates, tubes, structural shapes, castings, or machine parts, for further processing. Includes shipfitters.

Illustrative example: Shipfitter Apprentice

51-4193 Plating and Coating Machine Setters, Operators, and Tenders, Metal and Plastic

Set up, operate, or tend plating or coating machines to coat metal or plastic products with chromium, zinc, copper, cadmium, nickel, or other metal to protect or decorate surfaces. Includes electrolytic processes.

Illustrative examples: Anodizer, Galvanizer, Nickel Plater

51-4194 Tool Grinders, Filers, and Sharpeners

Perform precision smoothing, sharpening, polishing, or grinding of metal objects.

Illustrative example: Tool Grinding Machine Operator

51-4199 Metal Workers and Plastic Workers, All Other

All metal workers and plastic workers not listed separately.

Illustrative examples: Electrical Discharge Machine Setup Operator, Metal Rivet Machine Operator, Tin Recovery Worker

51-5100 Printing Workers

51-5110 Printing Workers

This broad occupation includes the following three detailed occupations:
51-5111 Prepress Technicians and Workers
51-5112 Printing Press Operators
51-5113 Print Binding and Finishing Workers

51-5111 Prepress Technicians and Workers

Format and proof text and images submitted by designers and clients into finished pages that can be printed. Includes digital and photo typesetting. May produce printing plates.

Illustrative examples: Digital Proofing and Platemaker, Photoengraver, Plate Mounter

51-5112 Printing Press Operators

Set up and operate digital, letterpress, lithographic, flexographic, gravure, or other printing machines. Includes short-run offset printing presses.

Illustrative examples: Gravure Press Operator, Offset Press Operator, Web Press Operator

51-5113 Print Binding and Finishing Workers

Bind books and other publications or finish printed products by hand or machine. May set up binding and finishing machines.

Illustrative examples: Bookbinder, Bookbinding Machine Operator

51-6000 Textile, Apparel, and Furnishings Workers

51-6010 Laundry and Dry-Cleaning Workers
This broad occupation is the same as the detailed occupation:
51-6011 Laundry and Dry-Cleaning Workers

51-6011 Laundry and Dry-Cleaning Workers
Operate or tend washing or dry-cleaning machines to wash or dry-clean industrial or household articles, such as cloth garments, suede, leather, furs, blankets, draperies, linens, rugs, and carpets. Includes spotters and dyers of these articles.

Illustrative examples: Laundry Attendant, Laundry Equipment Operator, Laundry Sorter

51-6020 Pressers, Textile, Garment, and Related Materials
This broad occupation is the same as the detailed occupation:
51-6021 Pressers, Textile, Garment, and Related Materials

51-6021 Pressers, Textile, Garment, and Related Materials
Press or shape articles by hand or machine.

Illustrative examples: Clothes Ironer, Pants Presser, Wool Presser

51-6030 Sewing Machine Operators
This broad occupation is the same as the detailed occupation:
51-6031 Sewing Machine Operators

51-6031 Sewing Machine Operators
Operate or tend sewing machines to join, reinforce, decorate, or perform related sewing operations in the manufacture of garment or nongarment products.

Illustrative examples: Blind Stitch Machine Operator, Button Sewing Machine Operator, Custom T-Shirt Embroidery Machine Operator

51-6040 Shoe and Leather Workers
This broad occupation includes the following two detailed occupations:
51-6041 Shoe and Leather Workers and Repairers
51-6042 Shoe Machine Operators and Tenders

51-6041 Shoe and Leather Workers and Repairers
Construct, decorate, or repair leather and leather-like products, such as luggage, shoes, and saddles.

Illustrative examples: Cobbler, Saddle Maker, Shoemaker

51-6042 Shoe Machine Operators and Tenders

Operate or tend a variety of machines to join, decorate, reinforce, or finish shoes and shoe parts.

Illustrative examples: Arch Cushion Press Operator, Lasting Machine Operator, Rasper Machine Operator

51-6050 Tailors, Dressmakers, and Sewers

This broad occupation includes the following two detailed occupations:
51-6051 Sewers, Hand
51-6052 Tailors, Dressmakers, and Custom Sewers

51-6051 Sewers, Hand

Sew, join, reinforce, or finish, usually with needle and thread, a variety of manufactured items. Includes weavers and stitchers. Excludes "Fabric Menders, Except Garment" (49-9093).

Illustrative examples: Hand Quilter, Hand Stitcher

51-6052 Tailors, Dressmakers, and Custom Sewers

Design, make, alter, repair, or fit garments.

Illustrative examples: Alterations Tailor, Coat Maker, Vest Maker

51-6060 Textile Machine Setters, Operators, and Tenders

This broad occupation includes the following four detailed occupations:
51-6061 Textile Bleaching and Dyeing Machine Operators and Tenders
51-6062 Textile Cutting Machine Setters, Operators, and Tenders
51-6063 Textile Knitting and Weaving Machine Setters, Operators, and Tenders
51-6064 Textile Winding, Twisting, and Drawing Out Machine Setters, Operators, and Tenders

51-6061 Textile Bleaching and Dyeing Machine Operators and Tenders

Operate or tend machines to bleach, shrink, wash, dye, or finish textiles or synthetic or glass fibers.

Illustrative examples: Cloth Dyer, Rug Dyer, Skein Yarn Dyer

51-6062 Textile Cutting Machine Setters, Operators, and Tenders

Set up, operate, or tend machines that cut textiles.

Illustrative examples: Canvas Cutter, Industrial Fabric Cutter, Welt Trimming Machine Operator

51-6063 Textile Knitting and Weaving Machine Setters, Operators, and Tenders

Set up, operate, or tend machines that knit, loop, weave, or draw in textiles. Excludes "Sewing Machine Operators" (51-6031).

Illustrative examples: Crochet Machine Operator, Jacquard Loom Weaver, Looping Machine Operator

51-6064 Textile Winding, Twisting, and Drawing Out Machine Setters, Operators, and Tenders

Set up, operate, or tend machines that wind or twist textiles; or draw out and combine sliver, such as wool, hemp, or synthetic fibers. Includes slubber machine and drawing frame operators.

Illustrative examples: Rope Machine Setter, Silk Winding Machine Operator

51-6090 Miscellaneous Textile, Apparel, and Furnishings Workers

This broad occupation includes the following four detailed occupations:
51-6091 Extruding and Forming Machine Setters, Operators, and Tenders, Synthetic and Glass Fibers
51-6092 Fabric and Apparel Patternmakers
51-6093 Upholsterers
51-6099 Textile, Apparel, and Furnishings Workers, All Other

51-6091 Extruding and Forming Machine Setters, Operators, and Tenders, Synthetic and Glass Fibers

Set up, operate, or tend machines that extrude and form continuous filaments from synthetic materials, such as liquid polymer, rayon, and fiberglass.

Illustrative examples: Fiber Machine Tender, Synthetic Filament Extruder

51-6092 Fabric and Apparel Patternmakers

Draw and construct sets of precision master fabric patterns or layouts. May also mark and cut fabrics and apparel.

Illustrative examples: Clothing Patternmaker, Embroidery Patternmaker, Fabric Pattern Grader

51-6093 Upholsterers

Make, repair, or replace upholstery for household furniture or transportation vehicles.

Illustrative examples: Aircraft Seat Upholsterer, Furniture Upholsterer

51-6099 Textile, Apparel, and Furnishings Workers, All Other

All textile, apparel, and furnishings workers not listed separately.

Illustrative examples: Apparel Embroidery Digitizer, Feltmaker, Hat Blocking Machine Operator

51-7000 Woodworkers

51-7010 Cabinetmakers and Bench Carpenters
This broad occupation is the same as the detailed occupation:
51-7011 Cabinetmakers and Bench Carpenters

51-7011 Cabinetmakers and Bench Carpenters
Cut, shape, and assemble wooden articles or set up and operate a variety of woodworking machines, such as power saws, jointers, and mortisers to surface, cut, or shape lumber or to fabricate parts for wood products. Excludes "Woodworking Machine Setters, Operators, and Tenders" (51-7040).

Illustrative examples: Cabinet Builder, Marquetry Worker, Wood Furniture Assembler

51-7020 Furniture Finishers
This broad occupation is the same as the detailed occupation:
51-7021 Furniture Finishers

51-7021 Furniture Finishers
Shape, finish, and refinish damaged, worn, or used furniture or new high-grade furniture to specified color or finish.

Illustrative examples: Furniture Sander, Piano Refinisher, Wood Cabinet Finisher

51-7030 Model Makers and Patternmakers, Wood
This broad occupation includes the following two detailed occupations:
51-7031 Model Makers, Wood
51-7032 Patternmakers, Wood

51-7031 Model Makers, Wood
Construct full-size and scale wooden precision models of products. Includes wood jig builders and loft workers.

Illustrative example: Architectural Wood Model Maker

51-7032 Patternmakers, Wood
Plan, lay out, and construct wooden unit or sectional patterns used in forming sand molds for castings.

Illustrative example: Wood Die Maker

51-7040 Woodworking Machine Setters, Operators, and Tenders
This broad occupation includes the following two detailed occupations:
51-7041 Sawing Machine Setters, Operators, and Tenders, Wood
51-7042 Woodworking Machine Setters, Operators, and Tenders, Except Sawing

51-7041 Sawing Machine Setters, Operators, and Tenders, Wood

Set up, operate, or tend wood sawing machines. May operate CNC equipment. Includes lead sawyers.

Illustrative examples: Buzzsaw Operator, Circle Saw Operator, Rip Saw Operator, Trim Saw Operator

51-7042 Woodworking Machine Setters, Operators, and Tenders, Except Sawing

Set up, operate, or tend woodworking machines, such as drill presses, lathes, shapers, routers, sanders, planers, and wood nailing machines. May operate CNC equipment.

Illustrative examples: Wood Dowel Machine Operator, Wood Lathe Operator, Wood Planer

51-7090 Miscellaneous Woodworkers

This broad occupation is the same as the detailed occupation:
51-7099 Woodworkers, All Other

51-7099 Woodworkers, All Other

All woodworkers not listed separately.

Illustrative examples: Pole Framer, Wood Carver, Wood Casket Assembler

51-8000 Plant and System Operators

51-8010 Power Plant Operators, Distributors, and Dispatchers

This broad occupation includes the following three detailed occupations:
51-8011 Nuclear Power Reactor Operators
51-8012 Power Distributors and Dispatchers
51-8013 Power Plant Operators

51-8011 Nuclear Power Reactor Operators

Operate or control nuclear reactors. Move control rods, start and stop equipment, monitor and adjust controls, and record data in logs. Implement emergency procedures when needed. May respond to abnormalities, determine cause, and recommend corrective action.

Illustrative examples: Nuclear Control Room Operator, Nuclear Reactor Operator, Nuclear Station Operator

51-8012 Power Distributors and Dispatchers

Coordinate, regulate, or distribute electricity or steam.

Illustrative examples: Steam Plant Control Room Operator, Substation Operator

51-8013 Power Plant Operators
Control, operate, or maintain machinery to generate electric power. Includes auxiliary equipment operators. Excludes "Nuclear Power Reactor Operators" (51-8011).

Illustrative examples: Hydroelectric Plant Operator, Powerhouse Operator

51-8020 Stationary Engineers and Boiler Operators
This broad occupation is the same as the detailed occupation:
51-8021 Stationary Engineers and Boiler Operators

51-8021 Stationary Engineers and Boiler Operators
Operate or maintain stationary engines, boilers, or other mechanical equipment to provide utilities for buildings or industrial processes. Operate equipment, such as steam engines, generators, motors, turbines, and steam boilers.

Illustrative examples: Boiler Engineer; Boiler Room Operator; Heating, Ventilation, and Air Conditioning (HVAC) Mechanic Boiler Operator

51-8030 Water and Wastewater Treatment Plant and System Operators
This broad occupation is the same as the detailed occupation:
51-8031 Water and Wastewater Treatment Plant and System Operators

51-8031 Water and Wastewater Treatment Plant and System Operators
Operate or control an entire process or system of machines, often through the use of control boards, to transfer or treat water or wastewater.

Illustrative examples: Liquid Waste Treatment Plant Operator, Sewage Plant Operator

51-8090 Miscellaneous Plant and System Operators
This broad occupation includes the following four detailed occupations:
51-8091 Chemical Plant and System Operators
51-8092 Gas Plant Operators
51-8093 Petroleum Pump System Operators, Refinery Operators, and Gaugers
51-8099 Plant and System Operators, All Other

51-8091 Chemical Plant and System Operators
Control or operate entire chemical processes or system of machines.

Illustrative examples: Nitric Acid Plant Operator, Pharmaceutical Manufacturing Machine Operator

51-8092 Gas Plant Operators
Distribute or process gas for utility companies and others by controlling compressors to maintain specified pressures on main pipelines.

Illustrative examples: Gas Controller, Gas Plant Dispatcher

51-8093 Petroleum Pump System Operators, Refinery Operators, and Gaugers

Operate or control petroleum refining or processing units. May specialize in controlling manifold and pumping systems, gauging or testing oil in storage tanks, or regulating the flow of oil into pipelines.

Illustrative examples: Hydrotreater Operator, Oil Pipeline Operator, Oil Refiner

51-8099 Plant and System Operators, All Other

All plant and system operators not listed separately.

Illustrative examples: Asphalt Plant Operator, Concrete Batch Plant Operator, Lime Filter Operator

51-9000 Other Production Occupations

51-9010 Chemical Processing Machine Setters, Operators, and Tenders

This broad occupation includes the following two detailed occupations:
51-9011 Chemical Equipment Operators and Tenders
51-9012 Separating, Filtering, Clarifying, Precipitating, and Still Machine Setters, Operators, and Tenders

51-9011 Chemical Equipment Operators and Tenders

Operate or tend equipment to control chemical changes or reactions in the processing of industrial or consumer products. Equipment used includes devulcanizers, steam-jacketed kettles, and reactor vessels. Excludes "Chemical Plant and System Operators" (51-8091).

Illustrative examples: Acid Purification Equipment Operator, Chemical Process Equipment Operator

51-9012 Separating, Filtering, Clarifying, Precipitating, and Still Machine Setters, Operators, and Tenders

Set up, operate, or tend continuous flow or vat-type equipment; filter presses; shaker screens; centrifuges; condenser tubes; precipitating, fermenting, or evaporating tanks; scrubbing towers; or batch stills. These machines extract, sort, or separate liquids, gases, or solids from other materials to recover a refined product. Includes dairy processing equipment operators. Excludes "Chemical Equipment Operators and Tenders" (51-9011).

Illustrative examples: Brewmaster, Fermentation Operator, Pasteurizer

51-9020 Crushing, Grinding, Polishing, Mixing, and Blending Workers

This broad occupation includes the following three detailed occupations:
51-9021 Crushing, Grinding, and Polishing Machine Setters, Operators, and Tenders
51-9022 Grinding and Polishing Workers, Hand

51-9023 Mixing and Blending Machine Setters, Operators, and Tenders

51-9021 Crushing, Grinding, and Polishing Machine Setters, Operators, and Tenders

Set up, operate, or tend machines to crush, grind, or polish materials, such as coal, glass, grain, stone, food, or rubber.

Illustrative examples: Beveling and Edging Machine Operator, Industrial Coffee Grinder, Marble and Granite Polisher, Pulverizer Operator

51-9022 Grinding and Polishing Workers, Hand

Grind, sand, or polish, using hand tools or hand-held power tools, a variety of metal, wood, stone, clay, plastic, or glass objects. Includes chippers, buffers, and finishers.

Illustrative examples: Hand Buffer, Hand Sander, Jewelry Polisher, Knife Grinder

51-9023 Mixing and Blending Machine Setters, Operators, and Tenders

Set up, operate, or tend machines to mix or blend materials, such as chemicals, tobacco, liquids, color pigments, or explosive ingredients. Excludes "Food Batchmakers" (51-3092).

Illustrative examples: Asphalt Blender, Clay Mixer, Ink Blender

51-9030 Cutting Workers

This broad occupation includes the following two detailed occupations:
51-9031 Cutters and Trimmers, Hand
51-9032 Cutting and Slicing Machine Setters, Operators, and Tenders

51-9031 Cutters and Trimmers, Hand

Use hand tools or hand-held power tools to cut and trim a variety of manufactured items, such as carpet, fabric, stone, glass, or rubber.

Illustrative examples: Fur Trimmer, Hand Cloth Cutter

51-9032 Cutting and Slicing Machine Setters, Operators, and Tenders

Set up, operate, or tend machines that cut or slice materials, such as glass, stone, cork, rubber, tobacco, food, paper, or insulating material. Excludes "Woodworking Machine Setters, Operators, and Tenders" (51-7040), "Cutting, Punching, and Press Machine Setters, Operators, and Tenders, Metal and Plastic" (51-4031), and "Textile Cutting Machine Setters, Operators, and Tenders" (51-6062).

Illustrative examples: Glass Cutting Machine Operator, Insulation Cutter, Rubber Trimmer

51-9040 Extruding, Forming, Pressing, and Compacting Machine Setters, Operators, and Tenders

This broad occupation is the same as the detailed occupation:
51-9041 Extruding, Forming, Pressing, and Compacting Machine Setters, Operators, and Tenders

51-9041 Extruding, Forming, Pressing, and Compacting Machine Setters, Operators, and Tenders
Set up, operate, or tend machines, such as glass forming machines, plodder machines, and tuber machines, to shape and form products, such as glassware, food, rubber, soap, brick, tile, clay, wax, tobacco, or cosmetics. Excludes "Paper Goods Machine Setters, Operators, and Tenders" (51-9196) and "Shoe Machine Operators and Tenders" (51-6042).

Illustrative examples: Brick Maker, Rubber Extrusion Operator, Sugar Presser

51-9050 Furnace, Kiln, Oven, Drier, and Kettle Operators and Tenders
This broad occupation is the same as the detailed occupation:
51-9051 Furnace, Kiln, Oven, Drier, and Kettle Operators and Tenders

51-9051 Furnace, Kiln, Oven, Drier, and Kettle Operators and Tenders
Operate or tend heating equipment other than basic metal, plastic, or food processing equipment. Includes activities, such as annealing glass, drying lumber, curing rubber, removing moisture from materials, or boiling soap.

Illustrative examples: Lime Kiln Operator, Lumber Kiln Operator, Rubber Curer

51-9060 Inspectors, Testers, Sorters, Samplers, and Weighers
This broad occupation is the same as the detailed occupation:
51-9061 Inspectors, Testers, Sorters, Samplers, and Weighers

51-9061 Inspectors, Testers, Sorters, Samplers, and Weighers
Inspect, test, sort, sample, or weigh nonagricultural raw materials or processed, machined, fabricated, or assembled parts or products for defects, wear, and deviations from specifications. May use precision measuring instruments and complex test equipment.

Illustrative examples: Machined Parts Quality Inspector, Petroleum Sampler

51-9070 Jewelers and Precious Stone and Metal Workers
This broad occupation is the same as the detailed occupation:
51-9071 Jewelers and Precious Stone and Metal Workers

51-9071 Jewelers and Precious Stone and Metal Workers
Design, fabricate, adjust, repair, or appraise jewelry, gold, silver, other precious metals, or gems. Includes diamond polishers and gem cutters, and persons who perform precision casting and modeling of molds, casting metal in molds, or setting precious and semi-precious stones for jewelry and related products.

Illustrative examples: Diamond Setter, Gemologist, Goldsmith

51-9080 Medical, Dental, and Ophthalmic Laboratory Technicians
This broad occupation includes the following three detailed occupations:
51-9081 Dental Laboratory Technicians
51-9082 Medical Appliance Technicians
51-9083 Ophthalmic Laboratory Technicians

51-9081 Dental Laboratory Technicians
Construct and repair full or partial dentures or dental appliances. Excludes "Dental Assistants" (31-9091).

Illustrative examples: Crown and Bridge Technician, Dental Ceramist, Orthodontic Technician

51-9082 Medical Appliance Technicians
Construct, fit, maintain, or repair medical supportive devices, such as braces, orthotics and prosthetic devices, joints, arch supports, and other surgical and medical appliances.

Illustrative examples: Brace Maker, Orthotics Technician, Prosthetics Technician

51-9083 Ophthalmic Laboratory Technicians
Cut, grind, and polish eyeglasses, contact lenses, or other precision optical elements. Assemble and mount lenses into frames or process other optical elements. Includes precision lens polishers or grinders, centerer-edgers, and lens mounters. Excludes "Opticians, Dispensing" (29-2081).

Illustrative examples: Eyeglass Maker, Lens Grinder, Precision Lens Centerer and Edger

51-9110 Packaging and Filling Machine Operators and Tenders
This broad occupation is the same as the detailed occupation:
51-9111 Packaging and Filling Machine Operators and Tenders

51-9111 Packaging and Filling Machine Operators and Tenders
Operate or tend machines to prepare industrial or consumer products for storage or shipment. Includes cannery workers who pack food products.

Illustrative examples: Bottle Capper, Keg Filler, Potato Chip Packaging Machine Operator

51-9120 Painting Workers
This broad occupation includes the following three detailed occupations:
51-9121 Coating, Painting, and Spraying Machine Setters, Operators, and Tenders
51-9122 Painters, Transportation Equipment
51-9123 Painting, Coating, and Decorating Workers

51-9121 Coating, Painting, and Spraying Machine Setters, Operators, and Tenders
Set up, operate, or tend machines to coat or paint any of a wide variety of products, including glassware, cloth, ceramics, metal, plastic, paper, or wood, with lacquer, silver, copper, rubber,

varnish, glaze, enamel, oil, or rust-proofing materials. Excludes "Plating and Coating Machine Setters, Operators, and Tenders, Metal and Plastic" (51-4193) and "Painters, Transportation Equipment" (51-9122).

Illustrative examples: Electrostatic Paint Operator, Lacquer Spray Booth Operator

51-9122 Painters, Transportation Equipment

Operate or tend painting machines to paint surfaces of transportation equipment, such as automobiles, buses, trucks, trains, boats, and airplanes. Includes painters in auto body repair facilities.

Illustrative examples: Aircraft Painter, Auto Painter, Railroad Car Painter

51-9123 Painting, Coating, and Decorating Workers

Paint, coat, or decorate articles such as furniture, glass, plateware, pottery, jewelry, toys, books, or leather. Excludes "Artists and Related Workers" (27-1010), "Designers" (27-1020), "Photographic Process Workers and Processing Machine Operators" (51-9151), and "Etchers and Engravers" (51-9194).

Illustrative examples: Ceramic Painter, China Decorator, Sign Painter

51-9140 Semiconductor Processors

This broad occupation is the same as the detailed occupation:
51-9141 Semiconductor Processors

51-9141 Semiconductor Processors

Perform any or all of the following functions in the manufacture of electronic semiconductors: load semiconductor material into furnace; saw formed ingots into segments; load individual segment into crystal growing chamber and monitor controls; locate crystal axis in ingot using x-ray equipment and saw ingots into wafers; and clean, polish, and load wafers into series of special purpose furnaces, chemical baths, and equipment used to form circuitry and change conductive properties.

Illustrative examples: Electronic Semiconductor Processor, Semiconductor Assembler, Wafer Fabricator

51-9150 Photographic Process Workers and Processing Machine Operators

This broad occupation is the same as the detailed occupation:
51-9151 Photographic Process Workers and Processing Machine Operators

51-9151 Photographic Process Workers and Processing Machine Operators

Perform work involved in developing and processing photographic images from film or digital media. May perform precision tasks such as editing photographic negatives and prints.

Illustrative examples: Digital Photo Printer, Photo Lab Specialist, Photo Retoucher

51-9190 Miscellaneous Production Workers
This broad occupation includes the following nine detailed occupations:
51-9191 Adhesive Bonding Machine Operators and Tenders
51-9192 Cleaning, Washing, and Metal Pickling Equipment Operators and Tenders
51-9193 Cooling and Freezing Equipment Operators and Tenders
51-9194 Etchers and Engravers
51-9195 Molders, Shapers, and Casters, Except Metal and Plastic
51-9196 Paper Goods Machine Setters, Operators, and Tenders
51-9197 Tire Builders
51-9198 Helpers–Production Workers
51-9199 Production Workers, All Other

51-9191 Adhesive Bonding Machine Operators and Tenders
Operate or tend bonding machines that use adhesives to join items for further processing or to form a completed product. Processes include joining veneer sheets into plywood; gluing paper; or joining rubber and rubberized fabric parts, plastic, simulated leather, or other materials. Excludes "Shoe Machine Operators and Tenders" (51-6042).

Illustrative examples: Glue Line Operator, Glue Reel Operator, Paper Gluing Operator

51-9192 Cleaning, Washing, and Metal Pickling Equipment Operators and Tenders
Operate or tend machines to wash or clean products, such as barrels or kegs, glass items, tin plate, food, pulp, coal, plastic, or rubber, to remove impurities.

Illustrative examples: Acid Dipper, Degreaser Operator, Immersion Metal Cleaner

51-9193 Cooling and Freezing Equipment Operators and Tenders
Operate or tend equipment, such as cooling and freezing units, refrigerators, batch freezers, and freezing tunnels, to cool or freeze products, food, blood plasma, and chemicals.

Illustrative examples: Chiller Tender, Refrigerating Machine Operator

51-9194 Etchers and Engravers
Engrave or etch metal, wood, rubber, or other materials. Includes such workers as etcher-circuit processors, pantograph engravers, and silk screen etchers. Photoengravers are included in "Prepress Technicians and Workers" (51-5111).

Illustrative examples: Glass Etcher, Metal Engraver

51-9195 Molders, Shapers, and Casters, Except Metal and Plastic
Mold, shape, form, cast, or carve products such as food products, figurines, tile, pipes, and candles consisting of clay, glass, plaster, concrete, stone, or combinations of materials.

Illustrative examples: Cigar Roller, Glass Blower, Neon Tube Bender

51-9196 Paper Goods Machine Setters, Operators, and Tenders

Set up, operate, or tend paper goods machines that perform a variety of functions, such as converting, sawing, corrugating, banding, wrapping, boxing, stitching, forming, or sealing paper or paperboard sheets into products.

Illustrative examples: Box Fabricator, Carton Making Machine Operator, Corrugator Operator

51-9197 Tire Builders

Operate machines to build tires.

Illustrative examples: Auto Tire Recapper, Retreader, Tire Molder

51-9198 Helpers—Production Workers

Help production workers by performing duties requiring less skill. Duties include supplying or holding materials or tools, and cleaning work area and equipment. Apprentice workers are classified in the appropriate production occupations (51-0000).

Illustrative examples: Blending Tank Helper, Commercial Baker Helper, Welder Helper

51-9199 Production Workers, All Other

All production workers not listed separately.

53-1000 Supervisors of Transportation and Material Moving Workers53-1010 Aircraft Cargo Handling Supervisors

This broad occupation is the same as the detailed occupation:
53-1011 Aircraft Cargo Handling Supervisors

53-1011 Aircraft Cargo Handling Supervisors

Supervise and coordinate the activities of ground crew in the loading, unloading, securing, and staging of aircraft cargo or baggage. May determine the quantity and orientation of cargo and compute aircraft center of gravity. May accompany aircraft as member of flight crew and monitor and handle cargo in flight, and assist and brief passengers on safety and emergency procedures. Includes loadmasters.

Illustrative examples: Air Cargo Ground Crew Supervisor, Air Cargo Ground Operations Supervisor, Airport Ramp Supervisor

53-1020 First-Line Supervisors of Helpers, Laborers, and Material Movers, Hand

This broad occupation is the same as the detailed occupation:
53-1021 First-Line Supervisors of Helpers, Laborers, and Material Movers, Hand

53-1021 First-Line Supervisors of Helpers, Laborers, and Material Movers, Hand

Directly supervise and coordinate the activities of helpers, laborers, or material movers.

Illustrative examples: Material Handling Crew Supervisor, Warehouse Supervisor

53-1030 First-Line Supervisors of Transportation and Material-Moving Machine and Vehicle Operators

This broad occupation is the same as the detailed occupation:
53-1031 First-Line Supervisors of Transportation and Material-Moving Machine and Vehicle Operators

53-1031 First-Line Supervisors of Transportation and Material-Moving Machine and Vehicle Operators

Directly supervise and coordinate activities of transportation and material-moving machine and vehicle operators and helpers.

Illustrative examples: Dock Operations Supervisor, Gas Station Supervisor, Refuse Collector Supervisor

53-2000 Air Transportation Workers

53-2010 Aircraft Pilots and Flight Engineers

This broad occupation includes the following two detailed occupations:
53-2011 Airline Pilots, Copilots, and Flight Engineers
53-2012 Commercial Pilots

53-2011 Airline Pilots, Copilots, and Flight Engineers

Pilot and navigate the flight of fixed-wing, multi-engine aircraft, usually on scheduled air carrier routes, for the transport of passengers and cargo. Requires Federal Air Transport Pilot certificate and rating for specific aircraft type used. Includes regional, National, and international airline pilots and flight instructors of airline pilots.

Illustrative examples: Airline Captain, Airline Pilot in Command, Charter Pilot (Air Transport Pilot Certificate Required), Charter Pilot (Airline)

53-2012 Commercial Pilots

Pilot and navigate the flight of fixed-winged aircraft on nonscheduled air carrier routes, or helicopters. Requires Commercial Pilot certificate. Includes charter pilots with similar certification, and air ambulance and air tour pilots. Excludes regional, National, and international airline pilots.

Illustrative examples: Aerial Crop Duster, Charter Pilot (Commercial Pilot Certificate Required), Flight Instructor (Commercial Pilots), Helicopter Pilot

53-2020 Air Traffic Controllers and Airfield Operations Specialists

This broad occupation includes the following two detailed occupations:
53-2021 Air Traffic Controllers
53-2022 Airfield Operations Specialists

53-2021 Air Traffic Controllers

Control air traffic on and within vicinity of airport and movement of air traffic between altitude sectors and control centers according to established procedures and policies. Authorize, regulate, and control commercial airline flights according to government or company regulations to expedite and ensure flight safety.

Illustrative examples: Air Traffic Control Operator, Control Tower Operator, Enroute Controller

53-2022 Airfield Operations Specialists

Ensure the safe takeoff and landing of commercial and military aircraft. Duties include coordination between air-traffic control and maintenance personnel; dispatching; using airfield landing and navigational aids; implementing airfield safety procedures; monitoring and maintaining flight records; and applying knowledge of weather information.

Illustrative examples: Aviation Operations Specialist, Flight Operations Coordinator

53-2030 Flight Attendants

This broad occupation is the same as the detailed occupation:
53-2031 Flight Attendants

53-2031 Flight Attendants

Provide personal services to ensure the safety, security, and comfort of airline passengers during flight. Greet passengers, verify tickets, explain use of safety equipment, and serve food or beverages.

Illustrative examples: Airline Flight Attendant, Airplane Flight Attendant

53-3000 Motor Vehicle Operators

53-3010 Ambulance Drivers and Attendants, Except Emergency Medical Technicians
This broad occupation is the same as the detailed occupation:
53-3011 Ambulance Drivers and Attendants, Except Emergency Medical Technicians

53-3011 Ambulance Drivers and Attendants, Except Emergency Medical Technicians
Drive ambulance or assist ambulance driver in transporting sick, injured, or convalescent persons. Assist in lifting patients.

Illustrative examples: Emergency Medical Services (EMS) Driver

53-3020 Bus Drivers
This broad occupation includes the following two detailed occupations:
53-3021 Bus Drivers, Transit and Intercity
53-3022 Bus Drivers, School or Special Client

53-3021 Bus Drivers, Transit and Intercity
Drive bus or motor coach, including regular route operations, charters, and private carriage. May assist passengers with baggage. May collect fares or tickets.

Illustrative examples: Motor Coach Bus Driver, Public Transit Bus Driver

53-3022 Bus Drivers, School or Special Client
Transport students or special clients, such as the elderly or persons with disabilities. Ensure adherence to safety rules. May assist passengers in boarding or exiting.

Illustrative examples: School Bus Operator, Special Education Bus Driver

53-3030 Driver/Sales Workers and Truck Drivers
This broad occupation includes the following three detailed occupations:
53-3031 Driver/Sales Workers
53-3032 Heavy and Tractor-Trailer Truck Drivers
53-3033 Light Truck or Delivery Services Drivers,

53-3031 Driver/Sales Workers
Drive truck or other vehicle over established routes or within an established territory and sell or deliver goods, such as food products, including restaurant take-out items, or pick up or deliver items such as commercial laundry. May also take orders, collect payment, or stock merchandise

at point of delivery. Includes newspaper delivery drivers. Excludes "Coin, Vending, and Amusement Machine Servicers and Repairers" (49-9091) and "Light Truck or Delivery Services Drivers" (53-3033).

Illustrative examples: Bakery Deliverer, Pizza Delivery Driver, Route Salesperson

53-3032 Heavy and Tractor-Trailer Truck Drivers
Drive a tractor-trailer combination or a truck with a capacity of at least 26,000 pounds Gross Vehicle Weight (GVW). May be required to unload truck. Requires commercial drivers' license.

Illustrative examples: Auto Carrier Driver, Cement Truck Driver, Moving Van Driver

53-3033 Light Truck or Delivery Services Drivers
Drive a light vehicle, such as a truck or van, with a capacity of less than 26,000 pounds Gross Vehicle Weight (GVW), primarily to deliver or pick up merchandise or to deliver packages. May load and unload vehicle. Excludes "Couriers and Messengers" (43-5021) and "Driver/Sales Workers" (53-3031).

Illustrative example: Pharmacy Delivery Driver

53-3040 Taxi Drivers and Chauffeurs
This broad occupation is the same as the detailed occupation:
53-3041 Taxi Drivers and Chauffeurs

53-3041 Taxi Drivers and Chauffeurs
Drive automobiles, vans, or limousines to transport passengers. May occasionally carry cargo. Includes hearse drivers. Excludes "Ambulance Drivers and Attendants, Except Emergency Medical Technicians" (53-3011) and "Bus Drivers" (53-3020).

Illustrative examples: Cab Driver, Courtesy Van Driver, Limousine Driver

53-3090 Miscellaneous Motor Vehicle Operators
This broad occupation is the same as the detailed occupation:
53-3099 Motor Vehicle Operators, All Other

53-3099 Motor Vehicle Operators, All Other
All motor vehicle operators not listed separately.

Illustrative examples: Ice-Resurfacing Machine Operator, Motorcycle Deliverer, Street Cleaning Equipment Operator

53-4000 Rail Transportation Workers

53-4010 Locomotive Engineers and Operators

This broad occupation includes the following three detailed occupations:

53-4011 Locomotive Engineers
53-4012 Locomotive Firers
53-4013 Rail Yard Engineers, Dinkey Operators, and Hostlers

53-4011 Locomotive Engineers

Drive electric, diesel-electric, steam, or gas-turbine-electric locomotives to transport passengers or freight. Interpret train orders, electronic or manual signals, and railroad rules and regulations.

Illustrative examples: Railroad Engineer, Train Engineer

53-4012 Locomotive Firers

Monitor locomotive instruments and watch for dragging equipment, obstacles on rights-of-way, and train signals during run. Watch for and relay traffic signals from yard workers to yard engineer in railroad yard.

Illustrative examples: Diesel Locomotive Firer, Dinkey Engine Firer, Railroad Firer

53-4013 Rail Yard Engineers, Dinkey Operators, and Hostlers

Drive switching or other locomotive or dinkey engines within railroad yard, industrial plant, quarry, construction project, or similar location.

Illustrative examples: Coal Tram Driver, Railcar Switcher

53-4020 Railroad Brake, Signal, and Switch Operators

This broad occupation is the same as the detailed occupation:
53-4021 Railroad Brake, Signal, and Switch Operators

53-4021 Railroad Brake, Signal, and Switch Operators

Operate railroad track switches. Couple or uncouple rolling stock to make up or break up trains. Signal engineers by hand or flagging. May inspect couplings, air hoses, journal boxes, and hand brakes.

Illustrative examples: Railway Switch Operator, Switch Coupler

53-4030 Railroad Conductors and Yardmasters

This broad occupation is the same as the detailed occupation:
53-4031 Railroad Conductors and Yardmasters

53-4031 Railroad Conductors and Yardmasters

Coordinate activities of switch-engine crew within railroad yard, industrial plant, or similar location. Conductors coordinate activities of train crew on passenger or freight trains. Yardmasters review train schedules and switching orders and coordinate activities of workers engaged in railroad traffic operations, such as the makeup or breakup of trains and yard switching.

Illustrative examples: Freight Conductor, Yard Conductor

53-4040 Subway and Streetcar Operators
This broad occupation is the same as the detailed occupation:
53-4041 Subway and Streetcar Operators

53-4041 Subway and Streetcar Operators
Operate subway or elevated suburban trains with no separate locomotive, or electric-powered streetcar, to transport passengers. May handle fares.

Illustrative examples: Light Rail Transit Operator, Tram Operator, Trolley Car Operator

53-4090 Miscellaneous Rail Transportation Workers
This broad occupation is the same as the detailed occupation:
53-4099 Rail Transportation Workers, All Other

53-4099 Rail Transportation Workers, All Other
All rail transportation workers not listed separately.

Illustrative examples: Railway Equipment Operator, Retarder Operator, Transfer Table Operator

53-5000 Water Transportation Workers

53-5010 Sailors and Marine Oilers
This broad occupation is the same as the detailed occupation:
53-5011 Sailors and Marine Oilers

53-5011 Sailors and Marine Oilers
Stand watch to look for obstructions in path of vessel, measure water depth, turn wheel on bridge, or use emergency equipment as directed by captain, mate, or pilot. Break out, rig, overhaul, and store cargo-handling gear, stationary rigging, and running gear. Perform a variety of maintenance tasks to preserve the painted surface of the ship and to maintain line and ship equipment. Must hold government-issued certification and tankerman certification when working aboard liquid-carrying vessels. Includes able seamen and ordinary seamen.

Illustrative examples: Deckhand, Merchant Mariner

53-5020 Ship and Boat Captains and Operators
This broad occupation includes the following two detailed occupations:
53-5021 Captains, Mates, and Pilots of Water Vessels
53-5022 Motorboat Operators

53-5021 Captains, Mates, and Pilots of Water Vessels

Command or supervise operations of ships and water vessels, such as tugboats and ferryboats. Required to hold license issued by U.S. Coast Guard. Excludes "Motorboat Operators" (53-5022).

Illustrative examples: Barge Captain, First Mate, Harbor Pilot, Port Captain

53-5022 Motorboat Operators

Operate small motor-driven boats. May assist in navigational activities.

Illustrative examples: Launch Operator, Speedboat Operator, Water Taxi Operator

53-5030 Ship Engineers

This broad occupation is the same as the detailed occupation:
53-5031 Ship Engineers

53-5031 Ship Engineers

Supervise and coordinate activities of crew engaged in operating and maintaining engines, boilers, deck machinery, and electrical, sanitary, and refrigeration equipment aboard ship.

Illustrative examples: Barge Engineer, Ferry Engineer, Tugboat Engineer

53-6000 Other Transportation Workers

53-6010 Bridge and Lock Tenders

This broad occupation is the same as the detailed occupation:
53-6011 Bridge and Lock Tenders

53-6011 Bridge and Lock Tenders

Operate and tend bridges, canal locks, and lighthouses to permit marine passage on inland waterways, near shores, and at danger points in waterway passages. May supervise such operations. Includes drawbridge operators, lock operators, and slip bridge operators.

Illustrative examples: Lighthouse Keeper, Lock and Dam Operator

53-6020 Parking Lot Attendants

This broad occupation is the same as the detailed occupation:
53-6021 Parking Lot Attendants

53-6021 Parking Lot Attendants

Park vehicles or issue tickets for customers in a parking lot or garage. May collect fee.

Illustrative examples: Parking Ramp Attendant, Valet Parker

53-6030 Automotive and Watercraft Service Attendants

This broad occupation is the same as the detailed occupation:
53-6031 Automotive and Watercraft Service Attendants

53-6031 Automotive and Watercraft Service Attendants

Service automobiles, buses, trucks, boats, and other automotive or marine vehicles with fuel, lubricants, and accessories. Collect payment for services and supplies. May lubricate vehicle, change motor oil, install antifreeze, or replace lights or other accessories, such as windshield wiper blades or fan belts. May repair or replace tires.

Illustrative examples: Gas and Oil Servicer, Gas Pump Attendant, Service Station Attendant

53-6040 Traffic Technicians

This broad occupation is the same as the detailed occupation:
53-6041 Traffic Technicians

53-6041 Traffic Technicians

Conduct field studies to determine traffic volume, speed, effectiveness of signals, adequacy of lighting, and other factors influencing traffic conditions, under direction of traffic engineer.

Illustrative examples: Highway Traffic Control Technician, Traffic Signal Technician, Transportation Technician

53-6050 Transportation Inspectors

This broad occupation is the same as the detailed occupation:
53-6051 Transportation Inspectors

53-6051 Transportation Inspectors

Inspect equipment or goods in connection with the safe transport of cargo or people. Includes rail transportation inspectors, such as freight inspectors; rail inspectors; and other inspectors of transportation vehicles, not elsewhere classified. Excludes "Transportation Security Screeners" (33-9093).

Illustrative examples: Aircraft Inspector, Motor Vehicle Emissions Inspector, Railroad Car Inspector

53-6060 Transportation Attendants, Except Flight Attendants

This broad occupation is the same as the detailed occupation:
53-6061 Transportation Attendants, Except Flight Attendants

53-6061 Transportation Attendants, Except Flight Attendants

Provide services to ensure the safety and comfort of passengers aboard ships, buses, trains, or within the station or terminal. Perform duties such as greeting passengers, explaining the use of safety equipment, serving meals or beverages, or answering questions related to travel. Excludes "Baggage Porters and Bellhops" (39-6011).
Illustrative examples: Ship Steward, Train Attendant

53-6090 Miscellaneous Transportation Workers
This broad occupation is the same as the detailed occupation:
53-6099 Transportation Workers, All Other

53-6099 Transportation Workers, All Other
All transportation workers not listed separately.

Illustrative examples: Airplane Refueler, Rickshaw Driver

53-7000 Material Moving Workers

53-7010 Conveyor Operators and Tenders
This broad occupation is the same as the detailed occupation:
53-7011 Conveyor Operators and Tenders

53-7011 Conveyor Operators and Tenders
Control or tend conveyors or conveyor systems that move materials or products to and from stockpiles, processing stations, departments, or vehicles. May control speed and routing of materials or products.

Illustrative examples: Conveyor Belt Operator, Grain Elevator Operator

53-7020 Crane and Tower Operators
This broad occupation is the same as the detailed occupation:
53-7021 Crane and Tower Operators

53-7021 Crane and Tower Operators
Operate mechanical boom and cable or tower and cable equipment to lift and move materials, machines, or products in many directions. Excludes "Excavating and Loading Machine and Dragline Operators" (53-7032).

Illustrative examples: Boom Crane Operator, Cherry Picker Operator, Coal Tower Operator

53-7030 Dredge, Excavating, and Loading Machine Operators
This broad occupation includes the following three detailed occupations:
53-7031 Dredge Operators
53-7032 Excavating and Loading Machine and Dragline Operators
53-7033 Loading Machine Operators, Underground Mining

53-7031 Dredge Operators
Operate dredge to remove sand, gravel, or other materials in order to excavate and maintain navigable channels in waterways.

Illustrative example: Dredger

193

53-7032 Excavating and Loading Machine and Dragline Operators

Operate or tend machinery equipped with scoops, shovels, or buckets, to excavate and load loose materials. Excludes "Dredge Operators" (53-7031).

Illustrative examples: Backhoe Operator, Payloader Operator, Shovel Operator

53-7033 Loading Machine Operators, Underground Mining

Operate underground loading machine to load coal, ore, or rock into shuttle or mine car or onto conveyors. Loading equipment may include power shovels, hoisting engines equipped with cable-drawn scraper or scoop, or machines equipped with gathering arms and conveyor.

Illustrative example: Coke Loader

53-7040 Hoist and Winch Operators

This broad occupation is the same as the detailed occupation:
53-7041 Hoist and Winch Operators

53-7041 Hoist and Winch Operators

Operate or tend hoists or winches to lift and pull loads using power-operated cable equipment. Excludes "Crane and Tower Operators" (53-7021).

Illustrative example: Winch Derrick Operator

53-7050 Industrial Truck and Tractor Operators

This broad occupation is the same as the detailed occupation:
53-7051 Industrial Truck and Tractor Operators

53-7051 Industrial Truck and Tractor Operators

Operate industrial trucks or tractors equipped to move materials around a warehouse, storage yard, factory, construction site, or similar location. Excludes "Logging Equipment Operators" (45-4022).

Illustrative examples: Forklift Operator, Stacker Operator

53-7060 Laborers and Material Movers, Hand

This broad occupation includes the following four detailed occupations:
53-7061 Cleaners of Vehicles and Equipment
53-7062 Laborers and Freight, Stock, and Material Movers, Hand
53-7063 Machine Feeders and Offbearers
53-7064 Packers and Packagers, Hand

53-7061 Cleaners of Vehicles and Equipment

Wash or otherwise clean vehicles, machinery, and other equipment. Use such materials as water, cleaning agents, brushes, cloths, and hoses. Excludes "Janitors and Cleaners, Except Maids and Housekeeping Cleaners" (37-2011).

Illustrative examples: Aircraft Cleaner, Auto Detailer, Car Wash Attendant

53-7062 Laborers and Freight, Stock, and Material Movers, Hand

Manually move freight, stock, or other materials or perform other general labor. Includes all manual laborers not elsewhere classified. Excludes "Material Moving Workers" (53-7011 through 53-7199) who use power equipment. Excludes "Construction Laborers" (47-2061) and "Helpers, Construction Trades" (47-3011 through 47-3019).

Illustrative examples: Cargo Handler, Wharf Laborer

53-7063 Machine Feeders and Offbearers

Feed materials into or remove materials from machines or equipment that is automatic or tended by other workers.

Illustrative examples: Hopper Filler, Spinning Doffer

53-7064 Packers and Packagers, Hand

Pack or package by hand a wide variety of products and materials.

Illustrative examples: Egg Packer, Gift Wrapper, Grocery Store Bagger

53-7070 Pumping Station Operators

This broad occupation includes the following three detailed occupations:
53-7071 Gas Compressor and Gas Pumping Station Operators
53-7072 Pump Operators, Except Wellhead Pumpers
53-7073 Wellhead Pumpers

53-7071 Gas Compressor and Gas Pumping Station Operators

Operate steam, gas, electric motor, or internal combustion engine driven compressors. Transmit, compress, or recover gases, such as butane, nitrogen, hydrogen, and natural gas.

Illustrative examples: Butane Compressor Operator, Gas Cylinder Processor, Liquid Natural Gas Plant Operator

53-7072 Pump Operators, Except Wellhead Pumpers

Tend, control, or operate power-driven, stationary, or portable pumps and manifold systems to transfer gases, oil, other liquids, slurries, or powdered materials to and from various vessels and processes.

Illustrative examples: Brewery Pumper, Fluid Pump Operator

53-7073 Wellhead Pumpers

Operate power pumps and auxiliary equipment to produce flow of oil or gas from wells in oil field.

Illustrative example: Oil Well Pumper

53-7080 Refuse and Recyclable Material Collectors
This broad occupation is the same as the detailed occupation:
53-7081 Refuse and Recyclable Material Collectors

53-7081 Refuse and Recyclable Material Collectors
Collect and dump refuse or recyclable materials from containers into truck. May drive truck.

Illustrative examples: Garbage Collector, Recyclable Materials Collector, Trash Collector

53-7110 Mine Shuttle Car Operators
This broad occupation is the same as the detailed occupation:
53-7111 Mine Shuttle Car Operators

53-7111 Mine Shuttle Car Operators
Operate diesel or electric-powered shuttle car in underground mine to transport materials from working face to mine cars or conveyor.

Illustrative example: Coal Hauler Operator

53-7120 Tank Car, Truck, and Ship Loaders
This broad occupation is the same as the detailed occupation:
53-7121 Tank Car, Truck, and Ship Loaders

53-7121 Tank Car, Truck, and Ship Loaders
Load and unload chemicals and bulk solids, such as coal, sand, and grain into or from tank cars, trucks, or ships using material moving equipment. May perform a variety of other tasks relating to shipment of products. May gauge or sample shipping tanks and test them for leaks.

Illustrative examples: Barge Loader, Rail Car Loader, Ship Unloader

53-7190 Miscellaneous Material Moving Workers
This broad occupation is the same as the detailed occupation:
53-7199 Material Moving Workers, All Other

53-7199 Material Moving Workers, All Other
All material moving workers not listed separately.

Illustrative example: Freight Elevator Operator

55-1000 Military Officer Special and Tactical Operations Leaders

55-1010 Military Officer Special and Tactical Operations Leaders
This broad occupation includes the following eight detailed occupations:
55-1011 Air Crew Officers
55-1012 Aircraft Launch and Recovery Officers
55-1013 Armored Assault Vehicle Officers
55-1014 Artillery and Missile Officers
55-1015 Command and Control Center Officers
55-1016 Infantry Officers
55-1017 Special Forces Officers
55-1019 Military Officer Special and Tactical Operations Leaders, All Other

55-1011 Air Crew Officers
Perform and direct in-flight duties to ensure the successful completion of combat, reconnaissance, transport, and search and rescue missions. Duties include operating aircraft communications and radar equipment, such as establishing satellite linkages and jamming enemy communications capabilities; operating aircraft weapons and defensive systems; conducting pre-flight, in-flight, and post-flight inspections of onboard equipment; and directing cargo and personnel drops.

Illustrative examples: Air Battle Manager, Airdrop Systems Technician, Special Project Airborne Electronics Evaluator

55-1012 Aircraft Launch and Recovery Officers
Plan and direct the operation and maintenance of catapults, arresting gear, and associated mechanical, hydraulic, and control systems involved primarily in aircraft carrier takeoff and landing operations. Duties include supervision of readiness and safety of arresting gear, launching equipment, barricades, and visual landing aid systems; planning and coordinating the design, development, and testing of launch and recovery systems; preparing specifications for catapult and arresting gear installations; evaluating design proposals; determining handling equipment needed for new aircraft; preparing technical data and instructions for operation of landing aids; and training personnel in carrier takeoff and landing procedures.

Illustrative examples: Catapult and Arresting Gear Officer, Flight Deck Officer, Landing Signal Officer

55-1013 Armored Assault Vehicle Officers
Direct the operation of tanks, light armor, and amphibious assault vehicle units during combat situations on land or in aquatic environments. Duties include directing crew members in the operation of targeting and firing systems; coordinating the operation of advanced onboard communications and navigation equipment; directing the transport of personnel and equipment during combat; formulating and implementing battle plans, including the tactical employment of armored vehicle units; and coordinating with infantry, artillery, and air support units.

Illustrative examples: Assault Amphibious Vehicle (AAV) Officer, Cavalry Officer, Tank Officer

55-1014 Artillery and Missile Officers

Manage personnel and weapons operations to destroy enemy positions, aircraft, and vessels. Duties include planning, targeting, and coordinating the tactical deployment of field artillery and air defense artillery missile systems units; directing the establishment and operation of fire control communications systems; targeting and launching intercontinental ballistic missiles; directing the storage and handling of nuclear munitions and components; overseeing security of weapons storage and launch facilities; and managing maintenance of weapons systems.

Illustrative examples: Air Defense Artillery Officer, Naval Surface Fire Support Planner, Targeting Acquisition Officer

55-1015 Command and Control Center Officers

Manage the operation of communications, detection, and weapons systems essential for controlling air, ground, and naval operations. Duties include managing critical communication links between air, naval, and ground forces; formulating and implementing emergency plans for natural and wartime disasters; coordinating emergency response teams and agencies; evaluating command center information and need for high-level military and government reporting; managing the operation of surveillance and detection systems; providing technical information and advice on capabilities and operational readiness; and directing operation of weapons targeting, firing, and launch computer systems.

Illustrative examples: Combat Information Center Officer, Command and Control Officer, Command and Control Systems Integrator

55-1016 Infantry Officers

Direct, train, and lead infantry units in ground combat operations. Duties include directing deployment of infantry weapons, vehicles, and equipment; directing location, construction, and camouflage of infantry positions and equipment; managing field communications operations; coordinating with armor, artillery, and air support units; performing strategic and tactical planning, including battle plan development; and leading basic reconnaissance operations.

Illustrative examples: Infantry Officer, Infantry Weapons Officer

55-1017 Special Forces Officers

Lead elite teams that implement unconventional operations by air, land, or sea during combat or peacetime. These activities include offensive raids, demolitions, reconnaissance, search and rescue, and counterterrorism. In addition to their combat training, special forces officers often have specialized training in swimming, diving, parachuting, survival, emergency medicine, and foreign languages. Duties include directing advanced reconnaissance operations and evaluating intelligence information; recruiting, training, and equipping friendly forces; leading raids and invasions on enemy territories; training personnel to implement individual missions and contingency plans; performing strategic and tactical planning for politically sensitive missions; and operating sophisticated communications equipment.

Illustrative examples: Parachute/Combatant Diver Officer, Sea-Air-Land Officer, Special Forces Officer

55-1019 Military Officer Special and Tactical Operations Leaders, All Other

All military officer special and tactical operations leaders not listed separately.

Illustrative examples: Chemical, Biological, Radiological, and Nuclear (CBRN) Officer, Joint Strategic Plans and Policy Officer, Special Technical Operations Officer

55-2000 First-Line Enlisted Military Supervisors

55-2010 First-Line Enlisted Military Supervisors
This broad occupation includes the following three detailed occupations:
55-2011 First-Line Supervisors of Air Crew Members
55-2012 First-Line Supervisors of Weapons Specialists/Crew Members
55-2013 First-Line Supervisors of All Other Tactical Operations Specialists

55-2011 First-Line Supervisors of Air Crew Members
Supervise and coordinate the activities of air crew members. Supervisors may also perform the same activities as the workers they supervise.

Illustrative examples: Airborne Mission Systems Superintendent, In-Flight Refueling Manager

55-2012 First-Line Supervisors of Weapons Specialists/Crew Members
Supervise and coordinate the activities of weapons specialists/crew members. Supervisors may also perform the same activities as the workers they supervise.

Illustrative examples: Armor Senior Sergeant, Field Artillery Senior Sergeant, Infantry Unit Leader

55-2013 First-Line Supervisors of All Other Tactical Operations Specialists
Supervise and coordinate the activities of all other tactical operations specialists not classified separately above. Supervisors may also perform the same activities as the workers they supervise.

Illustrative examples: Surface Ship USW Supervisor, Command Post Superintendent, Intelligence Chief

55-3000 Military Enlisted Tactical Operations and Air/Weapons Specialists and Crew Members

55-3010 Military Enlisted Tactical Operations and Air/Weapons Specialists and Crew Members
This broad occupation includes the following nine detailed occupations:
55-3011 Air Crew Members

55-3012 Aircraft Launch and Recovery Specialists
55-3013 Armored Assault Vehicle Crew Members
55-3014 Artillery and Missile Crew Members
55-3015 Command and Control Center Specialists
55-3016 Infantry
55-3017 Radar and Sonar Technicians
55-3018 Special Forces
55-3019 Military Enlisted Tactical Operations and Air/Weapons Specialists and Crew Members, All Other

55-3011 Air Crew Members

Perform in-flight duties to ensure the successful completion of combat, reconnaissance, transport, and search and rescue missions. Duties include operating aircraft communications and detection equipment, including establishing satellite linkages and jamming enemy communications capabilities; conducting pre-flight, in-flight, and post-flight inspections of onboard equipment; operating and maintaining aircraft weapons and defensive systems; operating and maintaining aircraft in-flight refueling systems; executing aircraft safety and emergency procedures; computing and verifying passenger, cargo, fuel, and emergency and special equipment weight and balance data; and conducting cargo and personnel drops.

Illustrative examples: Airborne and Air Delivery Specialist, Aviation Electronic Warfare Operator, In-Flight Refueling Craftsman

55-3012 Aircraft Launch and Recovery Specialists

Operate and maintain catapults, arresting gear, and associated mechanical, hydraulic, and control systems involved primarily in aircraft carrier takeoff and landing operations. Duties include installing and maintaining visual landing aids; testing and maintaining launch and recovery equipment using electric and mechanical test equipment and hand tools; activating airfield arresting systems, such as crash barriers and cables, during emergency landing situations; directing aircraft launch and recovery operations using hand or light signals; and maintaining logs of airplane launches, recoveries, and equipment maintenance.

Illustrative examples: Aircraft Launch and Recovery Equipment Maintenance Technician, C-13 Catapult Operator, Expeditionary Airfield Systems Technician

55-3013 Armored Assault Vehicle Crew Members

Operate tanks, light armor, and amphibious assault vehicles during combat situations on land or in aquatic environments. Duties include driving armored vehicles which require specialized training; operating and maintaining targeting and firing systems; operating and maintaining advanced onboard communications and navigation equipment; transporting personnel and equipment in a combat environment; and operating and maintaining auxiliary weapons, including machine guns and grenade launchers.

Illustrative examples: Assault Boat Coxswain, BRADLEY LINEBACKER Crewmember, M1A1 Tank Crewman

55-3014 Artillery and Missile Crew Members

Target, fire, and maintain weapons used to destroy enemy positions, aircraft, and vessels. Field artillery crew members predominantly use guns, cannons, and howitzers in ground combat operations, while air defense artillery crew members predominantly use missiles and rockets. Naval artillery crew members predominantly use torpedoes and missiles launched from a ship or submarine. Duties include testing, inspecting, and storing ammunition, missiles, and torpedoes; conducting preventive and routine maintenance on weapons and related equipment; establishing and maintaining radio and wire communications; and operating weapons targeting, firing, and launch computer systems.

Illustrative examples: Air and Missile Defense (AMD) Crewmember, Field Artillery Fire Control Man, Gunner's Mate

55-3015 Command and Control Center Specialists

Operate and monitor communications, detection, and weapons systems essential for controlling air, ground, and naval operations. Duties include maintaining and relaying critical communications between air, naval, and ground forces; implementing emergency plans for natural and wartime disasters; relaying command center information to high-level military and government decision makers; monitoring surveillance and detection systems, such as air defense; interpreting and evaluating tactical situations and making recommendations to superiors; and operating weapons targeting, firing, and launch computer systems.

Illustrative examples: Air Defense Command, Control, Communications, Computers and Intelligence Tactical Operations Center Enhanced Operator/Maintainer; C2 Tactical Analysis Technician; Command Post Craftsman

55-3016 Infantry

Operate weapons and equipment in ground combat operations. Duties include operating and maintaining weapons, such as rifles, machine guns, mortars, and hand grenades; locating, constructing, and camouflaging infantry positions and equipment; evaluating terrain and recording topographical information; operating and maintaining field communications equipment; assessing need for and directing supporting fire; placing explosives and performing minesweeping activities on land; and participating in basic reconnaissance operations.

Illustrative examples: Infantryman, Machine Gunner, Mortarman

55-3017 Radar and Sonar Technicians

Operate equipment using radio or sound wave technology to identify, track, and analyze objects or natural phenomena of military interest. Includes airborne, shipboard, and terrestrial positions. May perform minor maintenance.

Illustrative examples: Field Artillery Radar Operator, Sonar Subsystem Equipment Operator, Space Systems Operations Craftsman

55-3018 Special Forces

Implement unconventional operations by air, land, or sea during combat or peacetime as members of elite teams. These activities include offensive raids, demolitions, reconnaissance, search and rescue, and counterterrorism. In addition to their combat training, special forces members often have specialized training in swimming, diving, parachuting, survival, emergency medicine, and foreign languages. Duties include conducting advanced reconnaissance operations and collecting intelligence information; recruiting, training, and equipping friendly forces; conducting raids and invasions on enemy territories; laying and detonating explosives for demolition targets; locating, identifying, defusing, and disposing of ordnance; and operating and maintaining sophisticated communications equipment.

Illustrative examples: Combatant Swimmer (SEAL), Pararescue Craftsman, Special Forces Weapons Sergeant

55-3019 Military Enlisted Tactical Operations and Air/Weapons Specialists and Crew Members, All Other

All military enlisted tactical operations and air/weapons specialists and crew members not listed separately.

Illustrative examples: Electronic Warfare Specialist, Landing Support Specialist, Psychological Operations Specialist

Appendices

Appendix A: Crosswalk from the 2000 SOC to the 2010 SOC

Appendix A matches every detailed occupation from the 2000 SOC with the corresponding new 2010 SOC code(s) and title(s). A single asterisk (*) after the occupation code and title in the first column means that the occupation in the second column makes up only part of the occupation in the first column; that is, the asterisked 2000 SOC occupation has been divided into multiple new occupations. Likewise, a double asterisk (**) after the occupation code and title in the second column means that the occupation in the first column makes up only part of the occupation in the second column; that is, the double asterisked 2010 SOC occupation has been created from multiple 2000 SOC codes. Each occupation with the (*) or (**) notation appears multiple times in the chart.

For example, as shown below, the 2010 SOC occupation 11-9013 "Farmers, Ranchers, and Other Agricultural Managers**" (with two asterisks) was created from two 2000 SOC occupations: 11-9011 Farm, Ranch, and Other Agricultural Managers and 11-9012 Farmers and Ranchers. The 2000 SOC occupation; 11-9061 "Funeral Directors*" (with one asterisk) was divided into two occupations in the 2010 SOC: 11-9061 "Funeral Service Managers" and 39-4031 "Morticians, Undertakers, and Funeral Directors."

2000 SOC code	2000 SOC title	2010 SOC code	2010 SOC title
11-9011	Farm, Ranch, and Other Agricultural Managers	11-9013	Farmers, Ranchers, and Other Agricultural Managers**
11-9012	Farmers and Ranchers	11-9013	Farmers, Ranchers, and Other Agricultural Managers**
11-9061	Funeral Directors *	11-9061	Funeral Service Managers
11-9061	Funeral Directors*	39-4031	Morticians, Undertakers, and Funeral Directors

Appendix A: Crosswalk to the 2010 SOC

2000 SOC code	2000 SOC title	2010 SOC code	2010 SOC title
11-1011	Chief Executives	11-1011	Chief Executives
11-1021	General and Operations Managers	11-1021	General and Operations Managers
11-1031	Legislators	11-1031	Legislators
11-2011	Advertising and Promotions Managers	11-2011	Advertising and Promotions Managers
11-2021	Marketing Managers	11-2021	Marketing Managers
11-2022	Sales Managers	11-2022	Sales Managers
11-2031	Public Relations Managers	11-2031	Public Relations and Fundraising Managers
11-3011	Administrative Services Managers	11-3011	Administrative Services Managers
11-3021	Computer and Information Systems Managers	11-3021	Computer and Information Systems Managers
11-3031	Financial Managers	11-3031	Financial Managers
11-3041	Compensation and Benefits Managers	11-3111	Compensation and Benefits Managers
11-3042	Training and Development Managers	11-3131	Training and Development Managers
11-3049	Human Resources Managers, All Other	11-3121	Human Resources Managers
11-3051	Industrial Production Managers	11-3051	Industrial Production Managers
11-3061	Purchasing Managers	11-3061	Purchasing Managers
11-3071	Transportation, Storage, and Distribution Managers	11-3071	Transportation, Storage, and Distribution Managers
11-9011	Farm, Ranch, and Other Agricultural Managers	11-9013	Farmers, Ranchers, and Other Agricultural Managers**
11-9012	Farmers and Ranchers	11-9013	Farmers, Ranchers, and Other Agricultural Managers**
11-9021	Construction Managers	11-9021	Construction Managers
11-9031	Education Administrators, Preschool and Child Care Center/Program	11-9031	Education Administrators, Preschool and Childcare Center/Program
11-9032	Education Administrators, Elementary and Secondary School	11-9032	Education Administrators, Elementary and Secondary School
11-9033	Education Administrators, Postsecondary	11-9033	Education Administrators, Postsecondary
11-9039	Education Administrators, All Other	11-9039	Education Administrators, All Other
11-9041	Engineering Managers	11-9041	Architectural and Engineering Managers
11-9051	Food Service Managers	11-9051	Food Service Managers

Appendix A: Crosswalk to the 2010 SOC

2000 SOC code	2000 SOC title	2010 SOC code	2010 SOC title
11-9061	Funeral Directors *	11-9061	Funeral Service Managers
11-9061	Funeral Directors*	39-4031	Morticians, Undertakers, and Funeral Directors
11-9071	Gaming Managers	11-9071	Gaming Managers
11-9081	Lodging Managers	11-9081	Lodging Managers
11-9111	Medical and Health Services Managers	11-9111	Medical and Health Services Managers
11-9121	Natural Sciences Managers	11-9121	Natural Sciences Managers
11-9131	Postmasters and Mail Superintendents	11-9131	Postmasters and Mail Superintendents
11-9141	Property, Real Estate, and Community Association Managers	11-9141	Property, Real Estate, and Community Association Managers
11-9151	Social and Community Service Managers	11-9151	Social and Community Service Managers
11-9199	Managers, All Other	11-9199	Managers, All Other
13-1011	Agents and Business Managers of Artists, Performers, and Athletes	13-1011	Agents and Business Managers of Artists, Performers, and Athletes
13-1021	Purchasing Agents and Buyers, Farm Products	13-1021	Buyers and Purchasing Agents, Farm Products
13-1022	Wholesale and Retail Buyers, Except Farm Products	13-1022	Wholesale and Retail Buyers, Except Farm Products
13-1023	Purchasing Agents, Except Wholesale, Retail, and Farm Products	13-1023	Purchasing Agents, Except Wholesale, Retail, and Farm Products
13-1031	Claims Adjusters, Examiners, and Investigators	13-1031	Claims Adjusters, Examiners, and Investigators
13-1032	Insurance Appraisers, Auto Damage	13-1032	Insurance Appraisers, Auto Damage
13-1041	Compliance Officers, Except Agriculture, Construction, Health and Safety, and Transportation*	13-1041	Compliance Officers
13-1041	Compliance Officers, Except Agriculture, Construction, Health and Safety, and Transportation*	33-9093	Transportation Security Screeners**
13-1051	Cost Estimators	13-1051	Cost Estimators
13-1061	Emergency Management Specialists	11-9161	Emergency Management Directors
13-1071	Employment, Recruitment, and Placement Specialists	13-1071	Human Resources Specialists**
13-1072	Compensation, Benefits, and Job Analysis Specialists	13-1141	Compensation, Benefits, and Job Analysis Specialists
13-1073	Training and Development Specialists	13-1151	Training and Development Specialists
13-1079	Human Resources, Training, and Labor Relations Specialists, All Other*	13-1071	Human Resources Specialists**
13-1079	Human Resources, Training, and Labor Relations Specialists, All Other*	13-1075	Labor Relations Specialists

Appendix A: Crosswalk to the 2010 SOC

2000 SOC code	2000 SOC title	2010 SOC code	2010 SOC title
13-1081	Logisticians	13-1081	Logisticians
13-1111	Management Analysts	13-1111	Management Analysts
13-1121	Meeting and Convention Planners	13-1121	Meeting, Convention, and Event Planners**
13-1199	Business Operations Specialists, All Other*	13-1121	Meeting, Convention, and Event Planners**
13-1199	Business Operations Specialists, All Other*	13-1161	Market Research Analysts and Marketing Specialists**
13-1199	Business Operations Specialists, All Other*	13-1199	Business Operations Specialists, All Other**
13-2011	Accountants and Auditors	13-2011	Accountants and Auditors
13-2021	Appraisers and Assessors of Real Estate	13-2021	Appraisers and Assessors of Real Estate
13-2031	Budget Analysts	13-2031	Budget Analysts
13-2041	Credit Analysts	13-2041	Credit Analysts
13-2051	Financial Analysts	13-2051	Financial Analysts
13-2052	Personal Financial Advisors	13-2052	Personal Financial Advisors
13-2053	Insurance Underwriters	13-2053	Insurance Underwriters
13-2061	Financial Examiners	13-2061	Financial Examiners
13-2071	Loan Counselors	13-2071	Credit Counselors
13-2072	Loan Officers	13-2072	Loan Officers
13-2081	Tax Examiners, Collectors, and Revenue Agents	13-2081	Tax Examiners and Collectors, and Revenue Agents
13-2082	Tax Preparers	13-2082	Tax Preparers
13-2099	Financial Specialists, All Other	13-2099	Financial Specialists, All Other
15-1011	Computer and Information Scientists, Research	15-1111	Computer and Information Research Scientists
15-1021	Computer Programmers	15-1131	Computer Programmers
15-1031	Computer Software Engineers, Applications	15-1132	Software Developers, Applications
15-1032	Computer Software Engineers, Systems Software	15-1133	Software Developers, Systems Software
15-1041	Computer Support Specialists	15-1151	Computer User Support Specialists

Appendix A: Crosswalk to the 2010 SOC

2000 SOC code	2000 SOC title	2010 SOC code	2010 SOC title
15-1051	Computer Systems Analysts*	15-1143	Computer Network Architects**
15-1051	Computer Systems Analysts*	15-1121	Computer Systems Analysts
15-1061	Database Administrators	15-1141	Database Administrators
15-1071	Network and Computer Systems Administrators	15-1142	Network and Computer Systems Administrators**
15-1081	Network Systems and Data Communications Analysts*	15-1122	Information Security Analysts
15-1081	Network Systems and Data Communications Analysts*	15-1134	Web Developers
15-1081	Network Systems and Data Communications Analysts*	15-1142	Network and Computer Systems Administrators**
15-1081	Network Systems and Data Communications Analysts*	15-1143	Computer Network Architects**
15-1081	Network Systems and Data Communications Analysts*	15-1152	Computer Network Support Specialists
15-1099	Computer Specialists, All Other	15-1199	Computer Occupations, All Other
15-2011	Actuaries	15-2011	Actuaries
15-2021	Mathematicians	15-2021	Mathematicians
15-2031	Operations Research Analysts	15-2031	Operations Research Analysts
15-2041	Statisticians	15-2041	Statisticians
15-2091	Mathematical Technicians	15-2091	Mathematical Technicians
15-2099	Mathematical Science Occupations, All Other	15-2099	Mathematical Science Occupations, All Other
17-1011	Architects, Except Landscape and Naval	17-1011	Architects, Except Landscape and Naval
17-1012	Landscape Architects	17-1012	Landscape Architects
17-1021	Cartographers and Photogrammetrists	17-1021	Cartographers and Photogrammetrists
17-1022	Surveyors	17-1022	Surveyors
17-2011	Aerospace Engineers	17-2011	Aerospace Engineers
17-2021	Agricultural Engineers	17-2021	Agricultural Engineers
17-2031	Biomedical Engineers	17-2031	Biomedical Engineers
17-2041	Chemical Engineers	17-2041	Chemical Engineers
17-2051	Civil Engineers	17-2051	Civil Engineers

Appendix A: Crosswalk to the 2010 SOC

2000 SOC code	2000 SOC title	2010 SOC code	2010 SOC title
17-2061	Computer Hardware Engineers	17-2061	Computer Hardware Engineers
17-2071	Electrical Engineers	17-2071	Electrical Engineers
17-2072	Electronics Engineers, Except Computer	17-2072	Electronics Engineers, Except Computer
17-2081	Environmental Engineers	17-2081	Environmental Engineers
17-2111	Health and Safety Engineers, Except Mining Safety Engineers and Inspectors	17-2111	Health and Safety Engineers, Except Mining Safety Engineers and Inspectors
17-2112	Industrial Engineers	17-2112	Industrial Engineers
17-2121	Marine Engineers and Naval Architects	17-2121	Marine Engineers and Naval Architects
17-2131	Materials Engineers	17-2131	Materials Engineers
17-2141	Mechanical Engineers	17-2141	Mechanical Engineers
17-2151	Mining and Geological Engineers, Including Mining Safety Engineers	17-2151	Mining and Geological Engineers, Including Mining Safety Engineers
17-2161	Nuclear Engineers	17-2161	Nuclear Engineers
17-2171	Petroleum Engineers	17-2171	Petroleum Engineers
17-2199	Engineers, All Other	17-2199	Engineers, All Other
17-3011	Architectural and Civil Drafters	17-3011	Architectural and Civil Drafters
17-3012	Electrical and Electronics Drafters	17-3012	Electrical and Electronics Drafters
17-3013	Mechanical Drafters	17-3013	Mechanical Drafters
17-3019	Drafters, All Other	17-3019	Drafters, All Other
17-3021	Aerospace Engineering and Operations Technicians	17-3021	Aerospace Engineering and Operations Technicians
17-3022	Civil Engineering Technicians	17-3022	Civil Engineering Technicians
17-3023	Electrical and Electronic Engineering Technicians	17-3023	Electrical and Electronics Engineering Technicians
17-3024	Electro-Mechanical Technicians	17-3024	Electro-Mechanical Technicians
17-3025	Environmental Engineering Technicians	17-3025	Environmental Engineering Technicians
17-3026	Industrial Engineering Technicians	17-3026	Industrial Engineering Technicians
17-3027	Mechanical Engineering Technicians	17-3027	Mechanical Engineering Technicians
17-3029	Engineering Technicians, Except Drafters, All Other	17-3029	Engineering Technicians, Except Drafters, All Other

Appendix A: Crosswalk to the 2010 SOC

2000 SOC code	2000 SOC title	2010 SOC code	2010 SOC title
17-3031	Surveying and Mapping Technicians	17-3031	Surveying and Mapping Technicians
19-1011	Animal Scientists	19-1011	Animal Scientists
19-1012	Food Scientists and Technologists	19-1012	Food Scientists and Technologists
19-1013	Soil and Plant Scientists	19-1013	Soil and Plant Scientists
19-1021	Biochemists and Biophysicists	19-1021	Biochemists and Biophysicists
19-1022	Microbiologists	19-1022	Microbiologists
19-1023	Zoologists and Wildlife Biologists	19-1023	Zoologists and Wildlife Biologists
19-1029	Biological Scientists, All Other	19-1029	Biological Scientists, All Other
19-1031	Conservation Scientists	19-1031	Conservation Scientists
19-1032	Foresters	19-1032	Foresters
19-1041	Epidemiologists	19-1041	Epidemiologists
19-1042	Medical Scientists, Except Epidemiologists	19-1042	Medical Scientists, Except Epidemiologists
19-1099	Life Scientists, All Other	19-1099	Life Scientists, All Other
19-2011	Astronomers	19-2011	Astronomers
19-2012	Physicists	19-2012	Physicists
19-2021	Atmospheric and Space Scientists	19-2021	Atmospheric and Space Scientists
19-2031	Chemists	19-2031	Chemists
19-2032	Materials Scientists	19-2032	Materials Scientists
19-2041	Environmental Scientists and Specialists, Including Health	19-2041	Environmental Scientists and Specialists, Including Health
19-2042	Geoscientists, Except Hydrologists and Geographers	19-2042	Geoscientists, Except Hydrologists and Geographers
19-2043	Hydrologists	19-2043	Hydrologists
19-2099	Physical Scientists, All Other	19-2099	Physical Scientists, All Other
19-3011	Economists	19-3011	Economists
19-3021	Market Research Analysts	13-1161	Market Research Analysts and Marketing Specialists**
19-3022	Survey Researchers	19-3022	Survey Researchers

Appendix A: Crosswalk to the 2010 SOC

2000 SOC code	2000 SOC title	2010 SOC code	2010 SOC title
19-3031	Clinical, Counseling, and School Psychologists	19-3031	Clinical, Counseling, and School Psychologists
19-3032	Industrial-Organizational Psychologists	19-3032	Industrial-Organizational Psychologists
19-3039	Psychologists, All Other	19-3039	Psychologists, All Other
19-3041	Sociologists	19-3041	Sociologists
19-3051	Urban and Regional Planners	19-3051	Urban and Regional Planners
19-3091	Anthropologists and Archeologists	19-3091	Anthropologists and Archeologists
19-3092	Geographers	19-3092	Geographers
19-3093	Historians	19-3093	Historians
19-3094	Political Scientists	19-3094	Political Scientists
19-3099	Social Scientists and Related Workers, All Other	19-3099	Social Scientists and Related Workers, All Other
19-4011	Agricultural and Food Science Technicians	19-4011	Agricultural and Food Science Technicians
19-4021	Biological Technicians	19-4021	Biological Technicians
19-4031	Chemical Technicians	19-4031	Chemical Technicians
19-4041	Geological and Petroleum Technicians	19-4041	Geological and Petroleum Technicians
19-4051	Nuclear Technicians	19-4051	Nuclear Technicians
19-4061	Social Science Research Assistants	19-4061	Social Science Research Assistants
19-4091	Environmental Science and Protection Technicians, Including Health	19-4091	Environmental Science and Protection Technicians, Including Health
19-4092	Forensic Science Technicians	19-4092	Forensic Science Technicians
19-4093	Forest and Conservation Technicians	19-4093	Forest and Conservation Technicians
19-4099	Life, Physical, and Social Science Technicians, All Other	19-4099	Life, Physical, and Social Science Technicians, All Other
21-1011	Substance Abuse and Behavioral Disorder Counselors	21-1011	Substance Abuse and Behavioral Disorder Counselors
21-1012	Educational, Vocational, and School Counselors	21-1012	Educational, Guidance, School, and Vocational Counselors
21-1013	Marriage and Family Therapists	21-1013	Marriage and Family Therapists
21-1014	Mental Health Counselors	21-1014	Mental Health Counselors
21-1015	Rehabilitation Counselors	21-1015	Rehabilitation Counselors

Appendix A: Crosswalk to the 2010 SOC

2000 SOC code	2000 SOC title	2010 SOC code	2010 SOC title
21-1019	Counselors, All Other	21-1019	Counselors, All Other
21-1021	Child, Family, and School Social Workers	21-1021	Child, Family, and School Social Workers
21-1022	Medical and Public Health Social Workers	21-1022	Healthcare Social Workers
21-1023	Mental Health and Substance Abuse Social Workers	21-1023	Mental Health and Substance Abuse Social Workers
21-1029	Social Workers, All Other	21-1029	Social Workers, All Other
21-1091	Health Educators*	21-1091	Health Educators
21-1091	Health Educators*	21-1094	Community Health Workers**
21-1092	Probation Officers and Correctional Treatment Specialists	21-1092	Probation Officers and Correctional Treatment Specialists
21-1093	Social and Human Service Assistants	21-1093	Social and Human Service Assistants
21-1099	Community and Social Service Specialists, All Other*	21-1094	Community Health Workers**
21-1099	Community and Social Service Specialists, All Other*	21-1099	Community and Social Service Specialists, All Other
21-2011	Clergy	21-2011	Clergy
21-2021	Directors, Religious Activities and Education	21-2021	Directors, Religious Activities and Education
21-2099	Religious Workers, All Other	21-2099	Religious Workers, All Other
23-1011	Lawyers	23-1011	Lawyers
23-1021	Administrative Law Judges, Adjudicators, and Hearing Officers	23-1021	Administrative Law Judges, Adjudicators, and Hearing Officers
23-1022	Arbitrators, Mediators, and Conciliators	23-1022	Arbitrators, Mediators, and Conciliators
23-1023	Judges, Magistrate Judges, and Magistrates	23-1023	Judges, Magistrate Judges, and Magistrates
23-2011	Paralegals and Legal Assistants	23-2011	Paralegals and Legal Assistants**
23-2091	Court Reporters	23-2091	Court Reporters
23-2092	Law Clerks*	23-1012	Judicial Law Clerks
23-2092	Law Clerks*	23-2011	Paralegals and Legal Assistants**
23-2093	Title Examiners, Abstractors, and Searchers	23-2093	Title Examiners, Abstractors, and Searchers
23-2099	Legal Support Workers, All Other	23-2099	Legal Support Workers, All Other
25-1011	Business Teachers, Postsecondary	25-1011	Business Teachers, Postsecondary

Appendix A: Crosswalk to the 2010 SOC

2000 SOC code	2000 SOC title	2010 SOC code	2010 SOC title
25-1021	Computer Science Teachers, Postsecondary	25-1021	Computer Science Teachers, Postsecondary
25-1022	Mathematical Science Teachers, Postsecondary	25-1022	Mathematical Science Teachers, Postsecondary
25-1031	Architecture Teachers, Postsecondary	25-1031	Architecture Teachers, Postsecondary
25-1032	Engineering Teachers, Postsecondary	25-1032	Engineering Teachers, Postsecondary
25-1041	Agricultural Sciences Teachers, Postsecondary	25-1041	Agricultural Sciences Teachers, Postsecondary
25-1042	Biological Science Teachers, Postsecondary	25-1042	Biological Science Teachers, Postsecondary
25-1043	Forestry and Conservation Science Teachers, Postsecondary	25-1043	Forestry and Conservation Science Teachers, Postsecondary
25-1051	Atmospheric, Earth, Marine, and Space Sciences Teachers, Postsecondary	25-1051	Atmospheric, Earth, Marine, and Space Sciences Teachers, Postsecondary
25-1052	Chemistry Teachers, Postsecondary	25-1052	Chemistry Teachers, Postsecondary
25-1053	Environmental Science Teachers, Postsecondary	25-1053	Environmental Science Teachers, Postsecondary
25-1054	Physics Teachers, Postsecondary	25-1054	Physics Teachers, Postsecondary
25-1061	Anthropology and Archeology Teachers, Postsecondary	25-1061	Anthropology and Archeology Teachers, Postsecondary
25-1062	Area, Ethnic, and Cultural Studies Teachers, Postsecondary	25-1062	Area, Ethnic, and Cultural Studies Teachers, Postsecondary
25-1063	Economics Teachers, Postsecondary	25-1063	Economics Teachers, Postsecondary
25-1064	Geography Teachers, Postsecondary	25-1064	Geography Teachers, Postsecondary
25-1065	Political Science Teachers, Postsecondary	25-1065	Political Science Teachers, Postsecondary
25-1066	Psychology Teachers, Postsecondary	25-1066	Psychology Teachers, Postsecondary
25-1067	Sociology Teachers, Postsecondary	25-1067	Sociology Teachers, Postsecondary
25-1069	Social Sciences Teachers, Postsecondary, All Other	25-1069	Social Sciences Teachers, Postsecondary, All Other
25-1071	Health Specialties Teachers, Postsecondary	25-1071	Health Specialties Teachers, Postsecondary
25-1072	Nursing Instructors and Teachers, Postsecondary	25-1072	Nursing Instructors and Teachers, Postsecondary
25-1081	Education Teachers, Postsecondary	25-1081	Education Teachers, Postsecondary
25-1082	Library Science Teachers, Postsecondary	25-1082	Library Science Teachers, Postsecondary
25-1111	Criminal Justice and Law Enforcement Teachers, Postsecondary	25-1111	Criminal Justice and Law Enforcement Teachers, Postsecondary
25-1112	Law Teachers, Postsecondary	25-1112	Law Teachers, Postsecondary

Appendix A: Crosswalk to the 2010 SOC

2000 SOC code	2000 SOC title	2010 SOC code	2010 SOC title
25-1113	Social Work Teachers, Postsecondary	25-1113	Social Work Teachers, Postsecondary
25-1121	Art, Drama, and Music Teachers, Postsecondary	25-1121	Art, Drama, and Music Teachers, Postsecondary
25-1122	Communications Teachers, Postsecondary	25-1122	Communications Teachers, Postsecondary
25-1123	English Language and Literature Teachers, Postsecondary	25-1123	English Language and Literature Teachers, Postsecondary
25-1124	Foreign Language and Literature Teachers, Postsecondary	25-1124	Foreign Language and Literature Teachers, Postsecondary
25-1125	History Teachers, Postsecondary	25-1125	History Teachers, Postsecondary
25-1126	Philosophy and Religion Teachers, Postsecondary	25-1126	Philosophy and Religion Teachers, Postsecondary
25-1191	Graduate Teaching Assistants	25-1191	Graduate Teaching Assistants
25-1192	Home Economics Teachers, Postsecondary	25-1192	Home Economics Teachers, Postsecondary
25-1193	Recreation and Fitness Studies Teachers, Postsecondary	25-1193	Recreation and Fitness Studies Teachers, Postsecondary
25-1194	Vocational Education Teachers, Postsecondary	25-1194	Vocational Education Teachers, Postsecondary
25-1199	Postsecondary Teachers, All Other	25-1199	Postsecondary Teachers, All Other
25-2011	Preschool Teachers, Except Special Education	25-2011	Preschool Teachers, Except Special Education
25-2012	Kindergarten Teachers, Except Special Education	25-2012	Kindergarten Teachers, Except Special Education
25-2021	Elementary School Teachers, Except Special Education	25-2021	Elementary School Teachers, Except Special Education
25-2022	Middle School Teachers, Except Special and Vocational Education	25-2022	Middle School Teachers, Except Special and Career/Technical Education
25-2023	Vocational Education Teachers, Middle School	25-2023	Career/Technical Education Teachers, Middle School
25-2031	Secondary School Teachers, Except Special and Vocational Education	25-2031	Secondary School Teachers, Except Special and Career/Technical Education
25-2032	Vocational Education Teachers, Secondary School	25-2032	Career/Technical Education Teachers, Secondary School
25-2041	Special Education Teachers, Preschool, Kindergarten, and Elementary School*	25-2051	Special Education Teachers, Preschool
25-2041	Special Education Teachers, Preschool, Kindergarten, and Elementary School*	25-2052	Special Education Teachers, Kindergarten and Elementary School
25-2042	Special Education Teachers, Middle School	25-2053	Special Education Teachers, Middle School
25-2043	Special Education Teachers, Secondary School	25-2054	Special Education Teachers, Secondary School
25-3011	Adult Literacy, Remedial Education, and GED Teachers and Instructors	25-3011	Adult Basic and Secondary Education and Literacy Teachers and Instructors
25-3021	Self-Enrichment Education Teachers	25-3021	Self-Enrichment Education Teachers

Appendix A: Crosswalk to the 2010 SOC

2000 SOC code	2000 SOC title	2010 SOC code	2010 SOC title
27-4014	Sound Engineering Technicians	27-4014	Sound Engineering Technicians
27-4021	Photographers	27-4021	Photographers
27-4031	Camera Operators, Television, Video, and Motion Picture	27-4031	Camera Operators, Television, Video, and Motion Picture
27-4032	Film and Video Editors	27-4032	Film and Video Editors
27-4099	Media and Communication Equipment Workers, All Other	27-4099	Media and Communication Equipment Workers, All Other
29-1011	Chiropractors	29-1011	Chiropractors
29-1021	Dentists, General	29-1021	Dentists, General
29-1022	Oral and Maxillofacial Surgeons	29-1022	Oral and Maxillofacial Surgeons
29-1023	Orthodontists	29-1023	Orthodontists
29-1024	Prosthodontists	29-1024	Prosthodontists
29-1029	Dentists, All Other Specialists	29-1029	Dentists, All Other Specialists
29-1031	Dietitians and Nutritionists	29-1031	Dietitians and Nutritionists
29-1041	Optometrists	29-1041	Optometrists
29-1051	Pharmacists	29-1051	Pharmacists
29-1061	Anesthesiologists	29-1061	Anesthesiologists
29-1062	Family and General Practitioners	29-1062	Family and General Practitioners
29-1063	Internists, General	29-1063	Internists, General
29-1064	Obstetricians and Gynecologists	29-1064	Obstetricians and Gynecologists
29-1065	Pediatricians, General	29-1065	Pediatricians, General
29-1066	Psychiatrists	29-1066	Psychiatrists
29-1067	Surgeons	29-1067	Surgeons
29-1069	Physicians and Surgeons, All Other	29-1069	Physicians and Surgeons, All Other
29-1071	Physician Assistants	29-1071	Physician Assistants
29-1081	Podiatrists	29-1081	Podiatrists

Appendix A: Crosswalk to the 2010 SOC

2000 SOC code	2000 SOC title	2010 SOC code	2010 SOC title
29-1111	Registered Nurses*	29-1141	Registered Nurses
29-1111	Registered Nurses*	29-1151	Nurse Anesthetists
29-1111	Registered Nurses*	29-1161	Nurse Midwives
29-1111	Registered Nurses*	29-1171	Nurse Practitioners
29-1121	Audiologists	29-1181	Audiologists
29-1122	Occupational Therapists	29-1122	Occupational Therapists
29-1123	Physical Therapists	29-1123	Physical Therapists
29-1124	Radiation Therapists	29-1124	Radiation Therapists
29-1125	Recreational Therapists	29-1125	Recreational Therapists
29-1126	Respiratory Therapists	29-1126	Respiratory Therapists
29-1127	Speech-Language Pathologists	29-1127	Speech-Language Pathologists
29-1129	Therapists, All Other*	29-1128	Exercise Physiologists
29-1129	Therapists, All Other*	29-1129	Therapists, All Other
29-1131	Veterinarians	29-1131	Veterinarians
29-1199	Health Diagnosing and Treating Practitioners, All Other	29-1199	Health Diagnosing and Treating Practitioners, All Other
29-2011	Medical and Clinical Laboratory Technologists	29-2011	Medical and Clinical Laboratory Technologists
29-2012	Medical and Clinical Laboratory Technicians	29-2012	Medical and Clinical Laboratory Technicians
29-2021	Dental Hygienists	29-2021	Dental Hygienists
29-2031	Cardiovascular Technologists and Technicians	29-2031	Cardiovascular Technologists and Technicians
29-2032	Diagnostic Medical Sonographers	29-2032	Diagnostic Medical Sonographers
29-2033	Nuclear Medicine Technologists	29-2033	Nuclear Medicine Technologists
29-2034	Radiologic Technologists and Technicians*	29-2034	Radiologic Technologists
29-2034	Radiologic Technologists and Technicians*	29-2035	Magnetic Resonance Imaging Technologists
29-2041	Emergency Medical Technicians and Paramedics	29-2041	Emergency Medical Technicians and Paramedics
29-2051	Dietetic Technicians	29-2051	Dietetic Technicians

Appendix A: Crosswalk to the 2010 SOC

2000 SOC code	2000 SOC title	2010 SOC code	2010 SOC title
29-2052	Pharmacy Technicians	29-2052	Pharmacy Technicians
29-2053	Psychiatric Technicians	29-2053	Psychiatric Technicians
29-2054	Respiratory Therapy Technicians	29-2054	Respiratory Therapy Technicians
29-2055	Surgical Technologists	29-2055	Surgical Technologists
29-2056	Veterinary Technologists and Technicians	29-2056	Veterinary Technologists and Technicians
29-2061	Licensed Practical and Licensed Vocational Nurses	29-2061	Licensed Practical and Licensed Vocational Nurses
29-2071	Medical Records and Health Information Technicians	29-2071	Medical Records and Health Information Technicians
29-2081	Opticians, Dispensing	29-2081	Opticians, Dispensing
29-2091	Orthotists and Prosthetists	29-2091	Orthotists and Prosthetists
29-2099	Health Technologists and Technicians, All Other*	29-2092	Hearing Aid Specialists
29-2099	Health Technologists and Technicians, All Other*	29-2057	Ophthalmic Medical Technicians
29-2099	Health Technologists and Technicians, All Other*	29-2099	Health Technologists and Technicians, All Other
29-9011	Occupational Health and Safety Specialists	29-9011	Occupational Health and Safety Specialists
29-9012	Occupational Health and Safety Technicians	29-9012	Occupational Health and Safety Technicians
29-9091	Athletic Trainers	29-9091	Athletic Trainers
29-9099	Healthcare Practitioners and Technical Workers, All Other*	29-9092	Genetic Counselors
29-9099	Healthcare Practitioners and Technical Workers, All Other*	29-9099	Healthcare Practitioners and Technical Workers, All Other
31-1011	Home Health Aides	31-1011	Home Health Aides
31-1012	Nursing Aides, Orderlies, and Attendants*	31-1015	Orderlies
31-1012	Nursing Aides, Orderlies, and Attendants*	31-1014	Nursing Assistants
31-1013	Psychiatric Aides	31-1013	Psychiatric Aides
31-2011	Occupational Therapist Assistants	31-2011	Occupational Therapy Assistants
31-2012	Occupational Therapist Aides	31-2012	Occupational Therapy Aides
31-2021	Physical Therapist Assistants	31-2021	Physical Therapist Assistants
31-2022	Physical Therapist Aides	31-2022	Physical Therapist Aides

Appendix A: Crosswalk to the 2010 SOC

2000 SOC code	2000 SOC title	2010 SOC code	2010 SOC title
31-9011	Massage Therapists	31-9011	Massage Therapists
31-9091	Dental Assistants	31-9091	Dental Assistants
31-9092	Medical Assistants	31-9092	Medical Assistants
31-9093	Medical Equipment Preparers	31-9093	Medical Equipment Preparers
31-9094	Medical Transcriptionists	31-9094	Medical Transcriptionists
31-9095	Pharmacy Aides	31-9095	Pharmacy Aides
31-9096	Veterinary Assistants and Laboratory Animal Caretakers	31-9096	Veterinary Assistants and Laboratory Animal Caretakers
31-9099	Healthcare Support Workers, All Other*	31-9097	Phlebotomists
31-9099	Healthcare Support Workers, All Other*	31-9099	Healthcare Support Workers, All Other
33-1011	First-Line Supervisors/Managers of Correctional Officers	33-1011	First-Line Supervisors of Correctional Officers
33-1012	First-Line Supervisors/Managers of Police and Detectives	33-1012	First-Line Supervisors of Police and Detectives
33-1021	First-Line Supervisors/Managers of Fire Fighting and Prevention Workers	33-1021	First-Line Supervisors of Fire Fighting and Prevention Workers
33-1099	First-Line Supervisors/Managers, Protective Service Workers, All Other	33-1099	First-Line Supervisors of Protective Service Workers, All Other
33-2011	Fire Fighters	33-2011	Firefighters
33-2021	Fire Inspectors and Investigators	33-2021	Fire Inspectors and Investigators
33-2022	Forest Fire Inspectors and Prevention Specialists	33-2022	Forest Fire Inspectors and Prevention Specialists
33-3011	Bailiffs	33-3011	Bailiffs
33-3012	Correctional Officers and Jailers	33-3012	Correctional Officers and Jailers
33-3021	Detectives and Criminal Investigators	33-3021	Detectives and Criminal Investigators
33-3031	Fish and Game Wardens	33-3031	Fish and Game Wardens
33-3041	Parking Enforcement Workers	33-3041	Parking Enforcement Workers
33-3051	Police and Sheriff's Patrol Officers	33-3051	Police and Sheriff's Patrol Officers
33-3052	Transit and Railroad Police	33-3052	Transit and Railroad Police
33-9011	Animal Control Workers	33-9011	Animal Control Workers
33-9021	Private Detectives and Investigators	33-9021	Private Detectives and Investigators

Appendix A: Crosswalk to the 2010 SOC

2000 SOC code	2000 SOC title	2010 SOC code	2010 SOC title
33-9031	Gaming Surveillance Officers and Gaming Investigators	33-9031	Gaming Surveillance Officers and Gaming Investigators
33-9032	Security Guards*	33-9032	Security Guards
33-9032	Security Guards*	33-9093	Transportation Security Screeners**
33-9091	Crossing Guards	33-9091	Crossing Guards
33-9092	Lifeguards, Ski Patrol, and Other Recreational Protective Service Workers	33-9092	Lifeguards, Ski Patrol, and Other Recreational Protective Service Workers
33-9099	Protective Service Workers, All Other*	33-9093	Transportation Security Screeners**
33-9099	Protective Service Workers, All Other*	33-9099	Protective Service Workers, All Other
35-1011	Chefs and Head Cooks	35-1011	Chefs and Head Cooks
35-1012	First-Line Supervisors/Managers of Food Preparation and Serving Workers	35-1012	First-Line Supervisors of Food Preparation and Serving Workers
35-2011	Cooks, Fast Food	35-2011	Cooks, Fast Food
35-2012	Cooks, Institution and Cafeteria	35-2012	Cooks, Institution and Cafeteria
35-2013	Cooks, Private Household	35-2013	Cooks, Private Household
35-2014	Cooks, Restaurant	35-2014	Cooks, Restaurant
35-2015	Cooks, Short Order	35-2015	Cooks, Short Order
35-2019	Cooks, All Other	35-2019	Cooks, All Other
35-2021	Food Preparation Workers	35-2021	Food Preparation Workers
35-3011	Bartenders	35-3011	Bartenders
35-3021	Combined Food Preparation and Serving Workers, Including Fast Food	35-3021	Combined Food Preparation and Serving Workers, Including Fast Food
35-3022	Counter Attendants, Cafeteria, Food Concession, and Coffee Shop	35-3022	Counter Attendants, Cafeteria, Food Concession, and Coffee Shop
35-3031	Waiters and Waitresses	35-3031	Waiters and Waitresses
35-3041	Food Servers, Nonrestaurant	35-3041	Food Servers, Nonrestaurant
35-9011	Dining Room and Cafeteria Attendants and Bartender Helpers	35-9011	Dining Room and Cafeteria Attendants and Bartender Helpers
35-9021	Dishwashers	35-9021	Dishwashers
35-9031	Hosts and Hostesses, Restaurant, Lounge, and Coffee Shop	35-9031	Hosts and Hostesses, Restaurant, Lounge, and Coffee Shop
35-9099	Food Preparation and Serving Related Workers, All Other	35-9099	Food Preparation and Serving Related Workers, All Other

Appendix A: Crosswalk to the 2010 SOC

2000 SOC code	2000 SOC title	2010 SOC code	2010 SOC title
37-1011	First-Line Supervisors/Managers of Housekeeping and Janitorial Workers	37-1011	First-Line Supervisors of Housekeeping and Janitorial Workers
37-1012	First-Line Supervisors/Managers of Landscaping, Lawn Service, and Groundskeeping Workers	37-1012	First-Line Supervisors of Landscaping, Lawn Service, and Groundskeeping Workers
37-2011	Janitors and Cleaners, Except Maids and Housekeeping Cleaners	37-2011	Janitors and Cleaners, Except Maids and Housekeeping Cleaners
37-2012	Maids and Housekeeping Cleaners	37-2012	Maids and Housekeeping Cleaners
37-2019	Building Cleaning Workers, All Other	37-2019	Building Cleaning Workers, All Other
37-2021	Pest Control Workers	37-2021	Pest Control Workers
37-3011	Landscaping and Groundskeeping Workers	37-3011	Landscaping and Groundskeeping Workers
37-3012	Pesticide Handlers, Sprayers, and Applicators, Vegetation	37-3012	Pesticide Handlers, Sprayers, and Applicators, Vegetation
37-3013	Tree Trimmers and Pruners	37-3013	Tree Trimmers and Pruners
37-3019	Grounds Maintenance Workers, All Other	37-3019	Grounds Maintenance Workers, All Other
39-1011	Gaming Supervisors	39-1011	Gaming Supervisors
39-1012	Slot Key Persons	39-1012	Slot Supervisors
39-1021	First-Line Supervisors/Managers of Personal Service Workers	39-1021	First-Line Supervisors of Personal Service Workers
39-2011	Animal Trainers	39-2011	Animal Trainers
39-2021	Nonfarm Animal Caretakers	39-2021	Nonfarm Animal Caretakers
39-3011	Gaming Dealers	39-3011	Gaming Dealers
39-3012	Gaming and Sports Book Writers and Runners	39-3012	Gaming and Sports Book Writers and Runners
39-3019	Gaming Service Workers, All Other	39-3019	Gaming Service Workers, All Other
39-3021	Motion Picture Projectionists	39-3021	Motion Picture Projectionists
39-3031	Ushers, Lobby Attendants, and Ticket Takers	39-3031	Ushers, Lobby Attendants, and Ticket Takers
39-3091	Amusement and Recreation Attendants	39-3091	Amusement and Recreation Attendants
39-3092	Costume Attendants	39-3092	Costume Attendants
39-3093	Locker Room, Coatroom, and Dressing Room Attendants	39-3093	Locker Room, Coatroom, and Dressing Room Attendants
39-3099	Entertainment Attendants and Related Workers, All Other	39-3099	Entertainment Attendants and Related Workers, All Other
39-4011	Embalmers	39-4011	Embalmers

Appendix A: Crosswalk to the 2010 SOC

2000 SOC code	2000 SOC title	2010 SOC code	2010 SOC title
39-4021	Funeral Attendants	39-4021	Funeral Attendants
39-5011	Barbers	39-5011	Barbers
39-5012	Hairdressers, Hairstylists, and Cosmetologists	39-5012	Hairdressers, Hairstylists, and Cosmetologists
39-5091	Makeup Artists, Theatrical and Performance	39-5091	Makeup Artists, Theatrical and Performance
39-5092	Manicurists and Pedicurists	39-5092	Manicurists and Pedicurists
39-5093	Shampooers	39-5093	Shampooers
39-5094	Skin Care Specialists	39-5094	Skincare Specialists
39-6011	Baggage Porters and Bellhops	39-6011	Baggage Porters and Bellhops
39-6012	Concierges	39-6012	Concierges
39-6021	Tour Guides and Escorts	39-7011	Tour Guides and Escorts
39-6022	Travel Guides	39-7012	Travel Guides
39-6031	Flight Attendants	53-2031	Flight Attendants
39-6032	Transportation Attendants, Except Flight Attendants and Baggage Porters	53-6061	Transportation Attendants, Except Flight Attendants
39-9011	Child Care Workers	39-9011	Childcare Workers
39-9021	Personal and Home Care Aides	39-9021	Personal Care Aides
39-9031	Fitness Trainers and Aerobics Instructors	39-9031	Fitness Trainers and Aerobics Instructors
39-9032	Recreation Workers	39-9032	Recreation Workers
39-9041	Residential Advisors	39-9041	Residential Advisors
39-9099	Personal Care and Service Workers, All Other	39-9099	Personal Care and Service Workers, All Other
41-1011	First-Line Supervisors/Managers of Retail Sales Workers	41-1011	First-Line Supervisors of Retail Sales Workers
41-1012	First-Line Supervisors/Managers of Non-Retail Sales Workers	41-1012	First-Line Supervisors of Non-Retail Sales Workers
41-2011	Cashiers	41-2011	Cashiers
41-2012	Gaming Change Persons and Booth Cashiers	41-2012	Gaming Change Persons and Booth Cashiers
41-2021	Counter and Rental Clerks	41-2021	Counter and Rental Clerks
41-2022	Parts Salespersons	41-2022	Parts Salespersons

Appendix A: Crosswalk to the 2010 SOC

2000 SOC code	2000 SOC title	2010 SOC code	2010 SOC title
41-2031	Retail Salespersons	41-2031	Retail Salespersons
41-3011	Advertising Sales Agents	41-3011	Advertising Sales Agents
41-3021	Insurance Sales Agents	41-3021	Insurance Sales Agents
41-3031	Securities, Commodities, and Financial Services Sales Agents	41-3031	Securities, Commodities, and Financial Services Sales Agents
41-3041	Travel Agents	41-3041	Travel Agents
41-3099	Sales Representatives, Services, All Other	41-3099	Sales Representatives, Services, All Other
41-4011	Sales Representatives, Wholesale and Manufacturing, Technical and Scientific Products	41-4011	Sales Representatives, Wholesale and Manufacturing, Technical and Scientific Products
41-4012	Sales Representatives, Wholesale and Manufacturing, Except Technical and Scientific Products	41-4012	Sales Representatives, Wholesale and Manufacturing, Except Technical and Scientific Products
41-9011	Demonstrators and Product Promoters	41-9011	Demonstrators and Product Promoters
41-9012	Models	41-9012	Models
41-9021	Real Estate Brokers	41-9021	Real Estate Brokers
41-9022	Real Estate Sales Agents	41-9022	Real Estate Sales Agents
41-9031	Sales Engineers	41-9031	Sales Engineers
41-9041	Telemarketers	41-9041	Telemarketers
41-9091	Door-to-Door Sales Workers, News and Street Vendors, and Related Workers	41-9091	Door-to-Door Sales Workers, News and Street Vendors, and Related Workers
41-9099	Sales and Related Workers, All Other*	41-9099	Sales and Related Workers, All Other
41-9099	Sales and Related Workers, All Other*	13-1131	Fundraisers
43-1011	First-Line Supervisors/Managers of Office and Administrative Support Workers	43-1011	First-Line Supervisors of Office and Administrative Support Workers
43-2011	Switchboard Operators, Including Answering Service	43-2011	Switchboard Operators, Including Answering Service
43-2021	Telephone Operators	43-2021	Telephone Operators
43-2099	Communications Equipment Operators, All Other	43-2099	Communications Equipment Operators, All Other
43-3011	Bill and Account Collectors	43-3011	Bill and Account Collectors
43-3021	Billing and Posting Clerks and Machine Operators	43-3021	Billing and Posting Clerks
43-3031	Bookkeeping, Accounting, and Auditing Clerks	43-3031	Bookkeeping, Accounting, and Auditing Clerks
43-3041	Gaming Cage Workers	43-3041	Gaming Cage Workers

226

Appendix A: Crosswalk to the 2010 SOC

2000 SOC code	2000 SOC title	2010 SOC code	2010 SOC title
43-3051	Payroll and Timekeeping Clerks	43-3051	Payroll and Timekeeping Clerks
43-3061	Procurement Clerks	43-3061	Procurement Clerks
43-3071	Tellers	43-3071	Tellers
43-4011	Brokerage Clerks	43-4011	Brokerage Clerks
43-4021	Correspondence Clerks	43-4021	Correspondence Clerks
43-4031	Court, Municipal, and License Clerks	43-4031	Court, Municipal, and License Clerks
43-4041	Credit Authorizers, Checkers, and Clerks	43-4041	Credit Authorizers, Checkers, and Clerks
43-4051	Customer Service Representatives	43-4051	Customer Service Representatives
43-4061	Eligibility Interviewers, Government Programs	43-4061	Eligibility Interviewers, Government Programs
43-4071	File Clerks	43-4071	File Clerks
43-4081	Hotel, Motel, and Resort Desk Clerks	43-4081	Hotel, Motel, and Resort Desk Clerks
43-4111	Interviewers, Except Eligibility and Loan	43-4111	Interviewers, Except Eligibility and Loan
43-4121	Library Assistants, Clerical	43-4121	Library Assistants, Clerical
43-4131	Loan Interviewers and Clerks	43-4131	Loan Interviewers and Clerks
43-4141	New Accounts Clerks	43-4141	New Accounts Clerks
43-4151	Order Clerks	43-4151	Order Clerks
43-4161	Human Resources Assistants, Except Payroll and Timekeeping	43-4161	Human Resources Assistants, Except Payroll and Timekeeping
43-4171	Receptionists and Information Clerks	43-4171	Receptionists and Information Clerks
43-4181	Reservation and Transportation Ticket Agents and Travel Clerks	43-4181	Reservation and Transportation Ticket Agents and Travel Clerks
43-4199	Information and Record Clerks, All Other	43-4199	Information and Record Clerks, All Other
43-5011	Cargo and Freight Agents	43-5011	Cargo and Freight Agents
43-5021	Couriers and Messengers	43-5021	Couriers and Messengers
43-5031	Police, Fire, and Ambulance Dispatchers	43-5031	Police, Fire, and Ambulance Dispatchers
43-5032	Dispatchers, Except Police, Fire, and Ambulance	43-5032	Dispatchers, Except Police, Fire, and Ambulance
43-5041	Meter Readers, Utilities	43-5041	Meter Readers, Utilities

Appendix A: Crosswalk to the 2010 SOC

2000 SOC code	2000 SOC title	2010 SOC code	2010 SOC title
43-5051	Postal Service Clerks	43-5051	Postal Service Clerks
43-5052	Postal Service Mail Carriers	43-5052	Postal Service Mail Carriers
43-5053	Postal Service Mail Sorters, Processors, and Processing Machine Operators	43-5053	Postal Service Mail Sorters, Processors, and Processing Machine Operators
43-5061	Production, Planning, and Expediting Clerks	43-5061	Production, Planning, and Expediting Clerks
43-5071	Shipping, Receiving, and Traffic Clerks	43-5071	Shipping, Receiving, and Traffic Clerks
43-5081	Stock Clerks and Order Fillers	43-5081	Stock Clerks and Order Fillers
43-5111	Weighers, Measurers, Checkers, and Samplers, Recordkeeping	43-5111	Weighers, Measurers, Checkers, and Samplers, Recordkeeping
43-6011	Executive Secretaries and Administrative Assistants	43-6011	Executive Secretaries and Executive Administrative Assistants
43-6012	Legal Secretaries	43-6012	Legal Secretaries
43-6013	Medical Secretaries	43-6013	Medical Secretaries
43-6014	Secretaries, Except Legal, Medical, and Executive	43-6014	Secretaries and Administrative Assistants, Except Legal, Medical, and Executive
43-9011	Computer Operators	43-9011	Computer Operators
43-9021	Data Entry Keyers	43-9021	Data Entry Keyers
43-9022	Word Processors and Typists	43-9022	Word Processors and Typists
43-9031	Desktop Publishers	43-9031	Desktop Publishers
43-9041	Insurance Claims and Policy Processing Clerks	43-9041	Insurance Claims and Policy Processing Clerks
43-9051	Mail Clerks and Mail Machine Operators, Except Postal Service	43-9051	Mail Clerks and Mail Machine Operators, Except Postal Service
43-9061	Office Clerks, General	43-9061	Office Clerks, General
43-9071	Office Machine Operators, Except Computer	43-9071	Office Machine Operators, Except Computer
43-9081	Proofreaders and Copy Markers	43-9081	Proofreaders and Copy Markers
43-9111	Statistical Assistants	43-9111	Statistical Assistants
43-9199	Office and Administrative Support Workers, All Other*	43-3099	Financial Clerks, All Other
43-9199	Office and Administrative Support Workers, All Other*	43-9199	Office and Administrative Support Workers, All Other
45-1011	First-Line Supervisors/Managers of Farming, Fishing, and Forestry Workers	45-1011	First-Line Supervisors of Farming, Fishing, and Forestry Workers
45-1012	Farm Labor Contractors	13-1074	Farm Labor Contractors

2000 SOC code	2000 SOC title	2010 SOC code	2010 SOC title
45-2011	Agricultural Inspectors	45-2011	Agricultural Inspectors
45-2021	Animal Breeders	45-2021	Animal Breeders
45-2041	Graders and Sorters, Agricultural Products	45-2041	Graders and Sorters, Agricultural Products
45-2091	Agricultural Equipment Operators	45-2091	Agricultural Equipment Operators
45-2092	Farmworkers and Laborers, Crop, Nursery, and Greenhouse	45-2092	Farmworkers and Laborers, Crop, Nursery, and Greenhouse
45-2093	Farmworkers, Farm and Ranch Animals	45-2093	Farmworkers, Farm, Ranch, and Aquacultural Animals
45-2099	Agricultural Workers, All Other	45-2099	Agricultural Workers, All Other
45-3011	Fishers and Related Fishing Workers	45-3011	Fishers and Related Fishing Workers
45-3021	Hunters and Trappers	45-3021	Hunters and Trappers
45-4011	Forest and Conservation Workers	45-4011	Forest and Conservation Workers
45-4021	Fallers	45-4021	Fallers
45-4022	Logging Equipment Operators	45-4022	Logging Equipment Operators
45-4023	Log Graders and Scalers	45-4023	Log Graders and Scalers
45-4029	Logging Workers, All Other	45-4029	Logging Workers, All Other
47-1011	First-Line Supervisors/Managers of Construction Trades and Extraction Workers	47-1011	First-Line Supervisors of Construction Trades and Extraction Workers
47-2011	Boilermakers	47-2011	Boilermakers
47-2021	Brickmasons and Blockmasons	47-2021	Brickmasons and Blockmasons
47-2022	Stonemasons	47-2022	Stonemasons
47-2031	Carpenters	47-2031	Carpenters
47-2041	Carpet Installers	47-2041	Carpet Installers
47-2042	Floor Layers, Except Carpet, Wood, and Hard Tiles	47-2042	Floor Layers, Except Carpet, Wood, and Hard Tiles
47-2043	Floor Sanders and Finishers	47-2043	Floor Sanders and Finishers
47-2044	Tile and Marble Setters	47-2044	Tile and Marble Setters
47-2051	Cement Masons and Concrete Finishers	47-2051	Cement Masons and Concrete Finishers
47-2053	Terrazzo Workers and Finishers	47-2053	Terrazzo Workers and Finishers

Appendix A: Crosswalk to the 2010 SOC

2000 SOC code	2000 SOC title	2010 SOC code	2010 SOC title
47-2061	Construction Laborers	47-2061	Construction Laborers
47-2071	Paving, Surfacing, and Tamping Equipment Operators	47-2071	Paving, Surfacing, and Tamping Equipment Operators
47-2072	Pile-Driver Operators	47-2072	Pile-Driver Operators
47-2073	Operating Engineers and Other Construction Equipment Operators	47-2073	Operating Engineers and Other Construction Equipment Operators
47-2081	Drywall and Ceiling Tile Installers	47-2081	Drywall and Ceiling Tile Installers
47-2082	Tapers	47-2082	Tapers
47-2111	Electricians*	47-2111	Electricians
47-2111	Electricians*	47-2231	Solar Photovoltaic Installers**
47-2121	Glaziers	47-2121	Glaziers
47-2131	Insulation Workers, Floor, Ceiling, and Wall	47-2131	Insulation Workers, Floor, Ceiling, and Wall
47-2132	Insulation Workers, Mechanical	47-2132	Insulation Workers, Mechanical
47-2141	Painters, Construction and Maintenance	47-2141	Painters, Construction and Maintenance
47-2142	Paperhangers	47-2142	Paperhangers
47-2151	Pipelayers	47-2151	Pipelayers
47-2152	Plumbers, Pipefitters, and Steamfitters	47-2152	Plumbers, Pipefitters, and Steamfitters
47-2161	Plasterers and Stucco Masons	47-2161	Plasterers and Stucco Masons
47-2171	Reinforcing Iron and Rebar Workers	47-2171	Reinforcing Iron and Rebar Workers
47-2181	Roofers*	47-2181	Roofers
47-2181	Roofers*	47-2231	Solar Photovoltaic Installers**
47-2211	Sheet Metal Workers	47-2211	Sheet Metal Workers
47-2221	Structural Iron and Steel Workers	47-2221	Structural Iron and Steel Workers
47-3011	Helpers--Brickmasons, Blockmasons, Stonemasons, and Tile and Marble Setters	47-3011	Helpers--Brickmasons, Blockmasons, Stonemasons, and Tile and Marble Setters
47-3012	Helpers--Carpenters	47-3012	Helpers--Carpenters
47-3013	Helpers--Electricians	47-3013	Helpers--Electricians
47-3014	Helpers--Painters, Paperhangers, Plasterers, and Stucco Masons	47-3014	Helpers--Painters, Paperhangers, Plasterers, and Stucco Masons

Appendix A: Crosswalk to the 2010 SOC

2000 SOC code	2000 SOC title	2010 SOC code	2010 SOC title
47-3015	Helpers--Pipelayers, Plumbers, Pipefitters, and Steamfitters	47-3015	Helpers--Pipelayers, Plumbers, Pipefitters, and Steamfitters
47-3016	Helpers--Roofers	47-3016	Helpers--Roofers
47-3019	Helpers, Construction Trades, All Other	47-3019	Helpers, Construction Trades, All Other
47-4011	Construction and Building Inspectors	47-4011	Construction and Building Inspectors
47-4021	Elevator Installers and Repairers	47-4021	Elevator Installers and Repairers
47-4031	Fence Erectors	47-4031	Fence Erectors
47-4041	Hazardous Materials Removal Workers	47-4041	Hazardous Materials Removal Workers
47-4051	Highway Maintenance Workers	47-4051	Highway Maintenance Workers
47-4061	Rail-Track Laying and Maintenance Equipment Operators	47-4061	Rail-Track Laying and Maintenance Equipment Operators
47-4071	Septic Tank Servicers and Sewer Pipe Cleaners	47-4071	Septic Tank Servicers and Sewer Pipe Cleaners
47-4091	Segmental Pavers	47-4091	Segmental Pavers
47-4099	Construction and Related Workers, All Other*	47-2231	Solar Photovoltaic Installers**
47-4099	Construction and Related Workers, All Other*	47-4099	Construction and Related Workers, All Other
47-5011	Derrick Operators, Oil and Gas	47-5011	Derrick Operators, Oil and Gas
47-5012	Rotary Drill Operators, Oil and Gas	47-5012	Rotary Drill Operators, Oil and Gas
47-5013	Service Unit Operators, Oil, Gas, and Mining	47-5013	Service Unit Operators, Oil, Gas, and Mining
47-5021	Earth Drillers, Except Oil and Gas	47-5021	Earth Drillers, Except Oil and Gas
47-5031	Explosives Workers, Ordnance Handling Experts, and Blasters	47-5031	Explosives Workers, Ordnance Handling Experts, and Blasters
47-5041	Continuous Mining Machine Operators	47-5041	Continuous Mining Machine Operators
47-5042	Mine Cutting and Channeling Machine Operators	47-5042	Mine Cutting and Channeling Machine Operators
47-5049	Mining Machine Operators, All Other	47-5049	Mining Machine Operators, All Other
47-5051	Rock Splitters, Quarry	47-5051	Rock Splitters, Quarry
47-5061	Roof Bolters, Mining	47-5061	Roof Bolters, Mining
47-5071	Roustabouts, Oil and Gas	47-5071	Roustabouts, Oil and Gas
47-5081	Helpers--Extraction Workers	47-5081	Helpers--Extraction Workers

Appendix A: Crosswalk to the 2010 SOC

2000 SOC code	2000 SOC title	2010 SOC code	2010 SOC title
47-5099	Extraction Workers, All Other	47-5099	Extraction Workers, All Other
49-1011	First-Line Supervisors/Managers of Mechanics, Installers, and Repairers	49-1011	First-Line Supervisors of Mechanics, Installers, and Repairers
49-2011	Computer, Automated Teller, and Office Machine Repairers	49-2011	Computer, Automated Teller, and Office Machine Repairers
49-2021	Radio Mechanics	49-2021	Radio, Cellular, and Tower Equipment Installers and Repairers
49-2022	Telecommunications Equipment Installers and Repairers, Except Line Installers	49-2022	Telecommunications Equipment Installers and Repairers, Except Line Installers
49-2091	Avionics Technicians	49-2091	Avionics Technicians
49-2092	Electric Motor, Power Tool, and Related Repairers	49-2092	Electric Motor, Power Tool, and Related Repairers
49-2093	Electrical and Electronics Installers and Repairers, Transportation Equipment	49-2093	Electrical and Electronics Installers and Repairers, Transportation Equipment
49-2094	Electrical and Electronics Repairers, Commercial and Industrial Equipment	49-2094	Electrical and Electronics Repairers, Commercial and Industrial Equipment
49-2095	Electrical and Electronics Repairers, Powerhouse, Substation, and Relay	49-2095	Electrical and Electronics Repairers, Powerhouse, Substation, and Relay
49-2096	Electronic Equipment Installers and Repairers, Motor Vehicles	49-2096	Electronic Equipment Installers and Repairers, Motor Vehicles
49-2097	Electronic Home Entertainment Equipment Installers and Repairers	49-2097	Electronic Home Entertainment Equipment Installers and Repairers
49-2098	Security and Fire Alarm Systems Installers	49-2098	Security and Fire Alarm Systems Installers
49-3011	Aircraft Mechanics and Service Technicians	49-3011	Aircraft Mechanics and Service Technicians
49-3021	Automotive Body and Related Repairers	49-3021	Automotive Body and Related Repairers
49-3022	Automotive Glass Installers and Repairers	49-3022	Automotive Glass Installers and Repairers
49-3023	Automotive Service Technicians and Mechanics	49-3023	Automotive Service Technicians and Mechanics
49-3031	Bus and Truck Mechanics and Diesel Engine Specialists	49-3031	Bus and Truck Mechanics and Diesel Engine Specialists
49-3041	Farm Equipment Mechanics	49-3041	Farm Equipment Mechanics and Service Technicians
49-3042	Mobile Heavy Equipment Mechanics, Except Engines	49-3042	Mobile Heavy Equipment Mechanics, Except Engines
49-3043	Rail Car Repairers	49-3043	Rail Car Repairers
49-3051	Motorboat Mechanics	49-3051	Motorboat Mechanics and Service Technicians
49-3052	Motorcycle Mechanics	49-3052	Motorcycle Mechanics
49-3053	Outdoor Power Equipment and Other Small Engine Mechanics	49-3053	Outdoor Power Equipment and Other Small Engine Mechanics
49-3091	Bicycle Repairers	49-3091	Bicycle Repairers

Appendix A: Crosswalk to the 2010 SOC

2000 SOC code	2000 SOC title	2010 SOC code	2010 SOC title
49-3092	Recreational Vehicle Service Technicians	49-3092	Recreational Vehicle Service Technicians
49-3093	Tire Repairers and Changers	49-3093	Tire Repairers and Changers
49-9011	Mechanical Door Repairers	49-9011	Mechanical Door Repairers
49-9012	Control and Valve Installers and Repairers, Except Mechanical Door	49-9012	Control and Valve Installers and Repairers, Except Mechanical Door
49-9021	Heating, Air Conditioning, and Refrigeration Mechanics and Installers*	49-9021	Heating, Air Conditioning, and Refrigeration Mechanics and Installers
49-9021	Heating, Air Conditioning, and Refrigeration Mechanics and Installers*	47-2231	Solar Photovoltaic Installers**
49-9031	Home Appliance Repairers	49-9031	Home Appliance Repairers
49-9041	Industrial Machinery Mechanics	49-9041	Industrial Machinery Mechanics
49-9042	Maintenance and Repair Workers, General	49-9071	Maintenance and Repair Workers, General
49-9043	Maintenance Workers, Machinery	49-9043	Maintenance Workers, Machinery
49-9044	Millwrights	49-9044	Millwrights
49-9045	Refractory Materials Repairers, Except Brickmasons	49-9045	Refractory Materials Repairers, Except Brickmasons
49-9051	Electrical Power-Line Installers and Repairers	49-9051	Electrical Power-Line Installers and Repairers
49-9052	Telecommunications Line Installers and Repairers	49-9052	Telecommunications Line Installers and Repairers
49-9061	Camera and Photographic Equipment Repairers	49-9061	Camera and Photographic Equipment Repairers
49-9062	Medical Equipment Repairers	49-9062	Medical Equipment Repairers
49-9063	Musical Instrument Repairers and Tuners	49-9063	Musical Instrument Repairers and Tuners
49-9064	Watch Repairers	49-9064	Watch Repairers
49-9069	Precision Instrument and Equipment Repairers, All Other	49-9069	Precision Instrument and Equipment Repairers, All Other
49-9091	Coin, Vending, and Amusement Machine Servicers and Repairers	49-9091	Coin, Vending, and Amusement Machine Servicers and Repairers
49-9092	Commercial Divers	49-9092	Commercial Divers
49-9093	Fabric Menders, Except Garment	49-9093	Fabric Menders, Except Garment
49-9094	Locksmiths and Safe Repairers	49-9094	Locksmiths and Safe Repairers
49-9095	Manufactured Building and Mobile Home Installers	49-9095	Manufactured Building and Mobile Home Installers
49-9096	Riggers	49-9096	Riggers

Appendix A: Crosswalk to the 2010 SOC

2000 SOC code	2000 SOC title	2010 SOC code	2010 SOC title
49-9097	Signal and Track Switch Repairers	49-9097	Signal and Track Switch Repairers
49-9098	Helpers--Installation, Maintenance, and Repair Workers	49-9098	Helpers--Installation, Maintenance, and Repair Workers
49-9099	Installation, Maintenance, and Repair Workers, All Other*	47-2231	Solar Photovoltaic Installers**
49-9099	Installation, Maintenance, and Repair Workers, All Other*	49-9081	Wind Turbine Service Technicians
49-9099	Installation, Maintenance, and Repair Workers, All Other*	49-9099	Installation, Maintenance, and Repair Workers, All Other
51-1011	First-Line Supervisors/Managers of Production and Operating Workers	51-1011	First-Line Supervisors of Production and Operating Workers
51-2011	Aircraft Structure, Surfaces, Rigging, and Systems Assemblers	51-2011	Aircraft Structure, Surfaces, Rigging, and Systems Assemblers
51-2021	Coil Winders, Tapers, and Finishers	51-2021	Coil Winders, Tapers, and Finishers
51-2022	Electrical and Electronic Equipment Assemblers	51-2022	Electrical and Electronic Equipment Assemblers
51-2023	Electromechanical Equipment Assemblers	51-2023	Electromechanical Equipment Assemblers
51-2031	Engine and Other Machine Assemblers	51-2031	Engine and Other Machine Assemblers
51-2041	Structural Metal Fabricators and Fitters	51-2041	Structural Metal Fabricators and Fitters
51-2091	Fiberglass Laminators and Fabricators	51-2091	Fiberglass Laminators and Fabricators
51-2092	Team Assemblers	51-2092	Team Assemblers
51-2093	Timing Device Assemblers, Adjusters, and Calibrators	51-2093	Timing Device Assemblers and Adjusters
51-2099	Assemblers and Fabricators, All Other	51-2099	Assemblers and Fabricators, All Other
51-3011	Bakers	51-3011	Bakers
51-3021	Butchers and Meat Cutters	51-3021	Butchers and Meat Cutters
51-3022	Meat, Poultry, and Fish Cutters and Trimmers	51-3022	Meat, Poultry, and Fish Cutters and Trimmers
51-3023	Slaughterers and Meat Packers	51-3023	Slaughterers and Meat Packers
51-3091	Food and Tobacco Roasting, Baking, and Drying Machine Operators and Tenders	51-3091	Food and Tobacco Roasting, Baking, and Drying Machine Operators and Tenders
51-3092	Food Batchmakers	51-3092	Food Batchmakers
51-3093	Food Cooking Machine Operators and Tenders	51-3093	Food Cooking Machine Operators and Tenders
51-4011	Computer-Controlled Machine Tool Operators, Metal and Plastic	51-4011	Computer-Controlled Machine Tool Operators, Metal and Plastic
51-4012	Numerical Tool and Process Control Programmers	51-4012	Computer Numerically Controlled Machine Tool Programmers, Metal and Plastic

Appendix A: Crosswalk to the 2010 SOC

2000 SOC code	2000 SOC title	2010 SOC code	2010 SOC title
51-4021	Extruding and Drawing Machine Setters, Operators, and Tenders, Metal and Plastic	51-4021	Extruding and Drawing Machine Setters, Operators, and Tenders, Metal and Plastic
51-4022	Forging Machine Setters, Operators, and Tenders, Metal and Plastic	51-4022	Forging Machine Setters, Operators, and Tenders, Metal and Plastic
51-4023	Rolling Machine Setters, Operators, and Tenders, Metal and Plastic	51-4023	Rolling Machine Setters, Operators, and Tenders, Metal and Plastic
51-4031	Cutting, Punching, and Press Machine Setters, Operators, and Tenders, Metal and Plastic	51-4031	Cutting, Punching, and Press Machine Setters, Operators, and Tenders, Metal and Plastic
51-4032	Drilling and Boring Machine Tool Setters, Operators, and Tenders, Metal and Plastic	51-4032	Drilling and Boring Machine Tool Setters, Operators, and Tenders, Metal and Plastic
51-4033	Grinding, Lapping, Polishing, and Buffing Machine Tool Setters, Operators, and Tenders, Metal and Plastic	51-4033	Grinding, Lapping, Polishing, and Buffing Machine Tool Setters, Operators, and Tenders, Metal and Plastic
51-4034	Lathe and Turning Machine Tool Setters, Operators, and Tenders, Metal and Plastic	51-4034	Lathe and Turning Machine Tool Setters, Operators, and Tenders, Metal and Plastic
51-4035	Milling and Planing Machine Setters, Operators, and Tenders, Metal and Plastic	51-4035	Milling and Planing Machine Setters, Operators, and Tenders, Metal and Plastic
51-4041	Machinists	51-4041	Machinists
51-4051	Metal-Refining Furnace Operators and Tenders	51-4051	Metal-Refining Furnace Operators and Tenders
51-4052	Pourers and Casters, Metal	51-4052	Pourers and Casters, Metal
51-4061	Model Makers, Metal and Plastic	51-4061	Model Makers, Metal and Plastic
51-4062	Patternmakers, Metal and Plastic	51-4062	Patternmakers, Metal and Plastic
51-4071	Foundry Mold and Coremakers	51-4071	Foundry Mold and Coremakers
51-4072	Molding, Coremaking, and Casting Machine Setters, Operators, and Tenders, Metal and Plastic	51-4072	Molding, Coremaking, and Casting Machine Setters, Operators, and Tenders, Metal and Plastic
51-4081	Multiple Machine Tool Setters, Operators, and Tenders, Metal and Plastic	51-4081	Multiple Machine Tool Setters, Operators, and Tenders, Metal and Plastic
51-4111	Tool and Die Makers	51-4111	Tool and Die Makers
51-4121	Welders, Cutters, Solderers, and Brazers	51-4121	Welders, Cutters, Solderers, and Brazers
51-4122	Welding, Soldering, and Brazing Machine Setters, Operators, and Tenders	51-4122	Welding, Soldering, and Brazing Machine Setters, Operators, and Tenders
51-4191	Heat Treating Equipment Setters, Operators, and Tenders, Metal and Plastic	51-4191	Heat Treating Equipment Setters, Operators, and Tenders, Metal and Plastic
51-4192	Lay-Out Workers, Metal and Plastic	51-4192	Layout Workers, Metal and Plastic
51-4193	Plating and Coating Machine Setters, Operators, and Tenders, Metal and Plastic	51-4193	Plating and Coating Machine Setters, Operators, and Tenders, Metal and Plastic
51-4194	Tool Grinders, Filers, and Sharpeners	51-4194	Tool Grinders, Filers, and Sharpeners
51-4199	Metal Workers and Plastic Workers, All Other	51-4199	Metal Workers and Plastic Workers, All Other

2000 SOC code	2000 SOC title	2010 SOC code	2010 SOC title
51-5011	Bindery Workers	51-5113	Print Binding and Finishing Workers**
51-5012	Bookbinders	51-5113	Print Binding and Finishing Workers**
51-5021	Job Printers*	51-5112	Printing Press Operators**
51-5021	Job Printers*	51-5113	Print Binding and Finishing Workers**
51-5022	Prepress Technicians and Workers	51-5111	Prepress Technicians and Workers
51-5023	Printing Machine Operators	51-5112	Printing Press Operators**
51-6011	Laundry and Dry-Cleaning Workers	51-6011	Laundry and Dry-Cleaning Workers
51-6021	Pressers, Textile, Garment, and Related Materials	51-6021	Pressers, Textile, Garment, and Related Materials
51-6031	Sewing Machine Operators	51-6031	Sewing Machine Operators
51-6041	Shoe and Leather Workers and Repairers	51-6041	Shoe and Leather Workers and Repairers
51-6042	Shoe Machine Operators and Tenders	51-6042	Shoe Machine Operators and Tenders
51-6051	Sewers, Hand	51-6051	Sewers, Hand
51-6052	Tailors, Dressmakers, and Custom Sewers	51-6052	Tailors, Dressmakers, and Custom Sewers
51-6061	Textile Bleaching and Dyeing Machine Operators and Tenders	51-6061	Textile Bleaching and Dyeing Machine Operators and Tenders
51-6062	Textile Cutting Machine Setters, Operators, and Tenders	51-6062	Textile Cutting Machine Setters, Operators, and Tenders
51-6063	Textile Knitting and Weaving Machine Setters, Operators, and Tenders	51-6063	Textile Knitting and Weaving Machine Setters, Operators, and Tenders
51-6064	Textile Winding, Twisting, and Drawing Out Machine Setters, Operators, and Tenders	51-6064	Textile Winding, Twisting, and Drawing Out Machine Setters, Operators, and Tenders
51-6091	Extruding and Forming Machine Setters, Operators, and Tenders, Synthetic and Glass Fibers	51-6091	Extruding and Forming Machine Setters, Operators, and Tenders, Synthetic and Glass Fibers
51-6092	Fabric and Apparel Patternmakers	51-6092	Fabric and Apparel Patternmakers
51-6093	Upholsterers	51-6093	Upholsterers
51-6099	Textile, Apparel, and Furnishings Workers, All Other	51-6099	Textile, Apparel, and Furnishings Workers, All Other
51-7011	Cabinetmakers and Bench Carpenters	51-7011	Cabinetmakers and Bench Carpenters
51-7021	Furniture Finishers	51-7021	Furniture Finishers
51-7031	Model Makers, Wood	51-7031	Model Makers, Wood

Appendix A: Crosswalk to the 2010 SOC

2000 SOC code	2000 SOC title	2010 SOC code	2010 SOC title
51-7032	Patternmakers, Wood	51-7032	Patternmakers, Wood
51-7041	Sawing Machine Setters, Operators, and Tenders, Wood	51-7041	Sawing Machine Setters, Operators, and Tenders, Wood
51-7042	Woodworking Machine Setters, Operators, and Tenders, Except Sawing	51-7042	Woodworking Machine Setters, Operators, and Tenders, Except Sawing
51-7099	Woodworkers, All Other	51-7099	Woodworkers, All Other
51-8011	Nuclear Power Reactor Operators	51-8011	Nuclear Power Reactor Operators
51-8012	Power Distributors and Dispatchers	51-8012	Power Distributors and Dispatchers
51-8013	Power Plant Operators	51-8013	Power Plant Operators
51-8021	Stationary Engineers and Boiler Operators	51-8021	Stationary Engineers and Boiler Operators
51-8031	Water and Liquid Waste Treatment Plant and System Operators	51-8031	Water and Wastewater Treatment Plant and System Operators
51-8091	Chemical Plant and System Operators	51-8091	Chemical Plant and System Operators
51-8092	Gas Plant Operators	51-8092	Gas Plant Operators
51-8093	Petroleum Pump System Operators, Refinery Operators, and Gaugers	51-8093	Petroleum Pump System Operators, Refinery Operators, and Gaugers
51-8099	Plant and System Operators, All Other	51-8099	Plant and System Operators, All Other
51-9011	Chemical Equipment Operators and Tenders	51-9011	Chemical Equipment Operators and Tenders
51-9012	Separating, Filtering, Clarifying, Precipitating, and Still Machine Setters, Operators, and Tenders	51-9012	Separating, Filtering, Clarifying, Precipitating, and Still Machine Setters, Operators, and Tenders
51-9021	Crushing, Grinding, and Polishing Machine Setters, Operators, and Tenders	51-9021	Crushing, Grinding, and Polishing Machine Setters, Operators, and Tenders
51-9022	Grinding and Polishing Workers, Hand	51-9022	Grinding and Polishing Workers, Hand
51-9023	Mixing and Blending Machine Setters, Operators, and Tenders	51-9023	Mixing and Blending Machine Setters, Operators, and Tenders
51-9031	Cutters and Trimmers, Hand	51-9031	Cutters and Trimmers, Hand
51-9032	Cutting and Slicing Machine Setters, Operators, and Tenders	51-9032	Cutting and Slicing Machine Setters, Operators, and Tenders
51-9041	Extruding, Forming, Pressing, and Compacting Machine Setters, Operators, and Tenders	51-9041	Extruding, Forming, Pressing, and Compacting Machine Setters, Operators, and Tenders
51-9051	Furnace, Kiln, Oven, Drier, and Kettle Operators and Tenders	51-9051	Furnace, Kiln, Oven, Drier, and Kettle Operators and Tenders
51-9061	Inspectors, Testers, Sorters, Samplers, and Weighers	51-9061	Inspectors, Testers, Sorters, Samplers, and Weighers
51-9071	Jewelers and Precious Stone and Metal Workers	51-9071	Jewelers and Precious Stone and Metal Workers
51-9081	Dental Laboratory Technicians	51-9081	Dental Laboratory Technicians

2000 SOC code	2000 SOC title	2010 SOC code	2010 SOC title
51-9082	Medical Appliance Technicians	51-9082	Medical Appliance Technicians
51-9083	Ophthalmic Laboratory Technicians	51-9083	Ophthalmic Laboratory Technicians
51-9111	Packaging and Filling Machine Operators and Tenders	51-9111	Packaging and Filling Machine Operators and Tenders
51-9121	Coating, Painting, and Spraying Machine Setters, Operators, and Tenders	51-9121	Coating, Painting, and Spraying Machine Setters, Operators, and Tenders
51-9122	Painters, Transportation Equipment	51-9122	Painters, Transportation Equipment
51-9123	Painting, Coating, and Decorating Workers	51-9123	Painting, Coating, and Decorating Workers
51-9131	Photographic Process Workers	51-9151	Photographic Process Workers and Processing Machine Operators**
51-9132	Photographic Processing Machine Operators	51-9151	Photographic Process Workers and Processing Machine Operators**
51-9141	Semiconductor Processors	51-9141	Semiconductor Processors
51-9191	Cementing and Gluing Machine Operators and Tenders	51-9191	Adhesive Bonding Machine Operators and Tenders
51-9192	Cleaning, Washing, and Metal Pickling Equipment Operators and Tenders	51-9192	Cleaning, Washing, and Metal Pickling Equipment Operators and Tenders
51-9193	Cooling and Freezing Equipment Operators and Tenders	51-9193	Cooling and Freezing Equipment Operators and Tenders
51-9194	Etchers and Engravers	51-9194	Etchers and Engravers
51-9195	Molders, Shapers, and Casters, Except Metal and Plastic	51-9195	Molders, Shapers, and Casters, Except Metal and Plastic
51-9196	Paper Goods Machine Setters, Operators, and Tenders	51-9196	Paper Goods Machine Setters, Operators, and Tenders
51-9197	Tire Builders	51-9197	Tire Builders
51-9198	Helpers--Production Workers	51-9198	Helpers--Production Workers
51-9199	Production Workers, All Other*	51-9199	Production Workers, All Other
51-9199	Production Workers, All Other*	51-3099	Food Processing Workers, All Other
53-1011	Aircraft Cargo Handling Supervisors	53-1011	Aircraft Cargo Handling Supervisors
53-1021	First-Line Supervisors/Managers of Helpers, Laborers, and Material Movers, Hand	53-1021	First-Line Supervisors of Helpers, Laborers, and Material Movers, Hand
53-1031	First-Line Supervisors/Managers of Transportation and Material-Moving Machine and Vehicle Operators	53-1031	First-Line Supervisors of Transportation and Material-Moving Machine and Vehicle Operators
53-2011	Airline Pilots, Copilots, and Flight Engineers	53-2011	Airline Pilots, Copilots, and Flight Engineers
53-2012	Commercial Pilots	53-2012	Commercial Pilots
53-2021	Air Traffic Controllers	53-2021	Air Traffic Controllers

Appendix A: Crosswalk to the 2010 SOC

2000 SOC code	2000 SOC title	2010 SOC code	2010 SOC title
53-2022	Airfield Operations Specialists	53-2022	Airfield Operations Specialists
53-3011	Ambulance Drivers and Attendants, Except Emergency Medical Technicians	53-3011	Ambulance Drivers and Attendants, Except Emergency Medical Technicians
53-3021	Bus Drivers, Transit and Intercity	53-3021	Bus Drivers, Transit and Intercity
53-3022	Bus Drivers, School	53-3022	Bus Drivers, School or Special Client
53-3031	Driver/Sales Workers	53-3031	Driver/Sales Workers
53-3032	Truck Drivers, Heavy and Tractor-Trailer	53-3032	Heavy and Tractor-Trailer Truck Drivers
53-3033	Truck Drivers, Light or Delivery Services	53-3033	Light Truck or Delivery Services Drivers
53-3041	Taxi Drivers and Chauffeurs	53-3041	Taxi Drivers and Chauffeurs
53-3099	Motor Vehicle Operators, All Other	53-3099	Motor Vehicle Operators, All Other
53-4011	Locomotive Engineers	53-4011	Locomotive Engineers
53-4012	Locomotive Firers	53-4012	Locomotive Firers
53-4013	Rail Yard Engineers, Dinkey Operators, and Hostlers	53-4013	Rail Yard Engineers, Dinkey Operators, and Hostlers
53-4021	Railroad Brake, Signal, and Switch Operators	53-4021	Railroad Brake, Signal, and Switch Operators
53-4031	Railroad Conductors and Yardmasters	53-4031	Railroad Conductors and Yardmasters
53-4041	Subway and Streetcar Operators	53-4041	Subway and Streetcar Operators
53-4099	Rail Transportation Workers, All Other	53-4099	Rail Transportation Workers, All Other
53-5011	Sailors and Marine Oilers	53-5011	Sailors and Marine Oilers
53-5021	Captains, Mates, and Pilots of Water Vessels	53-5021	Captains, Mates, and Pilots of Water Vessels
53-5022	Motorboat Operators	53-5022	Motorboat Operators
53-5031	Ship Engineers	53-5031	Ship Engineers
53-6011	Bridge and Lock Tenders	53-6011	Bridge and Lock Tenders
53-6021	Parking Lot Attendants	53-6021	Parking Lot Attendants
53-6031	Service Station Attendants	53-6031	Automotive and Watercraft Service Attendants
53-6041	Traffic Technicians	53-6041	Traffic Technicians
53-6051	Transportation Inspectors	53-6051	Transportation Inspectors

Appendix A: Crosswalk to the 2010 SOC

2000 SOC code	2000 SOC title	2010 SOC code	2010 SOC title
53-6099	Transportation Workers, All Other	53-6099	Transportation Workers, All Other
53-7011	Conveyor Operators and Tenders	53-7011	Conveyor Operators and Tenders
53-7021	Crane and Tower Operators	53-7021	Crane and Tower Operators
53-7031	Dredge Operators	53-7031	Dredge Operators
53-7032	Excavating and Loading Machine and Dragline Operators	53-7032	Excavating and Loading Machine and Dragline Operators
53-7033	Loading Machine Operators, Underground Mining	53-7033	Loading Machine Operators, Underground Mining
53-7041	Hoist and Winch Operators	53-7041	Hoist and Winch Operators
53-7051	Industrial Truck and Tractor Operators	53-7051	Industrial Truck and Tractor Operators
53-7061	Cleaners of Vehicles and Equipment	53-7061	Cleaners of Vehicles and Equipment
53-7062	Laborers and Freight, Stock, and Material Movers, Hand	53-7062	Laborers and Freight, Stock, and Material Movers, Hand
53-7063	Machine Feeders and Offbearers	53-7063	Machine Feeders and Offbearers
53-7064	Packers and Packagers, Hand	53-7064	Packers and Packagers, Hand
53-7071	Gas Compressor and Gas Pumping Station Operators	53-7071	Gas Compressor and Gas Pumping Station Operators
53-7072	Pump Operators, Except Wellhead Pumpers	53-7072	Pump Operators, Except Wellhead Pumpers
53-7073	Wellhead Pumpers	53-7073	Wellhead Pumpers
53-7081	Refuse and Recyclable Material Collectors	53-7081	Refuse and Recyclable Material Collectors
53-7111	Shuttle Car Operators	53-7111	Mine Shuttle Car Operators
53-7121	Tank Car, Truck, and Ship Loaders	53-7121	Tank Car, Truck, and Ship Loaders
53-7199	Material Moving Workers, All Other	53-7199	Material Moving Workers, All Other
55-1011	Air Crew Officers	55-1011	Air Crew Officers
55-1012	Aircraft Launch and Recovery Officers	55-1012	Aircraft Launch and Recovery Officers
55-1013	Armored Assault Vehicle Officers	55-1013	Armored Assault Vehicle Officers
55-1014	Artillery and Missile Officers	55-1014	Artillery and Missile Officers
55-1015	Command and Control Center Officers	55-1015	Command and Control Center Officers
55-1016	Infantry Officers	55-1016	Infantry Officers

Appendix A: Crosswalk to the 2010 SOC

2000 SOC code	2000 SOC title	2010 SOC code	2010 SOC title
55-1017	Special Forces Officers	55-1017	Special Forces Officers
55-1019	Military Officer Special and Tactical Operations Leaders/Managers, All Other	55-1019	Military Officer Special and Tactical Operations Leaders, All Other
55-2011	First-Line Supervisors/Managers of Air Crew Members	55-2011	First-Line Supervisors of Air Crew Members
55-2012	First-Line Supervisors/Managers of Weapons Specialists/Crew Members	55-2012	First-Line Supervisors of Weapons Specialists/Crew Members
55-2013	First-Line Supervisors/Managers of All Other Tactical Operations Specialists	55-2013	First-Line Supervisors of All Other Tactical Operations Specialists
55-3011	Air Crew Members	55-3011	Air Crew Members
55-3012	Aircraft Launch and Recovery Specialists	55-3012	Aircraft Launch and Recovery Specialists
55-3013	Armored Assault Vehicle Crew Members	55-3013	Armored Assault Vehicle Crew Members
55-3014	Artillery and Missile Crew Members	55-3014	Artillery and Missile Crew Members
55-3015	Command and Control Center Specialists	55-3015	Command and Control Center Specialists
55-3016	Infantry	55-3016	Infantry
55-3017	Radar and Sonar Technicians	55-3017	Radar and Sonar Technicians
55-3018	Special Forces	55-3018	Special Forces
55-3019	Military Enlisted Tactical Operations and Air/Weapons Specialists and Crew Members, All Other	55-3019	Military Enlisted Tactical Operations and Air/Weapons Specialists and Crew Members, All Other

Appendix B: Crosswalk from the 2010 SOC to the 2000 SOC

Appendix B matches every detailed occupation from the 2010 SOC with the corresponding previous 2000 SOC code(s) and title(s). A double asterisk (**) after the occupation code and title in the first column means that the occupation in the second column makes up only part of the occupation in the first column; that is, the double asterisk 2010 SOC occupation has been created from multiple 2000 SOC codes. Likewise, a single asterisk (*) after the occupation code and title in the second column means that the occupation in the first column makes up only part of the occupation in the second column; that is, the asterisked 2000 SOC occupation has been divided into multiple new occupations. Each occupation with the (*) or (**) notation appears multiple times in the chart.

For example, as shown below, the 2010 SOC occupation 11-9013 "Farmers, Ranchers, and Other Agricultural Managers**" (with two asterisks) was created from two 2000 SOC occupations: 11-9011 Farm, Ranch, and Other Agricultural Managers and 11-9012 Farmers and Ranchers. The 2010 occupations 11-9061 "Funeral Service Managers" and 39-4031 "Morticians, Undertakers, and Funeral Directors" both came from the same 2000 SOC occupation; 11-9061 "Funeral Directors*" (with one asterisk).

2010 SOC code	2000 SOC title	2000 SOC code	2010 SOC title
11-9013	Farmers, Ranchers, and Other Agricultural Managers**	11-9011	Farm, Ranch, and Other Agricultural Managers
11-9013	Farmers, Ranchers, and Other Agricultural Managers**	11-9012	Farmers and Ranchers
11-9061	Funeral Service Managers	11-9061	Funeral Directors *
39-4031	Morticians, Undertakers, and Funeral Directors	11-9061	Funeral Directors *

2010 SOC code	2010 SOC title	2000 SOC code	2000 SOC title
11-1021	General and Operations Managers	11-1021	General and Operations Managers
11-1031	Legislators	11-1031	Legislators
11-2011	Advertising and Promotions Managers	11-2011	Advertising and Promotions Managers
11-2021	Marketing Managers	11-2021	Marketing Managers
11-2022	Sales Managers	11-2022	Sales Managers
11-2031	Public Relations and Fundraising Managers	11-2031	Public Relations Managers
11-3011	Administrative Services Managers	11-3011	Administrative Services Managers
11-3021	Computer and Information Systems Managers	11-3021	Computer and Information Systems Managers
11-3031	Financial Managers	11-3031	Financial Managers
11-3051	Industrial Production Managers	11-3051	Industrial Production Managers
11-3061	Purchasing Managers	11-3061	Purchasing Managers
11-3071	Transportation, Storage, and Distribution Managers	11-3071	Transportation, Storage, and Distribution Managers
11-3111	Compensation and Benefits Managers	11-3041	Compensation and Benefits Managers
11-3121	Human Resources Managers	11-3049	Human Resources Managers, All Other
11-3131	Training and Development Managers	11-3042	Training and Development Managers
11-9013	Farmers, Ranchers, and Other Agricultural Managers**	11-9011	Farm, Ranch, and Other Agricultural Managers
11-9013	Farmers, Ranchers, and Other Agricultural Managers**	11-9012	Farmers and Ranchers
11-9021	Construction Managers	11-9021	Construction Managers
11-9031	Education Administrators, Preschool and Childcare Center/Program	11-9031	Education Administrators, Preschool and Child Care Center/Program
11-9032	Education Administrators, Elementary and Secondary School	11-9032	Education Administrators, Elementary and Secondary School
11-9033	Education Administrators, Postsecondary	11-9033	Education Administrators, Postsecondary
11-9039	Education Administrators, All Other	11-9039	Education Administrators, All Other
11-9041	Architectural and Engineering Managers	11-9041	Engineering Managers
11-9051	Food Service Managers	11-9051	Food Service Managers

2010 SOC code	2010 SOC title	2000 SOC code	2000 SOC title
11-9061	Funeral Service Managers	11-9061	Funeral Directors *
11-9071	Gaming Managers	11-9071	Gaming Managers
11-9081	Lodging Managers	11-9081	Lodging Managers
11-9111	Medical and Health Services Managers	11-9111	Medical and Health Services Managers
11-9121	Natural Sciences Managers	11-9121	Natural Sciences Managers
11-9131	Postmasters and Mail Superintendents	11-9131	Postmasters and Mail Superintendents
11-9141	Property, Real Estate, and Community Association Managers	11-9141	Property, Real Estate, and Community Association Managers
11-9151	Social and Community Service Managers	11-9151	Social and Community Service Managers
11-9161	Emergency Management Directors	13-1061	Emergency Management Specialists
11-9199	Managers, All Other	11-9199	Managers, All Other
13-1011	Agents and Business Managers of Artists, Performers, and Athletes	13-1011	Agents and Business Managers of Artists, Performers, and Athletes
13-1021	Buyers and Purchasing Agents, Farm Products	13-1021	Purchasing Agents and Buyers, Farm Products
13-1022	Wholesale and Retail Buyers, Except Farm Products	13-1022	Wholesale and Retail Buyers, Except Farm Products
13-1023	Purchasing Agents, Except Wholesale, Retail, and Farm Products	13-1023	Purchasing Agents, Except Wholesale, Retail, and Farm Products
13-1031	Claims Adjusters, Examiners, and Investigators	13-1031	Claims Adjusters, Examiners, and Investigators
13-1032	Insurance Appraisers, Auto Damage	13-1032	Insurance Appraisers, Auto Damage
13-1041	Compliance Officers	13-1041	Compliance Officers, Except Agriculture, Construction, Health and Safety, and Transportation*
13-1051	Cost Estimators	13-1051	Cost Estimators
13-1071	Human Resources Specialists**	13-1071	Employment, Recruitment, and Placement Specialists
13-1071	Human Resources Specialists**	13-1079	Human Resources, Training, and Labor Relations Specialists, All Other*
13-1074	Farm Labor Contractors	45-1012	Farm Labor Contractors
13-1075	Labor Relations Specialists	13-1079	Human Resources, Training, and Labor Relations Specialists, All Other*
13-1081	Logisticians	13-1081	Logisticians
13-1111	Management Analysts	13-1111	Management Analysts

2010 SOC code	2010 SOC title	2000 SOC code	2000 SOC title
13-1121	Meeting, Convention, and Event Planners**	13-1121	Meeting and Convention Planners
13-1121	Meeting, Convention, and Event Planners**	13-1199	Business Operations Specialists, All Other*
13-1121	Meeting, Convention, and Event Planners**	27-3031	Public Relations Specialists*
13-1131	Fundraisers	41-9099	Sales and Related Workers, All Other*
13-1141	Compensation, Benefits, and Job Analysis Specialists	13-1072	Compensation, Benefits, and Job Analysis Specialists
13-1151	Training and Development Specialists	13-1073	Training and Development Specialists
13-1161	Market Research Analysts and Marketing Specialists**	13-1199	Business Operations Specialists, All Other*
13-1161	Market Research Analysts and Marketing Specialists**	19-3021	Market Research Analysts
13-1161	Market Research Analysts and Marketing Specialists**	27-3031	Public Relations Specialists*
13-1199	Business Operations Specialists, All Other**	13-1199	Business Operations Specialists, All Other*
13-2011	Accountants and Auditors	13-2011	Accountants and Auditors
13-2021	Appraisers and Assessors of Real Estate	13-2021	Appraisers and Assessors of Real Estate
13-2031	Budget Analysts	13-2031	Budget Analysts
13-2041	Credit Analysts	13-2041	Credit Analysts
13-2051	Financial Analysts	13-2051	Financial Analysts
13-2052	Personal Financial Advisors	13-2052	Personal Financial Advisors
13-2053	Insurance Underwriters	13-2053	Insurance Underwriters
13-2061	Financial Examiners	13-2061	Financial Examiners
13-2071	Credit Counselors	13-2071	Loan Counselors
13-2072	Loan Officers	13-2072	Loan Officers
13-2081	Tax Examiners and Collectors, and Revenue Agents	13-2081	Tax Examiners, Collectors, and Revenue Agents
13-2082	Tax Preparers	13-2082	Tax Preparers
13-2099	Financial Specialists, All Other	13-2099	Financial Specialists, All Other
15-1111	Computer and Information Research Scientists	15-1011	Computer and Information Scientists, Research
15-1121	Computer Systems Analysts	15-1051	Computer Systems Analysts*

Appendix B: Crosswalk to the 2000 SOC

2010 SOC code	2010 SOC title	2000 SOC code	2000 SOC title
15-1122	Information Security Analysts	15-1081	Network Systems and Data Communications Analysts*
15-1131	Computer Programmers	15-1021	Computer Programmers
15-1132	Software Developers, Applications	15-1031	Computer Software Engineers, Applications
15-1133	Software Developers, Systems Software	15-1032	Computer Software Engineers, Systems Software
15-1134	Web Developers	15-1081	Network Systems and Data Communications Analysts*
15-1141	Database Administrators	15-1061	Database Administrators
15-1142	Network and Computer Systems Administrators**	15-1071	Network and Computer Systems Administrators
15-1142	Network and Computer Systems Administrators**	15-1081	Network Systems and Data Communications Analysts*
15-1143	Computer Network Architects**	15-1051	Computer Systems Analysts*
15-1143	Computer Network Architects**	15-1081	Network Systems and Data Communications Analysts*
15-1151	Computer User Support Specialists	15-1041	Computer Support Specialists
15-1152	Computer Network Support Specialists	15-1081	Network Systems and Data Communications Analysts*
15-1199	Computer Occupations, All Other	15-1099	Computer Specialists, All Other
15-2011	Actuaries	15-2011	Actuaries
15-2021	Mathematicians	15-2021	Mathematicians
15-2031	Operations Research Analysts	15-2031	Operations Research Analysts
15-2041	Statisticians	15-2041	Statisticians
15-2091	Mathematical Technicians	15-2091	Mathematical Technicians
15-2099	Mathematical Science Occupations, All Other	15-2099	Mathematical Science Occupations, All Other
17-1011	Architects, Except Landscape and Naval	17-1011	Architects, Except Landscape and Naval
17-1012	Landscape Architects	17-1012	Landscape Architects
17-1021	Cartographers and Photogrammetrists	17-1021	Cartographers and Photogrammetrists
17-1022	Surveyors	17-1022	Surveyors
17-2011	Aerospace Engineers	17-2011	Aerospace Engineers
17-2021	Agricultural Engineers	17-2021	Agricultural Engineers

2010 SOC code	2010 SOC title	2000 SOC code	2000 SOC title
17-2031	Biomedical Engineers	17-2031	Biomedical Engineers
17-2041	Chemical Engineers	17-2041	Chemical Engineers
17-2051	Civil Engineers	17-2051	Civil Engineers
17-2061	Computer Hardware Engineers	17-2061	Computer Hardware Engineers
17-2071	Electrical Engineers	17-2071	Electrical Engineers
17-2072	Electronics Engineers, Except Computer	17-2072	Electronics Engineers, Except Computer
17-2081	Environmental Engineers	17-2081	Environmental Engineers
17-2111	Health and Safety Engineers, Except Mining Safety Engineers and Inspectors	17-2111	Health and Safety Engineers, Except Mining Safety Engineers and Inspectors
17-2112	Industrial Engineers	17-2112	Industrial Engineers
17-2121	Marine Engineers and Naval Architects	17-2121	Marine Engineers and Naval Architects
17-2131	Materials Engineers	17-2131	Materials Engineers
17-2141	Mechanical Engineers	17-2141	Mechanical Engineers
17-2151	Mining and Geological Engineers, Including Mining Safety Engineers	17-2151	Mining and Geological Engineers, Including Mining Safety Engineers
17-2161	Nuclear Engineers	17-2161	Nuclear Engineers
17-2171	Petroleum Engineers	17-2171	Petroleum Engineers
17-2199	Engineers, All Other	17-2199	Engineers, All Other
17-3011	Architectural and Civil Drafters	17-3011	Architectural and Civil Drafters
17-3012	Electrical and Electronics Drafters	17-3012	Electrical and Electronics Drafters
17-3013	Mechanical Drafters	17-3013	Mechanical Drafters
17-3019	Drafters, All Other	17-3019	Drafters, All Other
17-3021	Aerospace Engineering and Operations Technicians	17-3021	Aerospace Engineering and Operations Technicians
17-3022	Civil Engineering Technicians	17-3022	Civil Engineering Technicians
17-3023	Electrical and Electronics Engineering Technicians	17-3023	Electrical and Electronic Engineering Technicians
17-3024	Electro-Mechanical Technicians	17-3024	Electro-Mechanical Technicians
17-3025	Environmental Engineering Technicians	17-3025	Environmental Engineering Technicians

Appendix B: Crosswalk to the 2000 SOC

2010 SOC code	2010 SOC title	2000 SOC code	2000 SOC title
17-3026	Industrial Engineering Technicians	17-3026	Industrial Engineering Technicians
17-3027	Mechanical Engineering Technicians	17-3027	Mechanical Engineering Technicians
17-3029	Engineering Technicians, Except Drafters, All Other	17-3029	Engineering Technicians, Except Drafters, All Other
17-3031	Surveying and Mapping Technicians	17-3031	Surveying and Mapping Technicians
19-1011	Animal Scientists	19-1011	Animal Scientists
19-1012	Food Scientists and Technologists	19-1012	Food Scientists and Technologists
19-1013	Soil and Plant Scientists	19-1013	Soil and Plant Scientists
19-1021	Biochemists and Biophysicists	19-1021	Biochemists and Biophysicists
19-1022	Microbiologists	19-1022	Microbiologists
19-1023	Zoologists and Wildlife Biologists	19-1023	Zoologists and Wildlife Biologists
19-1029	Biological Scientists, All Other	19-1029	Biological Scientists, All Other
19-1031	Conservation Scientists	19-1031	Conservation Scientists
19-1032	Foresters	19-1032	Foresters
19-1041	Epidemiologists	19-1041	Epidemiologists
19-1042	Medical Scientists, Except Epidemiologists	19-1042	Medical Scientists, Except Epidemiologists
19-1099	Life Scientists, All Other	19-1099	Life Scientists, All Other
19-2011	Astronomers	19-2011	Astronomers
19-2012	Physicists	19-2012	Physicists
19-2021	Atmospheric and Space Scientists	19-2021	Atmospheric and Space Scientists
19-2031	Chemists	19-2031	Chemists
19-2032	Materials Scientists	19-2032	Materials Scientists
19-2041	Environmental Scientists and Specialists, Including Health	19-2041	Environmental Scientists and Specialists, Including Health
19-2042	Geoscientists, Except Hydrologists and Geographers	19-2042	Geoscientists, Except Hydrologists and Geographers
19-2043	Hydrologists	19-2043	Hydrologists
19-2099	Physical Scientists, All Other	19-2099	Physical Scientists, All Other

2010 SOC code	2010 SOC title	2000 SOC code	2000 SOC title
19-3011	Economists	19-3011	Economists
19-3022	Survey Researchers	19-3022	Survey Researchers
19-3031	Clinical, Counseling, and School Psychologists	19-3031	Clinical, Counseling, and School Psychologists
19-3032	Industrial-Organizational Psychologists	19-3032	Industrial-Organizational Psychologists
19-3039	Psychologists, All Other	19-3039	Psychologists, All Other
19-3041	Sociologists	19-3041	Sociologists
19-3051	Urban and Regional Planners	19-3051	Urban and Regional Planners
19-3091	Anthropologists and Archeologists	19-3091	Anthropologists and Archeologists
19-3092	Geographers	19-3092	Geographers
19-3093	Historians	19-3093	Historians
19-3094	Political Scientists	19-3094	Political Scientists
19-3099	Social Scientists and Related Workers, All Other	19-3099	Social Scientists and Related Workers, All Other
19-4011	Agricultural and Food Science Technicians	19-4011	Agricultural and Food Science Technicians
19-4021	Biological Technicians	19-4021	Biological Technicians
19-4031	Chemical Technicians	19-4031	Chemical Technicians
19-4041	Geological and Petroleum Technicians	19-4041	Geological and Petroleum Technicians
19-4051	Nuclear Technicians	19-4051	Nuclear Technicians
19-4061	Social Science Research Assistants	19-4061	Social Science Research Assistants
19-4091	Environmental Science and Protection Technicians, Including Health	19-4091	Environmental Science and Protection Technicians, Including Health
19-4092	Forensic Science Technicians	19-4092	Forensic Science Technicians
19-4093	Forest and Conservation Technicians	19-4093	Forest and Conservation Technicians
19-4099	Life, Physical, and Social Science Technicians, All Other	19-4099	Life, Physical, and Social Science Technicians, All Other
21-1011	Substance Abuse and Behavioral Disorder Counselors	21-1011	Substance Abuse and Behavioral Disorder Counselors
21-1012	Educational, Guidance, School, and Vocational Counselors	21-1012	Educational, Vocational, and School Counselors
21-1013	Marriage and Family Therapists	21-1013	Marriage and Family Therapists

Appendix B: Crosswalk to the 2000 SOC

2010 SOC code	2010 SOC title	2000 SOC code	2000 SOC title
21-1014	Mental Health Counselors	21-1014	Mental Health Counselors
21-1015	Rehabilitation Counselors	21-1015	Rehabilitation Counselors
21-1019	Counselors, All Other	21-1019	Counselors, All Other
21-1021	Child, Family, and School Social Workers	21-1021	Child, Family, and School Social Workers
21-1022	Healthcare Social Workers	21-1022	Medical and Public Health Social Workers
21-1023	Mental Health and Substance Abuse Social Workers	21-1023	Mental Health and Substance Abuse Social Workers
21-1029	Social Workers, All Other	21-1029	Social Workers, All Other
21-1091	Health Educators	21-1091	Health Educators*
21-1092	Probation Officers and Correctional Treatment Specialists	21-1092	Probation Officers and Correctional Treatment Specialists
21-1093	Social and Human Service Assistants	21-1093	Social and Human Service Assistants
21-1094	Community Health Workers**	21-1091	Health Educators*
21-1094	Community Health Workers**	21-1099	Community and Social Service Specialists, All Other*
21-1099	Community and Social Service Specialists, All Other	21-1099	Community and Social Service Specialists, All Other*
21-2011	Clergy	21-2011	Clergy
21-2021	Directors, Religious Activities and Education	21-2021	Directors, Religious Activities and Education
21-2099	Religious Workers, All Other	21-2099	Religious Workers, All Other
23-1011	Lawyers	23-1011	Lawyers
23-1012	Judicial Law Clerks	23-2092	Law Clerks*
23-1021	Administrative Law Judges, Adjudicators, and Hearing Officers	23-1021	Administrative Law Judges, Adjudicators, and Hearing Officers
23-1022	Arbitrators, Mediators, and Conciliators	23-1022	Arbitrators, Mediators, and Conciliators
23-1023	Judges, Magistrate Judges, and Magistrates	23-1023	Judges, Magistrate Judges, and Magistrates
23-2011	Paralegals and Legal Assistants**	23-2011	Paralegals and Legal Assistants
23-2011	Paralegals and Legal Assistants**	23-2092	Law Clerks*
23-2091	Court Reporters	23-2091	Court Reporters
23-2093	Title Examiners, Abstractors, and Searchers	23-2093	Title Examiners, Abstractors, and Searchers

2010 SOC code	2010 SOC title	2000 SOC code	2000 SOC title
23-2099	Legal Support Workers, All Other	23-2099	Legal Support Workers, All Other
25-1011	Business Teachers, Postsecondary	25-1011	Business Teachers, Postsecondary
25-1021	Computer Science Teachers, Postsecondary	25-1021	Computer Science Teachers, Postsecondary
25-1022	Mathematical Science Teachers, Postsecondary	25-1022	Mathematical Science Teachers, Postsecondary
25-1031	Architecture Teachers, Postsecondary	25-1031	Architecture Teachers, Postsecondary
25-1032	Engineering Teachers, Postsecondary	25-1032	Engineering Teachers, Postsecondary
25-1041	Agricultural Sciences Teachers, Postsecondary	25-1041	Agricultural Sciences Teachers, Postsecondary
25-1042	Biological Science Teachers, Postsecondary	25-1042	Biological Science Teachers, Postsecondary
25-1043	Forestry and Conservation Science Teachers, Postsecondary	25-1043	Forestry and Conservation Science Teachers, Postsecondary
25-1051	Atmospheric, Earth, Marine, and Space Sciences Teachers, Postsecondary	25-1051	Atmospheric, Earth, Marine, and Space Sciences Teachers, Postsecondary
25-1052	Chemistry Teachers, Postsecondary	25-1052	Chemistry Teachers, Postsecondary
25-1053	Environmental Science Teachers, Postsecondary	25-1053	Environmental Science Teachers, Postsecondary
25-1054	Physics Teachers, Postsecondary	25-1054	Physics Teachers, Postsecondary
25-1061	Anthropology and Archeology Teachers, Postsecondary	25-1061	Anthropology and Archeology Teachers, Postsecondary
25-1062	Area, Ethnic, and Cultural Studies Teachers, Postsecondary	25-1062	Area, Ethnic, and Cultural Studies Teachers, Postsecondary
25-1063	Economics Teachers, Postsecondary	25-1063	Economics Teachers, Postsecondary
25-1064	Geography Teachers, Postsecondary	25-1064	Geography Teachers, Postsecondary
25-1065	Political Science Teachers, Postsecondary	25-1065	Political Science Teachers, Postsecondary
25-1066	Psychology Teachers, Postsecondary	25-1066	Psychology Teachers, Postsecondary
25-1067	Sociology Teachers, Postsecondary	25-1067	Sociology Teachers, Postsecondary
25-1069	Social Sciences Teachers, Postsecondary, All Other	25-1069	Social Sciences Teachers, Postsecondary, All Other
25-1071	Health Specialties Teachers, Postsecondary	25-1071	Health Specialties Teachers, Postsecondary
25-1072	Nursing Instructors and Teachers, Postsecondary	25-1072	Nursing Instructors and Teachers, Postsecondary
25-1081	Education Teachers, Postsecondary	25-1081	Education Teachers, Postsecondary
25-1082	Library Science Teachers, Postsecondary	25-1082	Library Science Teachers, Postsecondary

Appendix B: Crosswalk to the 2000 SOC

2010 SOC code	2010 SOC title	2000 SOC code	2000 SOC title
25-1111	Criminal Justice and Law Enforcement Teachers, Postsecondary	25-1111	Criminal Justice and Law Enforcement Teachers, Postsecondary
25-1112	Law Teachers, Postsecondary	25-1112	Law Teachers, Postsecondary
25-1113	Social Work Teachers, Postsecondary	25-1113	Social Work Teachers, Postsecondary
25-1121	Art, Drama, and Music Teachers, Postsecondary	25-1121	Art, Drama, and Music Teachers, Postsecondary
25-1122	Communications Teachers, Postsecondary	25-1122	Communications Teachers, Postsecondary
25-1123	English Language and Literature Teachers, Postsecondary	25-1123	English Language and Literature Teachers, Postsecondary
25-1124	Foreign Language and Literature Teachers, Postsecondary	25-1124	Foreign Language and Literature Teachers, Postsecondary
25-1125	History Teachers, Postsecondary	25-1125	History Teachers, Postsecondary
25-1126	Philosophy and Religion Teachers, Postsecondary	25-1126	Philosophy and Religion Teachers, Postsecondary
25-1191	Graduate Teaching Assistants	25-1191	Graduate Teaching Assistants
25-1192	Home Economics Teachers, Postsecondary	25-1192	Home Economics Teachers, Postsecondary
25-1193	Recreation and Fitness Studies Teachers, Postsecondary	25-1193	Recreation and Fitness Studies Teachers, Postsecondary
25-1194	Vocational Education Teachers, Postsecondary	25-1194	Vocational Education Teachers, Postsecondary
25-1199	Postsecondary Teachers, All Other	25-1199	Postsecondary Teachers, All Other
25-2011	Preschool Teachers, Except Special Education	25-2011	Preschool Teachers, Except Special Education
25-2012	Kindergarten Teachers, Except Special Education	25-2012	Kindergarten Teachers, Except Special Education
25-2021	Elementary School Teachers, Except Special Education	25-2021	Elementary School Teachers, Except Special Education
25-2022	Middle School Teachers, Except Special and Career/Technical Education	25-2022	Middle School Teachers, Except Special and Vocational Education
25-2023	Career/Technical Education Teachers, Middle School	25-2023	Vocational Education Teachers, Middle School
25-2031	Secondary School Teachers, Except Special and Career/Technical Education	25-2031	Secondary School Teachers, Except Special and Vocational Education
25-2032	Career/Technical Education Teachers, Secondary School	25-2032	Vocational Education Teachers, Secondary School
25-2051	Special Education Teachers, Preschool	25-2041	Special Education Teachers, Preschool, Kindergarten, and Elementary School*
25-2052	Special Education Teachers, Kindergarten and Elementary School	25-2041	Special Education Teachers, Preschool, Kindergarten, and Elementary School*
25-2053	Special Education Teachers, Middle School	25-2042	Special Education Teachers, Middle School
25-2054	Special Education Teachers, Secondary School	25-2043	Special Education Teachers, Secondary School

2010 SOC code	2010 SOC title	2000 SOC code	2000 SOC title
25-2059	Special Education Teachers, All Other	25-3099	Teachers and Instructors, All Other*
25-3011	Adult Basic and Secondary Education and Literacy Teachers and Instructors	25-3011	Adult Literacy, Remedial Education, and GED Teachers and Instructors
25-3021	Self-Enrichment Education Teachers	25-3021	Self-Enrichment Education Teachers
25-3099	Teachers and Instructors, All Other	25-3099	Teachers and Instructors, All Other*
25-4011	Archivists	25-4011	Archivists
25-4012	Curators	25-4012	Curators
25-4013	Museum Technicians and Conservators	25-4013	Museum Technicians and Conservators
25-4021	Librarians	25-4021	Librarians
25-4031	Library Technicians	25-4031	Library Technicians
25-9011	Audio-Visual and Multimedia Collections Specialists	25-9011	Audio-Visual Collections Specialists
25-9021	Farm and Home Management Advisors	25-9021	Farm and Home Management Advisors
25-9031	Instructional Coordinators	25-9031	Instructional Coordinators
25-9041	Teacher Assistants	25-9041	Teacher Assistants
25-9099	Education, Training, and Library Workers, All Other	25-9099	Education, Training, and Library Workers, All Other
27-1011	Art Directors	27-1011	Art Directors
27-1012	Craft Artists	27-1012	Craft Artists
27-1013	Fine Artists, Including Painters, Sculptors, and Illustrators	27-1013	Fine Artists, Including Painters, Sculptors, and Illustrators
27-1014	Multimedia Artists and Animators	27-1014	Multi-Media Artists and Animators
27-1019	Artists and Related Workers, All Other	27-1019	Artists and Related Workers, All Other
27-1021	Commercial and Industrial Designers	27-1021	Commercial and Industrial Designers
27-1022	Fashion Designers	27-1022	Fashion Designers
27-1023	Floral Designers	27-1023	Floral Designers
27-1024	Graphic Designers	27-1024	Graphic Designers
27-1025	Interior Designers	27-1025	Interior Designers
27-1026	Merchandise Displayers and Window Trimmers	27-1026	Merchandise Displayers and Window Trimmers

Appendix B: Crosswalk to the 2000 SOC

2010 SOC code	2010 SOC title	2000 SOC code	2000 SOC title
27-1027	Set and Exhibit Designers	27-1027	Set and Exhibit Designers
27-1029	Designers, All Other	27-1029	Designers, All Other
27-2011	Actors	27-2011	Actors
27-2012	Producers and Directors	27-2012	Producers and Directors
27-2021	Athletes and Sports Competitors	27-2021	Athletes and Sports Competitors
27-2022	Coaches and Scouts	27-2022	Coaches and Scouts
27-2023	Umpires, Referees, and Other Sports Officials	27-2023	Umpires, Referees, and Other Sports Officials
27-2031	Dancers	27-2031	Dancers
27-2032	Choreographers	27-2032	Choreographers
27-2041	Music Directors and Composers	27-2041	Music Directors and Composers
27-2042	Musicians and Singers	27-2042	Musicians and Singers
27-2099	Entertainers and Performers, Sports and Related Workers, All Other	27-2099	Entertainers and Performers, Sports and Related Workers, All Other
27-3011	Radio and Television Announcers	27-3011	Radio and Television Announcers
27-3012	Public Address System and Other Announcers	27-3012	Public Address System and Other Announcers
27-3021	Broadcast News Analysts	27-3021	Broadcast News Analysts
27-3022	Reporters and Correspondents	27-3022	Reporters and Correspondents
27-3031	Public Relations Specialists	27-3031	Public Relations Specialists*
27-3041	Editors	27-3041	Editors
27-3042	Technical Writers	27-3042	Technical Writers
27-3043	Writers and Authors	27-3043	Writers and Authors
27-3091	Interpreters and Translators	27-3091	Interpreters and Translators
27-3099	Media and Communication Workers, All Other	27-3099	Media and Communication Workers, All Other
27-4011	Audio and Video Equipment Technicians	27-4011	Audio and Video Equipment Technicians
27-4012	Broadcast Technicians	27-4012	Broadcast Technicians
27-4013	Radio Operators	27-4013	Radio Operators

2010 SOC code	2010 SOC title	2000 SOC code	2000 SOC title
27-4014	Sound Engineering Technicians	27-4014	Sound Engineering Technicians
27-4021	Photographers	27-4021	Photographers
27-4031	Camera Operators, Television, Video, and Motion Picture	27-4031	Camera Operators, Television, Video, and Motion Picture
27-4032	Film and Video Editors	27-4032	Film and Video Editors
27-4099	Media and Communication Equipment Workers, All Other	27-4099	Media and Communication Equipment Workers, All Other
29-1011	Chiropractors	29-1011	Chiropractors
29-1021	Dentists, General	29-1021	Dentists, General
29-1022	Oral and Maxillofacial Surgeons	29-1022	Oral and Maxillofacial Surgeons
29-1023	Orthodontists	29-1023	Orthodontists
29-1024	Prosthodontists	29-1024	Prosthodontists
29-1029	Dentists, All Other Specialists	29-1029	Dentists, All Other Specialists
29-1031	Dietitians and Nutritionists	29-1031	Dietitians and Nutritionists
29-1041	Optometrists	29-1041	Optometrists
29-1051	Pharmacists	29-1051	Pharmacists
29-1061	Anesthesiologists	29-1061	Anesthesiologists
29-1062	Family and General Practitioners	29-1062	Family and General Practitioners
29-1063	Internists, General	29-1063	Internists, General
29-1064	Obstetricians and Gynecologists	29-1064	Obstetricians and Gynecologists
29-1065	Pediatricians, General	29-1065	Pediatricians, General
29-1066	Psychiatrists	29-1066	Psychiatrists
29-1067	Surgeons	29-1067	Surgeons
29-1069	Physicians and Surgeons, All Other	29-1069	Physicians and Surgeons, All Other
29-1071	Physician Assistants	29-1071	Physician Assistants
29-1081	Podiatrists	29-1081	Podiatrists
29-1122	Occupational Therapists	29-1122	Occupational Therapists

Appendix B: Crosswalk to the 2000 SOC

2010 SOC code	2010 SOC title	2000 SOC code	2000 SOC title
29-1123	Physical Therapists	29-1123	Physical Therapists
29-1124	Radiation Therapists	29-1124	Radiation Therapists
29-1125	Recreational Therapists	29-1125	Recreational Therapists
29-1126	Respiratory Therapists	29-1126	Respiratory Therapists
29-1127	Speech-Language Pathologists	29-1127	Speech-Language Pathologists
29-1128	Exercise Physiologists	29-1129	Therapists, All Other*
29-1129	Therapists, All Other	29-1129	Therapists, All Other*
29-1131	Veterinarians	29-1131	Veterinarians
29-1141	Registered Nurses	29-1111	Registered Nurses*
29-1151	Nurse Anesthetists	29-1111	Registered Nurses*
29-1161	Nurse Midwives	29-1111	Registered Nurses*
29-1171	Nurse Practitioners	29-1111	Registered Nurses*
29-1181	Audiologists	29-1121	Audiologists
29-1199	Health Diagnosing and Treating Practitioners, All Other	29-1199	Health Diagnosing and Treating Practitioners, All Other
29-2011	Medical and Clinical Laboratory Technologists	29-2011	Medical and Clinical Laboratory Technologists
29-2012	Medical and Clinical Laboratory Technicians	29-2012	Medical and Clinical Laboratory Technicians
29-2021	Dental Hygienists	29-2021	Dental Hygienists
29-2031	Cardiovascular Technologists and Technicians	29-2031	Cardiovascular Technologists and Technicians
29-2032	Diagnostic Medical Sonographers	29-2032	Diagnostic Medical Sonographers
29-2033	Nuclear Medicine Technologists	29-2033	Nuclear Medicine Technologists
29-2034	Radiologic Technologists	29-2034	Radiologic Technologists and Technicians*
29-2035	Magnetic Resonance Imaging Technologists	29-2034	Radiologic Technologists and Technicians*
29-2041	Emergency Medical Technicians and Paramedics	29-2041	Emergency Medical Technicians and Paramedics
29-2051	Dietetic Technicians	29-2051	Dietetic Technicians
29-2052	Pharmacy Technicians	29-2052	Pharmacy Technicians

Appendix B: Crosswalk to the 2000 SOC

2010 SOC code	2010 SOC title	2000 SOC code	2000 SOC title
29-2053	Psychiatric Technicians	29-2053	Psychiatric Technicians
29-2054	Respiratory Therapy Technicians	29-2054	Respiratory Therapy Technicians
29-2055	Surgical Technologists	29-2055	Surgical Technologists
29-2056	Veterinary Technologists and Technicians	29-2056	Veterinary Technologists and Technicians
29-2057	Ophthalmic Medical Technicians	29-2099	Health Technologists and Technicians, All Other*
29-2061	Licensed Practical and Licensed Vocational Nurses	29-2061	Licensed Practical and Licensed Vocational Nurses
29-2071	Medical Records and Health Information Technicians	29-2071	Medical Records and Health Information Technicians
29-2081	Opticians, Dispensing	29-2081	Opticians, Dispensing
29-2091	Orthotists and Prosthetists	29-2091	Orthotists and Prosthetists
29-2092	Hearing Aid Specialists	29-2099	Health Technologists and Technicians, All Other*
29-2099	Health Technologists and Technicians, All Other	29-2099	Health Technologists and Technicians, All Other*
29-9011	Occupational Health and Safety Specialists	29-9011	Occupational Health and Safety Specialists
29-9012	Occupational Health and Safety Technicians	29-9012	Occupational Health and Safety Technicians
29-9091	Athletic Trainers	29-9091	Athletic Trainers
29-9092	Genetic Counselors	29-9099	Healthcare Practitioners and Technical Workers, All Other*
29-9099	Healthcare Practitioners and Technical Workers, All Other	29-9099	Healthcare Practitioners and Technical Workers, All Other*
31-1011	Home Health Aides	31-1011	Home Health Aides
31-1013	Psychiatric Aides	31-1013	Psychiatric Aides
31-1014	Nursing Assistants	31-1012	Nursing Aides, Orderlies, and Attendants*
31-1015	Orderlies	31-1012	Nursing Aides, Orderlies, and Attendants*
31-2011	Occupational Therapy Assistants	31-2011	Occupational Therapist Assistants
31-2012	Occupational Therapy Aides	31-2012	Occupational Therapist Aides
31-2021	Physical Therapist Assistants	31-2021	Physical Therapist Assistants
31-2022	Physical Therapist Aides	31-2022	Physical Therapist Aides
31-9011	Massage Therapists	31-9011	Massage Therapists

2010 SOC code	2010 SOC title	2000 SOC code	2000 SOC title
31-9091	Dental Assistants	31-9091	Dental Assistants
31-9092	Medical Assistants	31-9092	Medical Assistants
31-9093	Medical Equipment Preparers	31-9093	Medical Equipment Preparers
31-9094	Medical Transcriptionists	31-9094	Medical Transcriptionists
31-9095	Pharmacy Aides	31-9095	Pharmacy Aides
31-9096	Veterinary Assistants and Laboratory Animal Caretakers	31-9096	Veterinary Assistants and Laboratory Animal Caretakers
31-9097	Phlebotomists	31-9099	Healthcare Support Workers, All Other*
31-9099	Healthcare Support Workers, All Other	31-9099	Healthcare Support Workers, All Other*
33-1011	First-Line Supervisors of Correctional Officers	33-1011	First-Line Supervisors/Managers of Correctional Officers
33-1012	First-Line Supervisors of Police and Detectives	33-1012	First-Line Supervisors/Managers of Police and Detectives
33-1021	First-Line Supervisors of Fire Fighting and Prevention Workers	33-1021	First-Line Supervisors/Managers of Fire Fighting and Prevention Workers
33-1099	First-Line Supervisors of Protective Service Workers, All Other	33-1099	First-Line Supervisors/Managers, Protective Service Workers, All Other
33-2011	Firefighters	33-2011	Fire Fighters
33-2021	Fire Inspectors and Investigators	33-2021	Fire Inspectors and Investigators
33-2022	Forest Fire Inspectors and Prevention Specialists	33-2022	Forest Fire Inspectors and Prevention Specialists
33-3011	Bailiffs	33-3011	Bailiffs
33-3012	Correctional Officers and Jailers	33-3012	Correctional Officers and Jailers
33-3021	Detectives and Criminal Investigators	33-3021	Detectives and Criminal Investigators
33-3031	Fish and Game Wardens	33-3031	Fish and Game Wardens
33-3041	Parking Enforcement Workers	33-3041	Parking Enforcement Workers
33-3051	Police and Sheriff's Patrol Officers	33-3051	Police and Sheriff's Patrol Officers
33-3052	Transit and Railroad Police	33-3052	Transit and Railroad Police
33-9011	Animal Control Workers	33-9011	Animal Control Workers
33-9021	Private Detectives and Investigators	33-9021	Private Detectives and Investigators
33-9031	Gaming Surveillance Officers and Gaming Investigators	33-9031	Gaming Surveillance Officers and Gaming Investigators

2010 SOC code	2010 SOC title	2000 SOC code	2000 SOC title
33-9032	Security Guards	33-9032	Security Guards*
33-9091	Crossing Guards	33-9091	Crossing Guards
33-9092	Lifeguards, Ski Patrol, and Other Recreational Protective Service Workers	33-9092	Lifeguards, Ski Patrol, and Other Recreational Protective Service Workers
33-9093	Transportation Security Screeners**	13-1041	Compliance Officers, Except Agriculture, Construction, Health and Safety, and Transportation*
33-9093	Transportation Security Screeners**	33-9032	Security Guards*
33-9093	Transportation Security Screeners**	33-9099	Protective Service Workers, All Other*
33-9099	Protective Service Workers, All Other	33-9099	Protective Service Workers, All Other*
35-1011	Chefs and Head Cooks	35-1011	Chefs and Head Cooks
35-1012	First-Line Supervisors of Food Preparation and Serving Workers	35-1012	First-Line Supervisors/Managers of Food Preparation and Serving Workers
35-2011	Cooks, Fast Food	35-2011	Cooks, Fast Food
35-2012	Cooks, Institution and Cafeteria	35-2012	Cooks, Institution and Cafeteria
35-2013	Cooks, Private Household	35-2013	Cooks, Private Household
35-2014	Cooks, Restaurant	35-2014	Cooks, Restaurant
35-2015	Cooks, Short Order	35-2015	Cooks, Short Order
35-2019	Cooks, All Other	35-2019	Cooks, All Other
35-2021	Food Preparation Workers	35-2021	Food Preparation Workers
35-3011	Bartenders	35-3011	Bartenders
35-3021	Combined Food Preparation and Serving Workers, Including Fast Food	35-3021	Combined Food Preparation and Serving Workers, Including Fast Food
35-3022	Counter Attendants, Cafeteria, Food Concession, and Coffee Shop	35-3022	Counter Attendants, Cafeteria, Food Concession, and Coffee Shop
35-3031	Waiters and Waitresses	35-3031	Waiters and Waitresses
35-3041	Food Servers, Nonrestaurant	35-3041	Food Servers, Nonrestaurant
35-9011	Dining Room and Cafeteria Attendants and Bartender Helpers	35-9011	Dining Room and Cafeteria Attendants and Bartender Helpers
35-9021	Dishwashers	35-9021	Dishwashers
35-9031	Hosts and Hostesses, Restaurant, Lounge, and Coffee Shop	35-9031	Hosts and Hostesses, Restaurant, Lounge, and Coffee Shop
35-9099	Food Preparation and Serving Related Workers, All Other	35-9099	Food Preparation and Serving Related Workers, All Other

Appendix B: Crosswalk to the 2000 SOC

2010 SOC code	2010 SOC title	2000 SOC code	2000 SOC title
37-1011	First-Line Supervisors of Housekeeping and Janitorial Workers	37-1011	First-Line Supervisors/Managers of Housekeeping and Janitorial Workers
37-1012	First-Line Supervisors of Landscaping, Lawn Service, and Groundskeeping Workers	37-1012	First-Line Supervisors/Managers of Landscaping, Lawn Service, and Groundskeeping Workers
37-2011	Janitors and Cleaners, Except Maids and Housekeeping Cleaners	37-2011	Janitors and Cleaners, Except Maids and Housekeeping Cleaners
37-2012	Maids and Housekeeping Cleaners	37-2012	Maids and Housekeeping Cleaners
37-2019	Building Cleaning Workers, All Other	37-2019	Building Cleaning Workers, All Other
37-2021	Pest Control Workers	37-2021	Pest Control Workers
37-3011	Landscaping and Groundskeeping Workers	37-3011	Landscaping and Groundskeeping Workers
37-3012	Pesticide Handlers, Sprayers, and Applicators, Vegetation	37-3012	Pesticide Handlers, Sprayers, and Applicators, Vegetation
37-3013	Tree Trimmers and Pruners	37-3013	Tree Trimmers and Pruners
37-3019	Grounds Maintenance Workers, All Other	37-3019	Grounds Maintenance Workers, All Other
39-1011	Gaming Supervisors	39-1011	Gaming Supervisors
39-1012	Slot Supervisors	39-1012	Slot Key Persons
39-1021	First-Line Supervisors of Personal Service Workers	39-1021	First-Line Supervisors/Managers of Personal Service Workers
39-2011	Animal Trainers	39-2011	Animal Trainers
39-2021	Nonfarm Animal Caretakers	39-2021	Nonfarm Animal Caretakers
39-3011	Gaming Dealers	39-3011	Gaming Dealers
39-3012	Gaming and Sports Book Writers and Runners	39-3012	Gaming and Sports Book Writers and Runners
39-3019	Gaming Service Workers, All Other	39-3019	Gaming Service Workers, All Other
39-3021	Motion Picture Projectionists	39-3021	Motion Picture Projectionists
39-3031	Ushers, Lobby Attendants, and Ticket Takers	39-3031	Ushers, Lobby Attendants, and Ticket Takers
39-3091	Amusement and Recreation Attendants	39-3091	Amusement and Recreation Attendants
39-3092	Costume Attendants	39-3092	Costume Attendants
39-3093	Locker Room, Coatroom, and Dressing Room Attendants	39-3093	Locker Room, Coatroom, and Dressing Room Attendants
39-3099	Entertainment Attendants and Related Workers, All Other	39-3099	Entertainment Attendants and Related Workers, All Other
39-4011	Embalmers	39-4011	Embalmers

Appendix B: Crosswalk to the 2000 SOC

2010 SOC code	2010 SOC title	2000 SOC code	2000 SOC title
39-4021	Funeral Attendants	39-4021	Funeral Attendants
39-4031	Morticians, Undertakers, and Funeral Directors	11-9061	Funeral Directors*
39-5011	Barbers	39-5011	Barbers
39-5012	Hairdressers, Hairstylists, and Cosmetologists	39-5012	Hairdressers, Hairstylists, and Cosmetologists
39-5091	Makeup Artists, Theatrical and Performance	39-5091	Makeup Artists, Theatrical and Performance
39-5092	Manicurists and Pedicurists	39-5092	Manicurists and Pedicurists
39-5093	Shampooers	39-5093	Shampooers
39-5094	Skincare Specialists	39-5094	Skin Care Specialists
39-6011	Baggage Porters and Bellhops	39-6011	Baggage Porters and Bellhops
39-6012	Concierges	39-6012	Concierges
39-7011	Tour Guides and Escorts	39-6021	Tour Guides and Escorts
39-7012	Travel Guides	39-6022	Travel Guides
39-9011	Childcare Workers	39-9011	Child Care Workers
39-9021	Personal Care Aides	39-9021	Personal and Home Care Aides
39-9031	Fitness Trainers and Aerobics Instructors	39-9031	Fitness Trainers and Aerobics Instructors
39-9032	Recreation Workers	39-9032	Recreation Workers
39-9041	Residential Advisors	39-9041	Residential Advisors
39-9099	Personal Care and Service Workers, All Other	39-9099	Personal Care and Service Workers, All Other
41-1011	First-Line Supervisors of Retail Sales Workers	41-1011	First-Line Supervisors/Managers of Retail Sales Workers
41-1012	First-Line Supervisors of Non-Retail Sales Workers	41-1012	First-Line Supervisors/Managers of Non-Retail Sales Workers
41-2011	Cashiers	41-2011	Cashiers
41-2012	Gaming Change Persons and Booth Cashiers	41-2012	Gaming Change Persons and Booth Cashiers
41-2021	Counter and Rental Clerks	41-2021	Counter and Rental Clerks
41-2022	Parts Salespersons	41-2022	Parts Salespersons
41-2031	Retail Salespersons	41-2031	Retail Salespersons

Appendix B: Crosswalk to the 2000 SOC

2010 SOC code	2010 SOC title	2000 SOC code	2000 SOC title
41-3011	Advertising Sales Agents	41-3011	Advertising Sales Agents
41-3021	Insurance Sales Agents	41-3021	Insurance Sales Agents
41-3031	Securities, Commodities, and Financial Services Sales Agents	41-3031	Securities, Commodities, and Financial Services Sales Agents
41-3041	Travel Agents	41-3041	Travel Agents
41-3099	Sales Representatives, Services, All Other	41-3099	Sales Representatives, Services, All Other
41-4011	Sales Representatives, Wholesale and Manufacturing, Technical and Scientific Products	41-4011	Sales Representatives, Wholesale and Manufacturing, Technical and Scientific Products
41-4012	Sales Representatives, Wholesale and Manufacturing, Except Technical and Scientific Products	41-4012	Sales Representatives, Wholesale and Manufacturing, Except Technical and Scientific Products
41-9011	Demonstrators and Product Promoters	41-9011	Demonstrators and Product Promoters
41-9012	Models	41-9012	Models
41-9021	Real Estate Brokers	41-9021	Real Estate Brokers
41-9022	Real Estate Sales Agents	41-9022	Real Estate Sales Agents
41-9031	Sales Engineers	41-9031	Sales Engineers
41-9041	Telemarketers	41-9041	Telemarketers
41-9091	Door-to-Door Sales Workers, News and Street Vendors, and Related Workers	41-9091	Door-to-Door Sales Workers, News and Street Vendors, and Related Workers
41-9099	Sales and Related Workers, All Other	41-9099	Sales and Related Workers, All Other*
43-1011	First-Line Supervisors of Office and Administrative Support Workers	43-1011	First-Line Supervisors/Managers of Office and Administrative Support Workers
43-2011	Switchboard Operators, Including Answering Service	43-2011	Switchboard Operators, Including Answering Service
43-2021	Telephone Operators	43-2021	Telephone Operators
43-2099	Communications Equipment Operators, All Other	43-2099	Communications Equipment Operators, All Other
43-3011	Bill and Account Collectors	43-3011	Bill and Account Collectors
43-3021	Billing and Posting Clerks	43-3021	Billing and Posting Clerks and Machine Operators
43-3031	Bookkeeping, Accounting, and Auditing Clerks	43-3031	Bookkeeping, Accounting, and Auditing Clerks
43-3041	Gaming Cage Workers	43-3041	Gaming Cage Workers
43-3051	Payroll and Timekeeping Clerks	43-3051	Payroll and Timekeeping Clerks

Appendix B: Crosswalk to the 2000 SOC

2010 SOC code	2010 SOC title	2000 SOC code	2000 SOC title
43-3061	Procurement Clerks	43-3061	Procurement Clerks
43-3071	Tellers	43-3071	Tellers
43-3099	Financial Clerks, All Other	43-9199	Office and Administrative Support Workers, All Other*
43-4011	Brokerage Clerks	43-4011	Brokerage Clerks
43-4021	Correspondence Clerks	43-4021	Correspondence Clerks
43-4031	Court, Municipal, and License Clerks	43-4031	Court, Municipal, and License Clerks
43-4041	Credit Authorizers, Checkers, and Clerks	43-4041	Credit Authorizers, Checkers, and Clerks
43-4051	Customer Service Representatives	43-4051	Customer Service Representatives
43-4061	Eligibility Interviewers, Government Programs	43-4061	Eligibility Interviewers, Government Programs
43-4071	File Clerks	43-4071	File Clerks
43-4081	Hotel, Motel, and Resort Desk Clerks	43-4081	Hotel, Motel, and Resort Desk Clerks
43-4111	Interviewers, Except Eligibility and Loan	43-4111	Interviewers, Except Eligibility and Loan
43-4121	Library Assistants, Clerical	43-4121	Library Assistants, Clerical
43-4131	Loan Interviewers and Clerks	43-4131	Loan Interviewers and Clerks
43-4141	New Accounts Clerks	43-4141	New Accounts Clerks
43-4151	Order Clerks	43-4151	Order Clerks
43-4161	Human Resources Assistants, Except Payroll and Timekeeping	43-4161	Human Resources Assistants, Except Payroll and Timekeeping
43-4171	Receptionists and Information Clerks	43-4171	Receptionists and Information Clerks
43-4181	Reservation and Transportation Ticket Agents and Travel Clerks	43-4181	Reservation and Transportation Ticket Agents and Travel Clerks
43-4199	Information and Record Clerks, All Other	43-4199	Information and Record Clerks, All Other
43-5011	Cargo and Freight Agents	43-5011	Cargo and Freight Agents
43-5021	Couriers and Messengers	43-5021	Couriers and Messengers
43-5031	Police, Fire, and Ambulance Dispatchers	43-5031	Police, Fire, and Ambulance Dispatchers
43-5032	Dispatchers, Except Police, Fire, and Ambulance	43-5032	Dispatchers, Except Police, Fire, and Ambulance
43-5041	Meter Readers, Utilities	43-5041	Meter Readers, Utilities

Appendix B: Crosswalk to the 2000 SOC

2010 SOC code	2010 SOC title	2000 SOC code	2000 SOC title
43-5051	Postal Service Clerks	43-5051	Postal Service Clerks
43-5052	Postal Service Mail Carriers	43-5052	Postal Service Mail Carriers
43-5053	Postal Service Mail Sorters, Processors, and Processing Machine Operators	43-5053	Postal Service Mail Sorters, Processors, and Processing Machine Operators
43-5061	Production, Planning, and Expediting Clerks	43-5061	Production, Planning, and Expediting Clerks
43-5071	Shipping, Receiving, and Traffic Clerks	43-5071	Shipping, Receiving, and Traffic Clerks
43-5081	Stock Clerks and Order Fillers	43-5081	Stock Clerks and Order Fillers
43-5111	Weighers, Measurers, Checkers, and Samplers, Recordkeeping	43-5111	Weighers, Measurers, Checkers, and Samplers, Recordkeeping
43-6011	Executive Secretaries and Executive Administrative Assistants	43-6011	Executive Secretaries and Administrative Assistants
43-6012	Legal Secretaries	43-6012	Legal Secretaries
43-6013	Medical Secretaries	43-6013	Medical Secretaries
43-6014	Secretaries and Administrative Assistants, Except Legal, Medical, and Executive	43-6014	Secretaries, Except Legal, Medical, and Executive
43-9011	Computer Operators	43-9011	Computer Operators
43-9021	Data Entry Keyers	43-9021	Data Entry Keyers
43-9022	Word Processors and Typists	43-9022	Word Processors and Typists
43-9031	Desktop Publishers	43-9031	Desktop Publishers
43-9041	Insurance Claims and Policy Processing Clerks	43-9041	Insurance Claims and Policy Processing Clerks
43-9051	Mail Clerks and Mail Machine Operators, Except Postal Service	43-9051	Mail Clerks and Mail Machine Operators, Except Postal Service
43-9061	Office Clerks, General	43-9061	Office Clerks, General
43-9071	Office Machine Operators, Except Computer	43-9071	Office Machine Operators, Except Computer
43-9081	Proofreaders and Copy Markers	43-9081	Proofreaders and Copy Markers
43-9111	Statistical Assistants	43-9111	Statistical Assistants
43-9199	Office and Administrative Support Workers, All Other	43-9199	Office and Administrative Support Workers, All Other*
45-1011	First-Line Supervisors of Farming, Fishing, and Forestry Workers	45-1011	First-Line Supervisors/Managers of Farming, Fishing, and Forestry Workers
45-2011	Agricultural Inspectors	45-2011	Agricultural Inspectors
45-2021	Animal Breeders	45-2021	Animal Breeders

Appendix B: Crosswalk to the 2000 SOC

2010 SOC code	2010 SOC title	2000 SOC code	2000 SOC title
45-2041	Graders and Sorters, Agricultural Products	45-2041	Graders and Sorters, Agricultural Products
45-2091	Agricultural Equipment Operators	45-2091	Agricultural Equipment Operators
45-2092	Farmworkers and Laborers, Crop, Nursery, and Greenhouse	45-2092	Farmworkers and Laborers, Crop, Nursery, and Greenhouse
45-2093	Farmworkers, Farm, Ranch, and Aquacultural Animals	45-2093	Farmworkers, Farm and Ranch Animals
45-2099	Agricultural Workers, All Other	45-2099	Agricultural Workers, All Other
45-3011	Fishers and Related Fishing Workers	45-3011	Fishers and Related Fishing Workers
45-3021	Hunters and Trappers	45-3021	Hunters and Trappers
45-4011	Forest and Conservation Workers	45-4011	Forest and Conservation Workers
45-4021	Fallers	45-4021	Fallers
45-4022	Logging Equipment Operators	45-4022	Logging Equipment Operators
45-4023	Log Graders and Scalers	45-4023	Log Graders and Scalers
45-4029	Logging Workers, All Other	45-4029	Logging Workers, All Other
47-1011	First-Line Supervisors of Construction Trades and Extraction Workers	47-1011	First-Line Supervisors/Managers of Construction Trades and Extraction Workers
47-2011	Boilermakers	47-2011	Boilermakers
47-2021	Brickmasons and Blockmasons	47-2021	Brickmasons and Blockmasons
47-2022	Stonemasons	47-2022	Stonemasons
47-2031	Carpenters	47-2031	Carpenters
47-2041	Carpet Installers	47-2041	Carpet Installers
47-2042	Floor Layers, Except Carpet, Wood, and Hard Tiles	47-2042	Floor Layers, Except Carpet, Wood, and Hard Tiles
47-2043	Floor Sanders and Finishers	47-2043	Floor Sanders and Finishers
47-2044	Tile and Marble Setters	47-2044	Tile and Marble Setters
47-2051	Cement Masons and Concrete Finishers	47-2051	Cement Masons and Concrete Finishers
47-2053	Terrazzo Workers and Finishers	47-2053	Terrazzo Workers and Finishers
47-2061	Construction Laborers	47-2061	Construction Laborers
47-2071	Paving, Surfacing, and Tamping Equipment Operators	47-2071	Paving, Surfacing, and Tamping Equipment Operators

2010 SOC code	2010 SOC title	2000 SOC code	2000 SOC title
47-2072	Pile-Driver Operators	47-2072	Pile-Driver Operators
47-2073	Operating Engineers and Other Construction Equipment Operators	47-2073	Operating Engineers and Other Construction Equipment Operators
47-2081	Drywall and Ceiling Tile Installers	47-2081	Drywall and Ceiling Tile Installers
47-2082	Tapers	47-2082	Tapers
47-2111	Electricians	47-2111	Electricians*
47-2121	Glaziers	47-2121	Glaziers
47-2131	Insulation Workers, Floor, Ceiling, and Wall	47-2131	Insulation Workers, Floor, Ceiling, and Wall
47-2132	Insulation Workers, Mechanical	47-2132	Insulation Workers, Mechanical
47-2141	Painters, Construction and Maintenance	47-2141	Painters, Construction and Maintenance
47-2142	Paperhangers	47-2142	Paperhangers
47-2151	Pipelayers	47-2151	Pipelayers
47-2152	Plumbers, Pipefitters, and Steamfitters	47-2152	Plumbers, Pipefitters, and Steamfitters
47-2161	Plasterers and Stucco Masons	47-2161	Plasterers and Stucco Masons
47-2171	Reinforcing Iron and Rebar Workers	47-2171	Reinforcing Iron and Rebar Workers
47-2181	Roofers	47-2181	Roofers*
47-2211	Sheet Metal Workers	47-2211	Sheet Metal Workers
47-2221	Structural Iron and Steel Workers	47-2221	Structural Iron and Steel Workers
47-2231	Solar Photovoltaic Installers**	47-2111	Electricians*
47-2231	Solar Photovoltaic Installers**	47-2181	Roofers*
47-2231	Solar Photovoltaic Installers**	47-4099	Construction and Related Workers, All Other*
47-2231	Solar Photovoltaic Installers**	49-9021	Heating, Air Conditioning, and Refrigeration Mechanics and Installers*
47-2231	Solar Photovoltaic Installers**	49-9099	Installation, Maintenance, and Repair Workers, All Other*
47-3011	Helpers--Brickmasons, Blockmasons, Stonemasons, and Tile and Marble Setters	47-3011	Helpers--Brickmasons, Blockmasons, Stonemasons, and Tile and Marble Setters
47-3012	Helpers--Carpenters	47-3012	Helpers--Carpenters
47-3013	Helpers--Electricians	47-3013	Helpers--Electricians

2010 SOC code	2010 SOC title	2000 SOC code	2000 SOC title
47-3014	Helpers--Painters, Paperhangers, Plasterers, and Stucco Masons	47-3014	Helpers--Painters, Paperhangers, Plasterers, and Stucco Masons
47-3015	Helpers--Pipelayers, Plumbers, Pipefitters, and Steamfitters	47-3015	Helpers--Pipelayers, Plumbers, Pipefitters, and Steamfitters
47-3016	Helpers--Roofers	47-3016	Helpers--Roofers
47-3019	Helpers, Construction Trades, All Other	47-3019	Helpers, Construction Trades, All Other
47-4011	Construction and Building Inspectors	47-4011	Construction and Building Inspectors
47-4021	Elevator Installers and Repairers	47-4021	Elevator Installers and Repairers
47-4031	Fence Erectors	47-4031	Fence Erectors
47-4041	Hazardous Materials Removal Workers	47-4041	Hazardous Materials Removal Workers
47-4051	Highway Maintenance Workers	47-4051	Highway Maintenance Workers
47-4061	Rail-Track Laying and Maintenance Equipment Operators	47-4061	Rail-Track Laying and Maintenance Equipment Operators
47-4071	Septic Tank Servicers and Sewer Pipe Cleaners	47-4071	Septic Tank Servicers and Sewer Pipe Cleaners
47-4091	Segmental Pavers	47-4091	Segmental Pavers
47-4099	Construction and Related Workers, All Other	47-4099	Construction and Related Workers, All Other*
47-5011	Derrick Operators, Oil and Gas	47-5011	Derrick Operators, Oil and Gas
47-5012	Rotary Drill Operators, Oil and Gas	47-5012	Rotary Drill Operators, Oil and Gas
47-5013	Service Unit Operators, Oil, Gas, and Mining	47-5013	Service Unit Operators, Oil, Gas, and Mining
47-5021	Earth Drillers, Except Oil and Gas	47-5021	Earth Drillers, Except Oil and Gas
47-5031	Explosives Workers, Ordnance Handling Experts, and Blasters	47-5031	Explosives Workers, Ordnance Handling Experts, and Blasters
47-5041	Continuous Mining Machine Operators	47-5041	Continuous Mining Machine Operators
47-5042	Mine Cutting and Channeling Machine Operators	47-5042	Mine Cutting and Channeling Machine Operators
47-5049	Mining Machine Operators, All Other	47-5049	Mining Machine Operators, All Other
47-5051	Rock Splitters, Quarry	47-5051	Rock Splitters, Quarry
47-5061	Roof Bolters, Mining	47-5061	Roof Bolters, Mining
47-5071	Roustabouts, Oil and Gas	47-5071	Roustabouts, Oil and Gas
47-5081	Helpers--Extraction Workers	47-5081	Helpers--Extraction Workers

2010 SOC code	2010 SOC title	2000 SOC code	2000 SOC title
47-5099	Extraction Workers, All Other	47-5099	Extraction Workers, All Other
49-1011	First-Line Supervisors of Mechanics, Installers, and Repairers	49-1011	First-Line Supervisors/Managers of Mechanics, Installers, and Repairers
49-2011	Computer, Automated Teller, and Office Machine Repairers	49-2011	Computer, Automated Teller, and Office Machine Repairers
49-2021	Radio, Cellular, and Tower Equipment Installers and Repairers	49-2021	Radio Mechanics
49-2022	Telecommunications Equipment Installers and Repairers, Except Line Installers	49-2022	Telecommunications Equipment Installers and Repairers, Except Line Installers
49-2091	Avionics Technicians	49-2091	Avionics Technicians
49-2092	Electric Motor, Power Tool, and Related Repairers	49-2092	Electric Motor, Power Tool, and Related Repairers
49-2093	Electrical and Electronics Installers and Repairers, Transportation Equipment	49-2093	Electrical and Electronics Installers and Repairers, Transportation Equipment
49-2094	Electrical and Electronics Repairers, Commercial and Industrial Equipment	49-2094	Electrical and Electronics Repairers, Commercial and Industrial Equipment
49-2095	Electrical and Electronics Repairers, Powerhouse, Substation, and Relay	49-2095	Electrical and Electronics Repairers, Powerhouse, Substation, and Relay
49-2096	Electronic Equipment Installers and Repairers, Motor Vehicles	49-2096	Electronic Equipment Installers and Repairers, Motor Vehicles
49-2097	Electronic Home Entertainment Equipment Installers and Repairers	49-2097	Electronic Home Entertainment Equipment Installers and Repairers
49-2098	Security and Fire Alarm Systems Installers	49-2098	Security and Fire Alarm Systems Installers
49-3011	Aircraft Mechanics and Service Technicians	49-3011	Aircraft Mechanics and Service Technicians
49-3021	Automotive Body and Related Repairers	49-3021	Automotive Body and Related Repairers
49-3022	Automotive Glass Installers and Repairers	49-3022	Automotive Glass Installers and Repairers
49-3023	Automotive Service Technicians and Mechanics	49-3023	Automotive Service Technicians and Mechanics
49-3031	Bus and Truck Mechanics and Diesel Engine Specialists	49-3031	Bus and Truck Mechanics and Diesel Engine Specialists
49-3041	Farm Equipment Mechanics and Service Technicians	49-3041	Farm Equipment Mechanics
49-3042	Mobile Heavy Equipment Mechanics, Except Engines	49-3042	Mobile Heavy Equipment Mechanics, Except Engines
49-3043	Rail Car Repairers	49-3043	Rail Car Repairers
49-3051	Motorboat Mechanics and Service Technicians	49-3051	Motorboat Mechanics
49-3052	Motorcycle Mechanics	49-3052	Motorcycle Mechanics
49-3053	Outdoor Power Equipment and Other Small Engine Mechanics	49-3053	Outdoor Power Equipment and Other Small Engine Mechanics
49-3091	Bicycle Repairers	49-3091	Bicycle Repairers

2010 SOC code	2010 SOC title	2000 SOC code	2000 SOC title
49-3092	Recreational Vehicle Service Technicians	49-3092	Recreational Vehicle Service Technicians
49-3093	Tire Repairers and Changers	49-3093	Tire Repairers and Changers
49-9011	Mechanical Door Repairers	49-9011	Mechanical Door Repairers
49-9012	Control and Valve Installers and Repairers, Except Mechanical Door	49-9012	Control and Valve Installers and Repairers, Except Mechanical Door
49-9021	Heating, Air Conditioning, and Refrigeration Mechanics and Installers	49-9021	Heating, Air Conditioning, and Refrigeration Mechanics and Installers*
49-9031	Home Appliance Repairers	49-9031	Home Appliance Repairers
49-9041	Industrial Machinery Mechanics	49-9041	Industrial Machinery Mechanics
49-9043	Maintenance Workers, Machinery	49-9043	Maintenance Workers, Machinery
49-9044	Millwrights	49-9044	Millwrights
49-9045	Refractory Materials Repairers, Except Brickmasons	49-9045	Refractory Materials Repairers, Except Brickmasons
49-9051	Electrical Power-Line Installers and Repairers	49-9051	Electrical Power-Line Installers and Repairers
49-9052	Telecommunications Line Installers and Repairers	49-9052	Telecommunications Line Installers and Repairers
49-9061	Camera and Photographic Equipment Repairers	49-9061	Camera and Photographic Equipment Repairers
49-9062	Medical Equipment Repairers	49-9062	Medical Equipment Repairers
49-9063	Musical Instrument Repairers and Tuners	49-9063	Musical Instrument Repairers and Tuners
49-9064	Watch Repairers	49-9064	Watch Repairers
49-9069	Precision Instrument and Equipment Repairers, All Other	49-9069	Precision Instrument and Equipment Repairers, All Other
49-9071	Maintenance and Repair Workers, General	49-9042	Maintenance and Repair Workers, General
49-9081	Wind Turbine Service Technicians	49-9099	Installation, Maintenance, and Repair Workers, All Other*
49-9091	Coin, Vending, and Amusement Machine Servicers and Repairers	49-9091	Coin, Vending, and Amusement Machine Servicers and Repairers
49-9092	Commercial Divers	49-9092	Commercial Divers
49-9093	Fabric Menders, Except Garment	49-9093	Fabric Menders, Except Garment
49-9094	Locksmiths and Safe Repairers	49-9094	Locksmiths and Safe Repairers
49-9095	Manufactured Building and Mobile Home Installers	49-9095	Manufactured Building and Mobile Home Installers
49-9096	Riggers	49-9096	Riggers

Appendix B: Crosswalk to the 2000 SOC

2010 SOC code	2010 SOC title	2000 SOC code	2000 SOC title
49-9097	Signal and Track Switch Repairers	49-9097	Signal and Track Switch Repairers
49-9098	Helpers--Installation, Maintenance, and Repair Workers	49-9098	Helpers--Installation, Maintenance, and Repair Workers
49-9099	Installation, Maintenance, and Repair Workers, All Other	49-9099	Installation, Maintenance, and Repair Workers, All Other*
51-1011	First-Line Supervisors of Production and Operating Workers	51-1011	First-Line Supervisors/Managers of Production and Operating Workers
51-2011	Aircraft Structure, Surfaces, Rigging, and Systems Assemblers	51-2011	Aircraft Structure, Surfaces, Rigging, and Systems Assemblers
51-2021	Coil Winders, Tapers, and Finishers	51-2021	Coil Winders, Tapers, and Finishers
51-2022	Electrical and Electronic Equipment Assemblers	51-2022	Electrical and Electronic Equipment Assemblers
51-2023	Electromechanical Equipment Assemblers	51-2023	Electromechanical Equipment Assemblers
51-2031	Engine and Other Machine Assemblers	51-2031	Engine and Other Machine Assemblers
51-2041	Structural Metal Fabricators and Fitters	51-2041	Structural Metal Fabricators and Fitters
51-2091	Fiberglass Laminators and Fabricators	51-2091	Fiberglass Laminators and Fabricators
51-2092	Team Assemblers	51-2092	Team Assemblers
51-2093	Timing Device Assemblers and Adjusters	51-2093	Timing Device Assemblers, Adjusters, and Calibrators
51-2099	Assemblers and Fabricators, All Other	51-2099	Assemblers and Fabricators, All Other
51-3011	Bakers	51-3011	Bakers
51-3021	Butchers and Meat Cutters	51-3021	Butchers and Meat Cutters
51-3022	Meat, Poultry, and Fish Cutters and Trimmers	51-3022	Meat, Poultry, and Fish Cutters and Trimmers
51-3023	Slaughterers and Meat Packers	51-3023	Slaughterers and Meat Packers
51-3091	Food and Tobacco Roasting, Baking, and Drying Machine Operators and Tenders	51-3091	Food and Tobacco Roasting, Baking, and Drying Machine Operators and Tenders
51-3092	Food Batchmakers	51-3092	Food Batchmakers
51-3093	Food Cooking Machine Operators and Tenders	51-3093	Food Cooking Machine Operators and Tenders
51-3099	Food Processing Workers, All Other	51-9199	Production Workers, All Other*
51-4011	Computer-Controlled Machine Tool Operators, Metal and Plastic	51-4011	Computer-Controlled Machine Tool Operators, Metal and Plastic
51-4012	Computer Numerically Controlled Machine Tool Programmers, Metal and Plastic	51-4012	Numerical Tool and Process Control Programmers
51-4021	Extruding and Drawing Machine Setters, Operators, and Tenders, Metal and Plastic	51-4021	Extruding and Drawing Machine Setters, Operators, and Tenders, Metal and Plastic

2010 SOC code	2010 SOC title	2000 SOC code	2000 SOC title
51-4022	Forging Machine Setters, Operators, and Tenders, Metal and Plastic	51-4022	Forging Machine Setters, Operators, and Tenders, Metal and Plastic
51-4023	Rolling Machine Setters, Operators, and Tenders, Metal and Plastic	51-4023	Rolling Machine Setters, Operators, and Tenders, Metal and Plastic
51-4031	Cutting, Punching, and Press Machine Setters, Operators, and Tenders, Metal and Plastic	51-4031	Cutting, Punching, and Press Machine Setters, Operators, and Tenders, Metal and Plastic
51-4032	Drilling and Boring Machine Tool Setters, Operators, and Tenders, Metal and Plastic	51-4032	Drilling and Boring Machine Tool Setters, Operators, and Tenders, Metal and Plastic
51-4033	Grinding, Lapping, Polishing, and Buffing Machine Tool Setters, Operators, and Tenders, Metal and Plastic	51-4033	Grinding, Lapping, Polishing, and Buffing Machine Tool Setters, Operators, and Tenders, Metal and Plastic
51-4034	Lathe and Turning Machine Tool Setters, Operators, and Tenders, Metal and Plastic	51-4034	Lathe and Turning Machine Tool Setters, Operators, and Tenders, Metal and Plastic
51-4035	Milling and Planing Machine Setters, Operators, and Tenders, Metal and Plastic	51-4035	Milling and Planing Machine Setters, Operators, and Tenders, Metal and Plastic
51-4041	Machinists	51-4041	Machinists
51-4051	Metal-Refining Furnace Operators and Tenders	51-4051	Metal-Refining Furnace Operators and Tenders
51-4052	Pourers and Casters, Metal	51-4052	Pourers and Casters, Metal
51-4061	Model Makers, Metal and Plastic	51-4061	Model Makers, Metal and Plastic
51-4062	Patternmakers, Metal and Plastic	51-4062	Patternmakers, Metal and Plastic
51-4071	Foundry Mold and Coremakers	51-4071	Foundry Mold and Coremakers
51-4072	Molding, Coremaking, and Casting Machine Setters, Operators, and Tenders, Metal and Plastic	51-4072	Molding, Coremaking, and Casting Machine Setters, Operators, and Tenders, Metal and Plastic
51-4081	Multiple Machine Tool Setters, Operators, and Tenders, Metal and Plastic	51-4081	Multiple Machine Tool Setters, Operators, and Tenders, Metal and Plastic
51-4111	Tool and Die Makers	51-4111	Tool and Die Makers
51-4121	Welders, Cutters, Solderers, and Brazers	51-4121	Welders, Cutters, Solderers, and Brazers
51-4122	Welding, Soldering, and Brazing Machine Setters, Operators, and Tenders	51-4122	Welding, Soldering, and Brazing Machine Setters, Operators, and Tenders
51-4191	Heat Treating Equipment Setters, Operators, and Tenders, Metal and Plastic	51-4191	Heat Treating Equipment Setters, Operators, and Tenders, Metal and Plastic
51-4192	Layout Workers, Metal and Plastic	51-4192	Lay-Out Workers, Metal and Plastic
51-4193	Plating and Coating Machine Setters, Operators, and Tenders, Metal and Plastic	51-4193	Plating and Coating Machine Setters, Operators, and Tenders, Metal and Plastic
51-4194	Tool Grinders, Filers, and Sharpeners	51-4194	Tool Grinders, Filers, and Sharpeners
51-4199	Metal Workers and Plastic Workers, All Other	51-4199	Metal Workers and Plastic Workers, All Other
51-5111	Prepress Technicians and Workers	51-5022	Prepress Technicians and Workers

2010 SOC code	2010 SOC title	2000 SOC code	2000 SOC title
51-5112	Printing Press Operators**	51-5021	Job Printers*
51-5112	Printing Press Operators**	51-5023	Printing Machine Operators
51-5113	Print Binding and Finishing Workers**	51-5011	Bindery Workers
51-5113	Print Binding and Finishing Workers**	51-5012	Bookbinders
51-5113	Print Binding and Finishing Workers**	51-5021	Job Printers*
51-6011	Laundry and Dry-Cleaning Workers	51-6011	Laundry and Dry-Cleaning Workers
51-6021	Pressers, Textile, Garment, and Related Materials	51-6021	Pressers, Textile, Garment, and Related Materials
51-6031	Sewing Machine Operators	51-6031	Sewing Machine Operators
51-6041	Shoe and Leather Workers and Repairers	51-6041	Shoe and Leather Workers and Repairers
51-6042	Shoe Machine Operators and Tenders	51-6042	Shoe Machine Operators and Tenders
51-6051	Sewers, Hand	51-6051	Sewers, Hand
51-6052	Tailors, Dressmakers, and Custom Sewers	51-6052	Tailors, Dressmakers, and Custom Sewers
51-6061	Textile Bleaching and Dyeing Machine Operators and Tenders	51-6061	Textile Bleaching and Dyeing Machine Operators and Tenders
51-6062	Textile Cutting Machine Setters, Operators, and Tenders	51-6062	Textile Cutting Machine Setters, Operators, and Tenders
51-6063	Textile Knitting and Weaving Machine Setters, Operators, and Tenders	51-6063	Textile Knitting and Weaving Machine Setters, Operators, and Tenders
51-6064	Textile Winding, Twisting, and Drawing Out Machine Setters, Operators, and Tenders	51-6064	Textile Winding, Twisting, and Drawing Out Machine Setters, Operators, and Tenders
51-6091	Extruding and Forming Machine Setters, Operators, and Tenders, Synthetic and Glass Fibers	51-6091	Extruding and Forming Machine Setters, Operators, and Tenders, Synthetic and Glass Fibers
51-6092	Fabric and Apparel Patternmakers	51-6092	Fabric and Apparel Patternmakers
51-6093	Upholsterers	51-6093	Upholsterers
51-6099	Textile, Apparel, and Furnishings Workers, All Other	51-6099	Textile, Apparel, and Furnishings Workers, All Other
51-7011	Cabinetmakers and Bench Carpenters	51-7011	Cabinetmakers and Bench Carpenters
51-7021	Furniture Finishers	51-7021	Furniture Finishers
51-7031	Model Makers, Wood	51-7031	Model Makers, Wood
51-7032	Patternmakers, Wood	51-7032	Patternmakers, Wood

2010 SOC code	2010 SOC title	2000 SOC code	2000 SOC title
51-7041	Sawing Machine Setters, Operators, and Tenders, Wood	51-7041	Sawing Machine Setters, Operators, and Tenders, Wood
51-7042	Woodworking Machine Setters, Operators, and Tenders, Except Sawing	51-7042	Woodworking Machine Setters, Operators, and Tenders, Except Sawing
51-7099	Woodworkers, All Other	51-7099	Woodworkers, All Other
51-8011	Nuclear Power Reactor Operators	51-8011	Nuclear Power Reactor Operators
51-8012	Power Distributors and Dispatchers	51-8012	Power Distributors and Dispatchers
51-8013	Power Plant Operators	51-8013	Power Plant Operators
51-8021	Stationary Engineers and Boiler Operators	51-8021	Stationary Engineers and Boiler Operators
51-8031	Water and Wastewater Treatment Plant and System Operators	51-8031	Water and Liquid Waste Treatment Plant and System Operators
51-8091	Chemical Plant and System Operators	51-8091	Chemical Plant and System Operators
51-8092	Gas Plant Operators	51-8092	Gas Plant Operators
51-8093	Petroleum Pump System Operators, Refinery Operators, and Gaugers	51-8093	Petroleum Pump System Operators, Refinery Operators, and Gaugers
51-8099	Plant and System Operators, All Other	51-8099	Plant and System Operators, All Other
51-9011	Chemical Equipment Operators and Tenders	51-9011	Chemical Equipment Operators and Tenders
51-9012	Separating, Filtering, Clarifying, Precipitating, and Still Machine Setters, Operators, and Tenders	51-9012	Separating, Filtering, Clarifying, Precipitating, and Still Machine Setters, Operators, and Tenders
51-9021	Crushing, Grinding, and Polishing Machine Setters, Operators, and Tenders	51-9021	Crushing, Grinding, and Polishing Machine Setters, Operators, and Tenders
51-9022	Grinding and Polishing Workers, Hand	51-9022	Grinding and Polishing Workers, Hand
51-9023	Mixing and Blending Machine Setters, Operators, and Tenders	51-9023	Mixing and Blending Machine Setters, Operators, and Tenders
51-9031	Cutters and Trimmers, Hand	51-9031	Cutters and Trimmers, Hand
51-9032	Cutting and Slicing Machine Setters, Operators, and Tenders	51-9032	Cutting and Slicing Machine Setters, Operators, and Tenders
51-9041	Extruding, Forming, Pressing, and Compacting Machine Setters, Operators, and Tenders	51-9041	Extruding, Forming, Pressing, and Compacting Machine Setters, Operators, and Tenders
51-9051	Furnace, Kiln, Oven, Drier, and Kettle Operators and Tenders	51-9051	Furnace, Kiln, Oven, Drier, and Kettle Operators and Tenders
51-9061	Inspectors, Testers, Sorters, Samplers, and Weighers	51-9061	Inspectors, Testers, Sorters, Samplers, and Weighers
51-9071	Jewelers and Precious Stone and Metal Workers	51-9071	Jewelers and Precious Stone and Metal Workers
51-9081	Dental Laboratory Technicians	51-9081	Dental Laboratory Technicians
51-9082	Medical Appliance Technicians	51-9082	Medical Appliance Technicians

2010 SOC code	2010 SOC title	2000 SOC code	2000 SOC title
51-9083	Ophthalmic Laboratory Technicians	51-9083	Ophthalmic Laboratory Technicians
51-9111	Packaging and Filling Machine Operators and Tenders	51-9111	Packaging and Filling Machine Operators and Tenders
51-9121	Coating, Painting, and Spraying Machine Setters, Operators, and Tenders	51-9121	Coating, Painting, and Spraying Machine Setters, Operators, and Tenders
51-9122	Painters, Transportation Equipment	51-9122	Painters, Transportation Equipment
51-9123	Painting, Coating, and Decorating Workers	51-9123	Painting, Coating, and Decorating Workers
51-9141	Semiconductor Processors	51-9141	Semiconductor Processors
51-9151	Photographic Process Workers and Processing Machine Operators**	51-9131	Photographic Process Workers
51-9151	Photographic Process Workers and Processing Machine Operators**	51-9132	Photographic Processing Machine Operators
51-9191	Adhesive Bonding Machine Operators and Tenders	51-9191	Cementing and Gluing Machine Operators and Tenders
51-9192	Cleaning, Washing, and Metal Pickling Equipment Operators and Tenders	51-9192	Cleaning, Washing, and Metal Pickling Equipment Operators and Tenders
51-9193	Cooling and Freezing Equipment Operators and Tenders	51-9193	Cooling and Freezing Equipment Operators and Tenders
51-9194	Etchers and Engravers	51-9194	Etchers and Engravers
51-9195	Molders, Shapers, and Casters, Except Metal and Plastic	51-9195	Molders, Shapers, and Casters, Except Metal and Plastic
51-9196	Paper Goods Machine Setters, Operators, and Tenders	51-9196	Paper Goods Machine Setters, Operators, and Tenders
51-9197	Tire Builders	51-9197	Tire Builders
51-9198	Helpers--Production Workers	51-9198	Helpers--Production Workers
51-9199	Production Workers, All Other	51-9199	Production Workers, All Other*
53-1011	Aircraft Cargo Handling Supervisors	53-1011	Aircraft Cargo Handling Supervisors
53-1021	First-Line Supervisors of Helpers, Laborers, and Material Movers, Hand	53-1021	First-Line Supervisors/Managers of Helpers, Laborers, and Material Movers, Hand
53-1031	First-Line Supervisors of Transportation and Material-Moving Machine and Vehicle Operators	53-1031	First-Line Supervisors/Managers of Transportation and Material-Moving Machine and Vehicle Operators
53-2011	Airline Pilots, Copilots, and Flight Engineers	53-2011	Airline Pilots, Copilots, and Flight Engineers
53-2012	Commercial Pilots	53-2012	Commercial Pilots
53-2021	Air Traffic Controllers	53-2021	Air Traffic Controllers
53-2022	Airfield Operations Specialists	53-2022	Airfield Operations Specialists
53-2031	Flight Attendants	39-6031	Flight Attendants

2010 SOC code	2010 SOC title	2000 SOC code	2000 SOC title
53-3011	Ambulance Drivers and Attendants, Except Emergency Medical Technicians	53-3011	Ambulance Drivers and Attendants, Except Emergency Medical Technicians
53-3021	Bus Drivers, Transit and Intercity	53-3021	Bus Drivers, Transit and Intercity
53-3022	Bus Drivers, School or Special Client	53-3022	Bus Drivers, School
53-3031	Driver/Sales Workers	53-3031	Driver/Sales Workers
53-3032	Heavy and Tractor-Trailer Truck Drivers	53-3032	Truck Drivers, Heavy and Tractor-Trailer
53-3033	Light Truck or Delivery Services Drivers	53-3033	Truck Drivers, Light or Delivery Services
53-3041	Taxi Drivers and Chauffeurs	53-3041	Taxi Drivers and Chauffeurs
53-3099	Motor Vehicle Operators, All Other	53-3099	Motor Vehicle Operators, All Other
53-4011	Locomotive Engineers	53-4011	Locomotive Engineers
53-4012	Locomotive Firers	53-4012	Locomotive Firers
53-4013	Rail Yard Engineers, Dinkey Operators, and Hostlers	53-4013	Rail Yard Engineers, Dinkey Operators, and Hostlers
53-4021	Railroad Brake, Signal, and Switch Operators	53-4021	Railroad Brake, Signal, and Switch Operators
53-4031	Railroad Conductors and Yardmasters	53-4031	Railroad Conductors and Yardmasters
53-4041	Subway and Streetcar Operators	53-4041	Subway and Streetcar Operators
53-4099	Rail Transportation Workers, All Other	53-4099	Rail Transportation Workers, All Other
53-5011	Sailors and Marine Oilers	53-5011	Sailors and Marine Oilers
53-5021	Captains, Mates, and Pilots of Water Vessels	53-5021	Captains, Mates, and Pilots of Water Vessels
53-5022	Motorboat Operators	53-5022	Motorboat Operators
53-5031	Ship Engineers	53-5031	Ship Engineers
53-6011	Bridge and Lock Tenders	53-6011	Bridge and Lock Tenders
53-6021	Parking Lot Attendants	53-6021	Parking Lot Attendants
53-6031	Automotive and Watercraft Service Attendants	53-6031	Service Station Attendants
53-6041	Traffic Technicians	53-6041	Traffic Technicians
53-6051	Transportation Inspectors	53-6051	Transportation Inspectors
53-6061	Transportation Attendants, Except Flight Attendants	39-6032	Transportation Attendants, Except Flight Attendants and Baggage Porters

2010 SOC code	2010 SOC title	2000 SOC code	2000 SOC title
53-6099	Transportation Workers, All Other	53-6099	Transportation Workers, All Other
53-7011	Conveyor Operators and Tenders	53-7011	Conveyor Operators and Tenders
53-7021	Crane and Tower Operators	53-7021	Crane and Tower Operators
53-7031	Dredge Operators	53-7031	Dredge Operators
53-7032	Excavating and Loading Machine and Dragline Operators	53-7032	Excavating and Loading Machine and Dragline Operators
53-7033	Loading Machine Operators, Underground Mining	53-7033	Loading Machine Operators, Underground Mining
53-7041	Hoist and Winch Operators	53-7041	Hoist and Winch Operators
53-7051	Industrial Truck and Tractor Operators	53-7051	Industrial Truck and Tractor Operators
53-7061	Cleaners of Vehicles and Equipment	53-7061	Cleaners of Vehicles and Equipment
53-7062	Laborers and Freight, Stock, and Material Movers, Hand	53-7062	Laborers and Freight, Stock, and Material Movers, Hand
53-7063	Machine Feeders and Offbearers	53-7063	Machine Feeders and Offbearers
53-7064	Packers and Packagers, Hand	53-7064	Packers and Packagers, Hand
53-7071	Gas Compressor and Gas Pumping Station Operators	53-7071	Gas Compressor and Gas Pumping Station Operators
53-7072	Pump Operators, Except Wellhead Pumpers	53-7072	Pump Operators, Except Wellhead Pumpers
53-7073	Wellhead Pumpers	53-7073	Wellhead Pumpers
53-7081	Refuse and Recyclable Material Collectors	53-7081	Refuse and Recyclable Material Collectors
53-7111	Mine Shuttle Car Operators	53-7111	Shuttle Car Operators
53-7121	Tank Car, Truck, and Ship Loaders	53-7121	Tank Car, Truck, and Ship Loaders
53-7199	Material Moving Workers, All Other	53-7199	Material Moving Workers, All Other
55-1011	Air Crew Officers	55-1011	Air Crew Officers
55-1012	Aircraft Launch and Recovery Officers	55-1012	Aircraft Launch and Recovery Officers
55-1013	Armored Assault Vehicle Officers	55-1013	Armored Assault Vehicle Officers
55-1014	Artillery and Missile Officers	55-1014	Artillery and Missile Officers
55-1015	Command and Control Center Officers	55-1015	Command and Control Center Officers
55-1016	Infantry Officers	55-1016	Infantry Officers

2010 SOC code	2010 SOC title	2000 SOC code	2000 SOC title
55-1017	Special Forces Officers	55-1017	Special Forces Officers
55-1019	Military Officer Special and Tactical Operations Leaders, All Other	55-1019	Military Officer Special and Tactical Operations Leaders/Managers, All Other
55-2011	First-Line Supervisors of Air Crew Members	55-2011	First-Line Supervisors/Managers of Air Crew Members
55-2012	First-Line Supervisors of Weapons Specialists/Crew Members	55-2012	First-Line Supervisors/Managers of Weapons Specialists/Crew Members
55-2013	First-Line Supervisors of All Other Tactical Operations Specialists	55-2013	First-Line Supervisors/Managers of All Other Tactical Operations Specialists
55-3011	Air Crew Members	55-3011	Air Crew Members
55-3012	Aircraft Launch and Recovery Specialists	55-3012	Aircraft Launch and Recovery Specialists
55-3013	Armored Assault Vehicle Crew Members	55-3013	Armored Assault Vehicle Crew Members
55-3014	Artillery and Missile Crew Members	55-3014	Artillery and Missile Crew Members
55-3015	Command and Control Center Specialists	55-3015	Command and Control Center Specialists
55-3016	Infantry	55-3016	Infantry
55-3017	Radar and Sonar Technicians	55-3017	Radar and Sonar Technicians
55-3018	Special Forces	55-3018	Special Forces
55-3019	Military Enlisted Tactical Operations and Air/Weapons Specialists and Crew Members, All Other	55-3019	Military Enlisted Tactical Operations and Air/Weapons Specialists and Crew Members, All Other

Appendix C: Type of Change by Detailed Occupation, 2010 SOC

2010 SOC detailed occupation	Type of change		SOC code	2010 SOC detailed occupation	Type of change
Chief Executives	E		13-1074	Farm Labor Contractors	C,E
General and Operations Managers	E		13-1075	Labor Relations Specialists	C,T,D
Legislators	E		13-1081	Logisticians	E
Advertising and Promotions Managers	E		13-1111	Management Analysts	E
Marketing Managers	E		13-1121	Meeting, Convention, and Event Planners	T,D
Sales Managers	E		13-1131	Fundraisers	C,T,D
Public Relations and Fundraising Managers	T,E		13-1141	Compensation, Benefits, and Job Analysis Specialists	C
Administrative Services Managers	E				
Computer and Information Systems Managers	E		13-1151	Training and Development Specialists	C,E
Financial Managers	E		13-1161	Market Research Analysts and Marketing Specialists	C,T,D
Industrial Production Managers	-				
Purchasing Managers	-		13-1199	Business Operations Specialists, All Other	D
Transportation, Storage, and Distribution Managers	E		13-2011	Accountants and Auditors	E
			13-2021	Appraisers and Assessors of Real Estate	E
Compensation and Benefits Managers	C,E		13-2031	Budget Analysts	E
Human Resources Managers	C,T,E		13-2041	Credit Analysts	E
Training and Development Managers	C		13-2051	Financial Analysts	-
Farmers, Ranchers, and Other Agricultural Managers	C,T,D		13-2052	Personal Financial Advisors	E
			13-2053	Insurance Underwriters	-
Construction Managers	E		13-2061	Financial Examiners	E
Education Administrators, Preschool and Childcare Center/Program	T,E		13-2071	Credit Counselors	T,E
			13-2072	Loan Officers	E
Education Administrators, Elementary and Secondary School	E		13-2081	Tax Examiners and Collectors, and Revenue Agents	T
Education Administrators, Postsecondary	-		13-2082	Tax Preparers	E
Education Administrators, All Other	-		13-2099	Financial Specialists, All Other	-
Architectural and Engineering Managers	T		15-1111	Computer and Information Research Scientists	C,T,E
Food Service Managers	E		15-1121	Computer Systems Analysts	C,D
Funeral Service Managers	T,D		15-1122	Information Security Analysts	C,T,D
Gaming Managers	E		15-1131	Computer Programmers	C,E
Lodging Managers	-		15-1132	Software Developers, Applications	C,T,E
Medical and Health Services Managers	E		15-1133	Software Developers, Systems Software	C,T,E
Natural Sciences Managers	E		15-1134	Web Developers	C,T,D
Postmasters and Mail Superintendents	E		15-1141	Database Administrators	C,E
Property, Real Estate, and Community Association Managers	E		15-1142	Network and Computer Systems Administrators	C,D
Social and Community Service Managers	E		15-1143	Computer Network Architects	C,T,D
Emergency Management Directors	C,T,E		15-1151	Computer User Support Specialists	C,T,E
Managers, All Other	-		15-1152	Computer Network Support Specialists	C,T,D
Agents and Business Managers of Artists, Performers, and Athletes	E		15-1199	Computer Occupations, All Other	C,T,E
			15-2011	Actuaries	E
Buyers and Purchasing Agents, Farm Products	T,E		15-2021	Mathematicians	E
			15-2031	Operations Research Analysts	E
Wholesale and Retail Buyers, Except Farm Products	E		15-2041	Statisticians	E
			15-2091	Mathematical Technicians	-
Purchasing Agents, Except Wholesale, Retail, and Farm Products	E		15-2099	Mathematical Science Occupations, All Other	-
			17-1011	Architects, Except Landscape and Naval	E
Claims Adjusters, Examiners, and Investigators	E		17-1012	Landscape Architects	E
			17-1021	Cartographers and Photogrammetrists	-
Insurance Appraisers, Auto Damage	E		17-1022	Surveyors	-
Compliance Officers	T,D		17-2011	Aerospace Engineers	E
Cost Estimators	-		17-2021	Agricultural Engineers	-
Human Resources Specialists	C,T,D		17-2031	Biomedical Engineers	-

C = Code Change, T = Title Change, D = Definition Content Change, E = Definition Editing Change

Appendix C: Type of Change by Detailed Occupation, 2010 SOC

SOC code	2010 SOC detailed occupation	Type of change
17-2041	Chemical Engineers	-
17-2051	Civil Engineers	E
17-2061	Computer Hardware Engineers	E
17-2071	Electrical Engineers	E
17-2072	Electronics Engineers, Except Computer	E
17-2081	Environmental Engineers	E
17-2111	Health and Safety Engineers, Except Mining Safety Engineers and Inspectors	-
17-2112	Industrial Engineers	E
17-2121	Marine Engineers and Naval Architects	-
17-2131	Materials Engineers	E
17-2141	Mechanical Engineers	E
17-2151	Mining and Geological Engineers, Including Mining Safety Engineers	E
17-2161	Nuclear Engineers	E
17-2171	Petroleum Engineers	E
17-2199	Engineers, All Other	-
17-3011	Architectural and Civil Drafters	E
17-3012	Electrical and Electronics Drafters	E
17-3013	Mechanical Drafters	-
17-3019	Drafters, All Other	-
17-3021	Aerospace Engineering and Operations Technicians	E
17-3022	Civil Engineering Technicians	-
17-3023	Electrical and Electronics Engineering Technicians	-
17-3024	Electro-Mechanical Technicians	E
17-3025	Environmental Engineering Technicians	E
17-3026	Industrial Engineering Technicians	E
17-3027	Mechanical Engineering Technicians	E
17-3029	Engineering Technicians, Except Drafters, All Other	-
17-3031	Surveying and Mapping Technicians	E
19-1011	Animal Scientists	-
19-1012	Food Scientists and Technologists	-
19-1013	Soil and Plant Scientists	E
19-1021	Biochemists and Biophysicists	E
19-1022	Microbiologists	-
19-1023	Zoologists and Wildlife Biologists	E
19-1029	Biological Scientists, All Other	-
19-1031	Conservation Scientists	E
19-1032	Foresters	E
19-1041	Epidemiologists	E
19-1042	Medical Scientists, Except Epidemiologists	E
19-1099	Life Scientists, All Other	-
19-2011	Astronomers	E
19-2012	Physicists	E
19-2021	Atmospheric and Space Scientists	E
19-2031	Chemists	E
19-2032	Materials Scientists	E
19-2041	Environmental Scientists and Specialists, Including Health	E
19-2042	Geoscientists, Except Hydrologists and Geographers	E

SOC code	2010 SOC detailed occupation
19-2043	Hydrologists
19-2099	Physical Scientists, All Other
19-3011	Economists
19-3022	Survey Researchers
19-3031	Clinical, Counseling, and School Psychologists
19-3032	Industrial-Organizational Psychologists
19-3039	Psychologists, All Other
19-3041	Sociologists
19-3051	Urban and Regional Planners
19-3091	Anthropologists and Archeologists
19-3092	Geographers
19-3093	Historians
19-3094	Political Scientists
19-3099	Social Scientists and Related Workers, All Other
19-4011	Agricultural and Food Science Technicians
19-4021	Biological Technicians
19-4031	Chemical Technicians
19-4041	Geological and Petroleum Technicians
19-4051	Nuclear Technicians
19-4061	Social Science Research Assistants
19-4091	Environmental Science and Protection Technicians, Including Health
19-4092	Forensic Science Technicians
19-4093	Forest and Conservation Technicians
19-4099	Life, Physical, and Social Science Technicians, All Other
21-1011	Substance Abuse and Behavioral Disorder Counselors
21-1012	Educational, Guidance, School, and Vocational Counselors
21-1013	Marriage and Family Therapists
21-1014	Mental Health Counselors
21-1015	Rehabilitation Counselors
21-1019	Counselors, All Other
21-1021	Child, Family, and School Social Workers
21-1022	Healthcare Social Workers
21-1023	Mental Health and Substance Abuse Social Workers
21-1029	Social Workers, All Other
21-1091	Health Educators
21-1092	Probation Officers and Correctional Treatment Specialists
21-1093	Social and Human Service Assistants
21-1094	Community Health Workers
21-1099	Community and Social Service Specialists, All Other
21-2011	Clergy
21-2021	Directors, Religious Activities and Education
21-2099	Religious Workers, All Other
23-1011	Lawyers
23-1012	Judicial Law Clerks

C = Code Change, T = Title Change, D = Definition Content Change, E = Definition Editing Change

Appendix C: Type of Change by Detailed Occupation, 2010 SOC

2010 SOC detailed occupation	Type of change	SOC code	2010 SOC detailed occupation	Type of change
Administrative Law Judges, Adjudicators, and Hearing Officers	E	25-1126	Philosophy and Religion Teachers, Postsecondary	E
Arbitrators, Mediators, and Conciliators	-	25-1191	Graduate Teaching Assistants	E
Judges, Magistrate Judges, and Magistrates	E	25-1192	Home Economics Teachers, Postsecondary	E
Paralegals and Legal Assistants	D	25-1193	Recreation and Fitness Studies Teachers, Postsecondary	E
Court Reporters	-			
Title Examiners, Abstractors, and Searchers	E	25-1194	Vocational Education Teachers, Postsecondary	E
Legal Support Workers, All Other	-			
Business Teachers, Postsecondary	E	25-1199	Postsecondary Teachers, All Other	-
Computer Science Teachers, Postsecondary	E	25-2011	Preschool Teachers, Except Special Education	E
Mathematical Science Teachers, Postsecondary	E	25-2012	Kindergarten Teachers, Except Special Education	E
Architecture Teachers, Postsecondary	E			
Engineering Teachers, Postsecondary	E	25-2021	Elementary School Teachers, Except Special Education	E
Agricultural Sciences Teachers, Postsecondary	E	25-2022	Middle School Teachers, Except Special and Career/Technical Education	T,E
Biological Science Teachers, Postsecondary	E			
Forestry and Conservation Science Teachers, Postsecondary	E	25-2023	Career/Technical Education Teachers, Middle School	T,E
Atmospheric, Earth, Marine, and Space Sciences Teachers, Postsecondary	E	25-2031	Secondary School Teachers, Except Special and Career/Technical Education	T,E
Chemistry Teachers, Postsecondary	E	25-2032	Career/Technical Education Teachers, Secondary School	T,E
Environmental Science Teachers, Postsecondary	E	25-2051	Special Education Teachers, Preschool	C,T,D
Physics Teachers, Postsecondary	E	25-2052	Special Education Teachers, Kindergarten and Elementary School	C,T,D
Anthropology and Archeology Teachers, Postsecondary	E			
Area, Ethnic, and Cultural Studies Teachers, Postsecondary	E	25-2053	Special Education Teachers, Middle School	C
		25-2054	Special Education Teachers, Secondary School	C
Economics Teachers, Postsecondary	E	25-2059	Special Education Teachers, All Other	C,T,D
Geography Teachers, Postsecondary	E	25-3011	Adult Basic and Secondary Education and Literacy Teachers and Instructors	T
Political Science Teachers, Postsecondary	E			
Psychology Teachers, Postsecondary	E	25-3021	Self-Enrichment Education Teachers	E
Sociology Teachers, Postsecondary	E	25-3099	Teachers and Instructors, All Other	D
Social Sciences Teachers, Postsecondary, All Other	-	25-4011	Archivists	-
		25-4012	Curators	E
Health Specialties Teachers, Postsecondary	E	25-4013	Museum Technicians and Conservators	E
Nursing Instructors and Teachers, Postsecondary	E	25-4021	Librarians	E
		25-4031	Library Technicians	E
Education Teachers, Postsecondary	E	25-9011	Audio-Visual and Multimedia Collections Specialists	T,E
Library Science Teachers, Postsecondary	E			
Criminal Justice and Law Enforcement Teachers, Postsecondary	E	25-9021	Farm and Home Management Advisors	E
Law Teachers, Postsecondary	E	25-9031	Instructional Coordinators	-
Social Work Teachers, Postsecondary	E	25-9041	Teacher Assistants	E
Art, Drama, and Music Teachers, Postsecondary	E	25-9099	Education, Training, and Library Workers, All Other	-
Communications Teachers, Postsecondary	E	27-1011	Art Directors	E
English Language and Literature Teachers, Postsecondary	E	27-1012	Craft Artists	-
		27-1013	Fine Artists, Including Painters, Sculptors, and Illustrators	E
Foreign Language and Literature Teachers, Postsecondary	E	27-1014	Multimedia Artists and Animators	T
		27-1019	Artists and Related Workers, All Other	-
History Teachers, Postsecondary	E	27-1021	Commercial and Industrial Designers	-
		27-1022	Fashion Designers	E

C = Code Change, T = Title Change, D = Definition Content Change, E = Definition Editing Change

Appendix C: Type of Change by Detailed Occupation, 2010 SOC

SOC code	2010 SOC detailed occupation	Type of change	SOC code	2010 SOC detailed occupation
27-1023	Floral Designers	-	29-1065	Pediatricians, General
27-1024	Graphic Designers	-	29-1066	Psychiatrists
27-1025	Interior Designers	-	29-1067	Surgeons
27-1026	Merchandise Displayers and Window Trimmers	-	29-1069	Physicians and Surgeons, All Other
27-1027	Set and Exhibit Designers	-	29-1071	Physician Assistants
27-1029	Designers, All Other	-	29-1081	Podiatrists
27-2011	Actors	E	29-1122	Occupational Therapists
27-2012	Producers and Directors	E	29-1123	Physical Therapists
27-2021	Athletes and Sports Competitors	-	29-1124	Radiation Therapists
27-2022	Coaches and Scouts	-	29-1125	Recreational Therapists
27-2023	Umpires, Referees, and Other Sports Officials	-	29-1126	Respiratory Therapists
			29-1127	Speech-Language Pathologists
27-2031	Dancers	E	29-1128	Exercise Physiologists
27-2032	Choreographers	E	29-1129	Therapists, All Other
27-2041	Music Directors and Composers	E	29-1131	Veterinarians
27-2042	Musicians and Singers	E	29-1141	Registered Nurses
27-2099	Entertainers and Performers, Sports and Related Workers, All Other	-	29-1151	Nurse Anesthetists
			29-1161	Nurse Midwives
27-3011	Radio and Television Announcers	E	29-1171	Nurse Practitioners
27-3012	Public Address System and Other Announcers	E	29-1181	Audiologists
			29-1199	Health Diagnosing and Treating Practitioners, All Other
27-3021	Broadcast News Analysts	-	29-2011	Medical and Clinical Laboratory Technologists
27-3022	Reporters and Correspondents	-		
27-3031	Public Relations Specialists	E	29-2012	Medical and Clinical Laboratory Technicians
27-3041	Editors	E	29-2021	Dental Hygienists
27-3042	Technical Writers	-	29-2031	Cardiovascular Technologists and Technicians
27-3043	Writers and Authors	-		
27-3091	Interpreters and Translators	E	29-2032	Diagnostic Medical Sonographers
27-3099	Media and Communication Workers, All Other	-	29-2033	Nuclear Medicine Technologists
			29-2034	Radiologic Technologists
27-4011	Audio and Video Equipment Technicians	E	29-2035	Magnetic Resonance Imaging Technologists
27-4012	Broadcast Technicians	E	29-2041	Emergency Medical Technicians and Paramedics
27-4013	Radio Operators	E		
27-4014	Sound Engineering Technicians	-	29-2051	Dietetic Technicians
27-4021	Photographers	E	29-2052	Pharmacy Technicians
27-4031	Camera Operators, Television, Video, and Motion Picture	E	29-2053	Psychiatric Technicians
			29-2054	Respiratory Therapy Technicians
27-4032	Film and Video Editors	E	29-2055	Surgical Technologists
27-4099	Media and Communication Equipment Workers, All Other	-	29-2056	Veterinary Technologists and Technicians
			29-2057	Ophthalmic Medical Technicians
29-1011	Chiropractors	E	29-2061	Licensed Practical and Licensed Vocational Nurses
29-1021	Dentists, General	E		
29-1022	Oral and Maxillofacial Surgeons	E	29-2071	Medical Records and Health Information Technicians
29-1023	Orthodontists	-		
29-1024	Prosthodontists	-	29-2081	Opticians, Dispensing
29-1029	Dentists, All Other Specialists	-	29-2091	Orthotists and Prosthetists
29-1031	Dietitians and Nutritionists	-	29-2092	Hearing Aid Specialists
29-1041	Optometrists	E	29-2099	Health Technologists and Technicians, All Other
29-1051	Pharmacists	-		
29-1061	Anesthesiologists	E	29-9011	Occupational Health and Safety Specialists
29-1062	Family and General Practitioners	E	29-9012	Occupational Health and Safety Technicians
29-1063	Internists, General	E	29-9091	Athletic Trainers
29-1064	Obstetricians and Gynecologists	E	29-9092	Genetic Counselors

C = Code Change, T = Title Change, D = Definition Content Change, E = Definition Editing Change

Appendix C: Type of Change by Detailed Occupation, 2010 SOC

2010 SOC detailed occupation	Type of change	SOC code	2010 SOC detailed occupation	Type of change
Healthcare Practitioners and Technical Workers, All Other	T,D	35-2013	Cooks, Private Household	E
Home Health Aides	E	35-2014	Cooks, Restaurant	E
Psychiatric Aides	E	35-2015	Cooks, Short Order	-
Nursing Assistants	C,T,D	35-2019	Cooks, All Other	-
Orderlies	C,T,D	35-2021	Food Preparation Workers	-
Occupational Therapy Assistants	T	35-3011	Bartenders	-
Occupational Therapy Aides	T	35-3021	Combined Food Preparation and Serving Workers, Including Fast Food	E
Physical Therapist Assistants	-	35-3022	Counter Attendants, Cafeteria, Food Concession, and Coffee Shop	E
Physical Therapist Aides	-			
Massage Therapists	E	35-3031	Waiters and Waitresses	-
Dental Assistants	E	35-3041	Food Servers, Nonrestaurant	E
Medical Assistants	E	35-9011	Dining Room and Cafeteria Attendants and Bartender Helpers	E
Medical Equipment Preparers	-			
Medical Transcriptionists	E	35-9021	Dishwashers	-
Pharmacy Aides	-	35-9031	Hosts and Hostesses, Restaurant, Lounge, and Coffee Shop	-
Veterinary Assistants and Laboratory Animal Caretakers	-			
Phlebotomists	C,T,D	35-9099	Food Preparation and Serving Related Workers, All Other	-
Healthcare Support Workers, All Other	D	37-1011	First-Line Supervisors of Housekeeping and Janitorial Workers	T,E
First-Line Supervisors of Correctional Officers	T,E			
First-Line Supervisors of Police and Detectives	T,E	37-1012	First-Line Supervisors of Landscaping, Lawn Service, and Groundskeeping Workers	T,E
First-Line Supervisors of Fire Fighting and Prevention Workers	T,E	37-2011	Janitors and Cleaners, Except Maids and Housekeeping Cleaners	-
First-Line Supervisors of Protective Service Workers, All Other	T	37-2012	Maids and Housekeeping Cleaners	E
		37-2019	Building Cleaning Workers, All Other	-
Firefighters	T,E	37-2021	Pest Control Workers	E
Fire Inspectors and Investigators	E	37-3011	Landscaping and Groundskeeping Workers	-
Forest Fire Inspectors and Prevention Specialists	E	37-3012	Pesticide Handlers, Sprayers, and Applicators, Vegetation	E
Bailiffs	-	37-3013	Tree Trimmers and Pruners	E
Correctional Officers and Jailers	-	37-3019	Grounds Maintenance Workers, All Other	-
Detectives and Criminal Investigators	-	39-1011	Gaming Supervisors	E
Fish and Game Wardens	-	39-1012	Slot Supervisor	T,E
Parking Enforcement Workers	E	39-1021	First-Line Supervisors of Personal Service Workers	T,E
Police and Sheriff's Patrol Officers	E			
Transit and Railroad Police	-	39-2011	Animal Trainers	-
Animal Control Workers	-	39-2021	Nonfarm Animal Caretakers	-
Private Detectives and Investigators	E	39-3011	Gaming Dealers	E
Gaming Surveillance Officers and Gaming Investigators	-	39-3012	Gaming and Sports Book Writers and Runners	E
		39-3019	Gaming Service Workers, All Other	E
Security Guards	D	39-3021	Motion Picture Projectionists	-
Crossing Guards	-	39-3031	Ushers, Lobby Attendants, and Ticket Takers	-
Lifeguards, Ski Patrol, and Other Recreational Protective Service Workers	-	39-3091	Amusement and Recreation Attendants	-
		39-3092	Costume Attendants	E
Transportation Security Screeners	C,T,D	39-3093	Locker Room, Coatroom, and Dressing Room Attendants	-
Protective Service Workers, All Other	D			
Chefs and Head Cooks	E	39-3099	Entertainment Attendants and Related Workers, All Other	-
First-Line Supervisors of Food Preparation and Serving Workers	T,E			
		39-4011	Embalmers	-
Cooks, Fast Food	E	39-4021	Funeral Attendants	-
Cooks, Institution and Cafeteria	-			

C = Code Change, T = Title Change, D = Definition Content Change, E = Definition Editing Change

SOC code	2010 SOC detailed occupation	Type of change
39-4031	Morticians, Undertakers, and Funeral Directors	C,T,D
39-5011	Barbers	-
39-5012	Hairdressers, Hairstylists, and Cosmetologists	E
39-5091	Makeup Artists, Theatrical and Performance	-
39-5092	Manicurists and Pedicurists	-
39-5093	Shampooers	-
39-5094	Skincare Specialists	T,E
39-6011	Baggage Porters and Bellhops	-
39-6012	Concierges	E
39-7011	Tour Guides and Escorts	C
39-7012	Travel Guides	C,E
39-9011	Childcare Workers	T,E
39-9021	Personal Care Aides	T,E
39-9031	Fitness Trainers and Aerobics Instructors	E
39-9032	Recreation Workers	-
39-9041	Residential Advisors	E
39-9099	Personal Care and Service Workers, All Other	-
41-1011	First-Line Supervisors of Retail Sales Workers	T,E
41-1012	First-Line Supervisors of Non-Retail Sales Workers	T,E
41-2011	Cashiers	E
41-2012	Gaming Change Persons and Booth Cashiers	E
41-2021	Counter and Rental Clerks	E
41-2022	Parts Salespersons	-
41-2031	Retail Salespersons	E
41-3011	Advertising Sales Agents	E
41-3021	Insurance Sales Agents	E
41-3031	Securities, Commodities, and Financial Services Sales Agents	E
41-3041	Travel Agents	E
41-3099	Sales Representatives, Services, All Other	-
41-4011	Sales Representatives, Wholesale and Manufacturing, Technical and Scientific Products	E
41-4012	Sales Representatives, Wholesale and Manufacturing, Except Technical and Scientific Products	-
41-9011	Demonstrators and Product Promoters	-
41-9012	Models	E
41-9021	Real Estate Brokers	-
41-9022	Real Estate Sales Agents	-
41-9031	Sales Engineers	-
41-9041	Telemarketers	E
41-9091	Door-to-Door Sales Workers, News and Street Vendors, and Related Workers	-
41-9099	Sales and Related Workers, All Other	D
43-1011	First-Line Supervisors of Office and Administrative Support Workers	T,E

SOC code	2010 SOC detailed occupation	Type of change
43-2011	Switchboard Operators, Including Answering Service	
43-2021	Telephone Operators	
43-2099	Communications Equipment Operators, All Other	
43-3011	Bill and Account Collectors	
43-3021	Billing and Posting Clerks	
43-3031	Bookkeeping, Accounting, and Auditing Clerks	
43-3041	Gaming Cage Workers	
43-3051	Payroll and Timekeeping Clerks	
43-3061	Procurement Clerks	
43-3071	Tellers	
43-3099	Financial Clerks, All Other	
43-4011	Brokerage Clerks	
43-4021	Correspondence Clerks	
43-4031	Court, Municipal, and License Clerks	
43-4041	Credit Authorizers, Checkers, and Clerks	
43-4051	Customer Service Representatives	
43-4061	Eligibility Interviewers, Government Programs	
43-4071	File Clerks	
43-4081	Hotel, Motel, and Resort Desk Clerks	
43-4111	Interviewers, Except Eligibility and Loan	
43-4121	Library Assistants, Clerical	
43-4131	Loan Interviewers and Clerks	
43-4141	New Accounts Clerks	
43-4151	Order Clerks	
43-4161	Human Resources Assistants, Except Payroll and Timekeeping	
43-4171	Receptionists and Information Clerks	
43-4181	Reservation and Transportation Ticket Agents and Travel Clerks	
43-4199	Information and Record Clerks, All Other	
43-5011	Cargo and Freight Agents	
43-5021	Couriers and Messengers	
43-5031	Police, Fire, and Ambulance Dispatchers	
43-5032	Dispatchers, Except Police, Fire, and Ambulance	
43-5041	Meter Readers, Utilities	
43-5051	Postal Service Clerks	
43-5052	Postal Service Mail Carriers	
43-5053	Postal Service Mail Sorters, Processors, and Processing Machine Operators	
43-5061	Production, Planning, and Expediting Clerks	
43-5071	Shipping, Receiving, and Traffic Clerks	
43-5081	Stock Clerks and Order Fillers	
43-5111	Weighers, Measurers, Checkers, and Samplers, Recordkeeping	
43-6011	Executive Secretaries and Executive Administrative Assistants	
43-6012	Legal Secretaries	
43-6013	Medical Secretaries	

C = Code Change, T = Title Change, D = Definition Content Change, E = Definition Editing Change

2010 SOC detailed occupation	Type of change	SOC code	2010 SOC detailed occupation	Type of change
Secretaries and Administrative Assistants, Except Legal, Medical, and Executive	T,E	47-2082	Tapers	-
		47-2111	Electricians	D
Computer Operators	E	47-2121	Glaziers	-
Data Entry Keyers	-	47-2131	Insulation Workers, Floor, Ceiling, and Wall	-
Word Processors and Typists	E	47-2132	Insulation Workers, Mechanical	-
Desktop Publishers	-	47-2141	Painters, Construction and Maintenance	-
Insurance Claims and Policy Processing Clerks	-	47-2142	Paperhangers	E
		47-2151	Pipelayers	-
Mail Clerks and Mail Machine Operators, Except Postal Service	-	47-2152	Plumbers, Pipefitters, and Steamfitters	E
		47-2161	Plasterers and Stucco Masons	-
Office Clerks, General	E	47-2171	Reinforcing Iron and Rebar Workers	-
Office Machine Operators, Except Computer	E	47-2181	Roofers	D
Proofreaders and Copy Markers	-	47-2211	Sheet Metal Workers	E
Statistical Assistants	-	47-2221	Structural Iron and Steel Workers	-
Office and Administrative Support Workers, All Other	D	47-2231	Solar Photovoltaic Installers	C,T,D
		47-3011	Helpers--Brickmasons, Blockmasons, Stonemasons, and Tile and Marble Setters	E
First-Line Supervisors of Farming, Fishing, and Forestry Workers	T,E	47-3012	Helpers--Carpenters	E
Agricultural Inspectors	-	47-3013	Helpers--Electricians	E
Animal Breeders	E	47-3014	Helpers--Painters, Paperhangers, Plasterers, and Stucco Masons	E
Graders and Sorters, Agricultural Products	-			
Agricultural Equipment Operators	-	47-3015	Helpers--Pipelayers, Plumbers, Pipefitters, and Steamfitters	E
Farmworkers and Laborers, Crop, Nursery, and Greenhouse	E	47-3016	Helpers--Roofers	E
Farmworkers, Farm, Ranch, and Aquacultural Animals	T	47-3019	Helpers, Construction Trades, All Other	-
		47-4011	Construction and Building Inspectors	-
Agricultural Workers, All Other	-	47-4021	Elevator Installers and Repairers	-
Fishers and Related Fishing Workers	E	47-4031	Fence Erectors	E
Hunters and Trappers	-	47-4041	Hazardous Materials Removal Workers	E
Forest and Conservation Workers	E	47-4051	Highway Maintenance Workers	-
Fallers	-	47-4061	Rail-Track Laying and Maintenance Equipment Operators	-
Logging Equipment Operators	E			
Log Graders and Scalers	E	47-4071	Septic Tank Servicers and Sewer Pipe Cleaners	-
Logging Workers, All Other	-			
First-Line Supervisors of Construction Trades and Extraction Workers	T	47-4091	Segmental Pavers	E
		47-4099	Construction and Related Workers, All Other	D
Boilermakers	-	47-5011	Derrick Operators, Oil and Gas	-
Brickmasons and Blockmasons	E	47-5012	Rotary Drill Operators, Oil and Gas	E
Stonemasons	-	47-5013	Service Unit Operators, Oil, Gas, and Mining	-
Carpenters	E	47-5021	Earth Drillers, Except Oil and Gas	E
Carpet Installers	-	47-5031	Explosives Workers, Ordnance Handling Experts, and Blasters	-
Floor Layers, Except Carpet, Wood, and Hard Tiles	-			
Floor Sanders and Finishers	-	47-5041	Continuous Mining Machine Operators	E
Tile and Marble Setters	-	47-5042	Mine Cutting and Channeling Machine Operators	E
Cement Masons and Concrete Finishers	E			
Terrazzo Workers and Finishers	-	47-5049	Mining Machine Operators, All Other	-
Construction Laborers	E	47-5051	Rock Splitters, Quarry	-
Paving, Surfacing, and Tamping Equipment Operators	-	47-5061	Roof Bolters, Mining	-
		47-5071	Roustabouts, Oil and Gas	-
Pile-Driver Operators	-	47-5081	Helpers--Extraction Workers	E
Operating Engineers and Other Construction Equipment Operators	E	47-5099	Extraction Workers, All Other	-
		49-1011	First-Line Supervisors of Mechanics, Installers, and Repairers	T,E
Drywall and Ceiling Tile Installers	-			

C = Code Change, T = Title Change, D = Definition Content Change, E = Definition Editing Change

SOC code	2010 SOC detailed occupation	Type of change	SOC code	2010 SOC detailed occupation
49-2011	Computer, Automated Teller, and Office Machine Repairers	-	49-9052	Telecommunications Line Installers and Repairers
49-2021	Radio, Cellular, and Tower Equipment, Installers and Repairers	T,E	49-9061	Camera and Photographic Equipment Repairers
49-2022	Telecommunications Equipment Installers and Repairers, Except Line Installers	E	49-9062	Medical Equipment Repairers
49-2091	Avionics Technicians	-	49-9063	Musical Instrument Repairers and Tuners
49-2092	Electric Motor, Power Tool, and Related Repairers	-	49-9064	Watch Repairers
49-2093	Electrical and Electronics Installers and Repairers, Transportation Equipment	-	49-9069	Precision Instrument and Equipment Repairers, All Other
49-2094	Electrical and Electronics Repairers, Commercial and Industrial Equipment	-	49-9071	Maintenance and Repair Workers, General
49-2095	Electrical and Electronics Repairers, Powerhouse, Substation, and Relay	-	49-9081	Wind Turbine Service Technicians
49-2096	Electronic Equipment Installers and Repairers, Motor Vehicles	-	49-9091	Coin, Vending, and Amusement Machine Servicers and Repairers
49-2097	Electronic Home Entertainment Equipment Installers and Repairers	-	49-9092	Commercial Divers
			49-9093	Fabric Menders, Except Garment
49-2098	Security and Fire Alarm Systems Installers	E	49-9094	Locksmiths and Safe Repairers
49-3011	Aircraft Mechanics and Service Technicians	-	49-9095	Manufactured Building and Mobile Home Installers
49-3021	Automotive Body and Related Repairers	-	49-9096	Riggers
49-3022	Automotive Glass Installers and Repairers	-	49-9097	Signal and Track Switch Repairers
49-3023	Automotive Service Technicians and Mechanics	-	49-9098	Helpers--Installation, Maintenance, and Repair Workers
49-3031	Bus and Truck Mechanics and Diesel Engine Specialists	E	49-9099	Installation, Maintenance, and Repair Workers, All Other
49-3041	Farm Equipment Mechanics and Service Technicians	T	51-1011	First-Line Supervisors of Production and Operating Workers
49-3042	Mobile Heavy Equipment Mechanics, Except Engines	-	51-2011	Aircraft Structure, Surfaces, Rigging, and Systems Assemblers
49-3043	Rail Car Repairers	-	51-2021	Coil Winders, Tapers, and Finishers
49-3051	Motorboat Mechanics and Service Technicians	T,E	51-2022	Electrical and Electronic Equipment Assemblers
49-3052	Motorcycle Mechanics	-	51-2023	Electromechanical Equipment Assemblers
49-3053	Outdoor Power Equipment and Other Small Engine Mechanics	E	51-2031	Engine and Other Machine Assemblers
			51-2041	Structural Metal Fabricators and Fitters
49-3091	Bicycle Repairers	-	51-2091	Fiberglass Laminators and Fabricators
49-3092	Recreational Vehicle Service Technicians	-	51-2092	Team Assemblers
49-3093	Tire Repairers and Changers	-	51-2093	Timing Device Assemblers and Adjusters
49-9011	Mechanical Door Repairers	E	51-2099	Assemblers and Fabricators, All Other
49-9012	Control and Valve Installers and Repairers, Except Mechanical Door	-	51-3011	Bakers
			51-3021	Butchers and Meat Cutters
49-9021	Heating, Air Conditioning, and Refrigeration Mechanics and Installers	D	51-3022	Meat, Poultry, and Fish Cutters and Trimmers
49-9031	Home Appliance Repairers	-	51-3023	Slaughterers and Meat Packers
49-9041	Industrial Machinery Mechanics	E	51-3091	Food and Tobacco Roasting, Baking, and Drying Machine Operators and Tenders
49-9043	Maintenance Workers, Machinery	E	51-3092	Food Batchmakers
49-9044	Millwrights	-	51-3093	Food Cooking Machine Operators and Tenders
49-9045	Refractory Materials Repairers, Except Brickmasons	E	51-3099	Food Processing Workers, All Other
49-9051	Electrical Power-Line Installers and Repairers	-	51-4011	Computer-Controlled Machine Tool Operators, Metal and Plastic
			51-4012	Computer Numerically Controlled Machine Tool Programmers, Metal and Plastic

C = Code Change, T = Title Change, D = Definition Content Change, E = Definition Editing Change

2010 SOC detailed occupation	Type of change	SOC code	2010 SOC detailed occupation	Type of change
Extruding and Drawing Machine Setters, Operators, and Tenders, Metal and Plastic	-	51-6062	Textile Cutting Machine Setters, Operators, and Tenders	-
Forging Machine Setters, Operators, and Tenders, Metal and Plastic	-	51-6063	Textile Knitting and Weaving Machine Setters, Operators, and Tenders	-
Rolling Machine Setters, Operators, and Tenders, Metal and Plastic	-	51-6064	Textile Winding, Twisting, and Drawing Out Machine Setters, Operators, and Tenders	-
Cutting, Punching, and Press Machine Setters, Operators, and Tenders, Metal and Plastic	-	51-6091	Extruding and Forming Machine Setters, Operators, and Tenders, Synthetic and Glass Fibers	-
Drilling and Boring Machine Tool Setters, Operators, and Tenders, Metal and Plastic	-	51-6092	Fabric and Apparel Patternmakers	-
		51-6093	Upholsterers	-
Grinding, Lapping, Polishing, and Buffing Machine Tool Setters, Operators, and Tenders, Metal and Plastic	-	51-6099	Textile, Apparel, and Furnishings Workers, All Other	-
		51-7011	Cabinetmakers and Bench Carpenters	E
Lathe and Turning Machine Tool Setters, Operators, and Tenders, Metal and Plastic	-	51-7021	Furniture Finishers	-
		51-7031	Model Makers, Wood	-
Milling and Planing Machine Setters, Operators, and Tenders, Metal and Plastic	-	51-7032	Patternmakers, Wood	-
Machinists	E	51-7041	Sawing Machine Setters, Operators, and Tenders, Wood	E
Metal-Refining Furnace Operators and Tenders	-	51-7042	Woodworking Machine Setters, Operators, and Tenders, Except Sawing	E
Pourers and Casters, Metal	-	51-7099	Woodworkers, All Other	-
Model Makers, Metal and Plastic	-	51-8011	Nuclear Power Reactor Operators	E
Patternmakers, Metal and Plastic	-	51-8012	Power Distributors and Dispatchers	-
Foundry Mold and Coremakers	-	51-8013	Power Plant Operators	-
Molding, Coremaking, and Casting Machine Setters, Operators, and Tenders, Metal and Plastic	-	51-8021	Stationary Engineers and Boiler Operators	-
		51-8031	Water and Wastewater Treatment Plant and System Operators	T,E
Multiple Machine Tool Setters, Operators, and Tenders, Metal and Plastic	-	51-8091	Chemical Plant and System Operators	E
Tool and Die Makers	-	51-8092	Gas Plant Operators	-
Welders, Cutters, Solderers, and Brazers	-	51-8093	Petroleum Pump System Operators, Refinery Operators, and Gaugers	E
Welding, Soldering, and Brazing Machine Setters, Operators, and Tenders	-	51-8099	Plant and System Operators, All Other	-
		51-9011	Chemical Equipment Operators and Tenders	-
Heat Treating Equipment Setters, Operators, and Tenders, Metal and Plastic	-	51-9012	Separating, Filtering, Clarifying, Precipitating, and Still Machine Setters, Operators, and Tenders	-
Layout Workers, Metal and Plastic	T			
Plating and Coating Machine Setters, Operators, and Tenders, Metal and Plastic	-	51-9021	Crushing, Grinding, and Polishing Machine Setters, Operators, and Tenders	-
Tool Grinders, Filers, and Sharpeners	-	51-9022	Grinding and Polishing Workers, Hand	-
Metal Workers and Plastic Workers, All Other	E	51-9023	Mixing and Blending Machine Setters, Operators, and Tenders	-
Prepress Technicians and Workers	C,E			
Printing Press Operators	C,T,D	51-9031	Cutters and Trimmers, Hand	-
Print Binding and Finishing Workers	C,T,D	51-9032	Cutting and Slicing Machine Setters, Operators, and Tenders	E
Laundry and Dry-Cleaning Workers	E			
Pressers, Textile, Garment, and Related Materials	-	51-9041	Extruding, Forming, Pressing, and Compacting Machine Setters, Operators, and Tenders	-
Sewing Machine Operators	-			
Shoe and Leather Workers and Repairers	-	51-9051	Furnace, Kiln, Oven, Drier, and Kettle Operators and Tenders	-
Shoe Machine Operators and Tenders	-			
Sewers, Hand	-	51-9061	Inspectors, Testers, Sorters, Samplers, and Weighers	-
Tailors, Dressmakers, and Custom Sewers	-			
Textile Bleaching and Dyeing Machine Operators and Tenders	-	51-9071	Jewelers and Precious Stone and Metal Workers	E

C = Code Change, T = Title Change, D = Definition Content Change, E = Definition Editing Change

Appendix C: Type of Change by Detailed Occupation, 2010 SOC

SOC code	2010 SOC detailed occupation	Type of change	SOC code	2010 SOC detailed occupation
51-9081	Dental Laboratory Technicians	-	53-5011	Sailors and Marine Oilers
51-9082	Medical Appliance Technicians	E	53-5021	Captains, Mates, and Pilots of Water Vessels
51-9083	Ophthalmic Laboratory Technicians	-	53-5022	Motorboat Operators
51-9111	Packaging and Filling Machine Operators and Tenders	-	53-5031	Ship Engineers
51-9121	Coating, Painting, and Spraying Machine Setters, Operators, and Tenders	E	53-6011	Bridge and Lock Tenders
			53-6021	Parking Lot Attendants
			53-6031	Automotive and Watercraft Service Attendants
51-9122	Painters, Transportation Equipment	-		
51-9123	Painting, Coating, and Decorating Workers	E	53-6041	Traffic Technicians
51-9141	Semiconductor Processors	E	53-6051	Transportation Inspectors
51-9151	Photographic Process Workers and Processing Machine Operators	C,T,D	53-6061	Transportation Attendants, Except Flight Attendants
51-9191	Adhesive Bonding Machine Operators and Tenders	T,E	53-6099	Transportation Workers, All Other
			53-7011	Conveyor Operators and Tenders
51-9192	Cleaning, Washing, and Metal Pickling Equipment Operators and Tenders	-	53-7021	Crane and Tower Operators
			53-7031	Dredge Operators
51-9193	Cooling and Freezing Equipment Operators and Tenders	-	53-7032	Excavating and Loading Machine and Dragline Operators
51-9194	Etchers and Engravers	E	53-7033	Loading Machine Operators, Underground Mining
51-9195	Molders, Shapers, and Casters, Except Metal and Plastic	-	53-7041	Hoist and Winch Operators
51-9196	Paper Goods Machine Setters, Operators, and Tenders	-	53-7051	Industrial Truck and Tractor Operators
			53-7061	Cleaners of Vehicles and Equipment
51-9197	Tire Builders	E	53-7062	Laborers and Freight, Stock, and Material Movers, Hand
51-9198	Helpers--Production Workers	E		
51-9199	Production Workers, All Other	D	53-7063	Machine Feeders and Offbearers
53-1011	Aircraft Cargo Handling Supervisors	E	53-7064	Packers and Packagers, Hand
53-1021	First-Line Supervisors of Helpers, Laborers, and Material Movers, Hand	T,E	53-7071	Gas Compressor and Gas Pumping Station Operators
53-1031	First-Line Supervisors of Transportation and Material-Moving Machine and Vehicle Operators	T	53-7072	Pump Operators, Except Wellhead Pumpers
			53-7073	Wellhead Pumpers
			53-7081	Refuse and Recyclable Material Collectors
53-2011	Airline Pilots, Copilots, and Flight Engineers	E	53-7111	Mine Shuttle Car Operators
53-2012	Commercial Pilots	E	53-7121	Tank Car, Truck, and Ship Loaders
53-2021	Air Traffic Controllers	-	53-7199	Material Moving Workers, All Other
53-2022	Airfield Operations Specialists	-	55-1011	Air Crew Officers
53-2031	Flight Attendants	C,E	55-1012	Aircraft Launch and Recovery Officers
53-3011	Ambulance Drivers and Attendants, Except Emergency Medical Technicians	-	55-1013	Armored Assault Vehicle Officers
			55-1014	Artillery and Missile Officers
53-3021	Bus Drivers, Transit and Intercity	-	55-1015	Command and Control Center Officers
53-3022	Bus Drivers, School or Special Client	T	55-1016	Infantry Officers
53-3031	Driver/Sales Workers	E	55-1017	Special Forces Officers
53-3032	Heavy and Tractor-Trailer Truck Drivers	T,E	55-1019	Military Officer Special and Tactical Operations Leaders, All Other
53-3033	Light Truck or Delivery Services Drivers	T,E		
53-3041	Taxi Drivers and Chauffeurs	E	55-2011	First-Line Supervisors of Air Crew Members
53-3099	Motor Vehicle Operators, All Other	-	55-2012	First-Line Supervisors of Weapons Specialists/Crew Members
53-4011	Locomotive Engineers	-		
53-4012	Locomotive Firers	-	55-2013	First-Line Supervisors of All Other Tactical Operations Specialists
53-4013	Rail Yard Engineers, Dinkey Operators, and Hostlers	-		
			55-3011	Air Crew Members
53-4021	Railroad Brake, Signal, and Switch Operators	-	55-3012	Aircraft Launch and Recovery Specialists
53-4031	Railroad Conductors and Yardmasters	E	55-3013	Armored Assault Vehicle Crew Members
53-4041	Subway and Streetcar Operators	E	55-3014	Artillery and Missile Crew Members
53-4099	Rail Transportation Workers, All Other	-	55-3015	Command and Control Center Specialists

C = Code Change, T = Title Change, D = Definition Content Change, E = Definition Editing Change

Appendix C: Type of Change by Detailed Occupation, 2010 SOC

2010 SOC detailed occupation	Type of change	SOC code	2010 SOC detailed occupation	Type of change
Infantry	-			
Radar and Sonar Technicians	-			
Special Forces	-			
Military Enlisted Tactical Operations and Air/Weapons Specialists and Crew Members, All Other	-			

C = Code Change, T = Title Change, D = Definition Content Change, E = Definition Editing Change

Alphabetical Index of Occupations

Alphabetical Index of Occupations

Alphabetical Index of Occupations

Civil Engineers	17-2050	Clerks, Classified Ad	43-4151
Civil Engineers	17-2051	Clerks, Commodities	43-4011
Claims Adjusters	13-1031	Clerks, Correspondence	43-4021
Claims Adjusters, Appraisers, Examiners, and Investigators	13-1030	Clerks, Counter	41-2021
		Clerks, Court	43-4031
Claims Adjusters, Examiners, and Investigators	13-1031	Clerks, Credit	43-4041
		Clerks, Customer Complaint	43-4051
Claims Examiners	13-1031	Clerks, Data Input	43-9021
Claims Investigators	13-1031	Clerks, Direct Mail	43-9051
Clarifying Machine Operators	51-9012	Clerks, Dividend	43-4011
Clarifying Machine Setters	51-9012	Clerks, Document	43-4071
Clarifying Machine Tenders	51-9012	Clerks, Dry Cleaning Counter	41-2021
Classified Ad Clerks	43-4151	Clerks, Election	43-4199
Clay Mine Cutting Machine Operators	47-5042	Clerks, Expediting	43-5061
Clay Mixers	51-9023	Clerks, File	43-4071
Cleaners of Equipment	53-7061	Clerks, Financial Reserve Clerk	43-3099
Cleaners of Vehicles	53-7061	Clerks, Financial, All Other	43-3099
Cleaners of Vehicles and Equipment	53-7061	Clerks, Fingerprint	43-9199
Cleaners, Aircraft	53-7061	Clerks, Flat Sorting Machine	43-5053
Cleaners, Except Maids and Housekeeping Cleaners	37-2011	Clerks, Foreign Exchange	43-3071
		Clerks, Hotel Desk	43-4081
Cleaners, House	37-2012	Clerks, Hotel Front Desk	43-4081
Cleaners, Housekeeping	37-2012	Clerks, Hotel Registration	43-4081
Cleaners, Immersion Metal	51-9192	Clerks, HR	43-4161
Cleaners, Septic Tank	47-4071	Clerks, Incoming Freight	43-5071
Cleaners, Sewer Pipe	47-4071	Clerks, Information	43-4171
Cleaners, Silverware	35-9021	Clerks, Information, All Other	43-4199
Cleaning Equipment Operators	51-9192	Clerks, Insurance Claims	43-9041
Cleaning Equipment Tenders	51-9192	Clerks, Insurance Policy Issue	43-9041
Cleaning Staff Supervisors	37-1011	Clerks, Insurance Policy Processing	43-9041
Cleaning, Washing, and Metal Pickling Equipment Operators and Tenders	51-9192	Clerks, Inventory Control	43-5081
		Clerks, Invoice Control	43-3021
Clergy	21-2010	Clerks, Judicial	23-1012
Clergy	21-2011	Clerks, Judicial Law	23-1012
Clerical Library Assistants	43-4121	Clerks, Land Leasing Information	43-4171
Clerical Supervisors	43-1011	Clerks, License	43-4031
Clerk Typists	43-9022	Clerks, Loan	43-4131
Clerks of Court	11-9199	Clerks, Mail Forwarding System Markup	43-5053
Clerks, Accounting	43-3031	Clerks, Mail, Except Postal Service	43-9051
Clerks, Accounts Receivable	43-3031	Clerks, Mailroom	43-9051
Clerks, Actuarial	43-9111	Clerks, Material Control	43-5061
Clerks, Administrative	43-9061	Clerks, Microfilm	43-4121
Clerks, Appointment	43-4171	Clerks, Money Order	43-3071
Clerks, Auditing	43-3031	Clerks, Mortgage Accounting	43-3031
Clerks, Banking Services	43-4141	Clerks, Motel Desk	43-4081
Clerks, Betting	39-3012	Clerks, Motor Vehicle License	43-4031
Clerks, Billing	43-3021	Clerks, Municipal	43-4031
Clerks, Bookkeeping	43-3031	Clerks, New Accounts	43-4141
Clerks, Braille and Talking Books	43-4121	Clerks, Office, General	43-9061
Clerks, Brokerage	43-4011	Clerks, Order	43-4151
Clerks, Bulk Mail	43-5051	Clerks, Outpatient Interviewing	43-4111
Clerks, Catalogue	43-4151	Clerks, Packaging	43-9051
Clerks, Circuit Court	43-4031		
Clerks, Circulation	43-4121		

Alphabetical Index of Occupations

Alphabetical Index of Occupations

Alphabetical Index of Occupations

Alphabetical Index of Occupations

Alphabetical Index of Occupations

Alphabetical Index of Occupations

Alphabetical Index of Occupations

Makers, Die	51-4111	Managers, Development	11-3131
Makers, Doll	51-2099	Managers, Distribution	11-3071
Makers, Eyeglass	51-9083	Managers, Distribution Center	11-3071
Makers, Fiberglass Ski	51-2091	Managers, District Sales	11-2022
Makers, Foundry Mold	51-4071	Managers, E-Learning	11-3131
Makers, Frozen Yogurt	51-3092	Managers, Engineering	11-9041
Makers, Jig Bore Tool	51-4111	Managers, Engineering Design	11-9041
Makers, Key	49-9094	Managers, Export	11-2022
Makers, Metal Gauge	51-4111	Managers, Facilities	11-3011
Makers, Metal Mock Up	51-4061	Managers, Financial	11-3031
Makers, Peanut Butter	51-3092	Managers, Fish Hatchery	11-9013
Makers, Saddle	51-6041	Managers, Food Service	11-9051
Makers, Salad	35-2021	Managers, Fundraising	11-2031
Makers, Sandwich	35-2021	Managers, Funeral Home	11-9061
Makers, Template	51-4061	Managers, Funeral Service	11-9061
Makers, Tool	51-4111	Managers, Gaming	11-9071
Makers, Vest	51-6052	Managers, General	11-1021
Makers, Wood Die	51-7032	Managers, Geophysical	11-9121
Makers, Yeast	51-3099	Managers, Global Engineering	11-9041
Makeup Artists, Performance	39-5091	Managers, Health Services	11-9111
Makeup Artists, Theatrical	39-5091	Managers, Homeowner Association	11-9141
Makeup Artists, Theatrical and Performance	39-5091	Managers, Hotel	11-9081
Malariologists	19-1041	Managers, Human Resources	11-3121
Management Analysts	13-1110	Managers, Industrial Production	11-3051
Management Analysts	13-1111	Managers, In-Flight Refueling	55-2011
Management Consultants	13-1111	Managers, Information Systems	11-3021
Management Information Systems Directors	11-3021	Managers, Internet Marketing	11-2021
Management Occupations	11-0000	Managers, Job Analysis	11-3111
Management Psychologists	19-3032	Managers, Job Analysis	11-3121
Managers, Administrative Services	11-3011	Managers, Labor Training	11-3131
Managers, Advertising	11-2011	Managers, Land	11-9141
Managers, Air Battle	55-1011	Managers, Leased Housing Unit	11-9141
Managers, All Other	11-9199	Managers, Leasing Property	11-9141
Managers, Animal Husbandry	11-9013	Managers, Lodging	11-9081
Managers, Apartment	11-9141	Managers, Logistics	11-3071
Managers, Architectural	11-9041	Managers, Marketing	11-2021
Managers, Band	13-1011	Managers, Medical Services	11-9111
Managers, Bar	35-1012	Managers, Mental Health Program	11-9111
Managers, Benefits	11-3111	Managers, Miscellaneous	11-9190
Managers, Building	11-9141	Managers, Natural Sciences	11-9121
Managers, Building Rental	11-9141	Managers, Operations	11-1021
Managers, Carpentry	11-9021	Managers, Orchard	11-9013
Managers, Casino	11-9071	Managers, Other Agricultural	11-9013
Managers, Community Association	11-9141	Managers, Personnel	11-3121
Managers, Community Service	11-9151	Managers, Plant	11-3051
Managers, Compensation	11-3111	Managers, Plumbing	11-9021
Managers, Computer Systems	11-3021	Managers, Position Description	11-3111
Managers, Condominium Association	11-9141	Managers, Position Description	11-3121
Managers, Construction	11-9021	Managers, Procurement	11-3061
Managers, Contracting	11-3061	Managers, Production Control	11-3051
Managers, Dairy Farm	11-9013	Managers, Promotions	11-2011
Managers, Delicatessen Department	41-1011	Managers, Property	11-9141

Alphabetical Index of Occupations

Alphabetical Index of Occupations

Alphabetical Index of Occupations

Alphabetical Index of Occupations

Alphabetical Index of Occupations

Alphabetical Index of Occupations

Alphabetical Index of Occupations

Reviewers, Loan	13-2072
Rewinders, Armature	49-2092
Rheologists	19-2012
Rickshaw Drivers	53-6099
Rig Supervisors	47-1011
Riggers	49-9096
Riggers, Acrobatic	49-9096
Riggers, Crane	49-9096
Riggers, Yard	49-9096
Rigging Slingers	45-4029
Right of Way Agents	41-9022
Right-Of-Way Managers	11-9141
Ringmasters	27-3012
Rip Saw Operators	51-7041
River Expedition Guides	39-7012
Riveters, Aircraft	51-2011
Road Graders	47-2071
Road Patchers	47-4051
Road Sign Installers	47-4051
Roasters, Coffee	51-3091
Roasting, Baking, and Drying Machine Operators and Tenders, Food and Tobacco	51-3091
Robotics Testing Technicians	17-3024
Rock Dust Sprayers	47-5049
Rock Splitters, Quarry	47-5050
Rock Splitters, Quarry	47-5051
Rod Buster Helpers	47-3019
Rod Busters	47-2171
Rodent Exterminators	37-2021
Rollers, Brass	51-4023
Rollers, Cigar	51-9195
Rollers, Steel	51-4023
Rolling Machine Operators, Metal and Plastic	51-4023
Rolling Machine Setters, Metal and Plastic	51-4023
Rolling Machine Setters, Operators, and Tenders, Metal and Plastic	51-4023
Rolling Machine Tenders, Metal and Plastic	51-4023
Roof Bolter Helpers	47-5081
Roof Bolters, Mining	47-5060
Roof Bolters, Mining	47-5061
Roof Bolting Coal Miners	47-5061
Roofers	47-2180
Roofers	47-2181
Roofers Helpers	47-3016
Roofers, Hot Tar	47-2181
Roofers, Shingles	47-2181
Roofers, Terra Cotta	47-2181
Room Service Food Servers	35-3041
Rope Machine Setters	51-6064
Ropers, Log	45-4029
Rotary Derrick Operators	47-5011
Rotary Drill Operators, Gas	47-5012
Rotary Drill Operators, Oil	47-5012

Rotary Drill Operators, Oil and Gas	47-5012
Roughnecks, Oil Rig	47-5071
Roulette Dealers	39-3011
Roustabouts, Gas	47-5071
Roustabouts, Oil	47-5071
Roustabouts, Oil and Gas	47-5070
Roustabouts, Oil and Gas	47-5071
Roustabouts, Oil Field	47-5071
Route Delivery Clerks	43-5071
Route Salespersons	53-3031
Routers, Cargo	43-5011
Rubber Curers	51-9051
Rubber Extrusion Operators	51-9041
Rubber Trimmers	51-9032
Rug Dyers	51-6061
Runners, Gaming Book	39-3012
Runners, Keno	39-3012
Runners, Office	43-5021
Runners, Sports Book	39-3012
Rural Route Carriers	43-5052
Rural Sociologists	19-3041
Russian History Professors	25-1125
Russian Language Professors	25-1124
RV Mechanics	49-3092
Saddle Makers	51-6041
Safe and Vault Installers	49-9094
Safe and Vault Mechanics	49-9094
Safe Repairers	49-9094
Safety Deposit Clerks	43-3099
Safety Engineers, Except Mining Safety Engineers and Inspectors	17-2111
Sail Repairers	49-9093
Sailing Instructors	25-3021
Sailors	53-5011
Sailors and Marine Oilers	53-5010
Sailors and Marine Oilers	53-5011
Salad Makers	35-2021
Sales Agents, Advertising	41-3011
Sales Agents, Commodities	41-3031
Sales Agents, Financial Services	41-3031
Sales Agents, Insurance	41-3021
Sales Agents, Pest Control Service	41-3099
Sales Agents, Real Estate	41-9022
Sales Agents, Securities	41-3031
Sales and Related Occupations	41-0000
Sales and Related Workers, All Other	41-9099
Sales and Related Workers, Miscellaneous	41-9090
Sales Directors	11-2022
Sales Engineers	41-9030
Sales Engineers	41-9031
Sales Engineers, Aerospace Products	41-9031
Sales Managers	11-2022

Alphabetical Index of Occupations

Alphabetical Index of Occupations

Alphabetical Index of Occupations